S0-AHY-573

AWAKENINGS

New York City
Police Detective
Sara Pezzini is the
reluctant bearer of
the Witchblade, an
ancient and mysterious
mystical gauntlet that
has bonded itself to
her. Sara must
resist the
gauntlet's
all-consuming
thirst for battle,
all the while
solving the
city's strangest
crimes-many of
which invariably
seem to lead
back to the
WITCHBLADE!

WITCHBLADE

To find the
comics shop
nearest you call
1-888-COMICBOOK

image

for Image Comics
publisher Erik Larsen

Witchblade created by:
**Marc Silvestri, David Wohl,
Brian Haberlin and Michael Turner**

for Top Cow Productions
Marc Silvestri_chief executive officer
Matt Hawkins_president / chief operating officer
Renae Geerlings_editor in chief
Chaz Riggs_production manager
Rob Levin_editor
Annie Pham_marketing director
Peter Lam_webmaster
Phil Smith_trades and submissions
Viet Duc Nguyen
    and Lena Leal-Floyd-interns

For this edition,
Book Design and Layout by:
Phil Smith

ISBN # 1-58240-635-9
Witchblade volume 11 trade paperback 2006 First Printing.
Published by Image Comics Inc. Office of Publication: 1942 University Ave., Suite 305 Berkeley, CA 94704. $14.99 US, $16.70 CAN.
Originally published as *Witchblade* issues #86-#92. *Witchblade* is ©2006 Top Cow Productions, Inc. "Witchblade," the *Witchblade*
logos, and the likeness of all featured characters are registered trademarks of Top Cow Productions, Inc. All rights reserved. *Dawn* is
©2006 Joseph Michael Linsner. "Dawn" the *Dawn* logo, and her distinctive likeness is a trademark of Joseph Michael Linsner. All
rights reserved.The characters, events and stories in this publication are entirely fictional. With the exception of artwork used for
review purposes, none of the contents of this book may be reprinted in any form without the express written consent of Top Cow
Productions, Inc. **Printed in Canada**

Table of Contents:

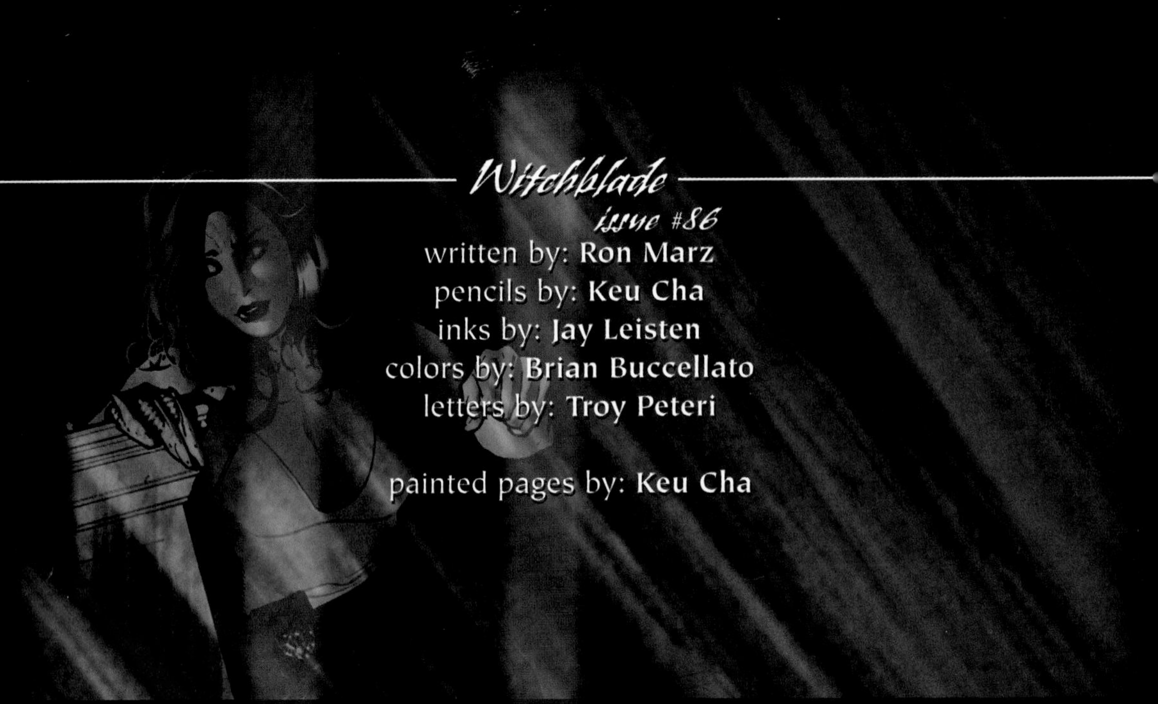

Witchblade

issue #86

written by: **Ron Marz**
pencils by: **Keu Cha**
inks by: **Jay Leisten**
colors by: **Brian Buccellato**
letters by: **Troy Peteri**

painted pages by: **Keu Cha**

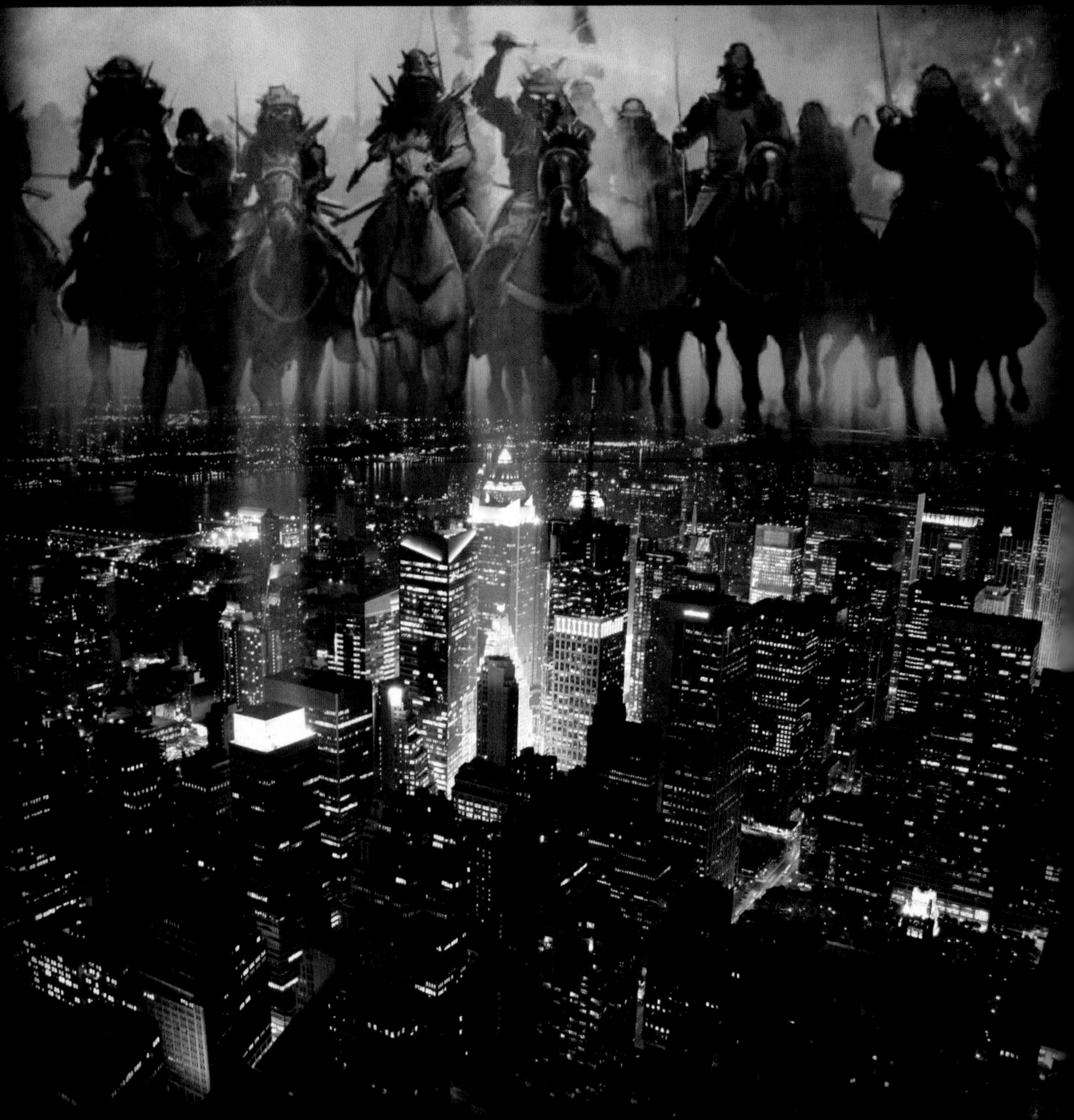

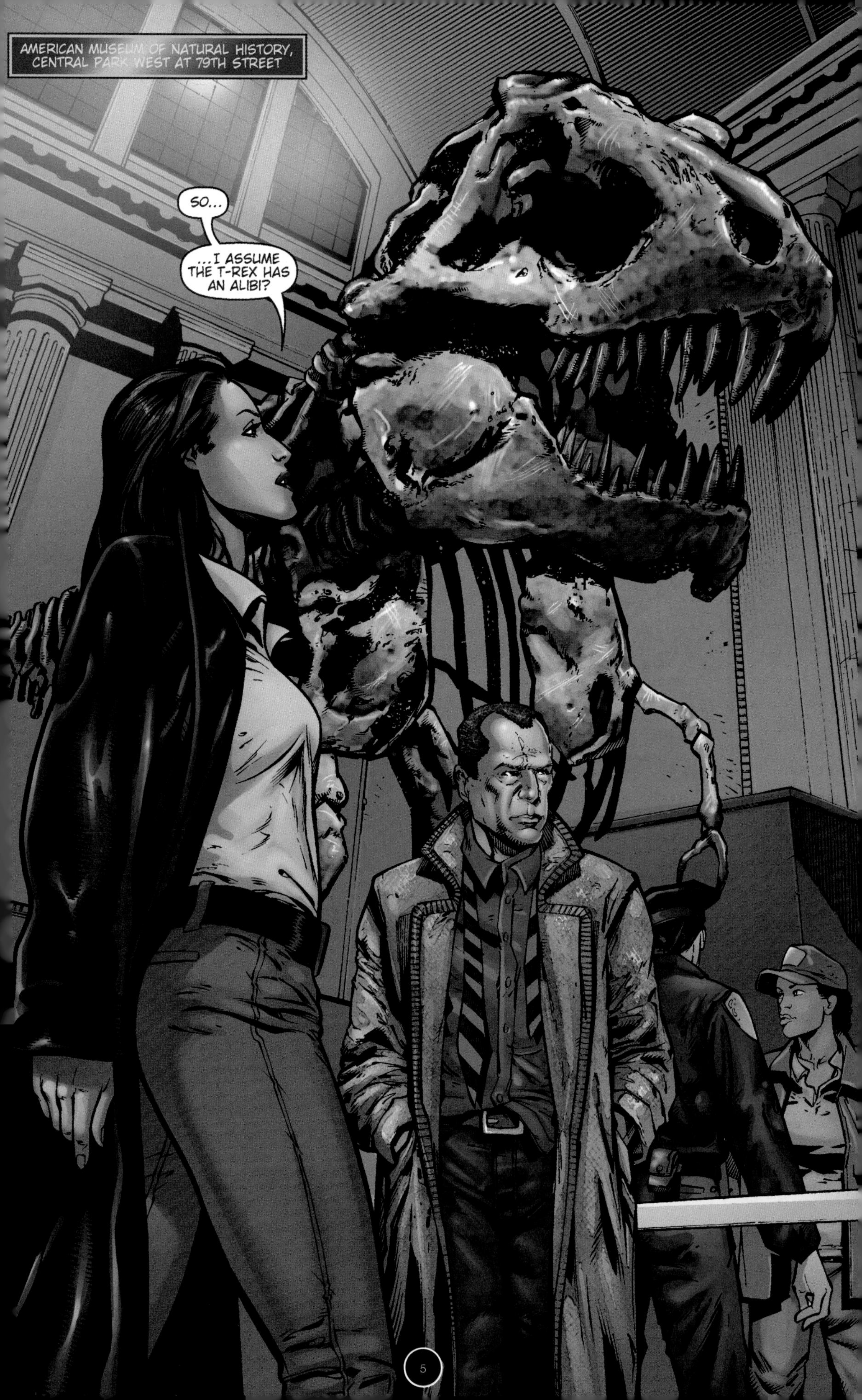
AMERICAN MUSEUM OF NATURAL HISTORY, CENTRAL PARK WEST AT 79TH STREET
SO...
...I ASSUME THE T-REX HAS AN ALIBI?

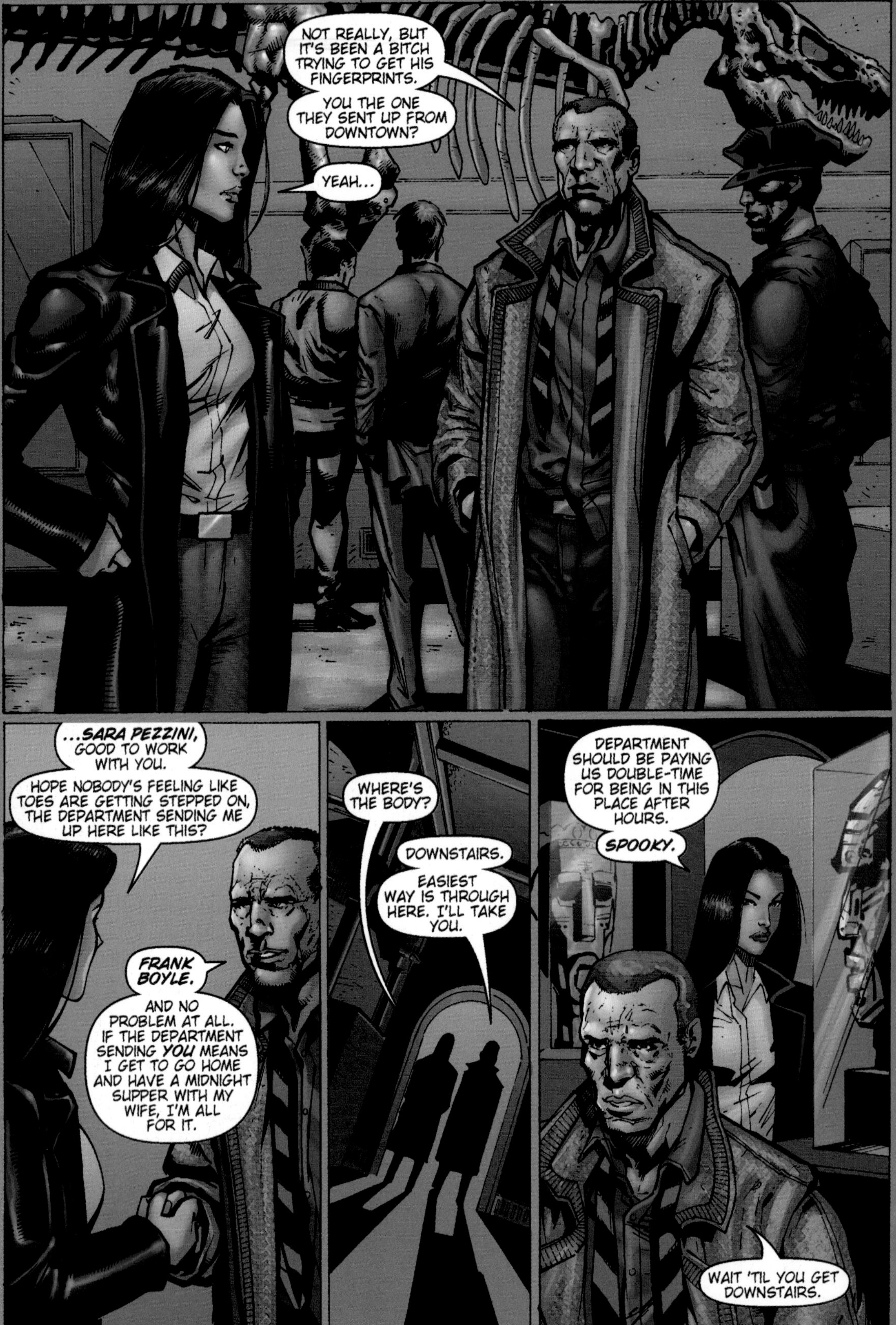
NOT REALLY, BUT IT'S BEEN A BITCH TRYING TO GET HIS FINGERPRINTS.
YOU THE ONE THEY SENT UP FROM DOWNTOWN?
YEAH...
...SARA PEZZINI, GOOD TO WORK WITH YOU.
HOPE NOBODY'S FEELING LIKE TOES ARE GETTING STEPPED ON, THE DEPARTMENT SENDING ME UP HERE LIKE THIS?
FRANK BOYLE.
AND NO PROBLEM AT ALL. IF THE DEPARTMENT SENDING YOU MEANS I GET TO GO HOME AND HAVE A MIDNIGHT SUPPER WITH MY WIFE, I'M ALL FOR IT.
WHERE'S THE BODY?
DOWNSTAIRS.
EASIEST WAY IS THROUGH HERE. I'LL TAKE YOU.
DEPARTMENT SHOULD BE PAYING US DOUBLE-TIME FOR BEING IN THIS PLACE AFTER HOURS.
SPOOKY.
WAIT 'TIL YOU GET DOWNSTAIRS.

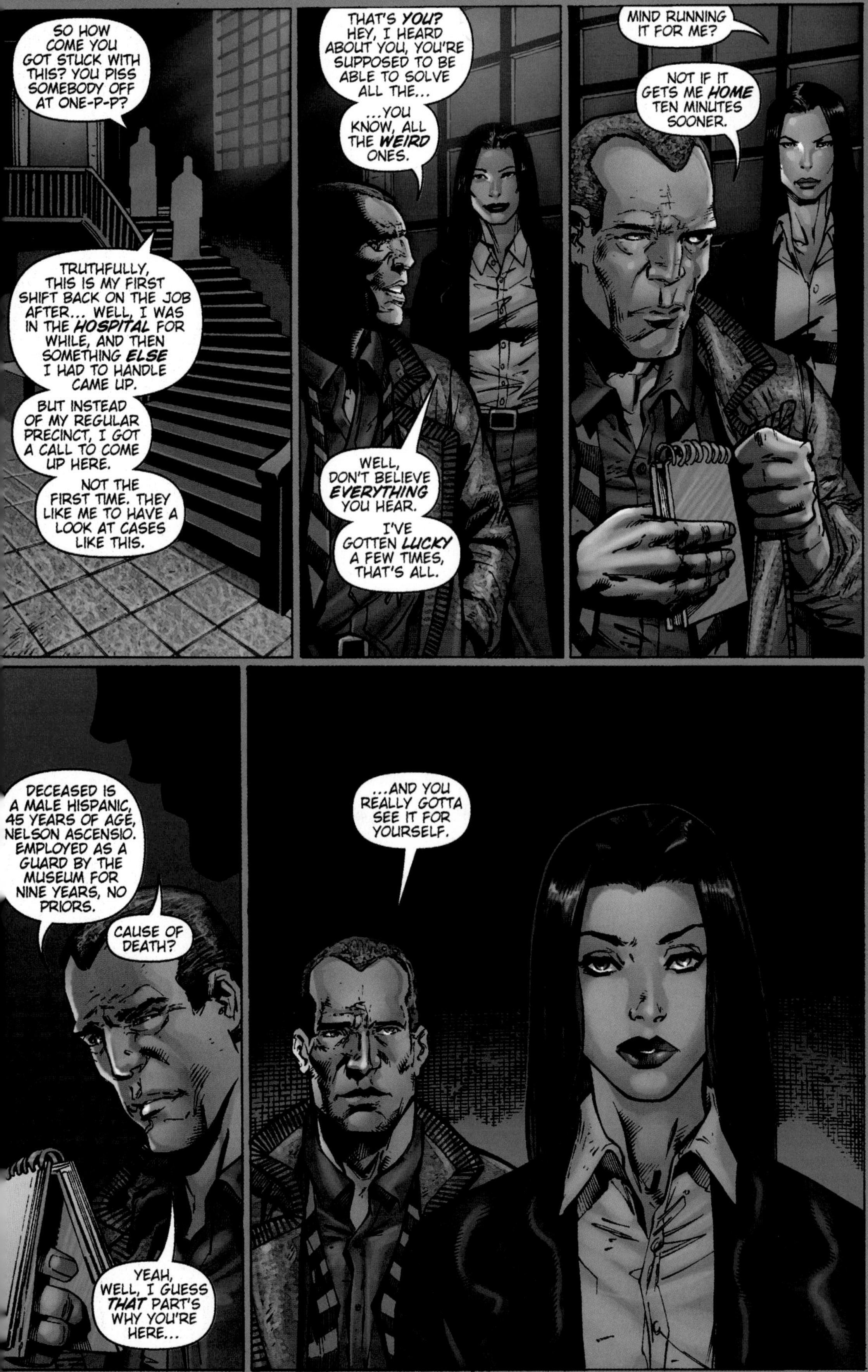
SO HOW COME YOU GOT STUCK WITH THIS? YOU PISS SOMEBODY OFF AT ONE-P-P?
TRUTHFULLY, THIS IS MY FIRST SHIFT BACK ON THE JOB AFTER... WELL, I WAS IN THE HOSPITAL FOR WHILE, AND THEN SOMETHING ELSE I HAD TO HANDLE CAME UP.
BUT INSTEAD OF MY REGULAR PRECINCT, I GOT A CALL TO COME UP HERE.
NOT THE FIRST TIME. THEY LIKE ME TO HAVE A LOOK AT CASES LIKE THIS.
THAT'S YOU? HEY, I HEARD ABOUT YOU, YOU'RE SUPPOSED TO BE ABLE TO SOLVE ALL THE...
...YOU KNOW, ALL THE WEIRD ONES.
WELL, DON'T BELIEVE EVERYTHING YOU HEAR.
I'VE GOTTEN LUCKY A FEW TIMES, THAT'S ALL.
MIND RUNNING IT FOR ME?
NOT IF IT GETS ME HOME TEN MINUTES SOONER.
DECEASED IS A MALE HISPANIC, 45 YEARS OF AGE, NELSON ASCENSIO. EMPLOYED AS A GUARD BY THE MUSEUM FOR NINE YEARS, NO PRIORS.
CAUSE OF DEATH?
YEAH, WELL, I GUESS THAT PART'S WHY YOU'RE HERE...
...AND YOU REALLY GOTTA SEE IT FOR YOURSELF.

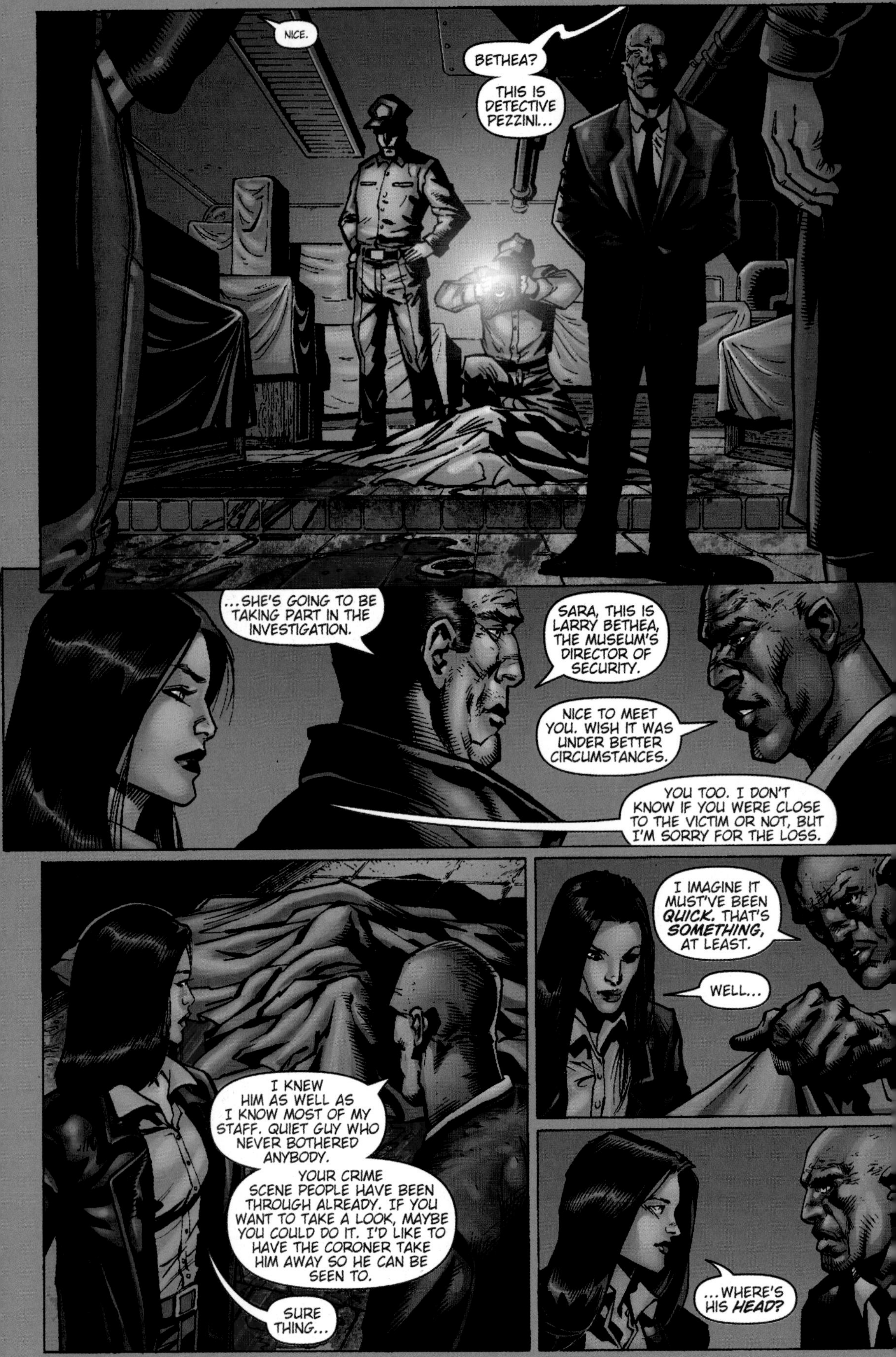

NICE.
BETHEA?
THIS IS DETECTIVE PEZZINI...
...SHE'S GOING TO BE TAKING PART IN THE INVESTIGATION.
SARA, THIS IS LARRY BETHEA, THE MUSEUM'S DIRECTOR OF SECURITY.
NICE TO MEET YOU. WISH IT WAS UNDER BETTER CIRCUMSTANCES.
YOU TOO. I DON'T KNOW IF YOU WERE CLOSE TO THE VICTIM OR NOT, BUT I'M SORRY FOR THE LOSS.
I KNEW HIM AS WELL AS I KNOW MOST OF MY STAFF. QUIET GUY WHO NEVER BOTHERED ANYBODY.
YOUR CRIME SCENE PEOPLE HAVE BEEN THROUGH ALREADY. IF YOU WANT TO TAKE A LOOK, MAYBE YOU COULD DO IT. I'D LIKE TO HAVE THE CORONER TAKE HIM AWAY SO HE CAN BE SEEN TO.
SURE THING...
I IMAGINE IT MUST'VE BEEN ***QUICK.*** THAT'S ***SOMETHING,*** AT LEAST.
WELL...
...WHERE'S HIS ***HEAD?***

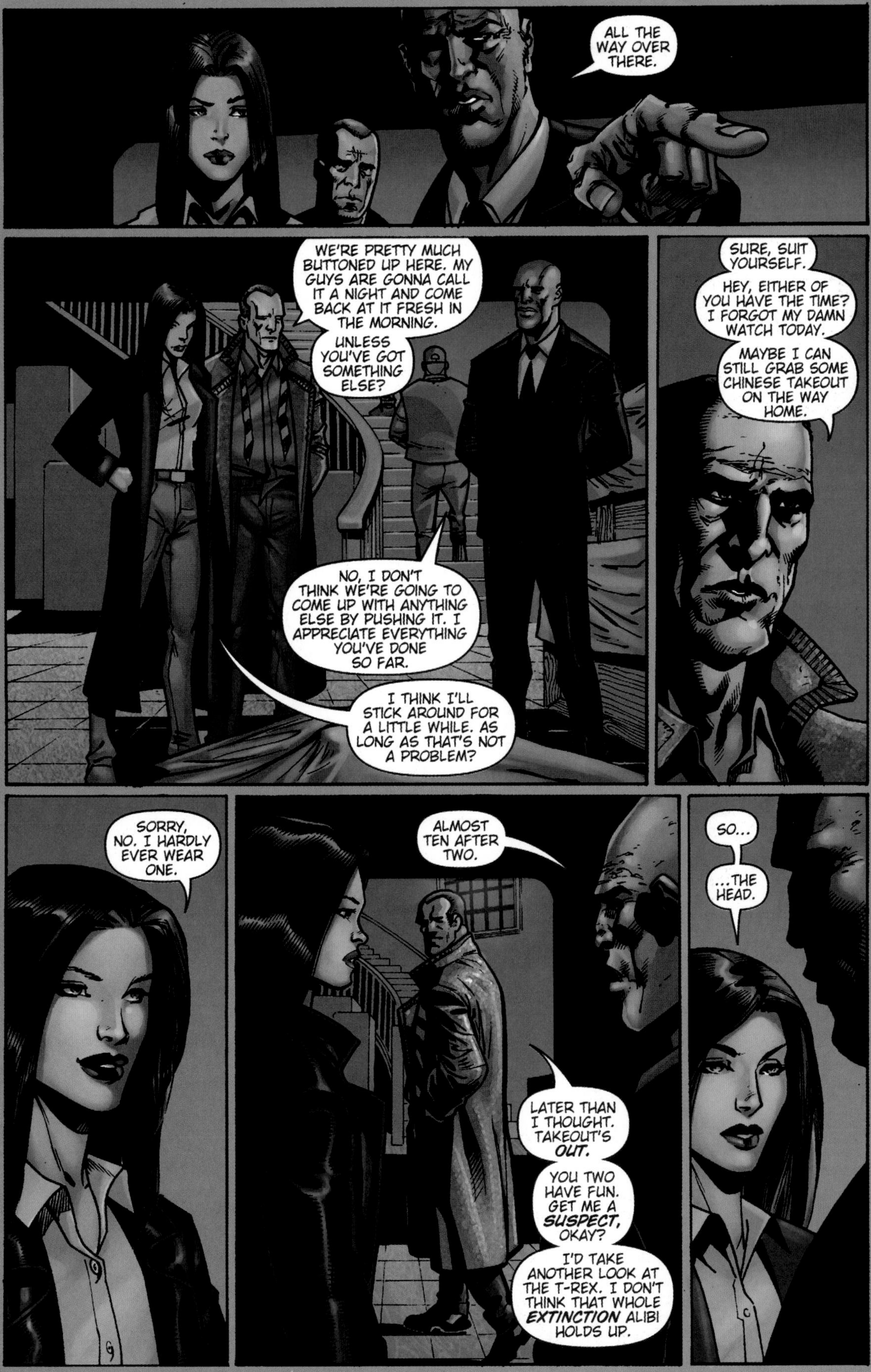
ALL THE WAY OVER THERE.
WE'RE PRETTY MUCH BUTTONED UP HERE. MY GUYS ARE GONNA CALL IT A NIGHT AND COME BACK AT IT FRESH IN THE MORNING.
UNLESS YOU'VE GOT SOMETHING ELSE?
NO, I DON'T THINK WE'RE GOING TO COME UP WITH ANYTHING ELSE BY PUSHING IT. I APPRECIATE EVERYTHING YOU'VE DONE SO FAR.
I THINK I'LL STICK AROUND FOR A LITTLE WHILE. AS LONG AS THAT'S NOT A PROBLEM?
SURE, SUIT YOURSELF.
HEY, EITHER OF YOU HAVE THE TIME? I FORGOT MY DAMN WATCH TODAY.
MAYBE I CAN STILL GRAB SOME CHINESE TAKEOUT ON THE WAY HOME.
SORRY, NO. I HARDLY EVER WEAR ONE.
ALMOST TEN AFTER TWO.
LATER THAN I THOUGHT. TAKEOUT'S **OUT.**
YOU TWO HAVE FUN. GET ME A **SUSPECT,** OKAY?
I'D TAKE ANOTHER LOOK AT THE T-REX. I DON'T THINK THAT WHOLE **EXTINCTION** ALIBI HOLDS UP.
SO...
...THE HEAD.

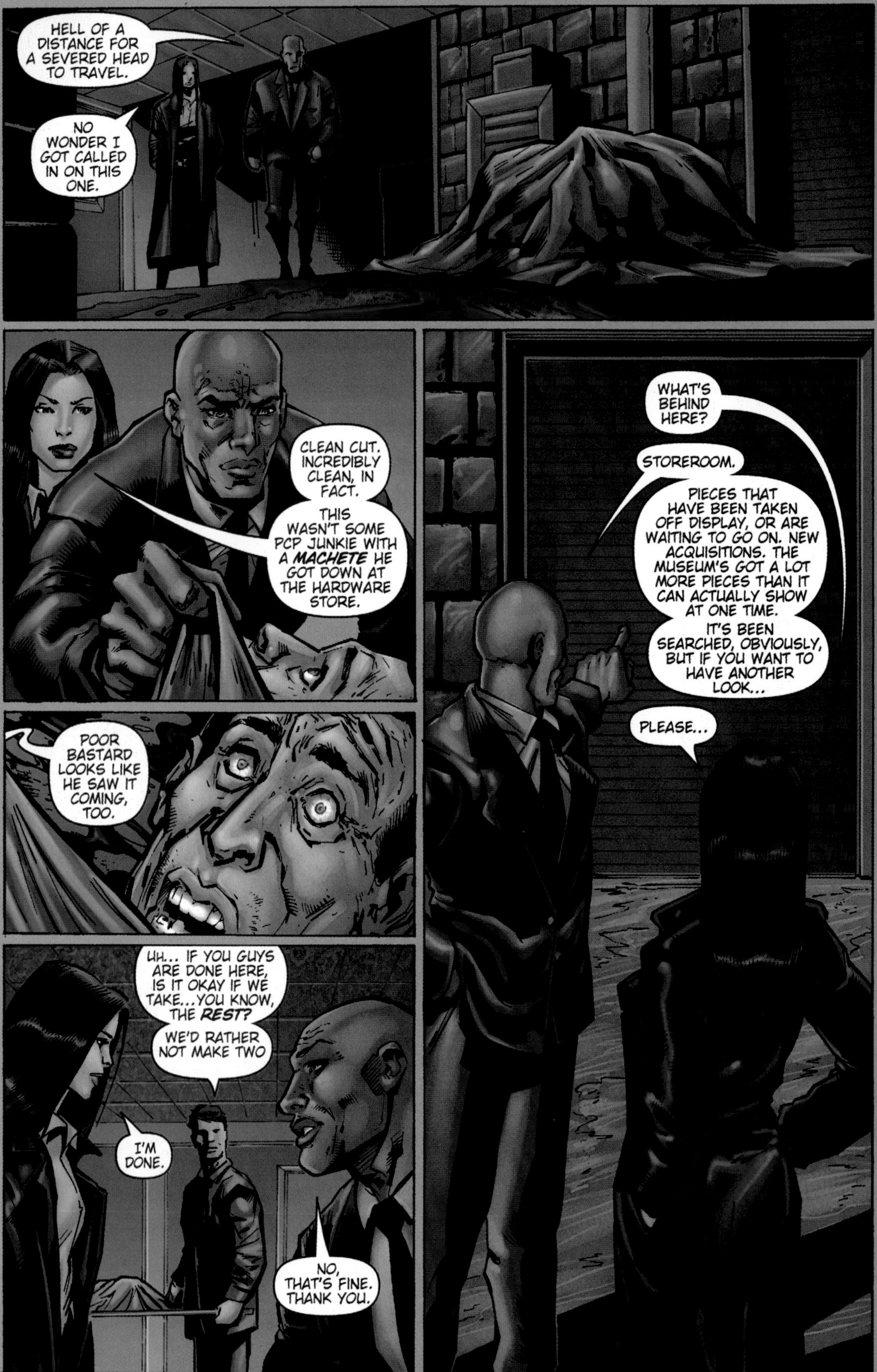
HELL OF A DISTANCE FOR A SEVERED HEAD TO TRAVEL.
NO WONDER I GOT CALLED IN ON THIS ONE.
CLEAN CUT. INCREDIBLY CLEAN, IN FACT.
THIS WASN'T SOME PCP JUNKIE WITH A MACHETE HE GOT DOWN AT THE HARDWARE STORE.
POOR BASTARD LOOKS LIKE HE SAW IT COMING, TOO.
UH... IF YOU GUYS ARE DONE HERE, IS IT OKAY IF WE TAKE...YOU KNOW, THE REST?
WE'D RATHER NOT MAKE TWO
I'M DONE.
NO, THAT'S FINE. THANK YOU.
WHAT'S BEHIND HERE?
STOREROOM.
PIECES THAT HAVE BEEN TAKEN OFF DISPLAY, OR ARE WAITING TO GO ON. NEW ACQUISITIONS. THE MUSEUM'S GOT A LOT MORE PIECES THAN IT CAN ACTUALLY SHOW AT ONE TIME.
IT'S BEEN SEARCHED, OBVIOUSLY, BUT IF YOU WANT TO HAVE ANOTHER LOOK...
PLEASE...

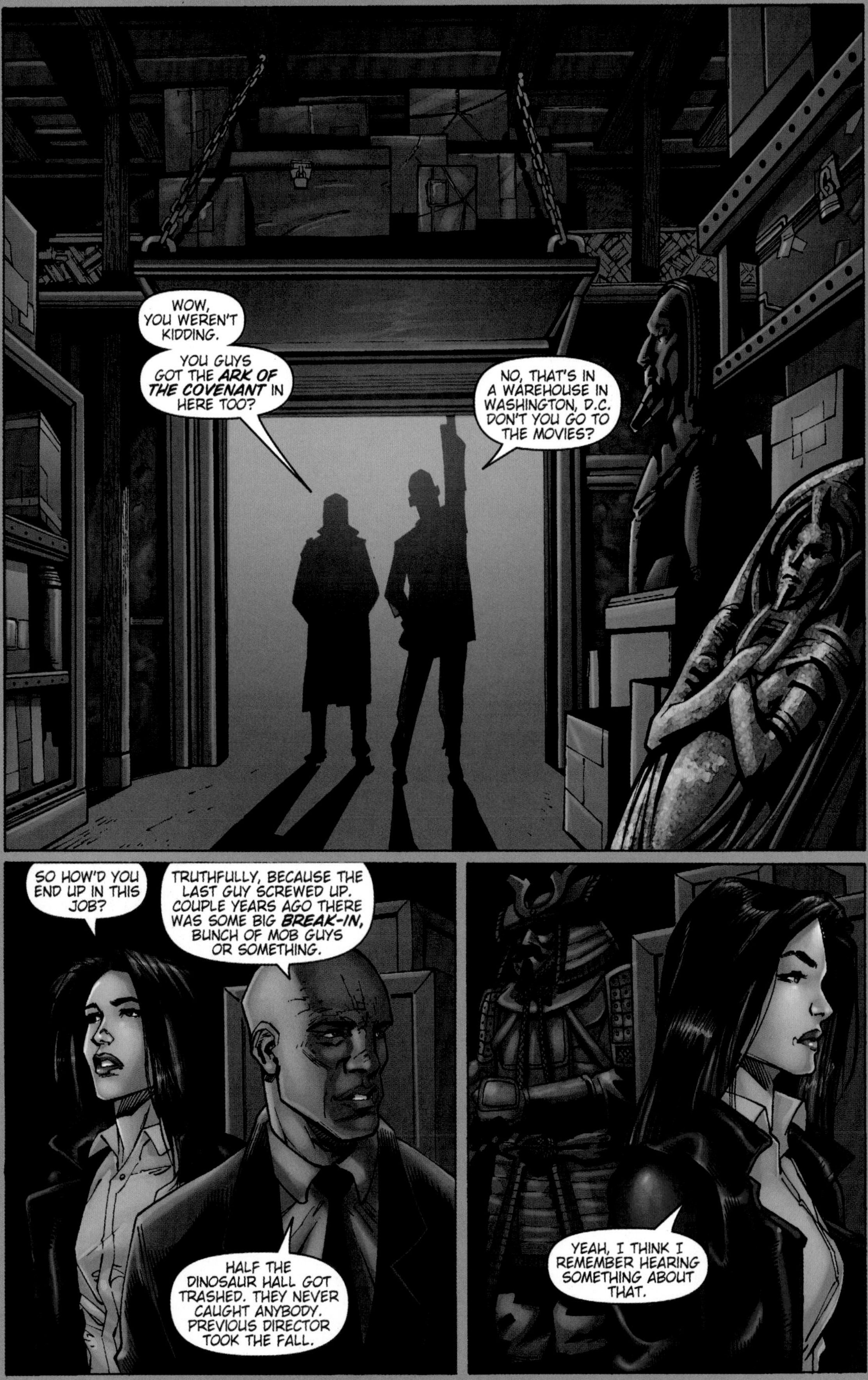

WOW, YOU WEREN'T KIDDING.
YOU GUYS GOT THE ARK OF THE COVENANT IN HERE TOO?
NO, THAT'S IN A WAREHOUSE IN WASHINGTON, D.C. DON'T YOU GO TO THE MOVIES?
SO HOW'D YOU END UP IN THIS JOB?
TRUTHFULLY, BECAUSE THE LAST GUY SCREWED UP. COUPLE YEARS AGO THERE WAS SOME BIG BREAK-IN, BUNCH OF MOB GUYS OR SOMETHING.
HALF THE DINOSAUR HALL GOT TRASHED. THEY NEVER CAUGHT ANYBODY. PREVIOUS DIRECTOR TOOK THE FALL.
YEAH, I THINK I REMEMBER HEARING SOMETHING ABOUT THAT.

I DIDN'T NECESSARILY WANT THE JOB TO COME TO ME BECAUSE OF SOMEBODY ELSE'S MISFORTUNE, BUT THIS IS THE ONLY JOB I'VE EVER WANTED.

I GREW UP IN HARLEM, 126TH STREET.

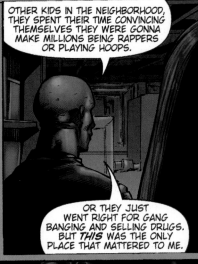

OTHER KIDS IN THE NEIGHBORHOOD, THEY SPENT THEIR TIME CONVINCING THEMSELVES THEY WERE GONNA MAKE MILLIONS BEING RAPPERS OR PLAYING HOOPS.

OR THEY JUST WENT RIGHT FOR GANG BANGING AND SELLING DRUGS. BUT *THIS* WAS THE ONLY PLACE THAT MATTERED TO ME.

EVERY CHANCE I GOT, I HOPPED THE SUBWAY AND CAME HERE. SPEND THE WHOLE DAY HERE, UNTIL THE SECURITY GUARDS WOULD SHOO EVERYBODY OUT AT CLOSING TIME.

BEST PLACE IN THE WORLD, AS FAR AS I WAS CONCERNED. I COULDN'T IMAGINE WANTING TO BE ANYWHERE ELSE.

BUT I KNEW I WASN'T EVER GOING TO BE ONE OF THE *SCIENTISTS* WHO WORKED HERE.

BUT I THOUGHT, SECURITY GUARD GETS TO BE HERE ALL DAY AND GETS PAID FOR IT. WHAT COULD BE BETTER THAN THAT?

SO I GOT A JOB AS A GUARD AND WORKED MY WAY UP. THOUGH AFTER *THIS*...

...I EXPECT SOMEBODY *ELSE* IS GONNA HAVE THIS JOB.

WHAT ABOUT YOU? ALWAYS WANT TO BE A COP?

NOT MUCH CHOICE. *FATHER* WAS A COP.

NEVER OCCURRED TO ME THAT I COULD BE ANYTHING *ELSE*.

YOU LIKE IT?

I LIKE IT WELL ENOUGH.

AND IT'S NOT LIKE I ACTUALLY KNOW HOW TO *DO* ANYTHING ELSE.

I DUNNO.

I GUESS YOU COULD SAY THAT MY LIFE HASN'T TURNED OUT QUITE THE WAY I EXPECTED.

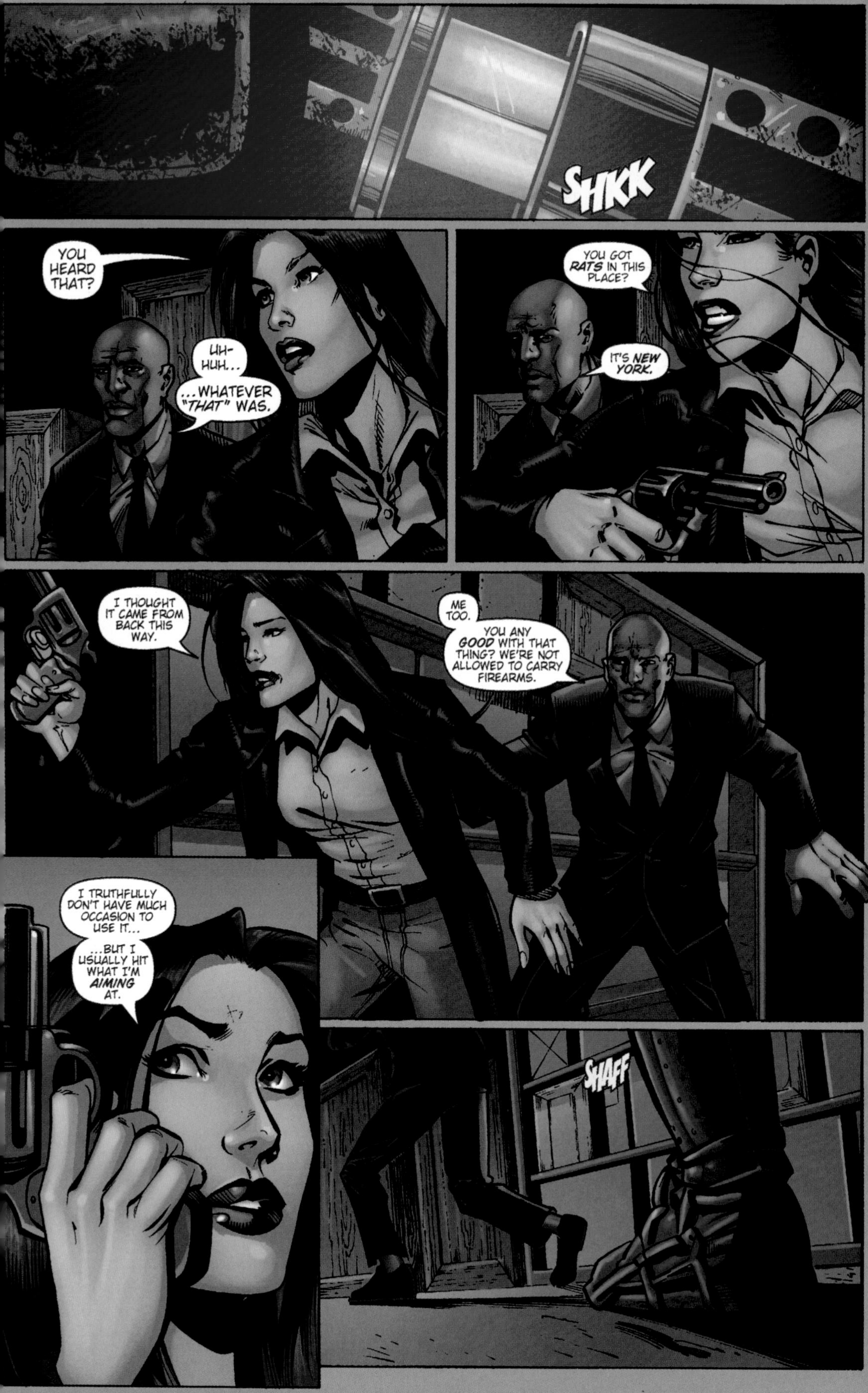

SHKK
YOU HEARD THAT?
UH-HUH...
...WHATEVER "THAT" WAS.
YOU GOT RATS IN THIS PLACE?
IT'S NEW YORK.
I THOUGHT IT CAME FROM BACK THIS WAY.
ME TOO.
YOU ANY GOOD WITH THAT THING? WE'RE NOT ALLOWED TO CARRY FIREARMS.
I TRUTHFULLY DON'T HAVE MUCH OCCASION TO USE IT...
...BUT I USUALLY HIT WHAT I'M AIMING AT.
SHAFF

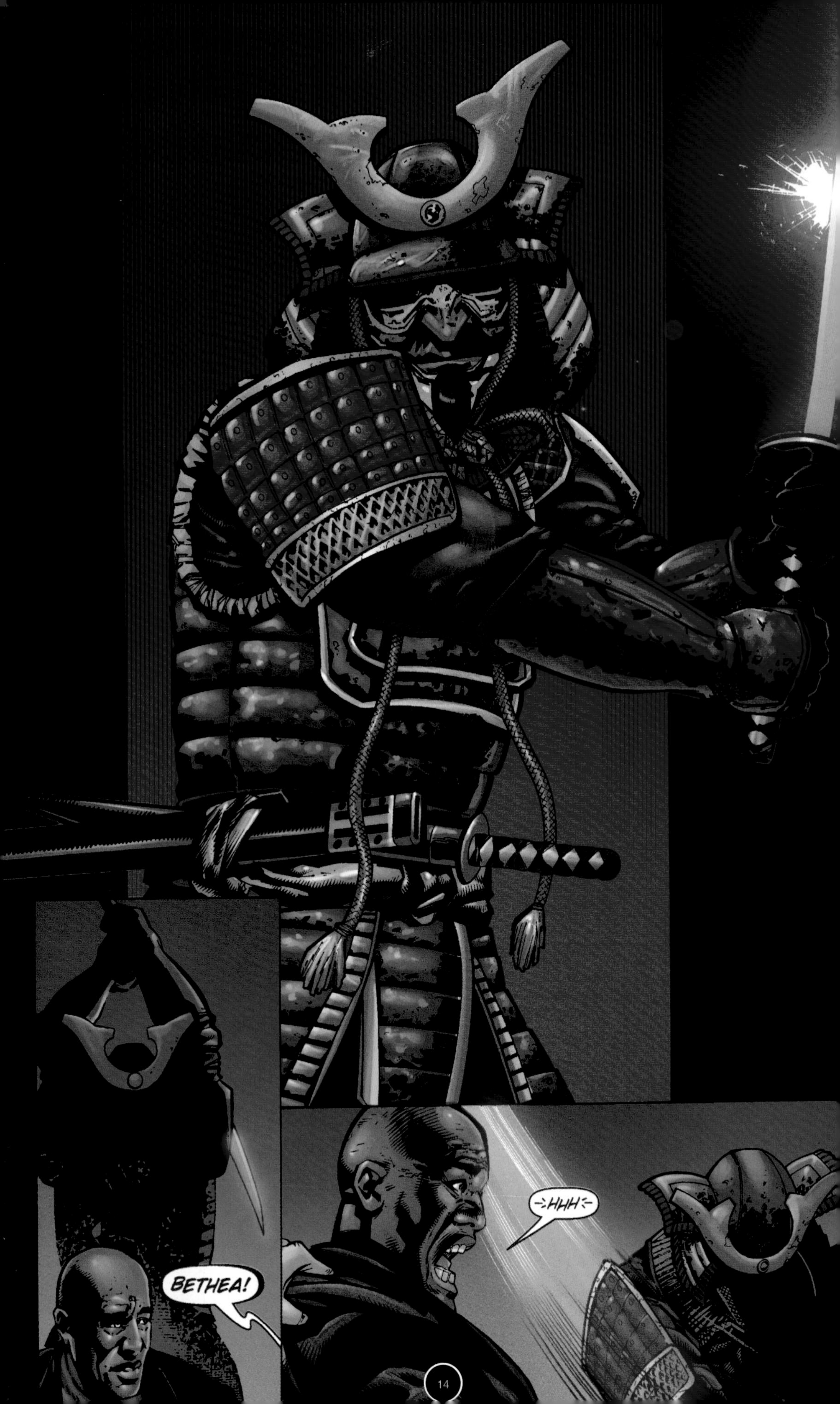

BETHEA!
HHH

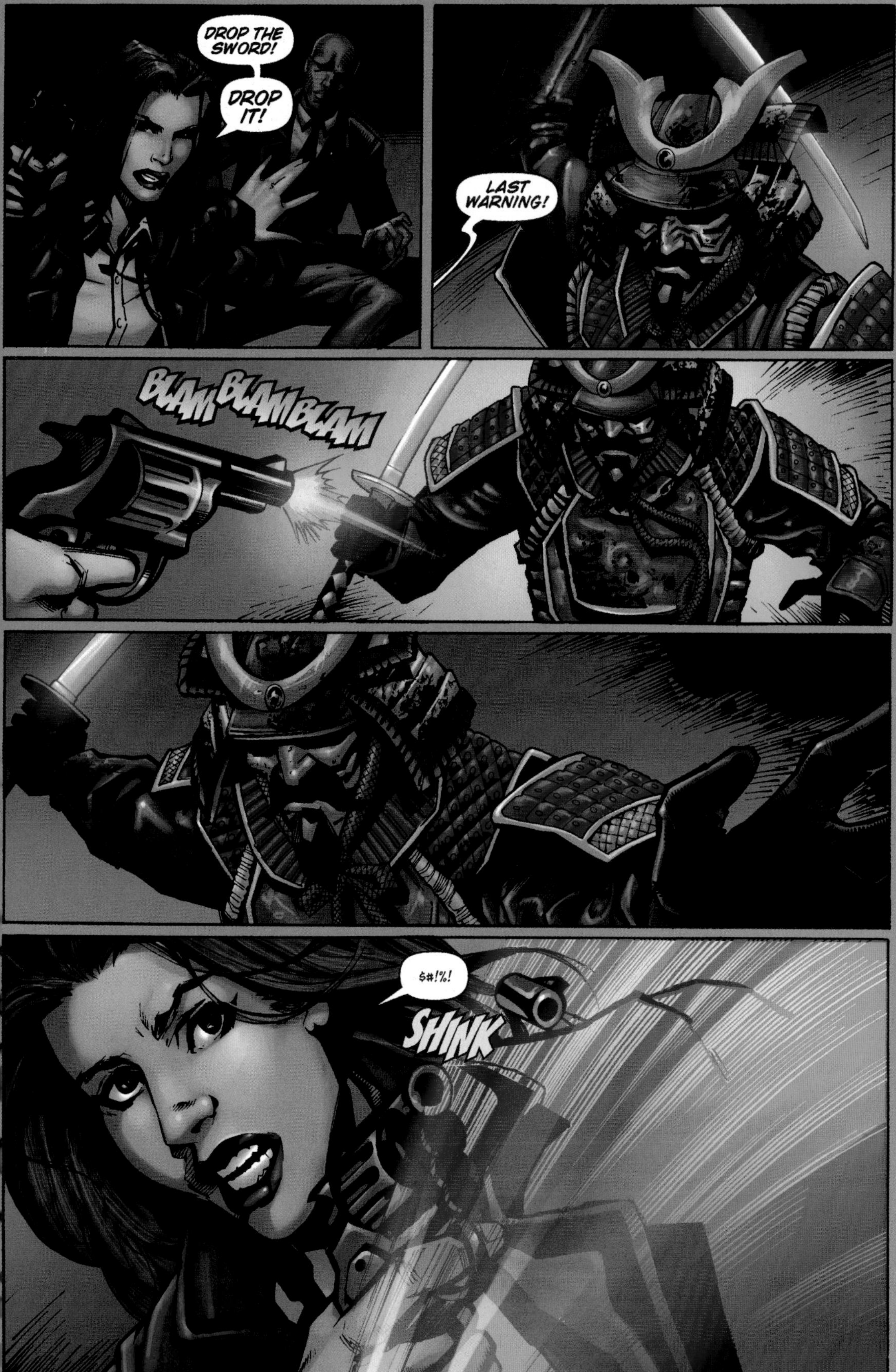
DROP THE SWORD!
DROP IT!
LAST WARNING!
BLAM BLAMBLAM
$#!%!
SHINK

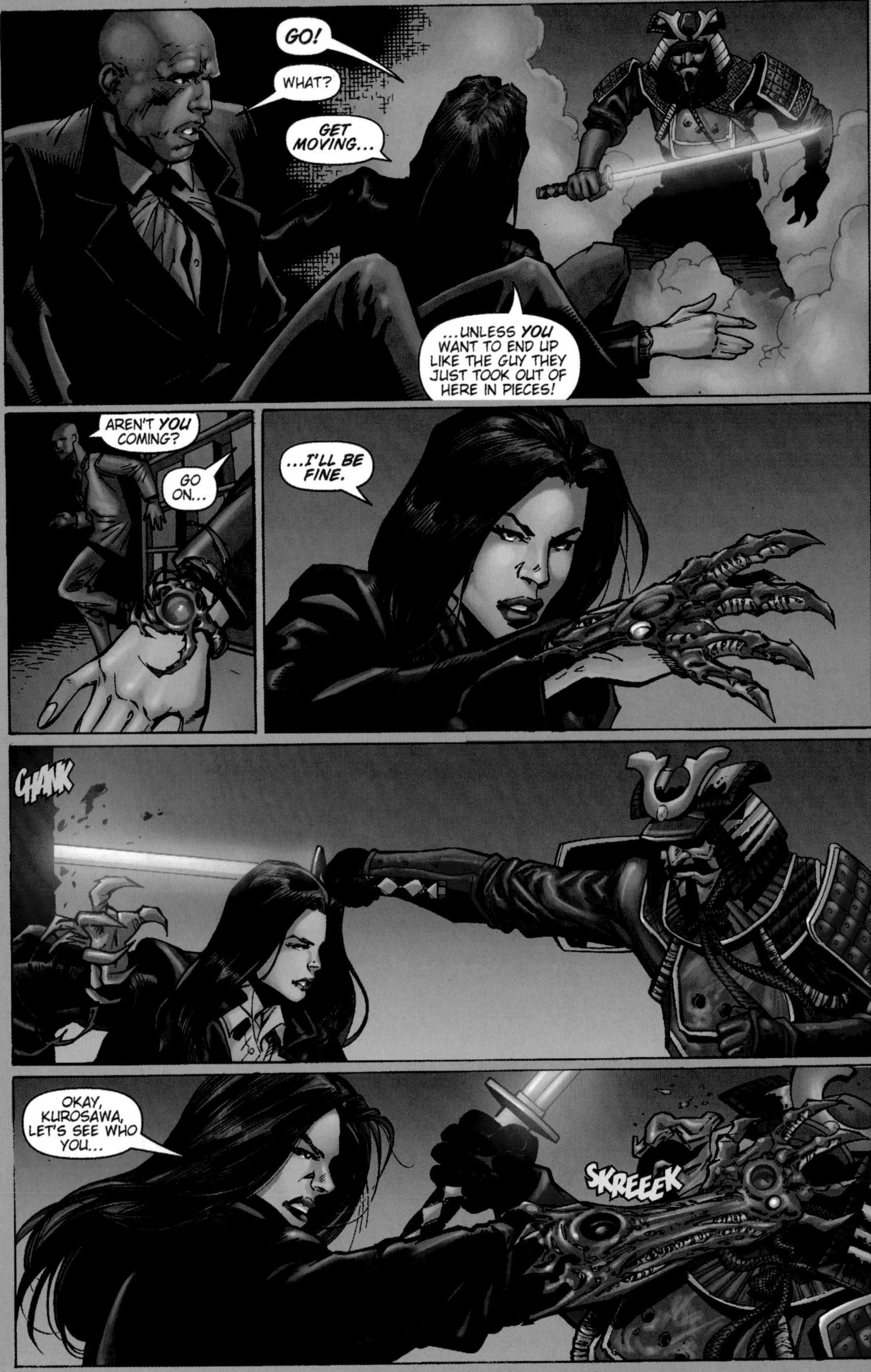
GO!
WHAT?
GET MOVING...
...UNLESS YOU WANT TO END UP LIKE THE GUY THEY JUST TOOK OUT OF HERE IN PIECES!
AREN'T YOU COMING?
GO ON...
...I'LL BE FINE.
CHANK
OKAY, KUROSAWA, LET'S SEE WHO YOU...
SKREEEK

...ARE?

AAHN!

WHUD

FIRST DAY BACK ON THE JOB...

...I GET A DAMN SAMURAI GHOST...

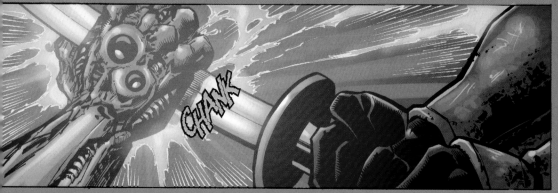

CHANK

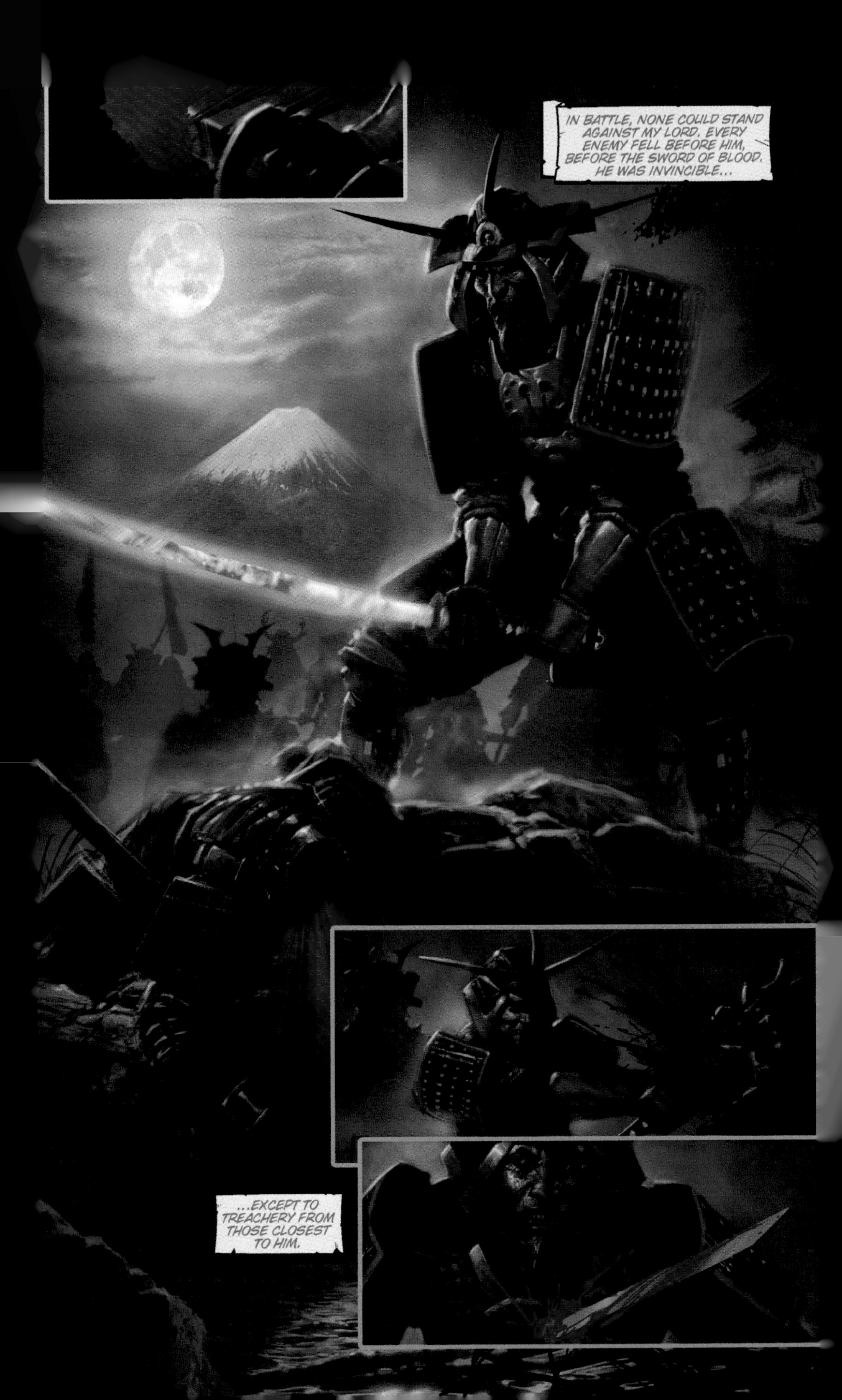
IN BATTLE, NONE COULD STAND AGAINST MY LORD. EVERY ENEMY FELL BEFORE HIM, BEFORE THE SWORD OF BLOOD. HE WAS INVINCIBLE...
...EXCEPT TO TREACHERY FROM THOSE CLOSEST TO HIM.

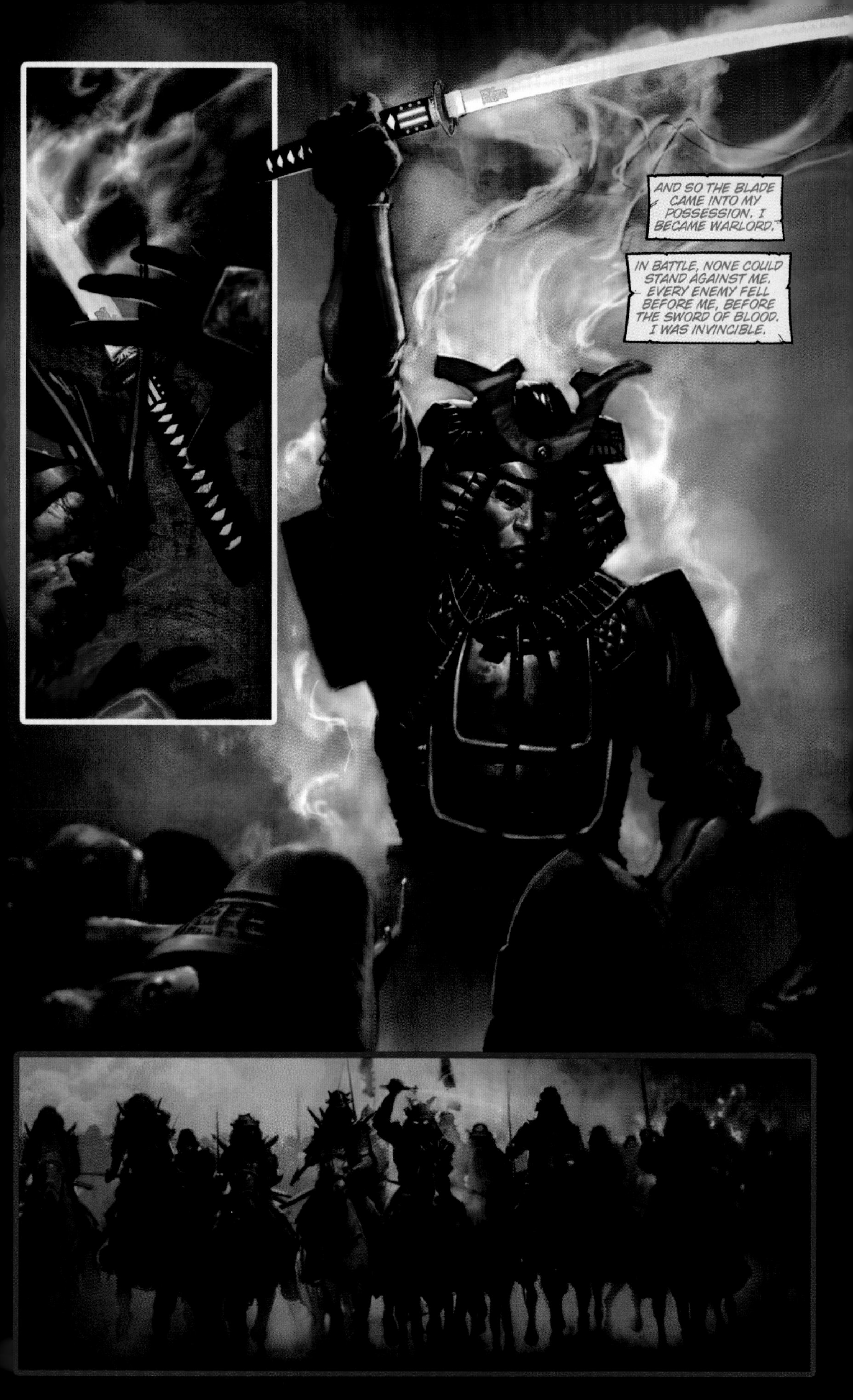
AND SO THE BLADE CAME INTO MY POSSESSION. I BECAME WARLORD.
IN BATTLE, NONE COULD STAND AGAINST ME. EVERY ENEMY FELL BEFORE ME, BEFORE THE SWORD OF BLOOD. I WAS INVINCIBLE.

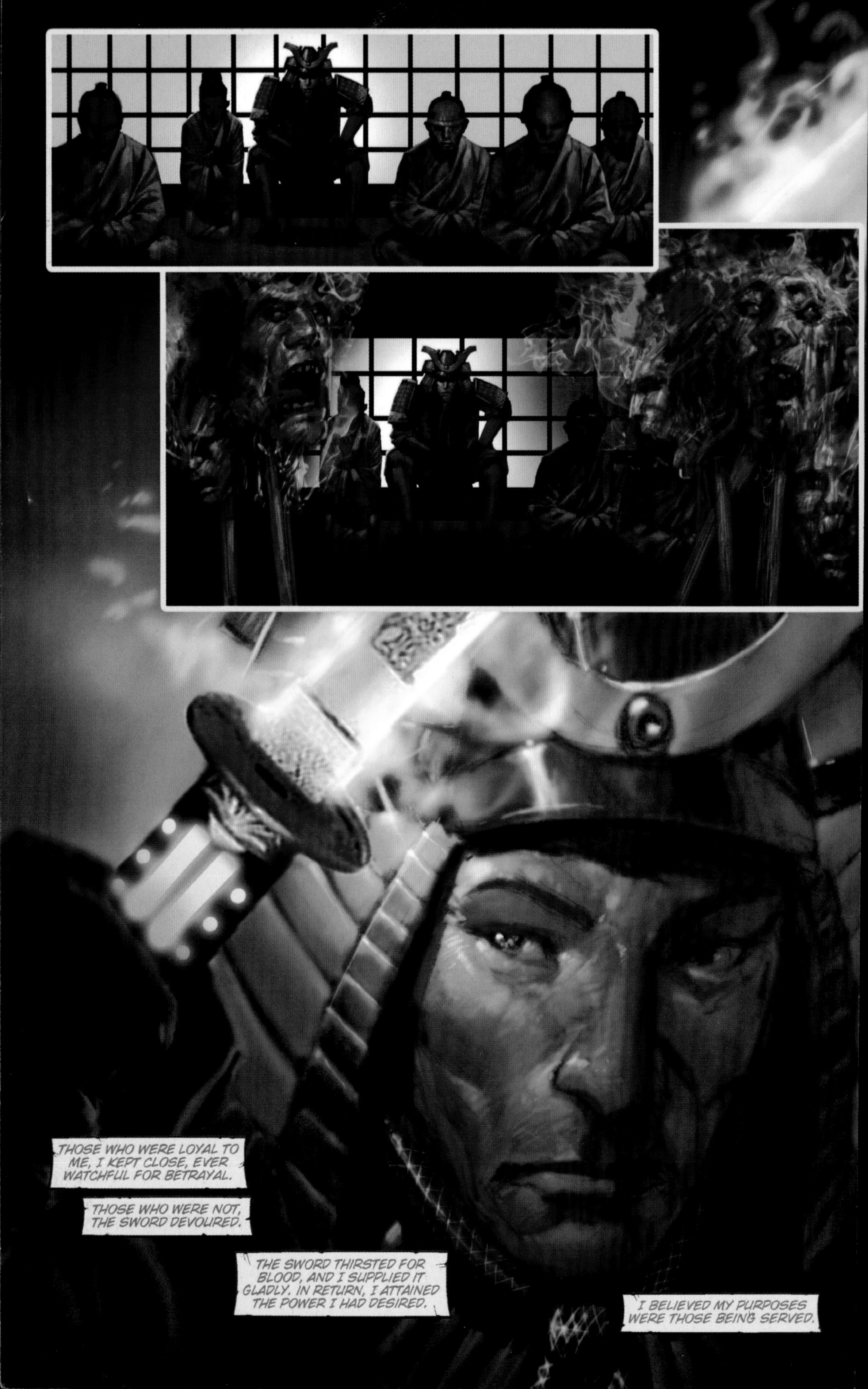
THOSE WHO WERE LOYAL TO ME, I KEPT CLOSE, EVER WATCHFUL FOR BETRAYAL.
THOSE WHO WERE NOT, THE SWORD DEVOURED.
THE SWORD THIRSTED FOR BLOOD, AND I SUPPLIED IT GLADLY. IN RETURN, I ATTAINED THE POWER I HAD DESIRED.
I BELIEVED MY PURPOSES WERE THOSE BEING SERVED.

YET I WAS MISTAKEN. IT WAS I WHO SERVED. I WHO WAS HELD IN THRALL...

...EVEN IN MY DOTAGE...

...IN DEATH...

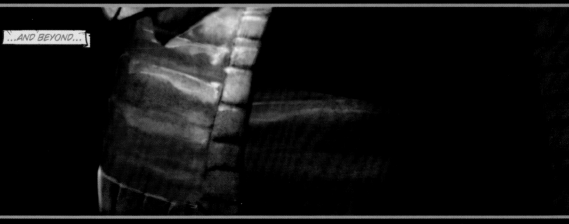

...AND BEYOND...

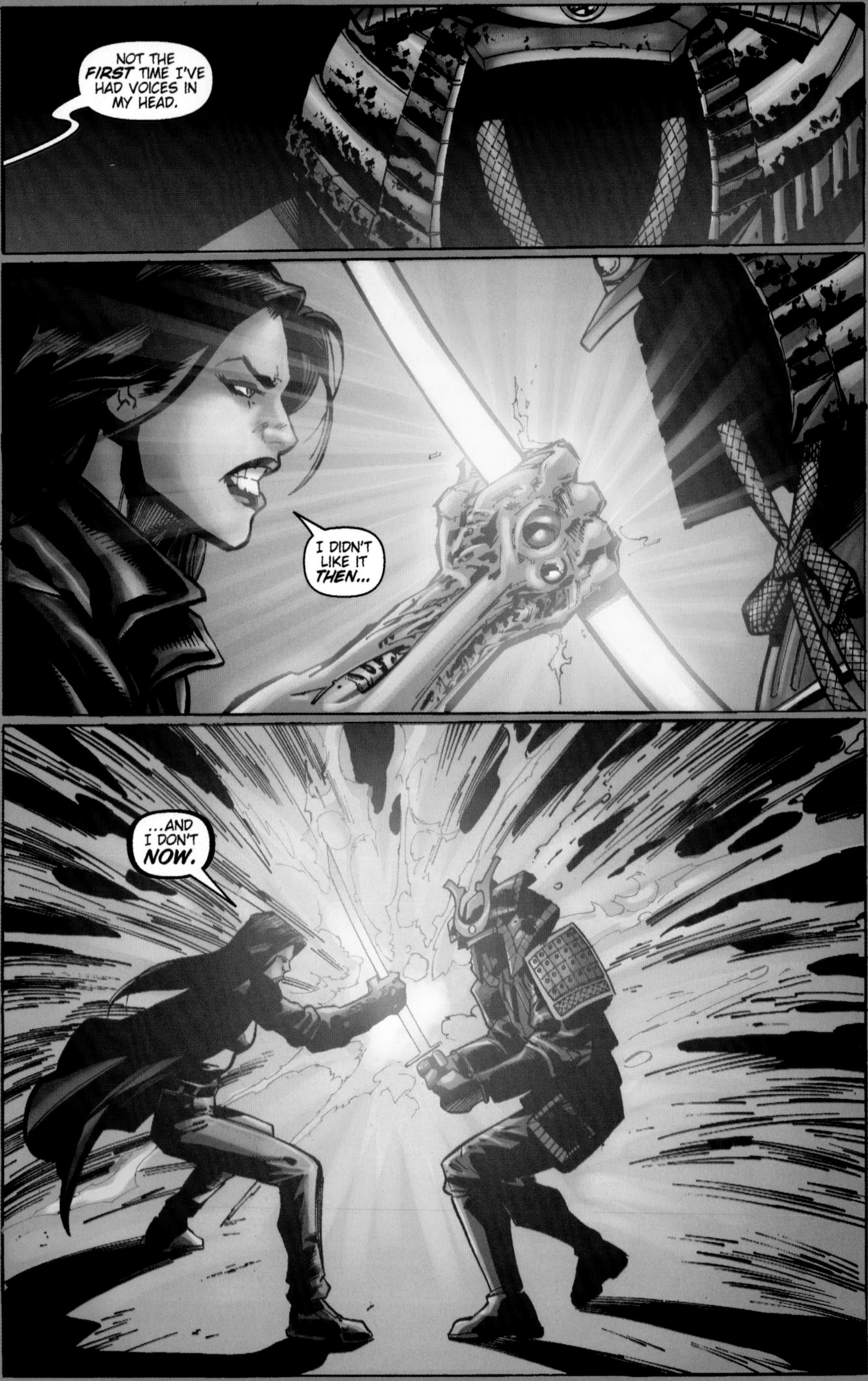
NOT THE FIRST TIME I'VE HAD VOICES IN MY HEAD.
I DIDN'T LIKE IT THEN...
...AND I DON'T NOW.

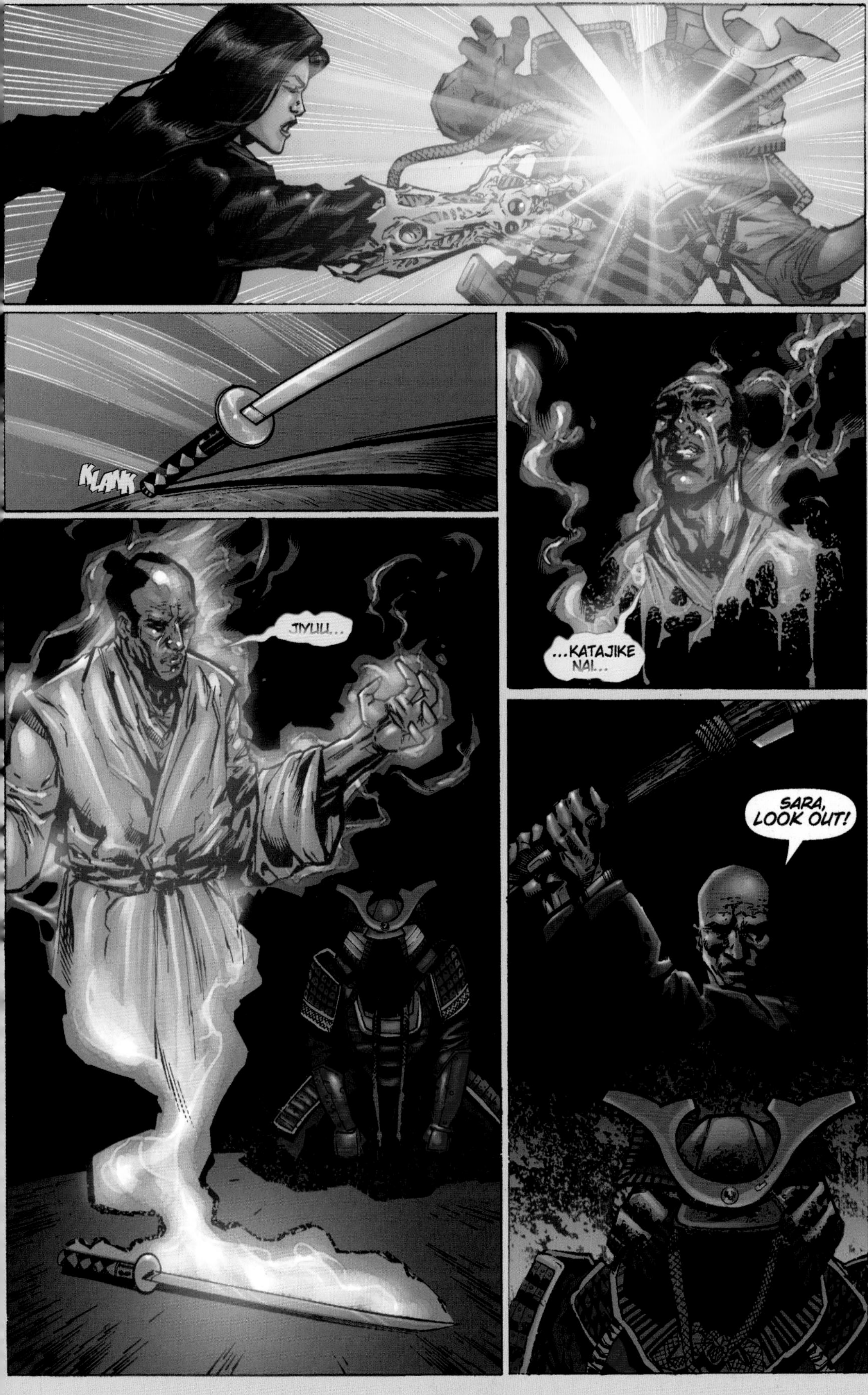
KLANK
JIYUU...
...KATAJIKE NAI...
SARA, LOOK OUT!

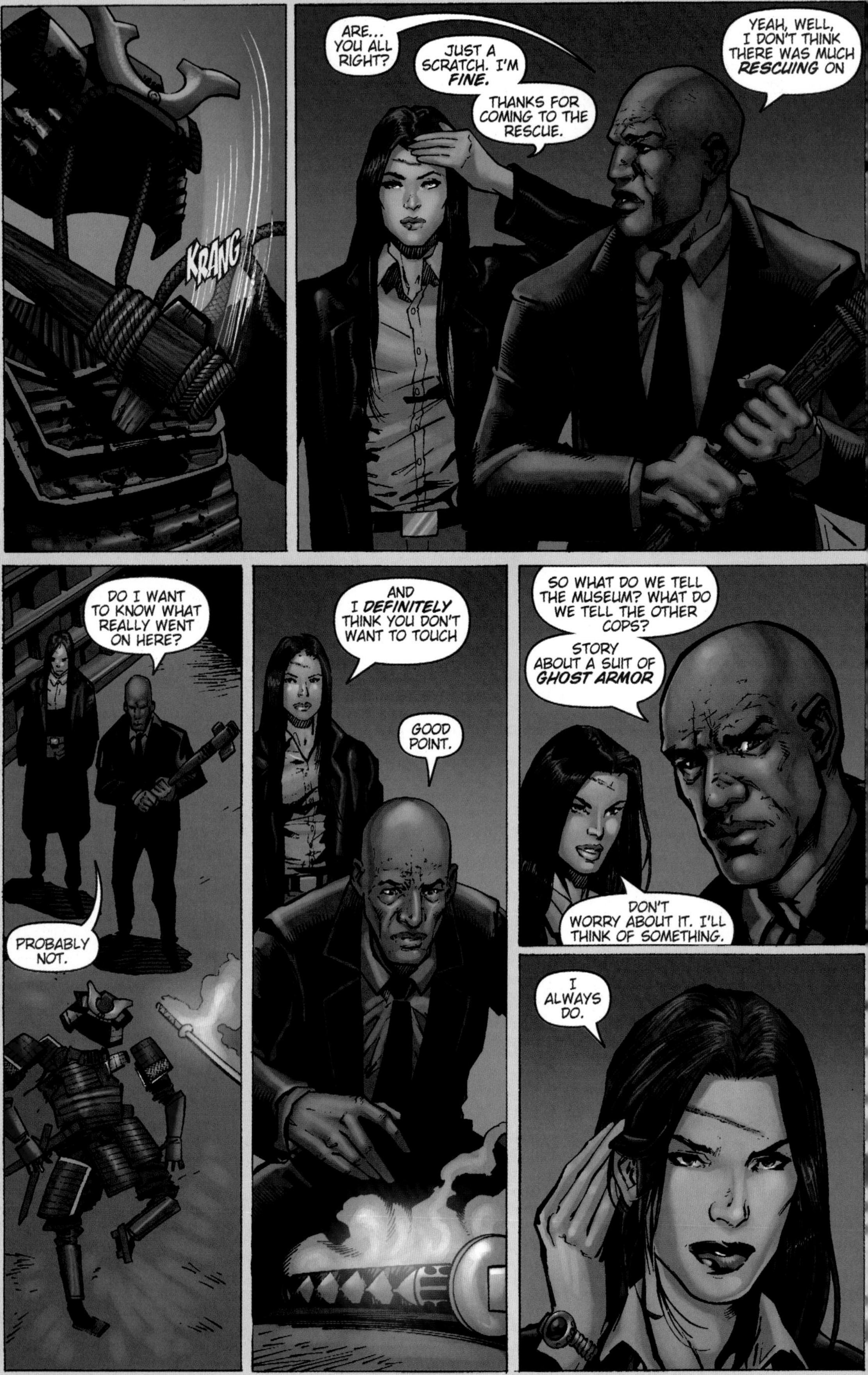
KRANG
ARE... YOU ALL RIGHT?
JUST A SCRATCH. I'M FINE.
THANKS FOR COMING TO THE RESCUE.
YEAH, WELL, I DON'T THINK THERE WAS MUCH RESCUING ON
DO I WANT TO KNOW WHAT REALLY WENT ON HERE?
PROBABLY NOT.
AND I DEFINITELY THINK YOU DON'T WANT TO TOUCH
GOOD POINT.
SO WHAT DO WE TELL THE MUSEUM? WHAT DO WE TELL THE OTHER COPS?
STORY ABOUT A SUIT OF GHOST ARMOR
DON'T WORRY ABOUT IT. I'LL THINK OF SOMETHING.
I ALWAYS DO.

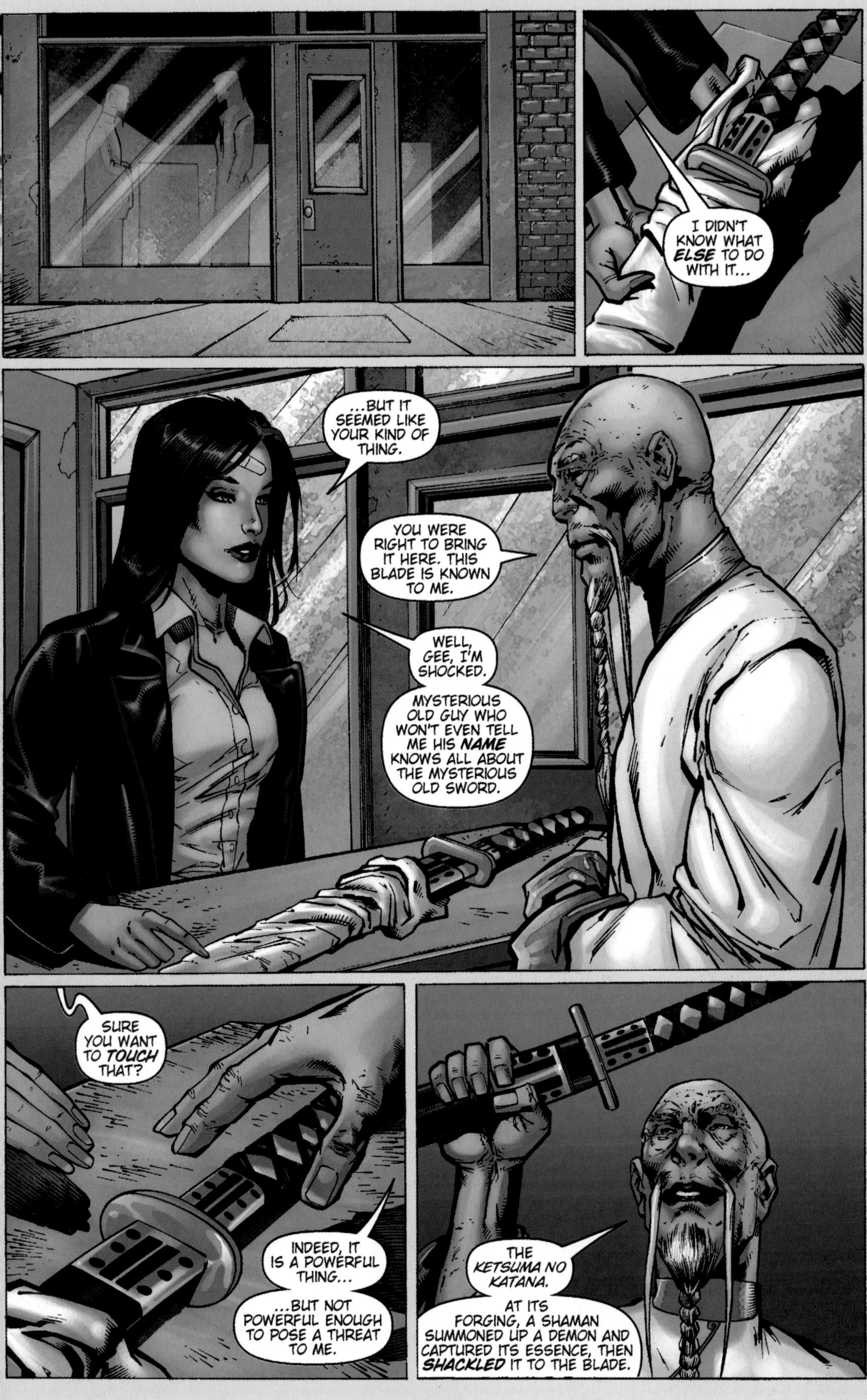
I DIDN'T KNOW WHAT ELSE TO DO WITH IT...
...BUT IT SEEMED LIKE YOUR KIND OF THING.
YOU WERE RIGHT TO BRING IT HERE. THIS BLADE IS KNOWN TO ME.
WELL, GEE, I'M SHOCKED.
MYSTERIOUS OLD GUY WHO WON'T EVEN TELL ME HIS NAME KNOWS ALL ABOUT THE MYSTERIOUS OLD SWORD.
SURE YOU WANT TO TOUCH THAT?
INDEED, IT IS A POWERFUL THING...
...BUT NOT POWERFUL ENOUGH TO POSE A THREAT TO ME.
THE KETSUMA NO KATANA.
AT ITS FORGING, A SHAMAN SUMMONED UP A DEMON AND CAPTURED ITS ESSENCE, THEN SHACKLED IT TO THE BLADE.

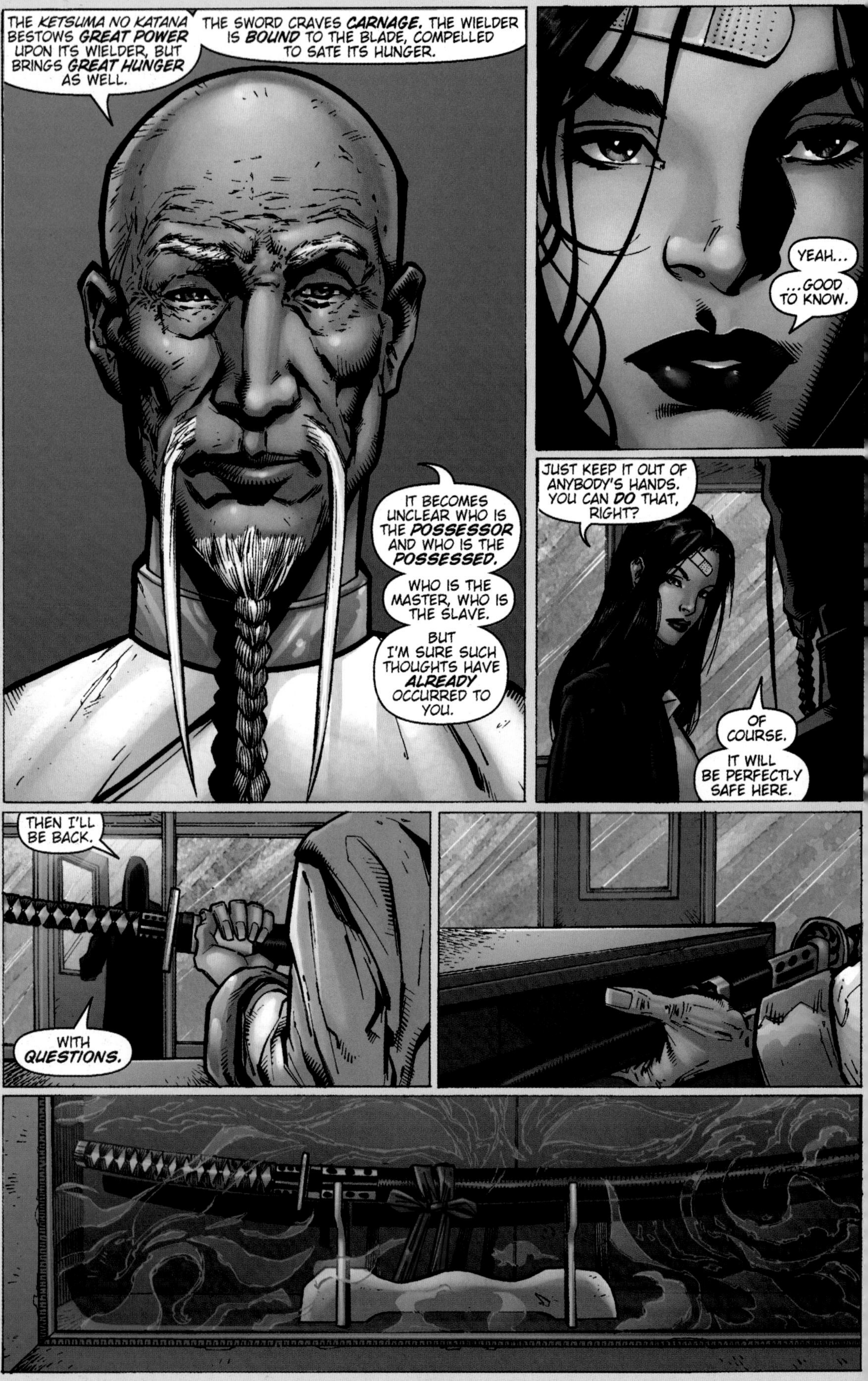
THE *KETSUMA NO KATANA* BESTOWS **GREAT POWER** UPON ITS WIELDER, BUT BRINGS **GREAT HUNGER** AS WELL.
THE SWORD CRAVES **CARNAGE.** THE WIELDER IS **BOUND** TO THE BLADE, COMPELLED TO SATE ITS HUNGER.
YEAH...
...GOOD TO KNOW.
IT BECOMES UNCLEAR WHO IS THE **POSSESSOR** AND WHO IS THE **POSSESSED.**
WHO IS THE MASTER, WHO IS THE SLAVE.
BUT I'M SURE SUCH THOUGHTS HAVE **ALREADY** OCCURRED TO YOU.
JUST KEEP IT OUT OF ANYBODY'S HANDS. YOU CAN **DO** THAT, RIGHT?
OF COURSE.
IT WILL BE PERFECTLY SAFE HERE.
THEN I'LL BE BACK.
WITH **QUESTIONS.**

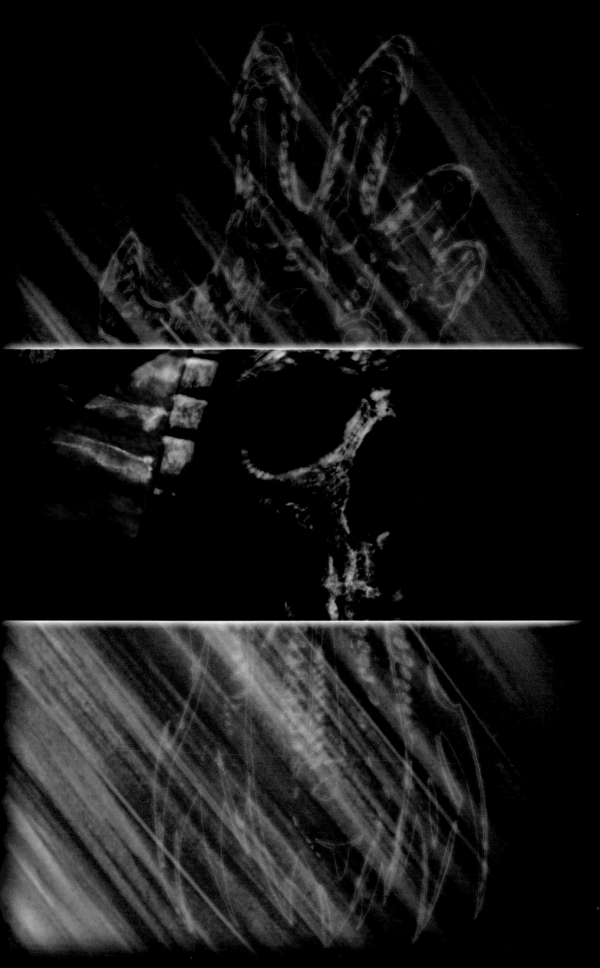

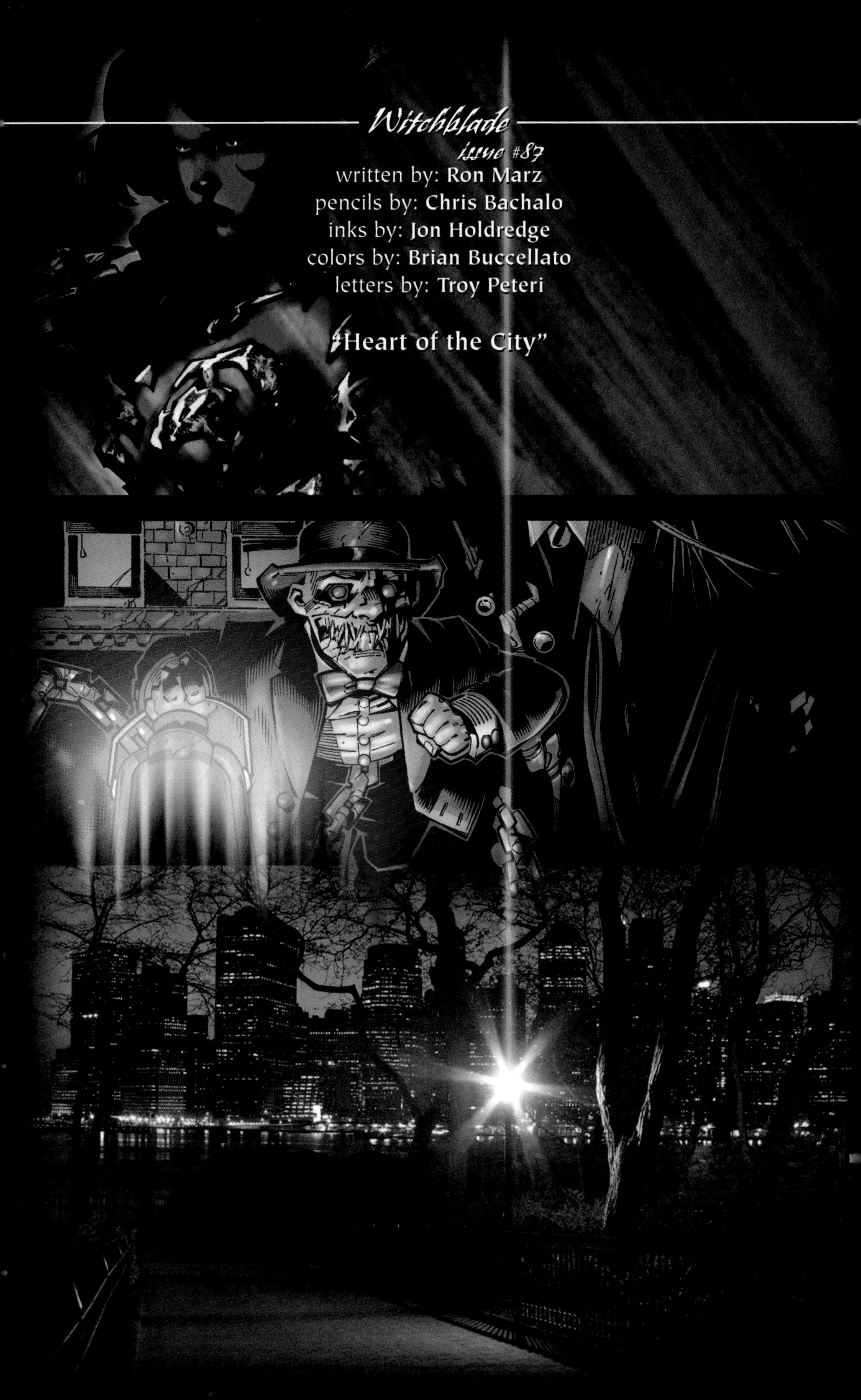
Witchblade
issue #87
written by: Ron Marz
pencils by: Chris Bachalo
inks by: Jon Holdredge
colors by: Brian Buccellato
letters by: Troy Peteri
"Heart of the City"

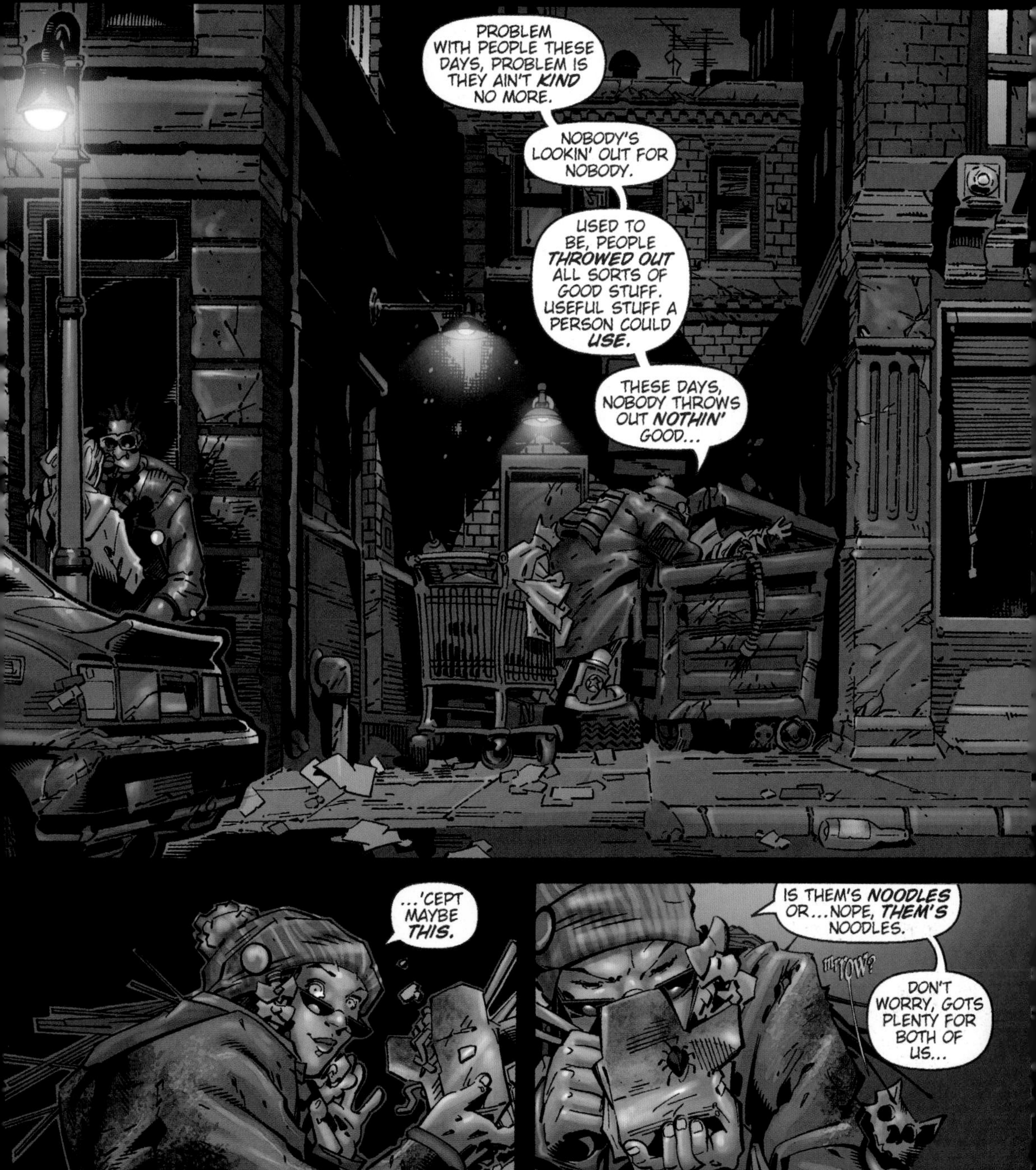
PROBLEM WITH PEOPLE THESE DAYS, PROBLEM IS THEY AIN'T KIND NO MORE.
NOBODY'S LOOKIN' OUT FOR NOBODY.
USED TO BE, PEOPLE THROWED OUT ALL SORTS OF GOOD STUFF. USEFUL STUFF A PERSON COULD USE.
THESE DAYS, NOBODY THROWS OUT NOTHIN' GOOD...
...'CEPT MAYBE THIS.
IS THEM'S NOODLES OR...NOPE, THEM'S NOODLES.
DON'T WORRY, GOTS PLENTY FOR BOTH OF US...

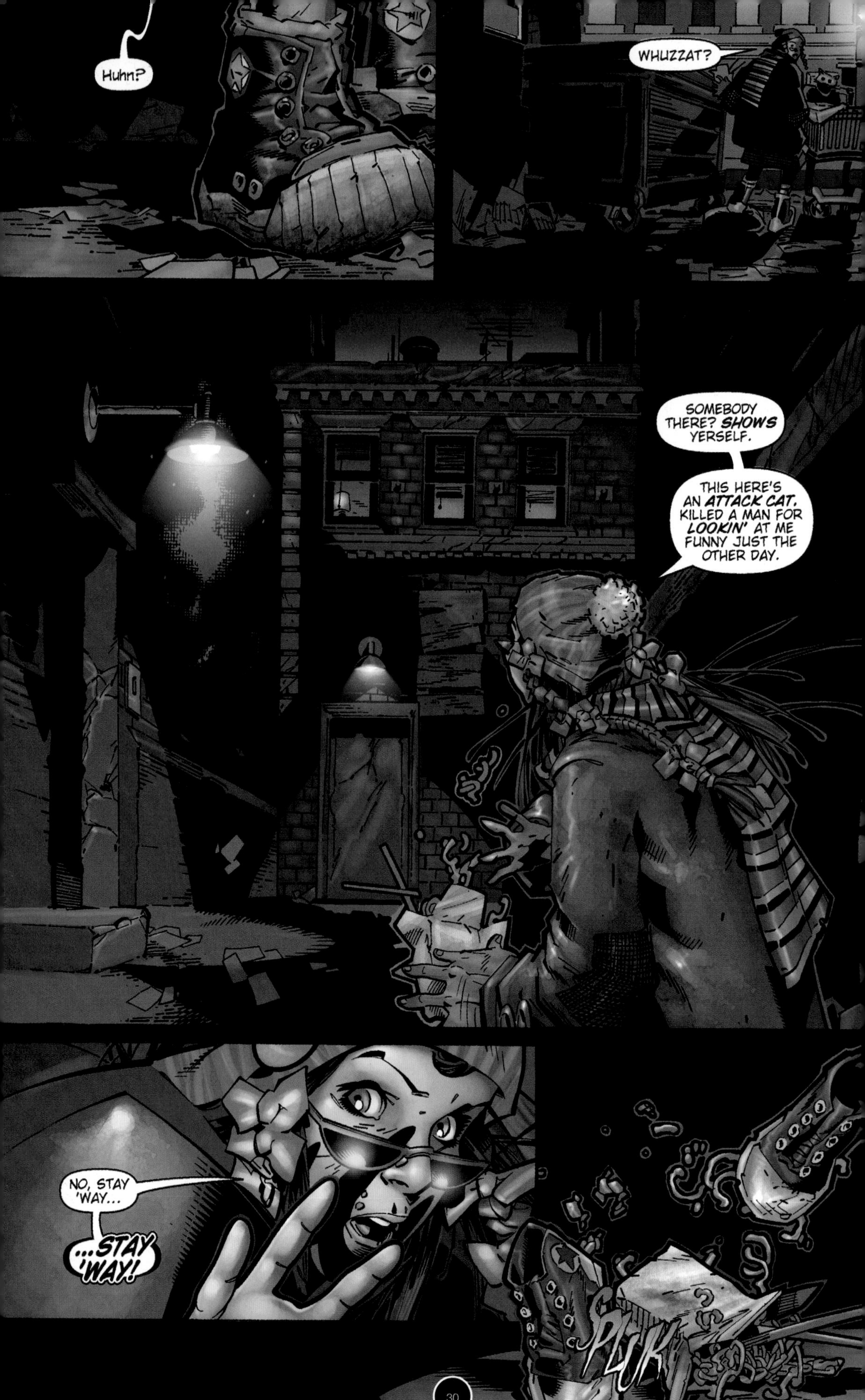
Huhn?
WHUZZAT?
SOMEBODY THERE? SHOWS YERSELF.
THIS HERE'S AN ATTACK CAT. KILLED A MAN FOR LOOKIN' AT ME FUNNY JUST THE OTHER DAY.
NO, STAY 'WAY...
...STAY 'WAY!
PLUK

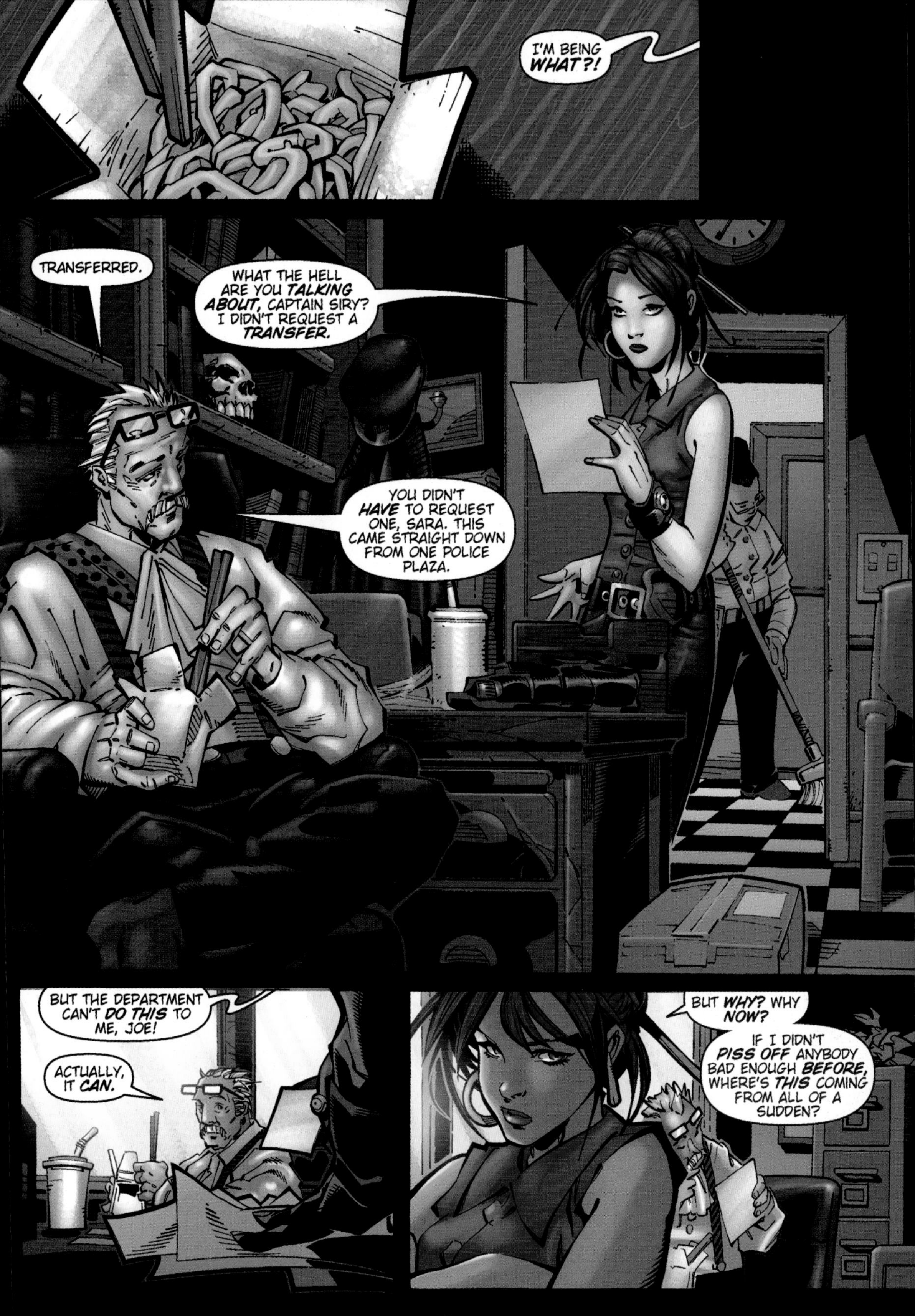

I'M BEING WHAT?!
TRANSFERRED.
WHAT THE HELL ARE YOU TALKING ABOUT, CAPTAIN SIRY? I DIDN'T REQUEST A TRANSFER.
YOU DIDN'T HAVE TO REQUEST ONE, SARA. THIS CAME STRAIGHT DOWN FROM ONE POLICE PLAZA.
BUT THE DEPARTMENT CAN'T DO THIS TO ME, JOE!
ACTUALLY, IT CAN.
BUT WHY? WHY NOW?
IF I DIDN'T PISS OFF ANYBODY BAD ENOUGH BEFORE, WHERE'S THIS COMING FROM ALL OF A SUDDEN?

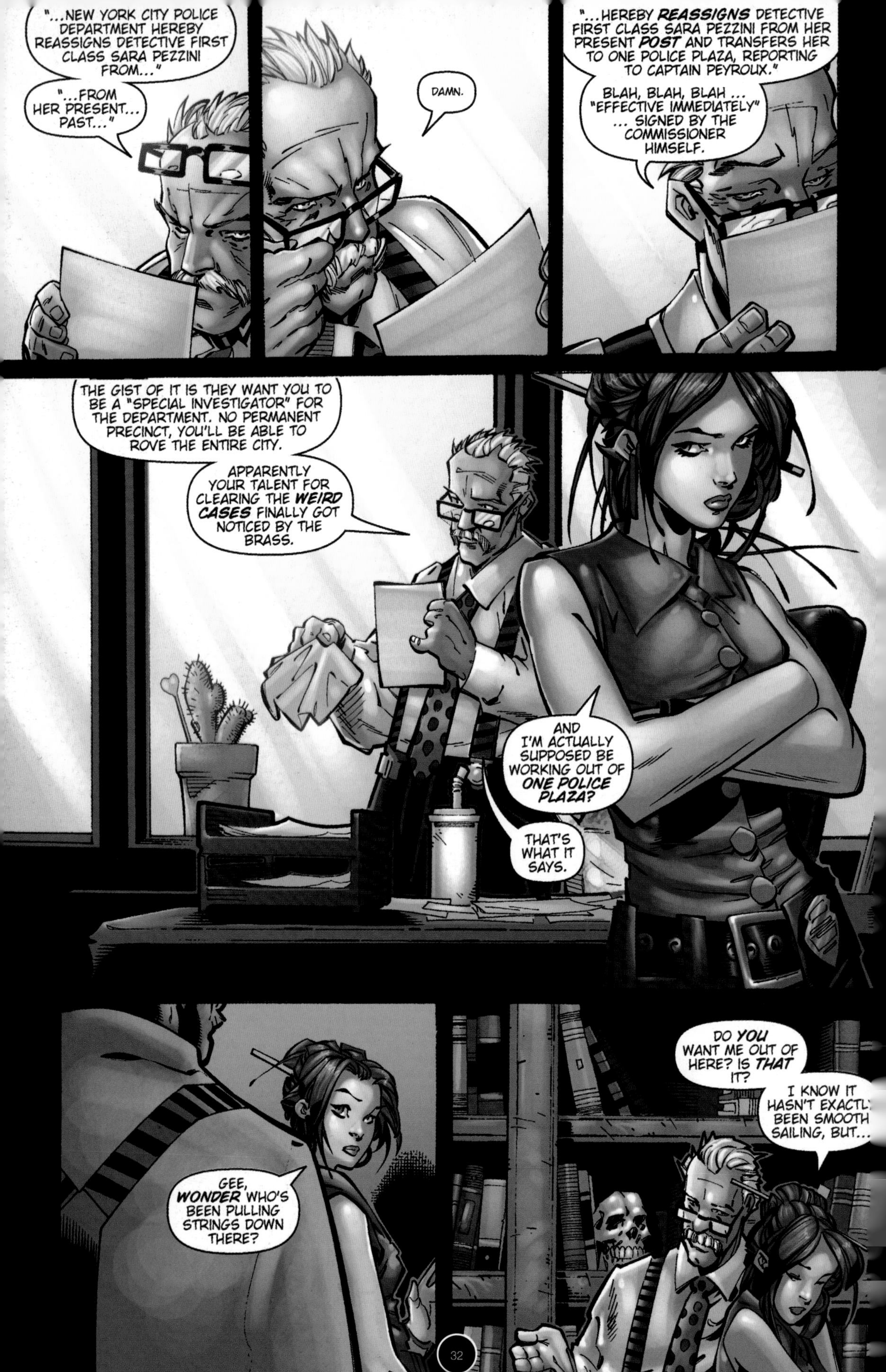
"...NEW YORK CITY POLICE DEPARTMENT HEREBY REASSIGNS DETECTIVE FIRST CLASS SARA PEZZINI FROM..."
"...FROM HER PRESENT... PAST..."
DAMN.
"...HEREBY REASSIGNS DETECTIVE FIRST CLASS SARA PEZZINI FROM HER PRESENT POST AND TRANSFERS HER TO ONE POLICE PLAZA, REPORTING TO CAPTAIN PEYROUX."
BLAH, BLAH, BLAH ... "EFFECTIVE IMMEDIATELY" ... SIGNED BY THE COMMISSIONER HIMSELF.
THE GIST OF IT IS THEY WANT YOU TO BE A "SPECIAL INVESTIGATOR" FOR THE DEPARTMENT. NO PERMANENT PRECINCT, YOU'LL BE ABLE TO ROVE THE ENTIRE CITY.
APPARENTLY YOUR TALENT FOR CLEARING THE WEIRD CASES FINALLY GOT NOTICED BY THE BRASS.
AND I'M ACTUALLY SUPPOSED BE WORKING OUT OF ONE POLICE PLAZA?
THAT'S WHAT IT SAYS.
GEE, WONDER WHO'S BEEN PULLING STRINGS DOWN THERE?
DO YOU WANT ME OUT OF HERE? IS THAT IT?
I KNOW IT HASN'T EXACTL BEEN SMOOTH SAILING, BUT...

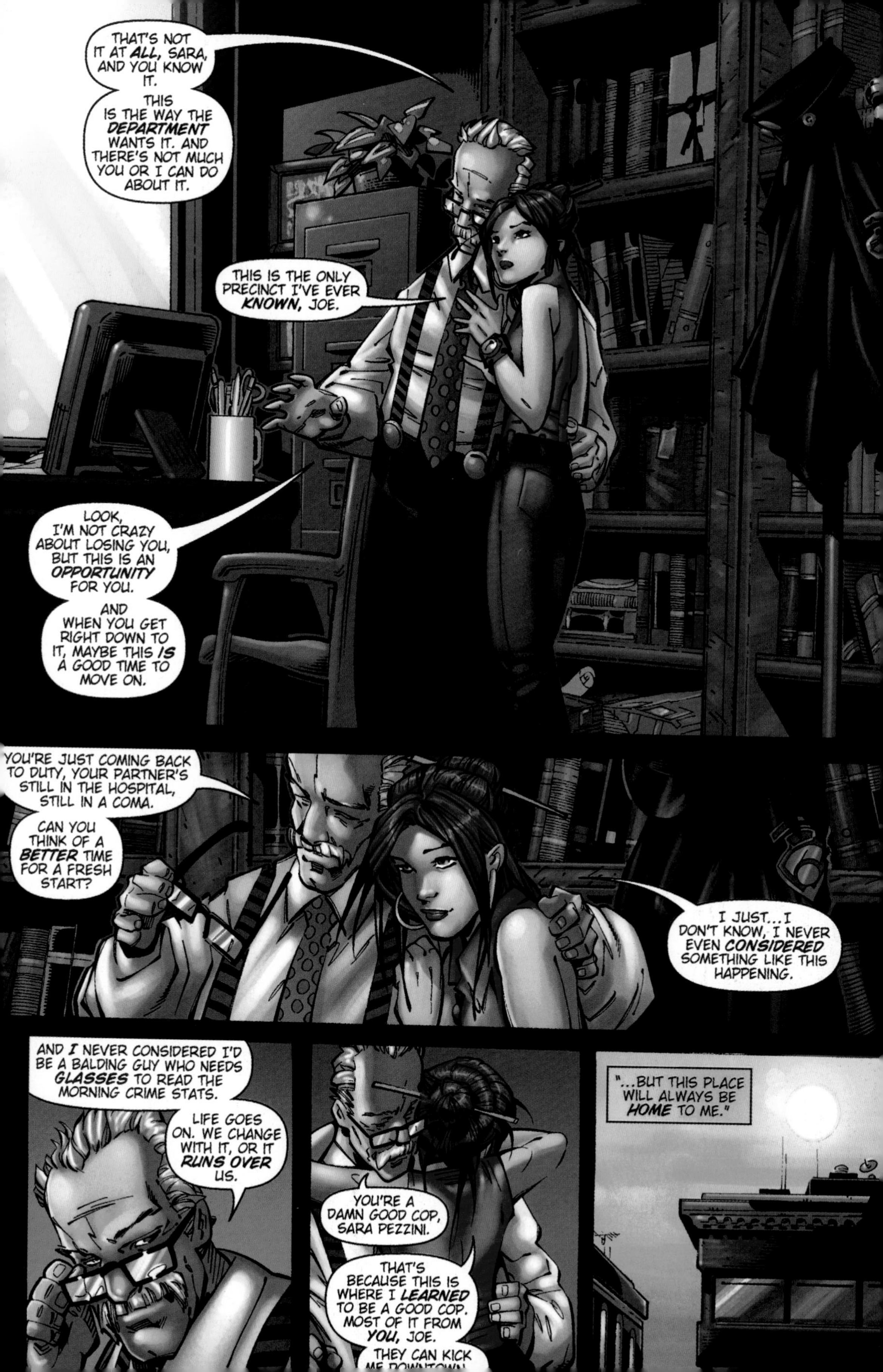
THAT'S NOT IT AT ALL, SARA, AND YOU KNOW IT.
THIS IS THE WAY THE DEPARTMENT WANTS IT. AND THERE'S NOT MUCH YOU OR I CAN DO ABOUT IT.
THIS IS THE ONLY PRECINCT I'VE EVER KNOWN, JOE.
LOOK, I'M NOT CRAZY ABOUT LOSING YOU, BUT THIS IS AN OPPORTUNITY FOR YOU.
AND WHEN YOU GET RIGHT DOWN TO IT, MAYBE THIS IS A GOOD TIME TO MOVE ON.
YOU'RE JUST COMING BACK TO DUTY, YOUR PARTNER'S STILL IN THE HOSPITAL, STILL IN A COMA.
CAN YOU THINK OF A BETTER TIME FOR A FRESH START?
I JUST...I DON'T KNOW, I NEVER EVEN CONSIDERED SOMETHING LIKE THIS HAPPENING.
AND I NEVER CONSIDERED I'D BE A BALDING GUY WHO NEEDS GLASSES TO READ THE MORNING CRIME STATS.
LIFE GOES ON. WE CHANGE WITH IT, OR IT RUNS OVER US.
YOU'RE A DAMN GOOD COP, SARA PEZZINI.
THAT'S BECAUSE THIS IS WHERE I LEARNED TO BE A GOOD COP. MOST OF IT FROM YOU, JOE.
THEY CAN KICK
"...BUT THIS PLACE WILL ALWAYS BE HOME TO ME."

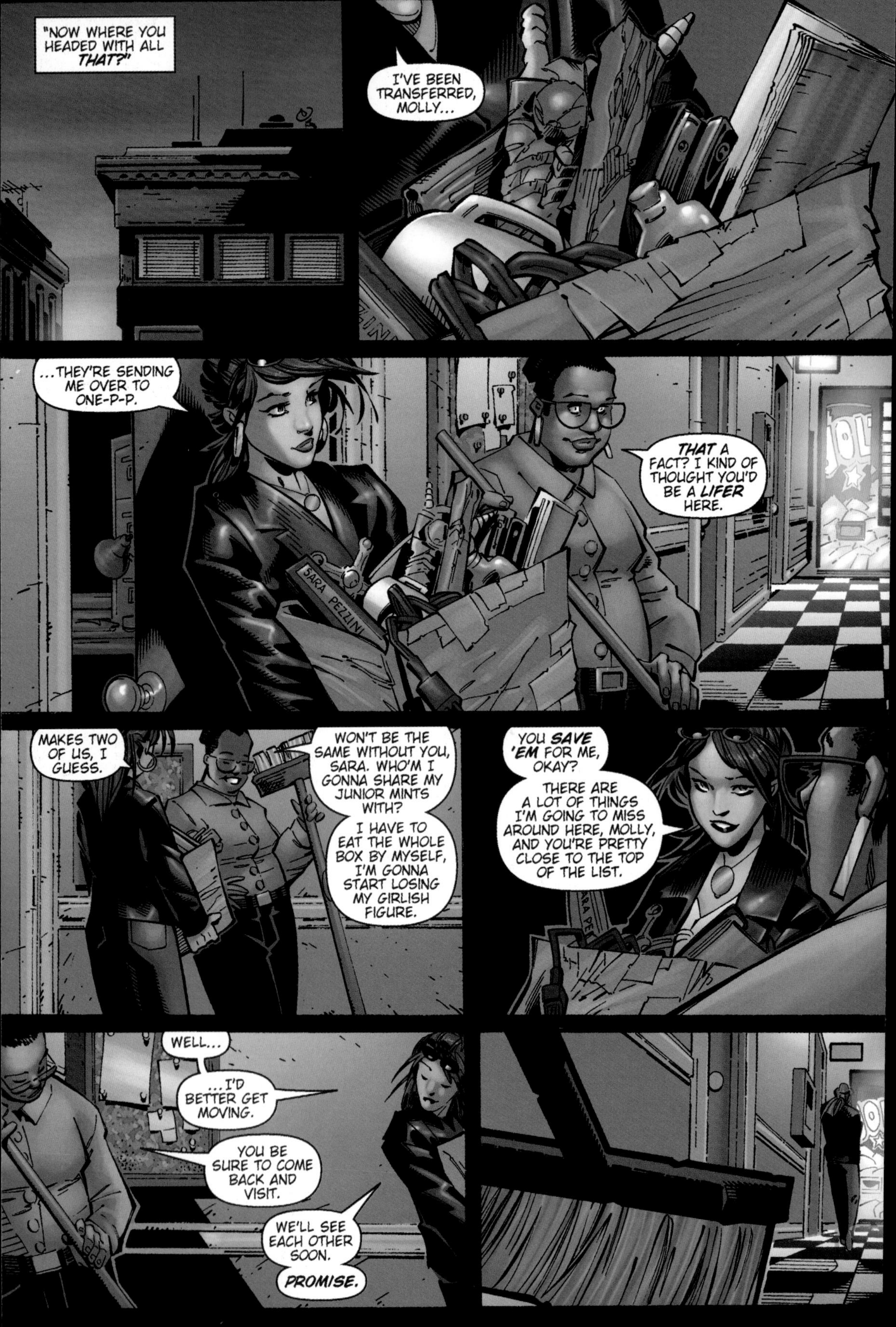
"NOW WHERE YOU HEADED WITH ALL *THAT?*"
I'VE BEEN TRANSFERRED, MOLLY...
...THEY'RE SENDING ME OVER TO ONE-P-P.
THAT A FACT? I KIND OF THOUGHT YOU'D BE A *LIFER* HERE.
SARA PEZZINI
MAKES TWO OF US, I GUESS.
WON'T BE THE SAME WITHOUT YOU, SARA. WHO'M I GONNA SHARE MY JUNIOR MINTS WITH?
I HAVE TO EAT THE WHOLE BOX BY MYSELF, I'M GONNA START LOSING MY GIRLISH FIGURE.
YOU *SAVE 'EM* FOR ME, OKAY?
THERE ARE A LOT OF THINGS I'M GOING TO MISS AROUND HERE, MOLLY, AND YOU'RE PRETTY CLOSE TO THE TOP OF THE LIST.
WELL...
...I'D BETTER GET MOVING.
YOU BE SURE TO COME BACK AND VISIT.
WE'LL SEE EACH OTHER SOON.
PROMISE.

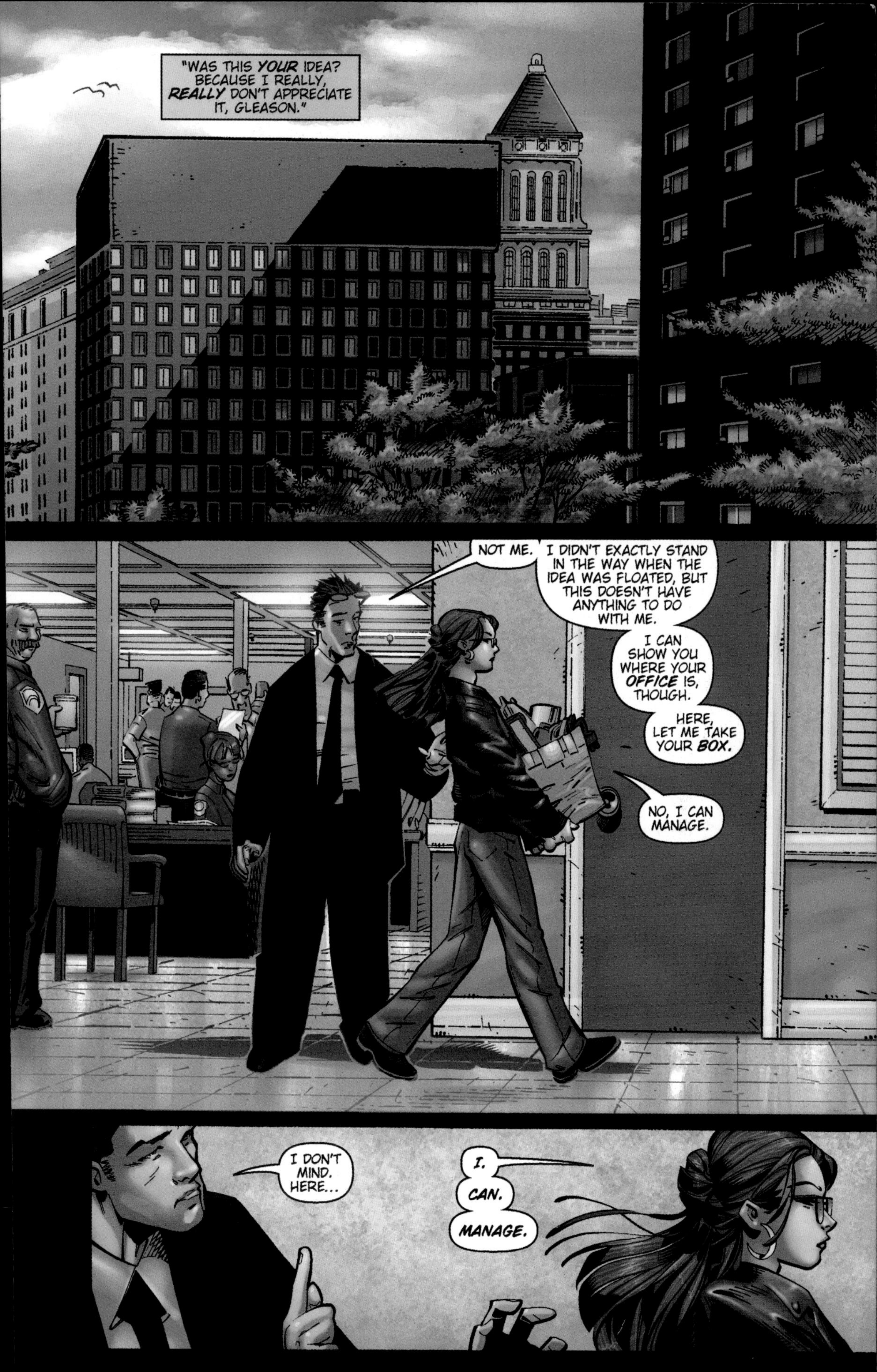
"WAS THIS YOUR IDEA? BECAUSE I REALLY, REALLY DON'T APPRECIATE IT, GLEASON."
NOT ME.
I DIDN'T EXACTLY STAND IN THE WAY WHEN THE IDEA WAS FLOATED, BUT THIS DOESN'T HAVE ANYTHING TO DO WITH ME.
I CAN SHOW YOU WHERE YOUR OFFICE IS, THOUGH.
HERE, LET ME TAKE YOUR BOX.
NO, I CAN MANAGE.
I DON'T MIND. HERE...
I.
CAN.
MANAGE.

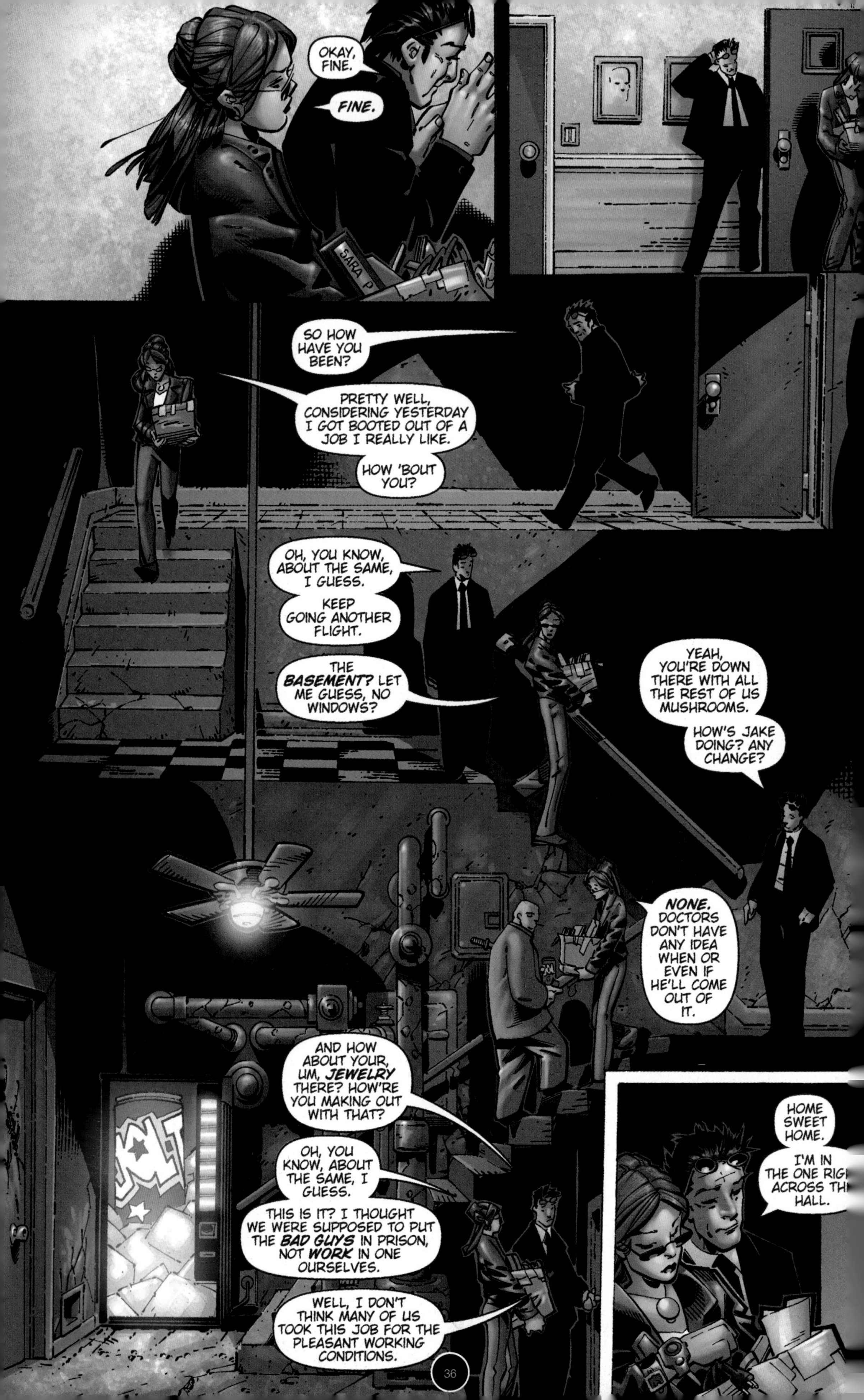
OKAY, FINE.
FINE.
SARA P
SO HOW HAVE YOU BEEN?
PRETTY WELL, CONSIDERING YESTERDAY I GOT BOOTED OUT OF A JOB I REALLY LIKE.
HOW 'BOUT YOU?
OH, YOU KNOW, ABOUT THE SAME, I GUESS.
KEEP GOING ANOTHER FLIGHT.
THE BASEMENT? LET ME GUESS, NO WINDOWS?
YEAH, YOU'RE DOWN THERE WITH ALL THE REST OF US MUSHROOMS.
HOW'S JAKE DOING? ANY CHANGE?
NONE. DOCTORS DON'T HAVE ANY IDEA WHEN OR EVEN IF HE'LL COME OUT OF IT.
AND HOW ABOUT YOUR, UM, JEWELRY THERE? HOW'RE YOU MAKING OUT WITH THAT?
OH, YOU KNOW, ABOUT THE SAME, I GUESS.
THIS IS IT? I THOUGHT WE WERE SUPPOSED TO PUT THE BAD GUYS IN PRISON, NOT WORK IN ONE OURSELVES.
WELL, I DON'T THINK MANY OF US TOOK THIS JOB FOR THE PLEASANT WORKING CONDITIONS.
HOME SWEET HOME.
I'M IN THE ONE RIG ACROSS TH HALL.

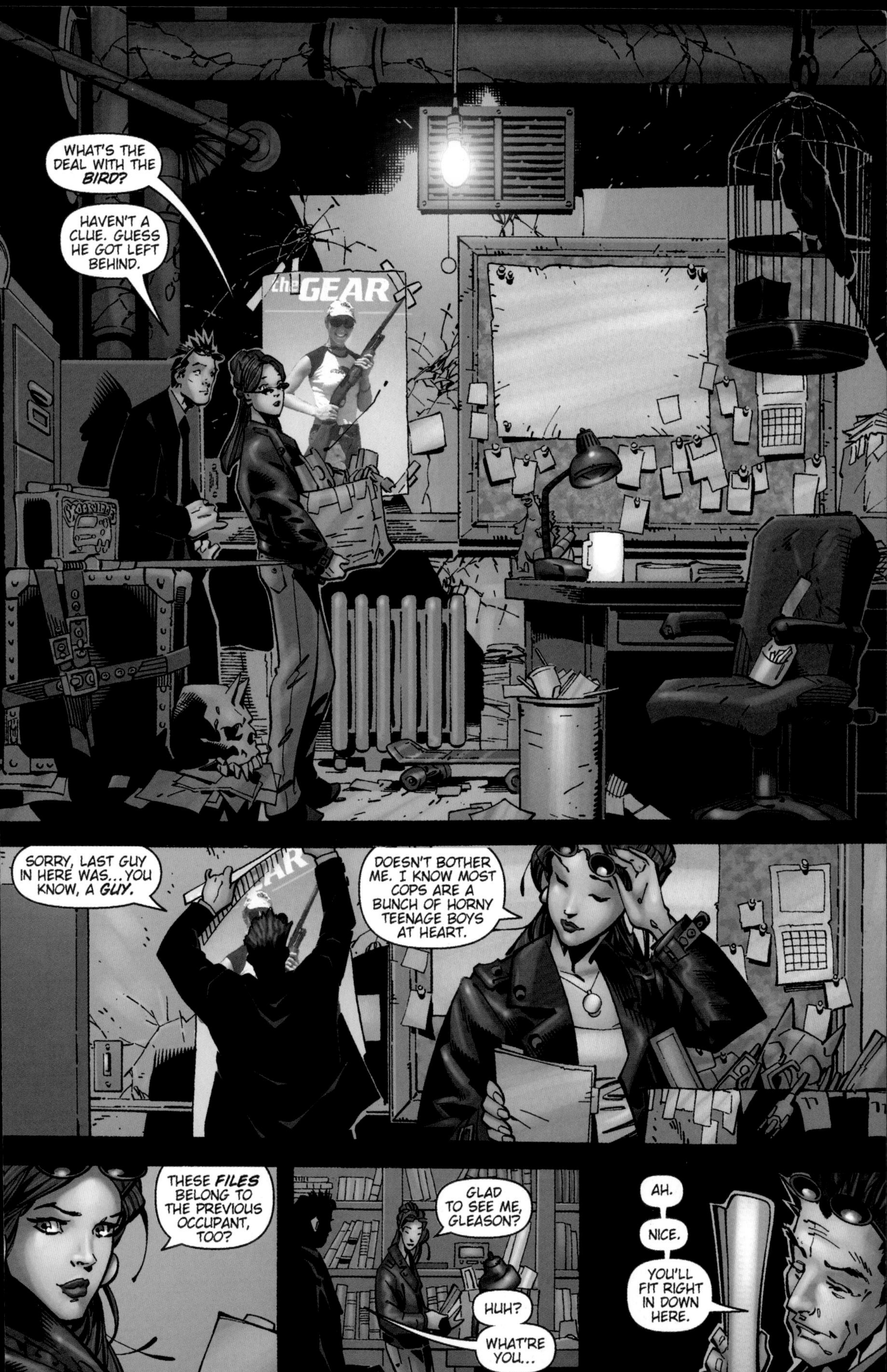
WHAT'S THE DEAL WITH THE BIRD?
HAVEN'T A CLUE. GUESS HE GOT LEFT BEHIND.
the GEAR
SORRY, LAST GUY IN HERE WAS...YOU KNOW, A GUY.
DOESN'T BOTHER ME. I KNOW MOST COPS ARE A BUNCH OF HORNY TEENAGE BOYS AT HEART.
THESE FILES BELONG TO THE PREVIOUS OCCUPANT, TOO?
GLAD TO SEE ME, GLEASON?
HUH?
WHAT'RE YOU...
AH.
NICE.
YOU'LL FIT RIGHT IN DOWN HERE.

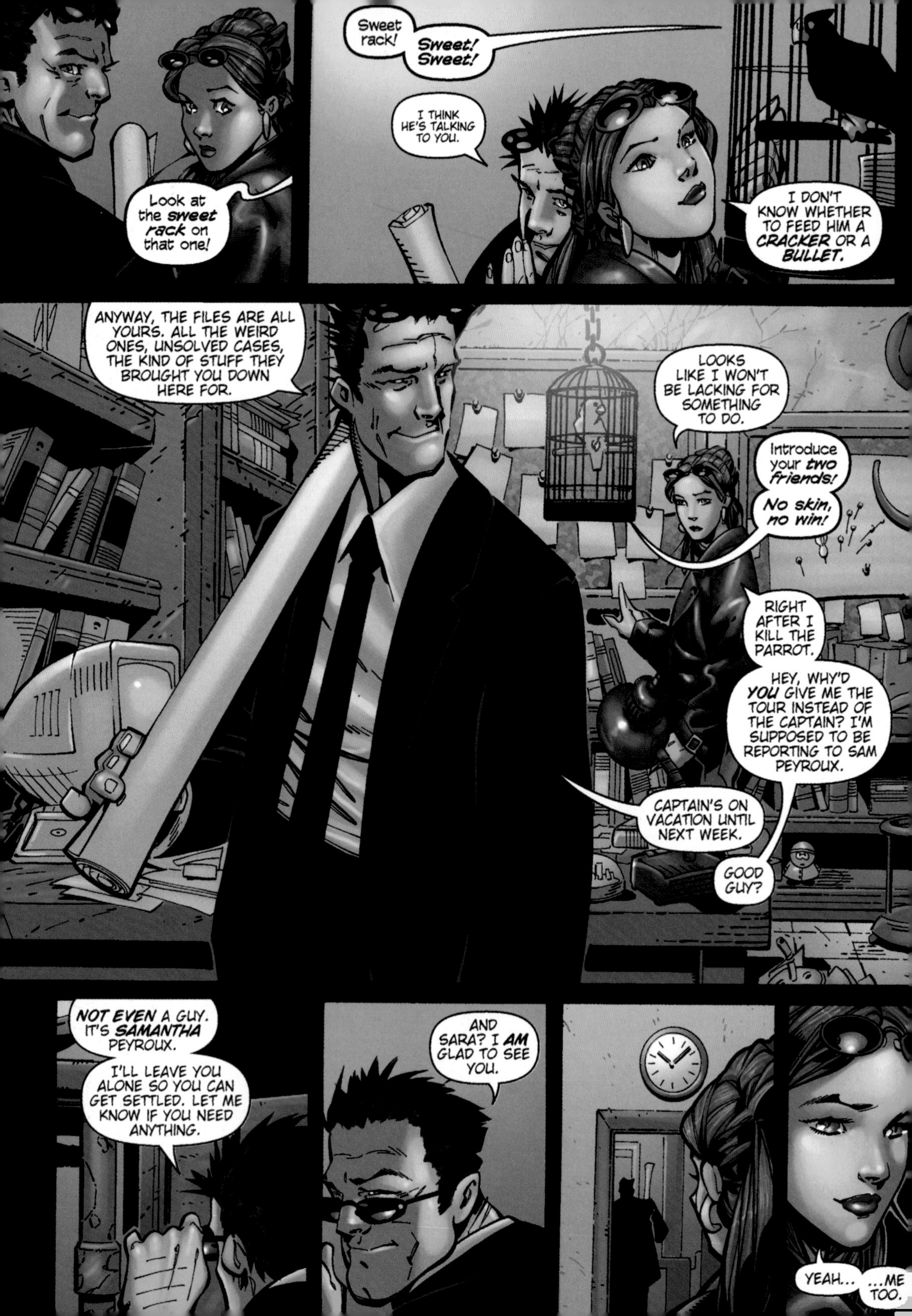
Look at the sweet rack on that one!
Sweet rack! Sweet! Sweet!
I THINK HE'S TALKING TO YOU.
I DON'T KNOW WHETHER TO FEED HIM A CRACKER OR A BULLET.
ANYWAY, THE FILES ARE ALL YOURS. ALL THE WEIRD ONES, UNSOLVED CASES, THE KIND OF STUFF THEY BROUGHT YOU DOWN HERE FOR.
LOOKS LIKE I WON'T BE LACKING FOR SOMETHING TO DO.
Introduce your two friends!
No skin, no win!
RIGHT AFTER I KILL THE PARROT.
HEY, WHY'D YOU GIVE ME THE TOUR INSTEAD OF THE CAPTAIN? I'M SUPPOSED TO BE REPORTING TO SAM PEYROUX.
CAPTAIN'S ON VACATION UNTIL NEXT WEEK.
GOOD GUY?
NOT EVEN A GUY. IT'S SAMANTHA PEYROUX.
I'LL LEAVE YOU ALONE SO YOU CAN GET SETTLED. LET ME KNOW IF YOU NEED ANYTHING.
AND SARA? I AM GLAD TO SEE YOU.
YEAH...
...ME TOO.

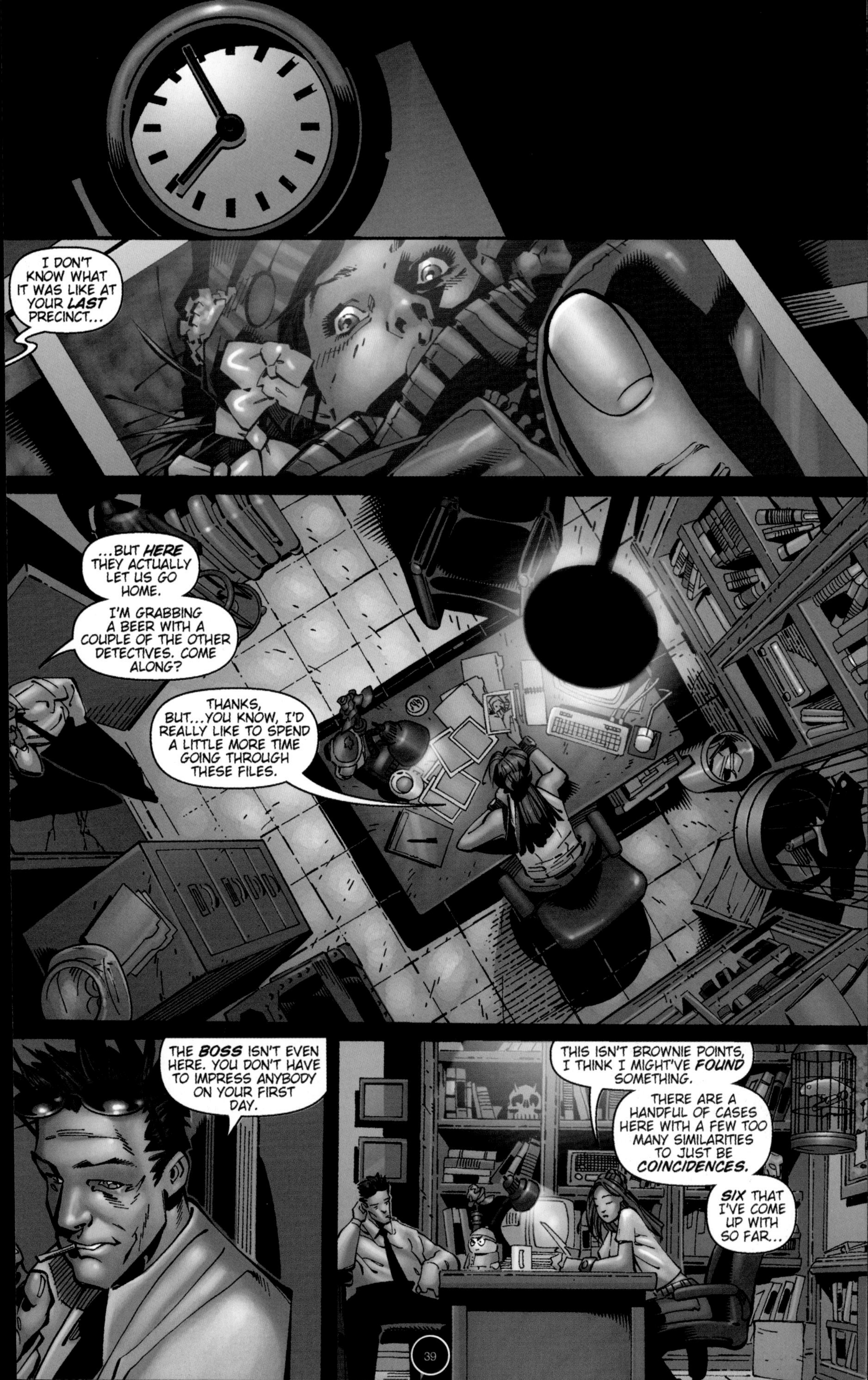
I DON'T KNOW WHAT IT WAS LIKE AT YOUR LAST PRECINCT...
...BUT HERE THEY ACTUALLY LET US GO HOME.
I'M GRABBING A BEER WITH A COUPLE OF THE OTHER DETECTIVES. COME ALONG?
THANKS, BUT...YOU KNOW, I'D REALLY LIKE TO SPEND A LITTLE MORE TIME GOING THROUGH THESE FILES.
THE BOSS ISN'T EVEN HERE. YOU DON'T HAVE TO IMPRESS ANYBODY ON YOUR FIRST DAY.
THIS ISN'T BROWNIE POINTS, I THINK I MIGHT'VE FOUND SOMETHING.
THERE ARE A HANDFUL OF CASES HERE WITH A FEW TOO MANY SIMILARITIES TO JUST BE COINCIDENCES.
SIX THAT I'VE COME UP WITH SO FAR...

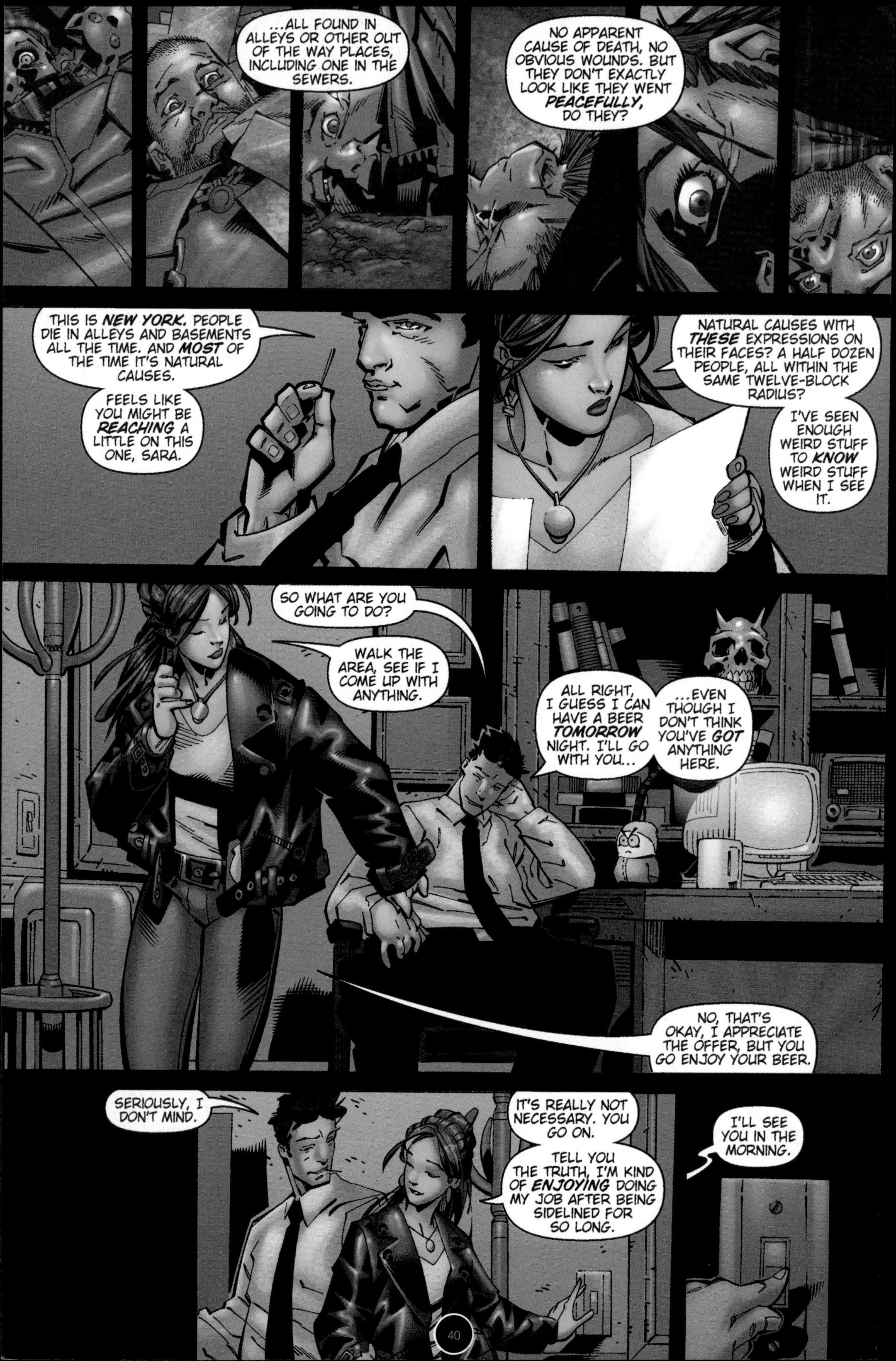

...ALL FOUND IN ALLEYS OR OTHER OUT OF THE WAY PLACES, INCLUDING ONE IN THE SEWERS.
NO APPARENT CAUSE OF DEATH, NO OBVIOUS WOUNDS. BUT THEY DON'T EXACTLY LOOK LIKE THEY WENT PEACEFULLY, DO THEY?
THIS IS NEW YORK. PEOPLE DIE IN ALLEYS AND BASEMENTS ALL THE TIME. AND MOST OF THE TIME IT'S NATURAL CAUSES.
FEELS LIKE YOU MIGHT BE REACHING A LITTLE ON THIS ONE, SARA.
NATURAL CAUSES WITH THESE EXPRESSIONS ON THEIR FACES? A HALF DOZEN PEOPLE, ALL WITHIN THE SAME TWELVE-BLOCK RADIUS?
I'VE SEEN ENOUGH WEIRD STUFF TO KNOW WEIRD STUFF WHEN I SEE IT.
SO WHAT ARE YOU GOING TO DO?
WALK THE AREA, SEE IF I COME UP WITH ANYTHING.
ALL RIGHT, I GUESS I CAN HAVE A BEER TOMORROW NIGHT. I'LL GO WITH YOU...
...EVEN THOUGH I DON'T THINK YOU'VE GOT ANYTHING HERE.
NO, THAT'S OKAY, I APPRECIATE THE OFFER, BUT YOU GO ENJOY YOUR BEER.
SERIOUSLY, I DON'T MIND.
IT'S REALLY NOT NECESSARY. YOU GO ON.
TELL YOU THE TRUTH, I'M KIND OF ENJOYING DOING MY JOB AFTER BEING SIDELINED FOR SO LONG.
I'LL SEE YOU IN THE MORNING.

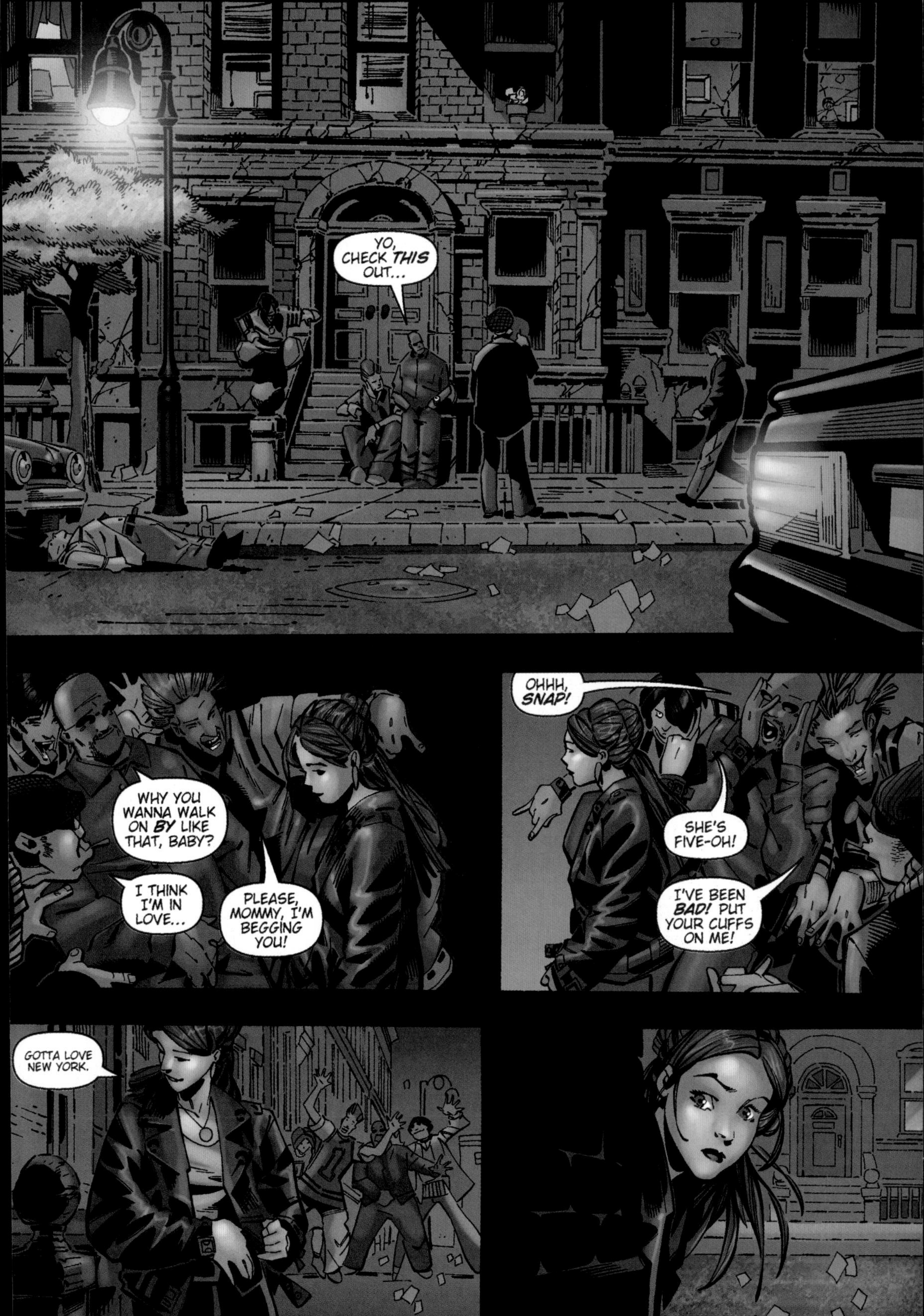
YO, CHECK THIS OUT...
WHY YOU WANNA WALK ON BY LIKE THAT, BABY?
I THINK I'M IN LOVE...
PLEASE, MOMMY, I'M BEGGING YOU!
OHHH, SNAP!
SHE'S FIVE-OH!
I'VE BEEN BAD! PUT YOUR CUFFS ON ME!
GOTTA LOVE NEW YORK.

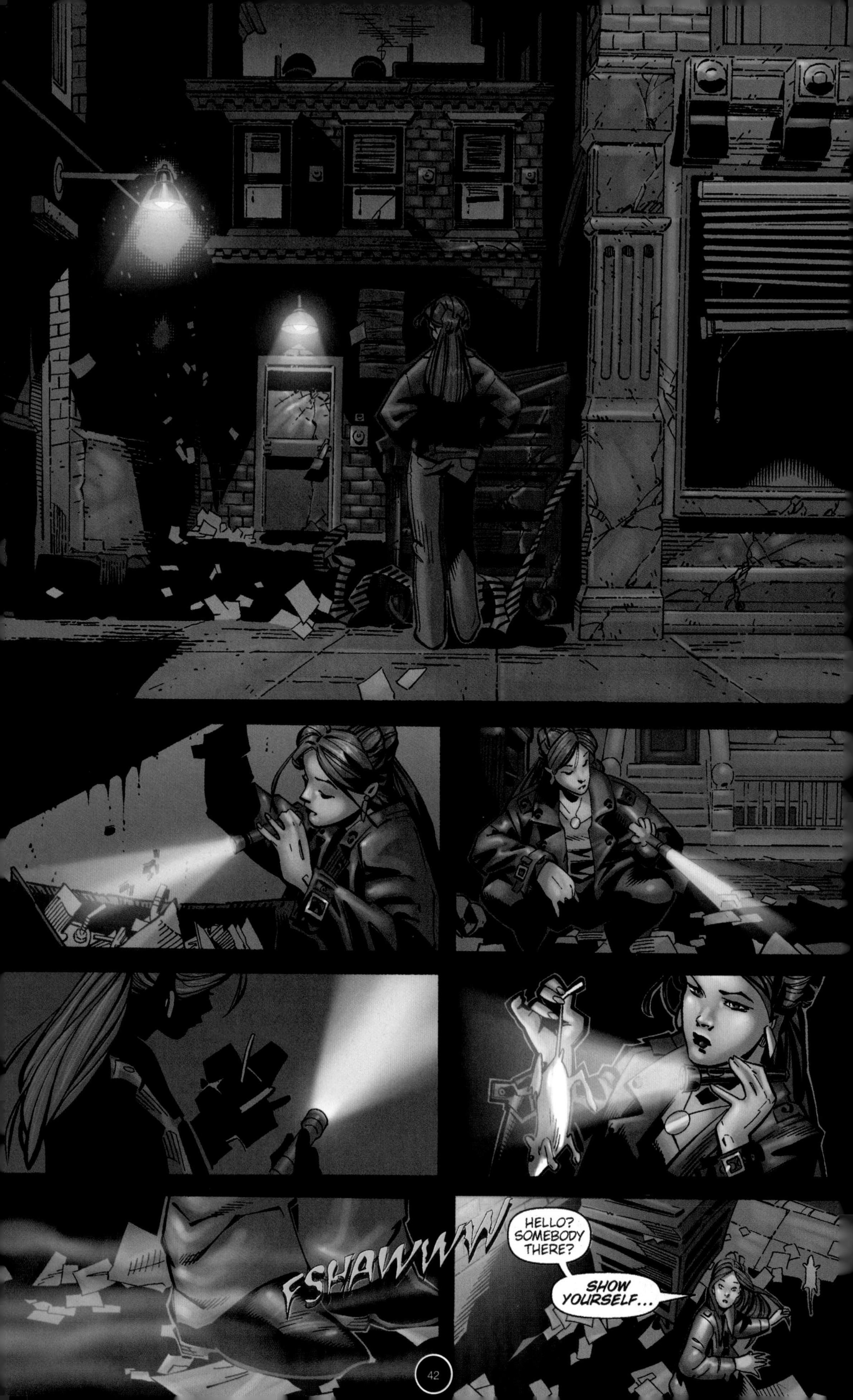
FSHAWWW
HELLO? SOMEBODY THERE?
SHOW YOURSELF...

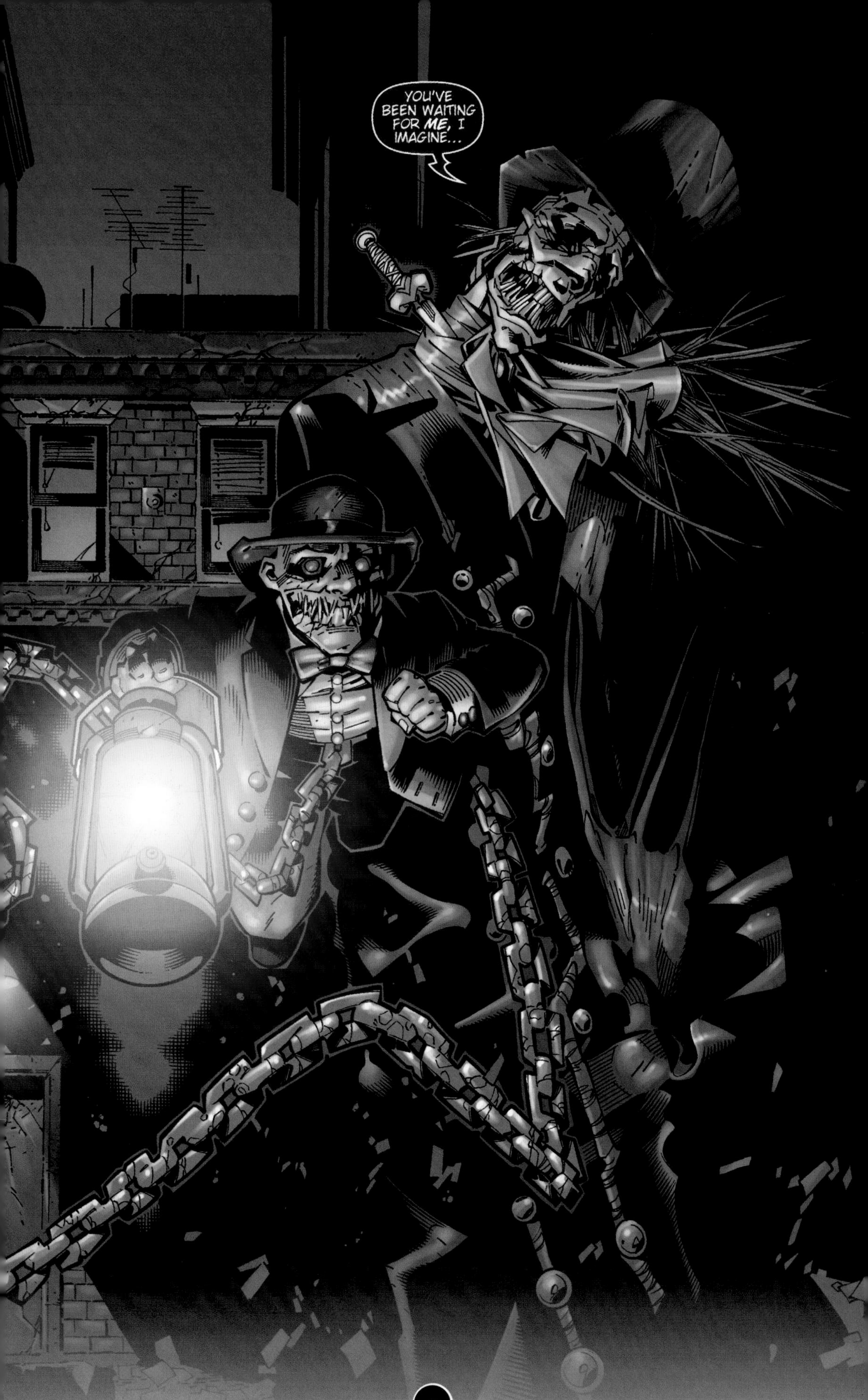
YOU'VE BEEN WAITING FOR ***ME,*** I IMAGINE...

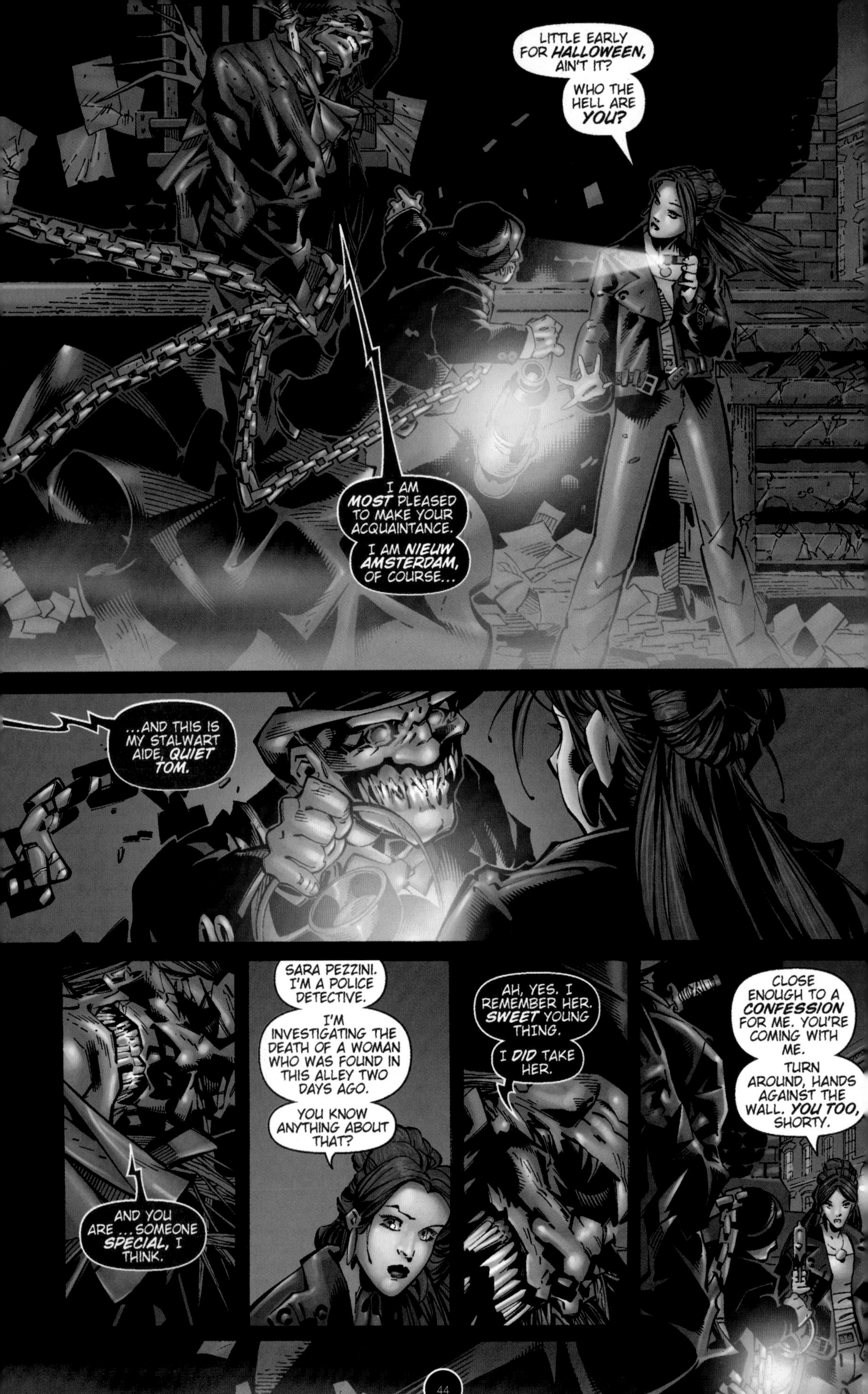
LITTLE EARLY FOR HALLOWEEN, AIN'T IT?
WHO THE HELL ARE YOU?
I AM MOST PLEASED TO MAKE YOUR ACQUAINTANCE.
I AM NIEUW AMSTERDAM, OF COURSE...
...AND THIS IS MY STALWART AIDE, QUIET TOM.
AND YOU ARE ... SOMEONE SPECIAL, I THINK.
SARA PEZZINI. I'M A POLICE DETECTIVE.
I'M INVESTIGATING THE DEATH OF A WOMAN WHO WAS FOUND IN THIS ALLEY TWO DAYS AGO.
YOU KNOW ANYTHING ABOUT THAT?
AH, YES. I REMEMBER HER. SWEET YOUNG THING.
I DID TAKE HER.
CLOSE ENOUGH TO A CONFESSION FOR ME. YOU'RE COMING WITH ME.
TURN AROUND, HANDS AGAINST THE WALL. YOU TOO, SHORTY.

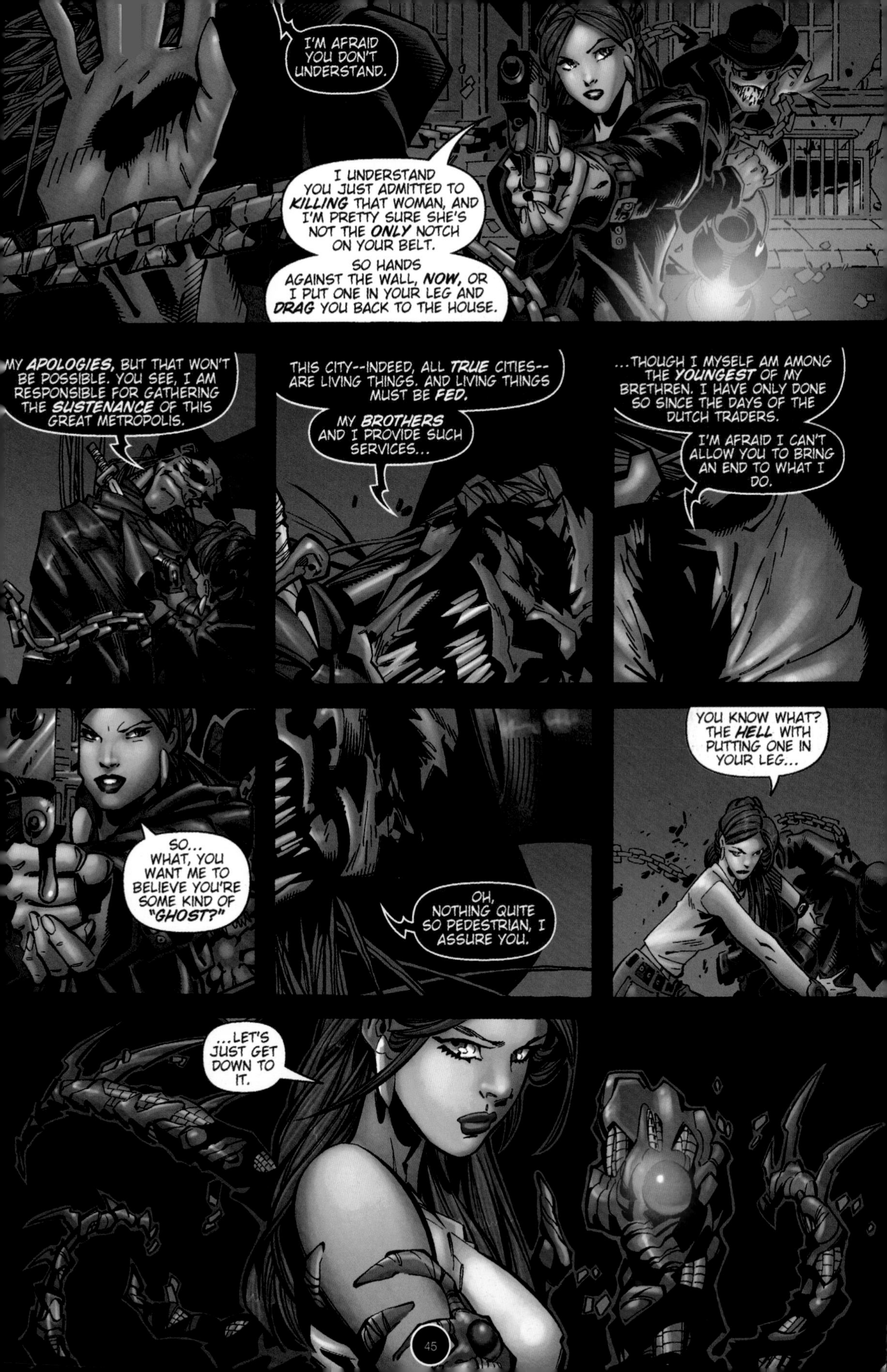
I'M AFRAID YOU DON'T UNDERSTAND.
I UNDERSTAND YOU JUST ADMITTED TO KILLING THAT WOMAN, AND I'M PRETTY SURE SHE'S NOT THE ONLY NOTCH ON YOUR BELT.
SO HANDS AGAINST THE WALL, NOW, OR I PUT ONE IN YOUR LEG AND DRAG YOU BACK TO THE HOUSE.
MY APOLOGIES, BUT THAT WON'T BE POSSIBLE. YOU SEE, I AM RESPONSIBLE FOR GATHERING THE SUSTENANCE OF THIS GREAT METROPOLIS.
THIS CITY--INDEED, ALL TRUE CITIES--ARE LIVING THINGS. AND LIVING THINGS MUST BE FED.
MY BROTHERS AND I PROVIDE SUCH SERVICES...
...THOUGH I MYSELF AM AMONG THE YOUNGEST OF MY BRETHREN. I HAVE ONLY DONE SO SINCE THE DAYS OF THE DUTCH TRADERS.
I'M AFRAID I CAN'T ALLOW YOU TO BRING AN END TO WHAT I DO.
SO... WHAT, YOU WANT ME TO BELIEVE YOU'RE SOME KIND OF "GHOST?"
OH, NOTHING QUITE SO PEDESTRIAN, I ASSURE YOU.
YOU KNOW WHAT? THE HELL WITH PUTTING ONE IN YOUR LEG...
...LET'S JUST GET DOWN TO IT.

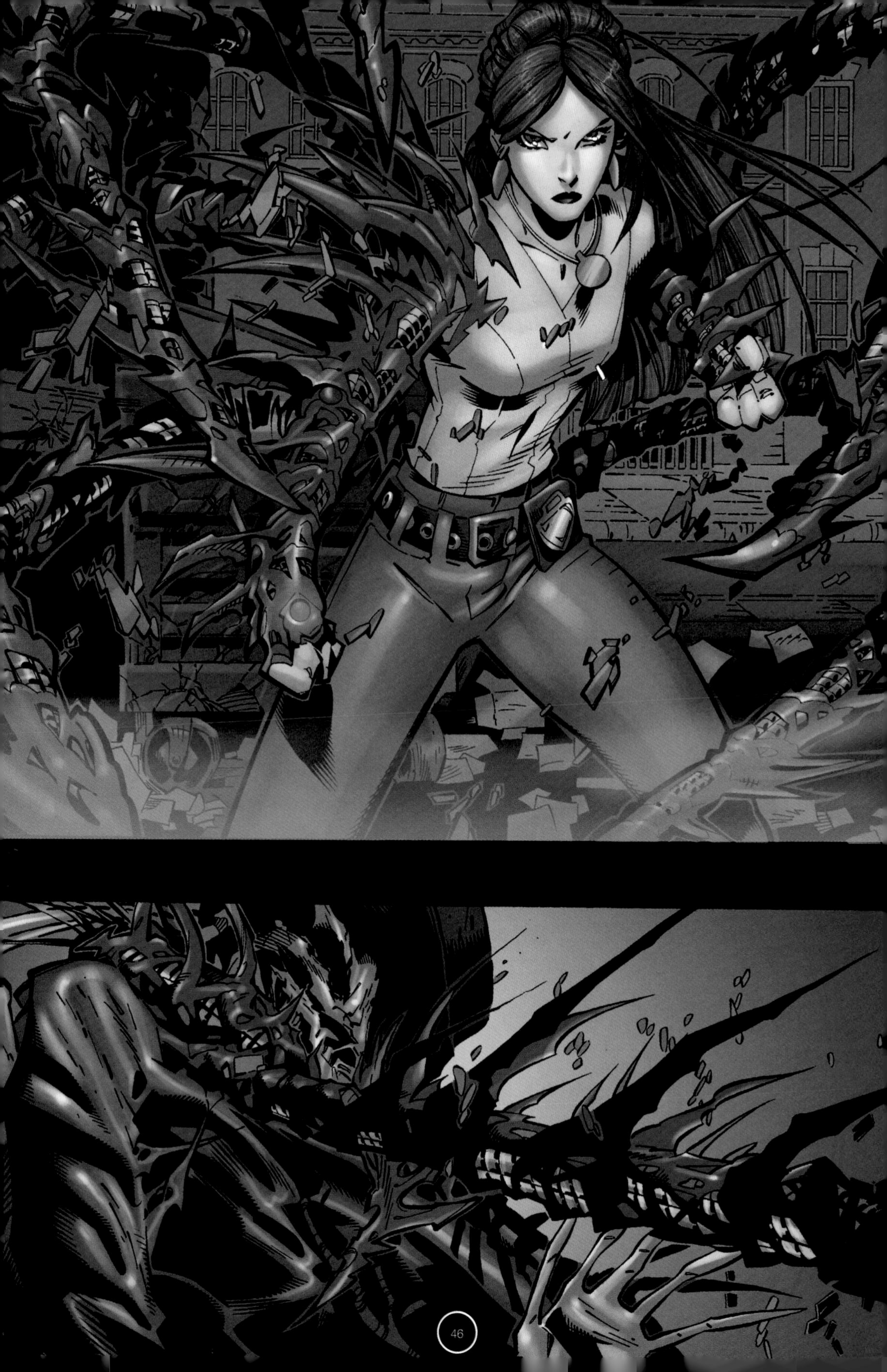

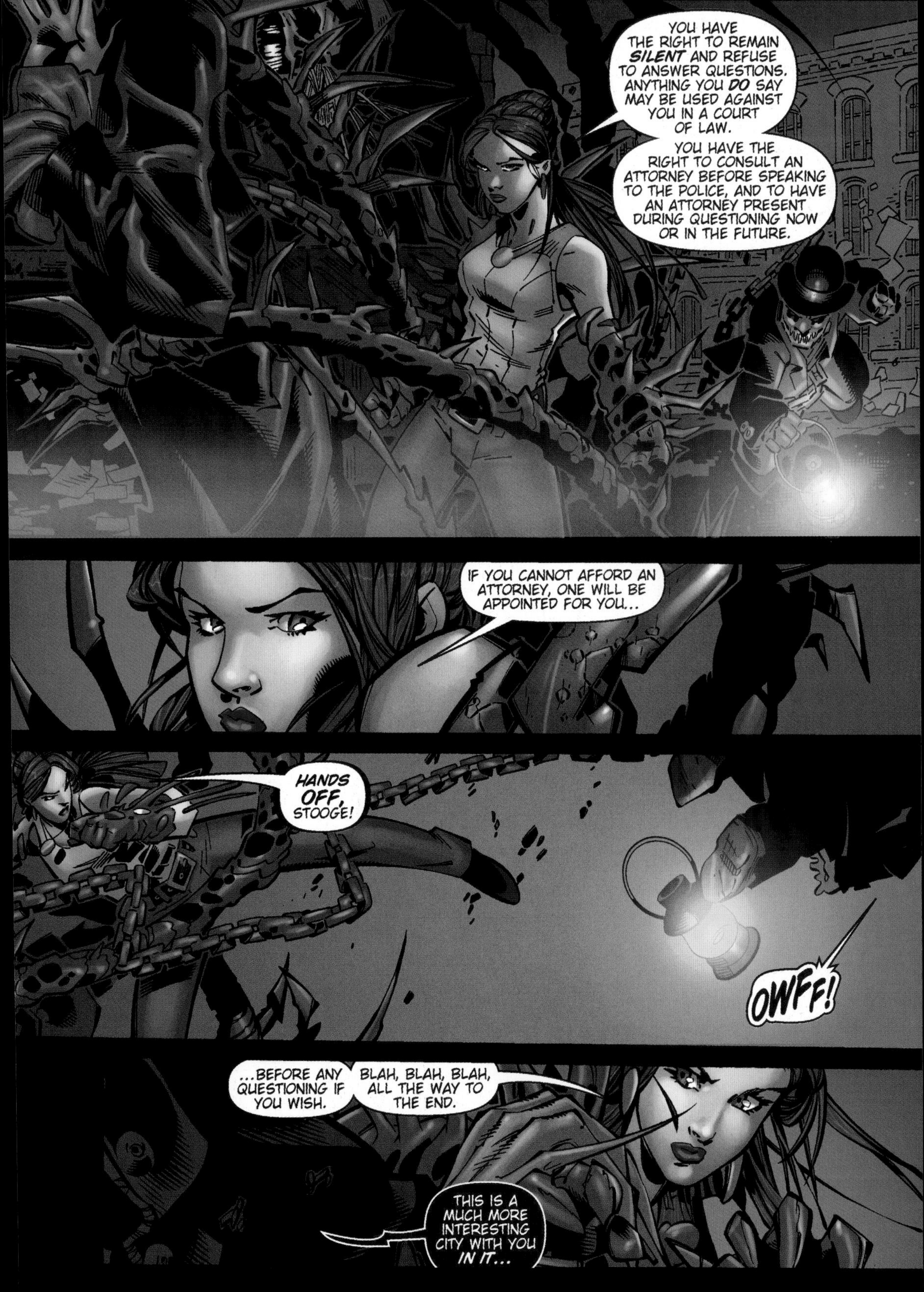
YOU HAVE THE RIGHT TO REMAIN SILENT AND REFUSE TO ANSWER QUESTIONS. ANYTHING YOU DO SAY MAY BE USED AGAINST YOU IN A COURT OF LAW.
YOU HAVE THE RIGHT TO CONSULT AN ATTORNEY BEFORE SPEAKING TO THE POLICE, AND TO HAVE AN ATTORNEY PRESENT DURING QUESTIONING NOW OR IN THE FUTURE.
IF YOU CANNOT AFFORD AN ATTORNEY, ONE WILL BE APPOINTED FOR YOU...
HANDS OFF, STOOGE!
OWFF!
...BEFORE ANY QUESTIONING IF YOU WISH.
BLAH, BLAH, BLAH, ALL THE WAY TO THE END.
THIS IS A MUCH MORE INTERESTING CITY WITH YOU IN IT...

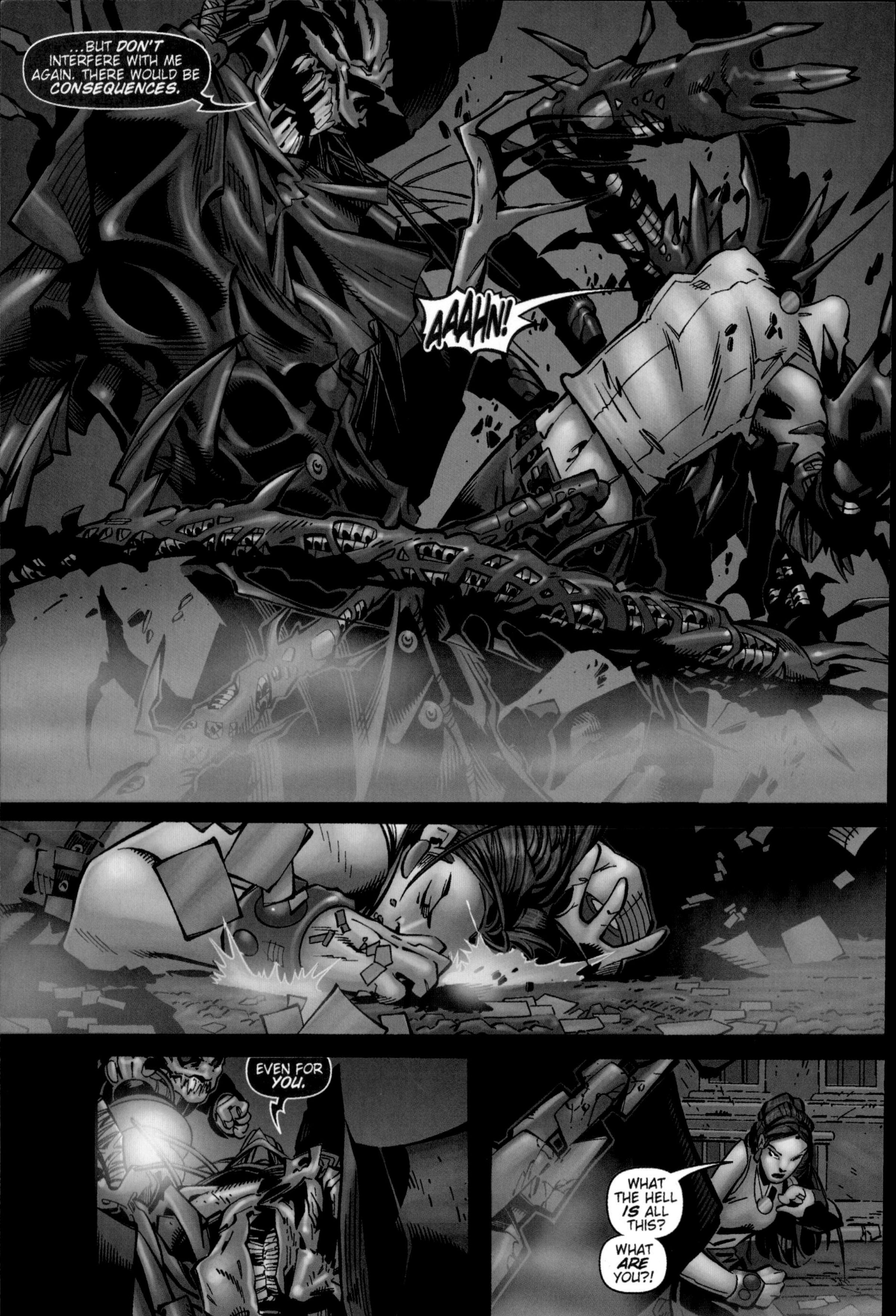

...BUT DON'T INTERFERE WITH ME AGAIN. THERE WOULD BE CONSEQUENCES.
AAAHN!
EVEN FOR YOU.
WHAT THE HELL IS ALL THIS?
WHAT ARE YOU?!

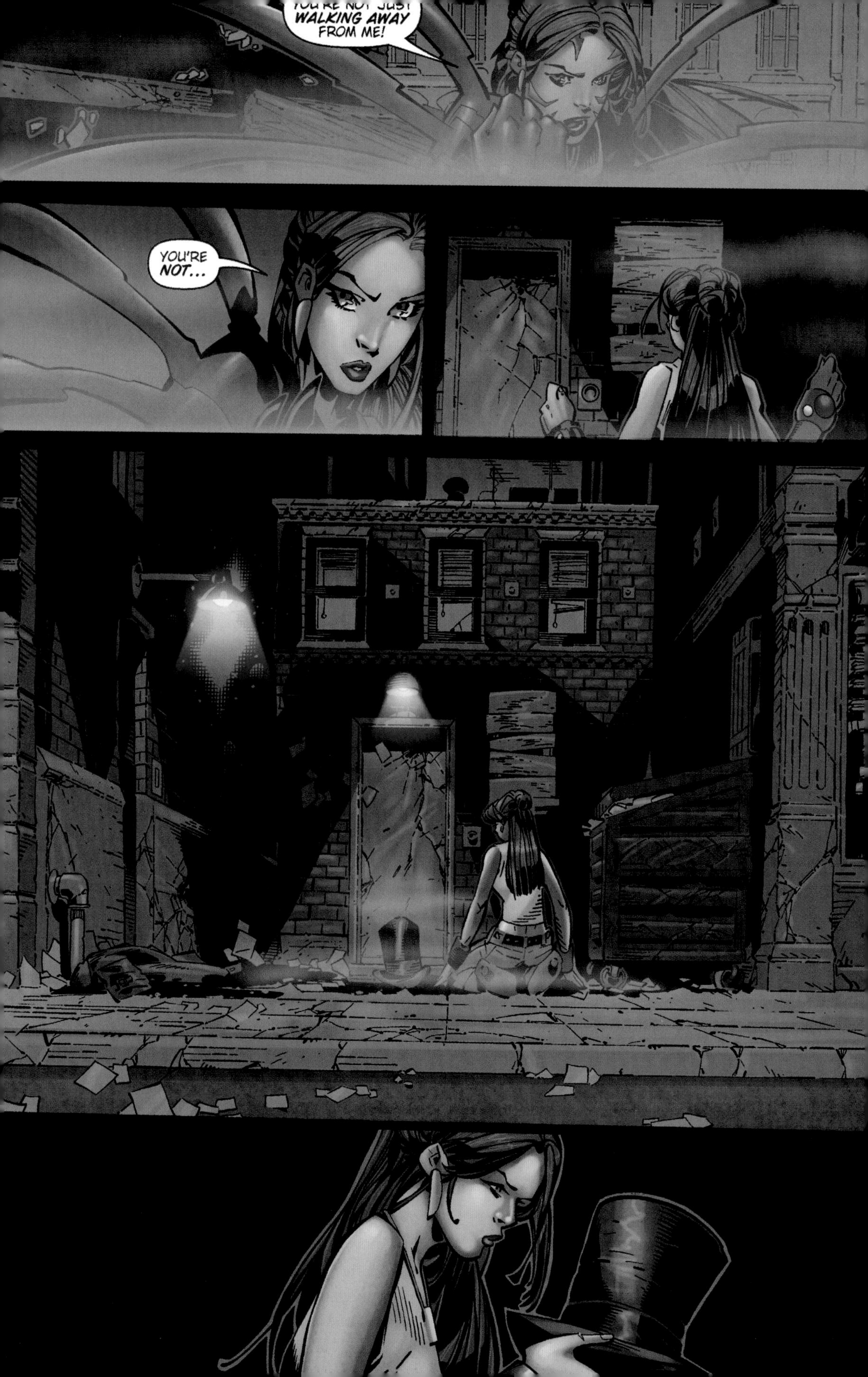
YOU'RE NOT JUST WALKING AWAY FROM ME!
YOU'RE NOT...

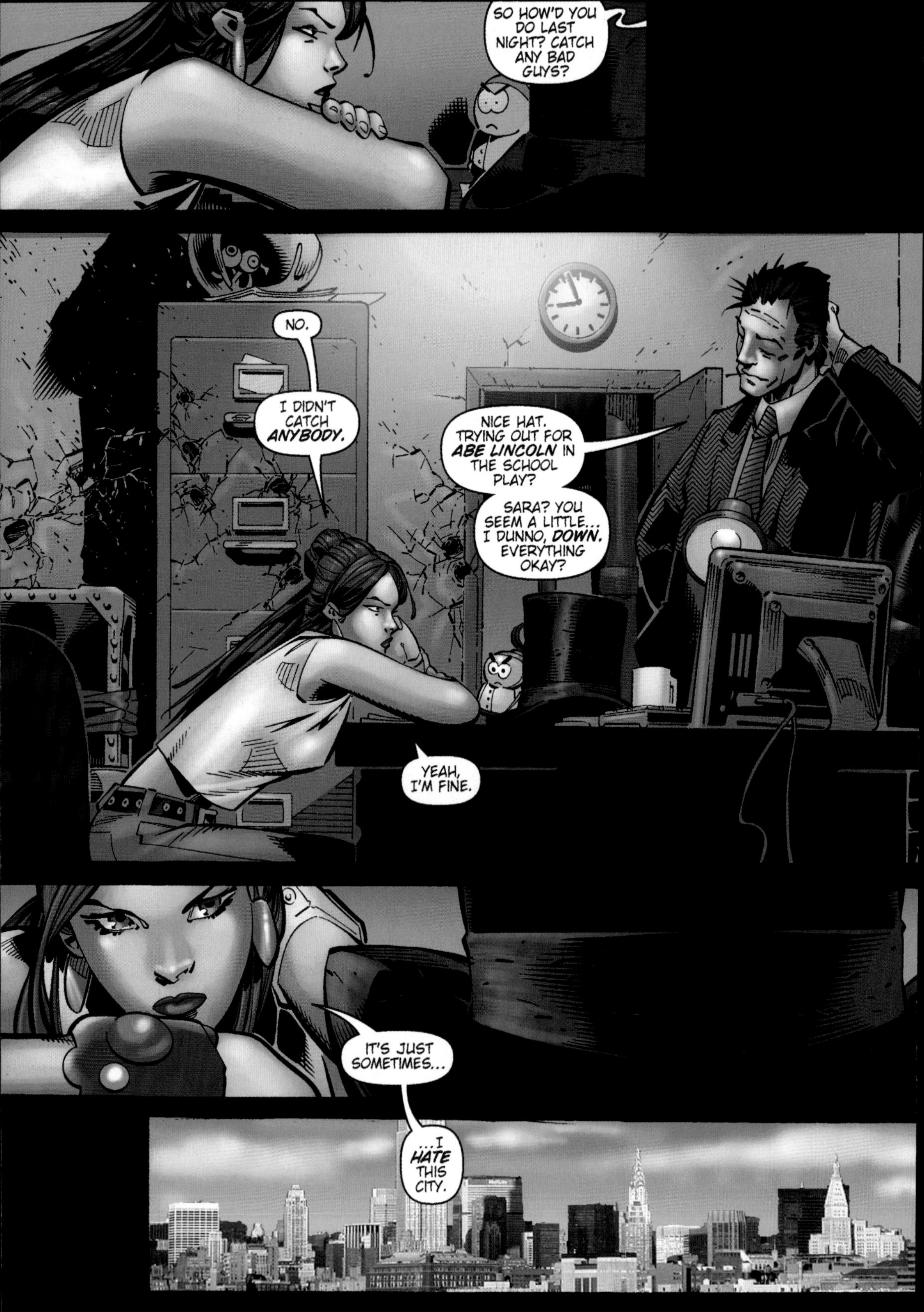
SO HOW'D YOU DO LAST NIGHT? CATCH ANY BAD GUYS?
NO.
I DIDN'T CATCH ANYBODY.
NICE HAT. TRYING OUT FOR ABE LINCOLN IN THE SCHOOL PLAY?
SARA? YOU SEEM A LITTLE... I DUNNO, DOWN. EVERYTHING OKAY?
YEAH, I'M FINE.
IT'S JUST SOMETIMES...
...I HATE THIS CITY.

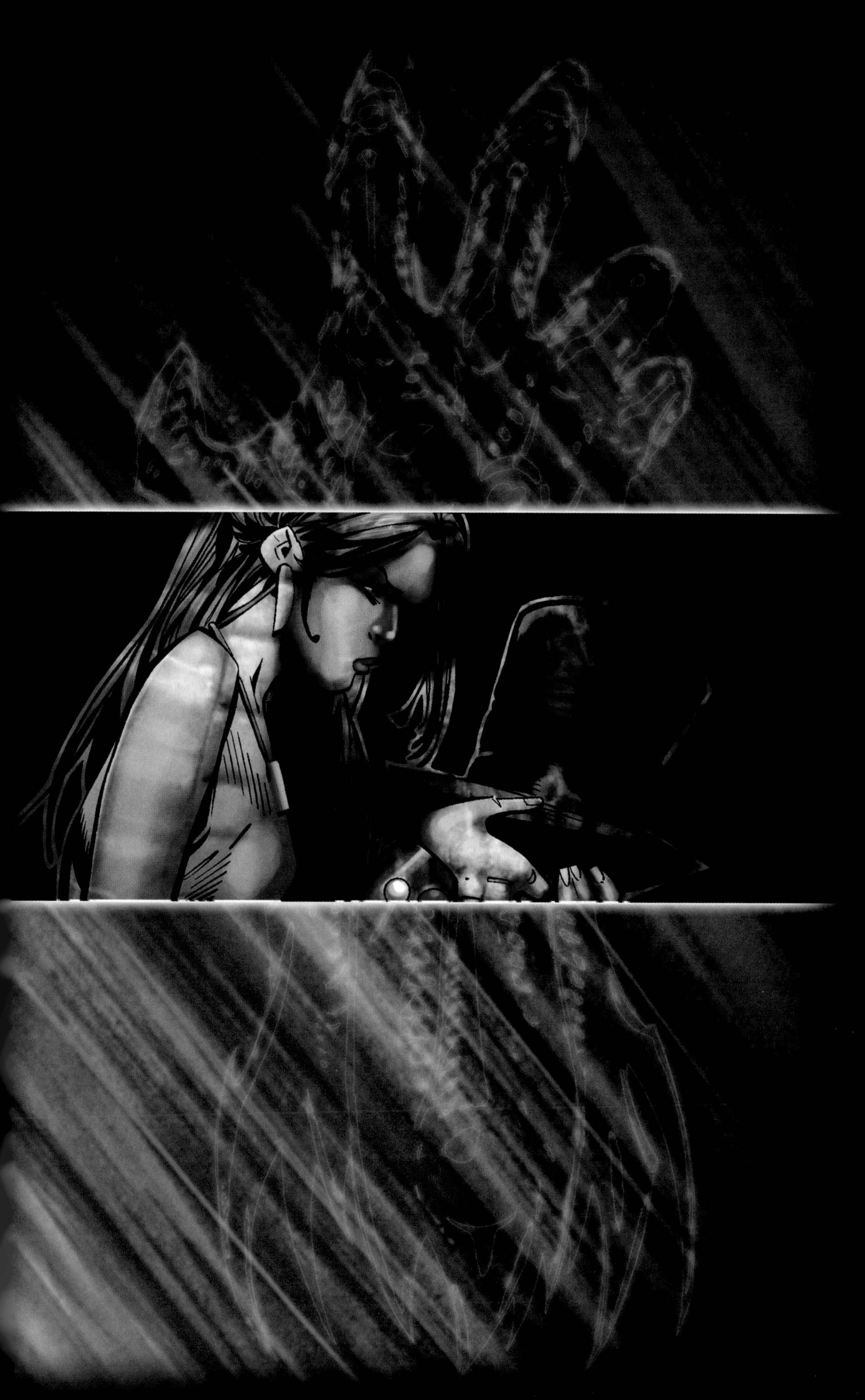

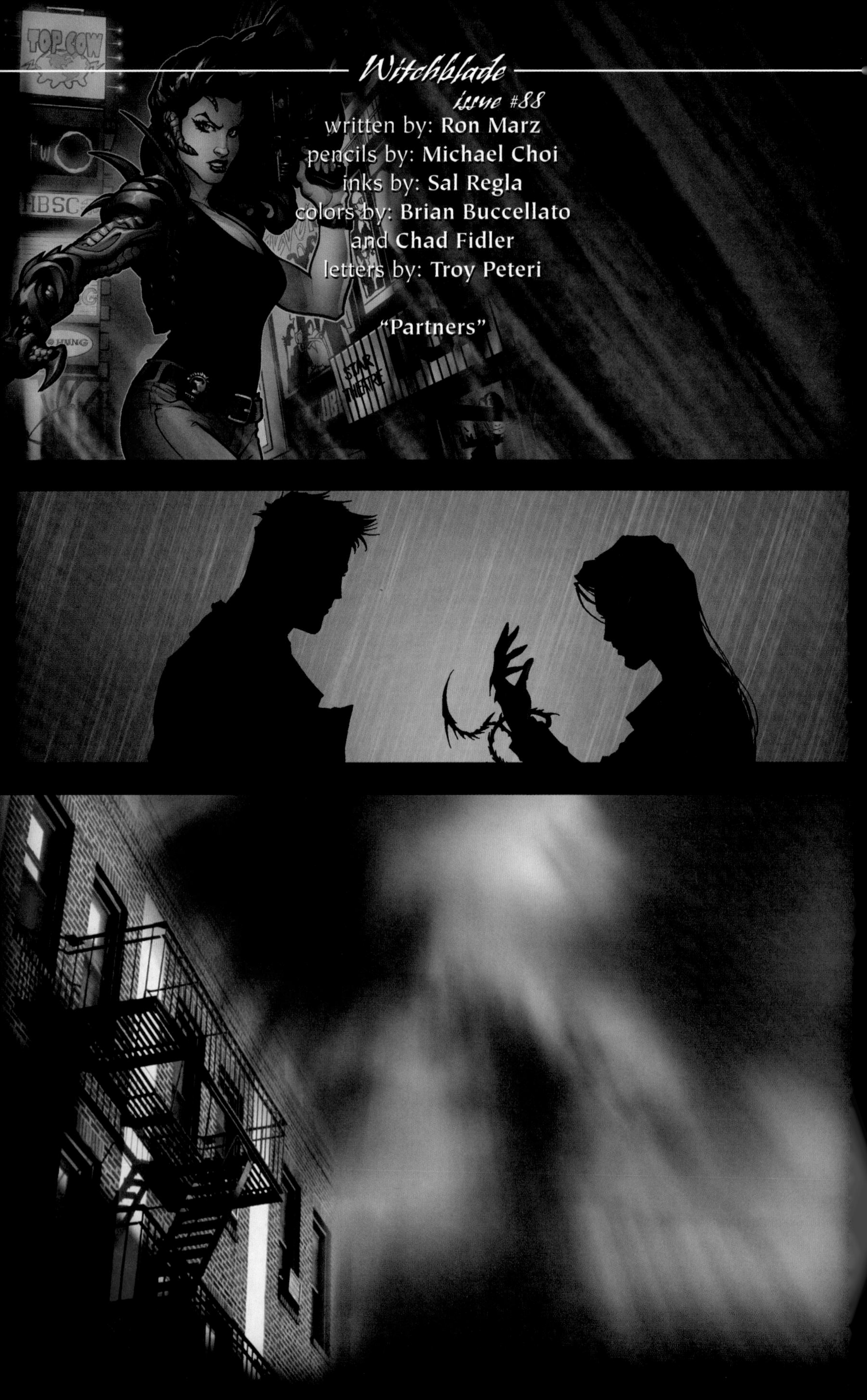
Witchblade
issue #88
written by: Ron Marz
pencils by: Michael Choi
inks by: Sal Regla
colors by: Brian Buccellato
and Chad Fidler
letters by: Troy Peteri
"Partners"
TOP COW
STAR THEATRE

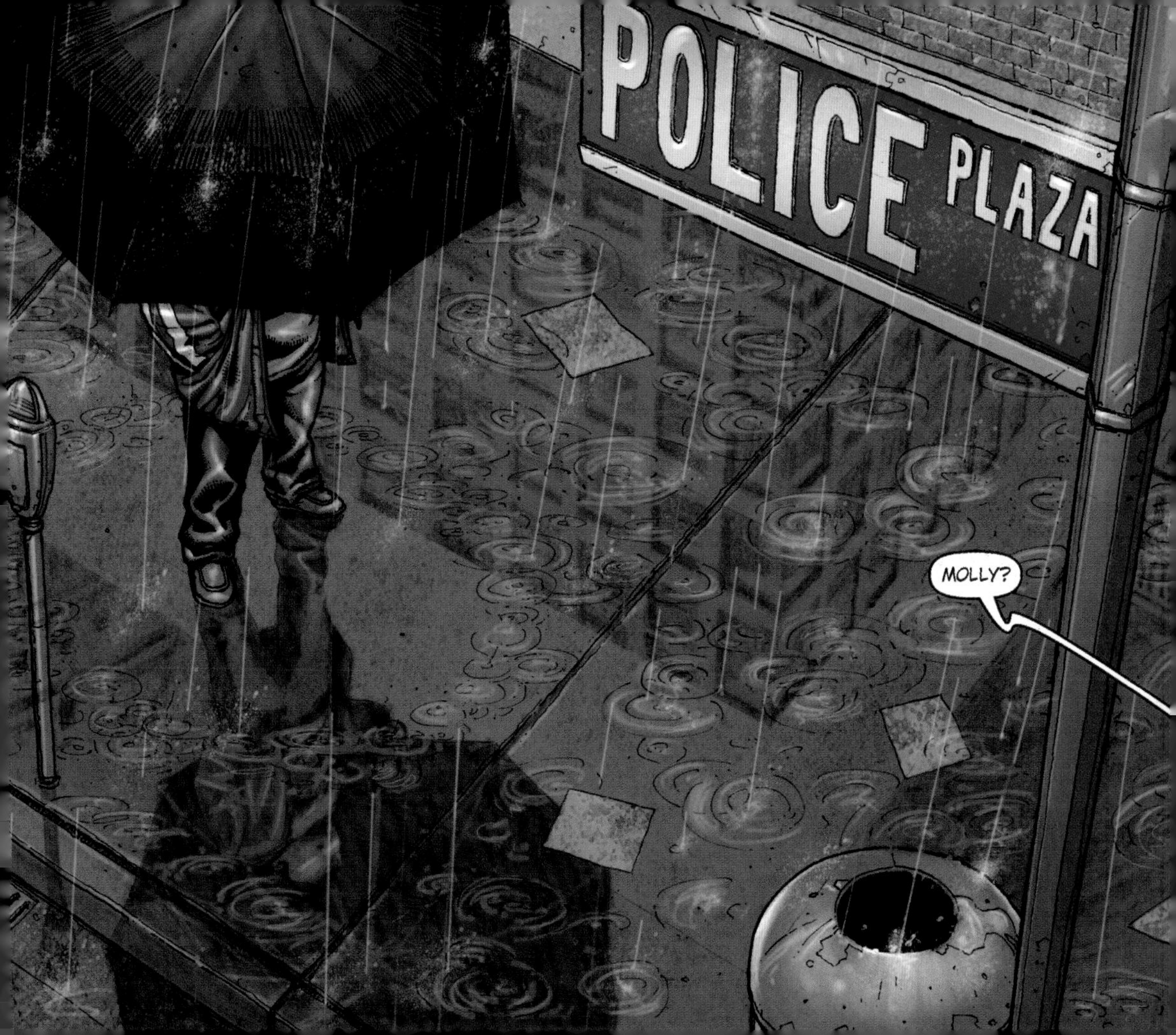
POLICE PLAZA
MOLLY?

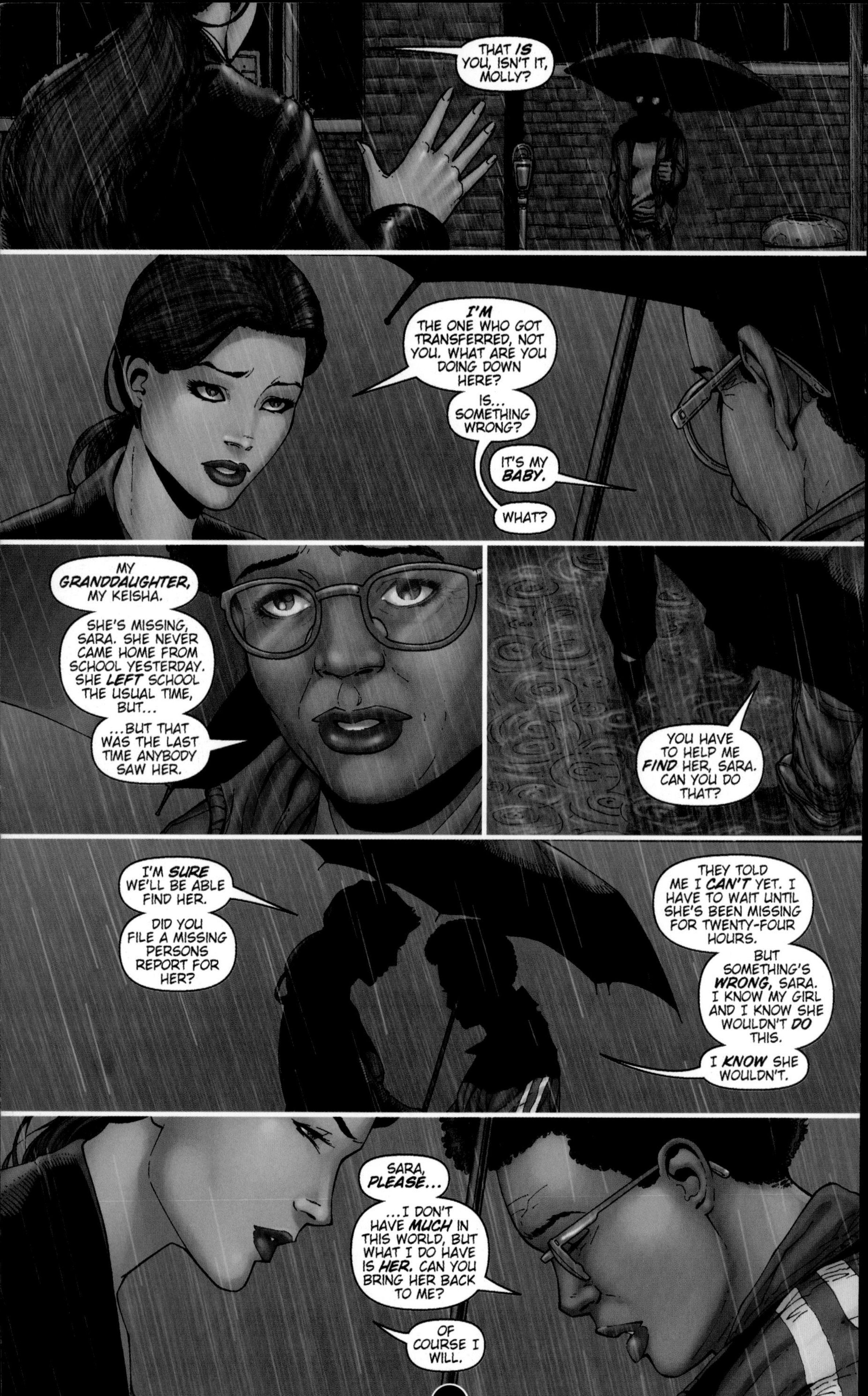
THAT *IS* YOU, ISN'T IT, MOLLY?
I'M THE ONE WHO GOT TRANSFERRED, NOT YOU. WHAT ARE YOU DOING DOWN HERE?
IS... SOMETHING WRONG?
IT'S MY *BABY.*
WHAT?
MY *GRANDDAUGHTER,* MY KEISHA.
SHE'S MISSING, SARA. SHE NEVER CAME HOME FROM SCHOOL YESTERDAY. SHE *LEFT* SCHOOL THE USUAL TIME, BUT...
...BUT THAT WAS THE LAST TIME ANYBODY SAW HER.
YOU HAVE TO HELP ME *FIND* HER, SARA. CAN YOU DO THAT?
I'M *SURE* WE'LL BE ABLE FIND HER.
DID YOU FILE A MISSING PERSONS REPORT FOR HER?
THEY TOLD ME I *CAN'T* YET. I HAVE TO WAIT UNTIL SHE'S BEEN MISSING FOR TWENTY-FOUR HOURS.
BUT SOMETHING'S *WRONG,* SARA. I KNOW MY GIRL AND I KNOW SHE WOULDN'T *DO* THIS.
I *KNOW* SHE WOULDN'T.
SARA, *PLEASE...*
...I DON'T HAVE *MUCH* IN THIS WORLD, BUT WHAT I DO HAVE IS *HER.* CAN YOU BRING HER BACK TO ME?
OF COURSE I WILL.

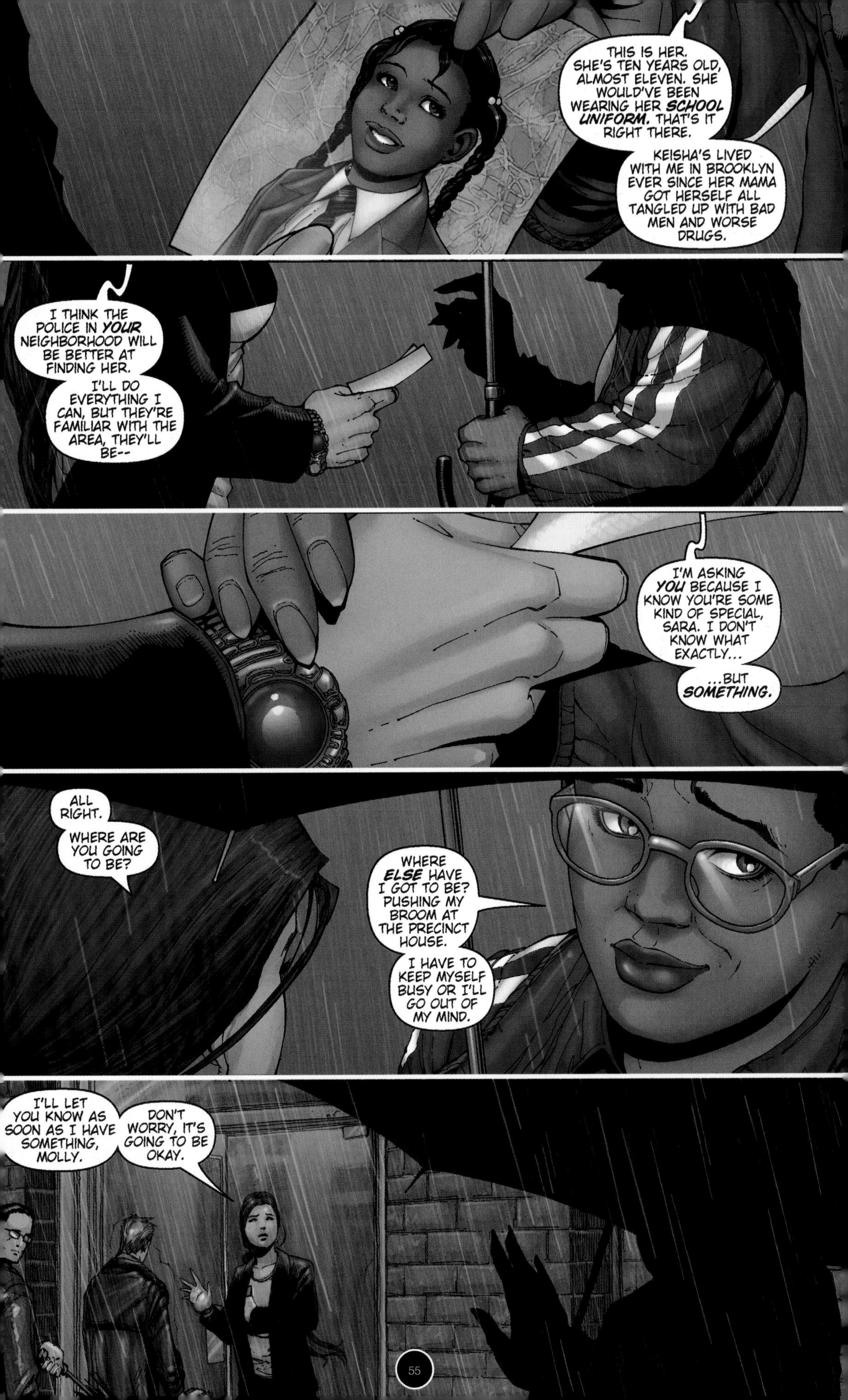
THIS IS HER. SHE'S TEN YEARS OLD, ALMOST ELEVEN. SHE WOULD'VE BEEN WEARING HER SCHOOL UNIFORM. THAT'S IT RIGHT THERE.
KEISHA'S LIVED WITH ME IN BROOKLYN EVER SINCE HER MAMA GOT HERSELF ALL TANGLED UP WITH BAD MEN AND WORSE DRUGS.
I THINK THE POLICE IN YOUR NEIGHBORHOOD WILL BE BETTER AT FINDING HER.
I'LL DO EVERYTHING I CAN, BUT THEY'RE FAMILIAR WITH THE AREA, THEY'LL BE--
I'M ASKING YOU BECAUSE I KNOW YOU'RE SOME KIND OF SPECIAL, SARA. I DON'T KNOW WHAT EXACTLY...
...BUT SOMETHING.
ALL RIGHT.
WHERE ARE YOU GOING TO BE?
WHERE ELSE HAVE I GOT TO BE? PUSHING MY BROOM AT THE PRECINCT HOUSE.
I HAVE TO KEEP MYSELF BUSY OR I'LL GO OUT OF MY MIND.
I'LL LET YOU KNOW AS SOON AS I HAVE SOMETHING, MOLLY.
DON'T WORRY, IT'S GOING TO BE OKAY.

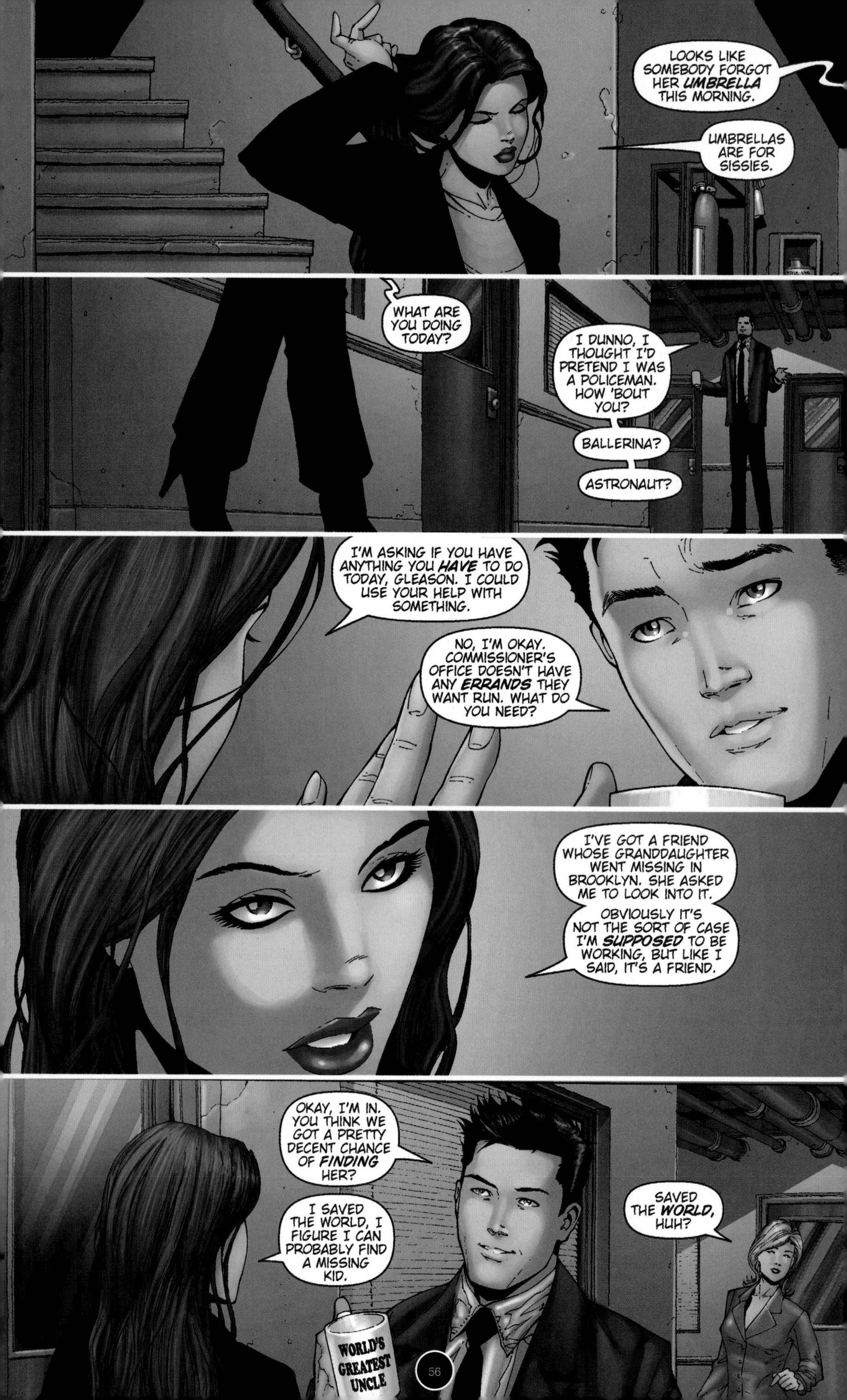
LOOKS LIKE SOMEBODY FORGOT HER *UMBRELLA* THIS MORNING.
UMBRELLAS ARE FOR SISSIES.
WHAT ARE YOU DOING TODAY?
I DUNNO, I THOUGHT I'D PRETEND I WAS A POLICEMAN. HOW 'BOUT YOU?
BALLERINA?
ASTRONAUT?
I'M ASKING IF YOU HAVE ANYTHING YOU *HAVE* TO DO TODAY, GLEASON. I COULD USE YOUR HELP WITH SOMETHING.
NO, I'M OKAY. COMMISSIONER'S OFFICE DOESN'T HAVE ANY *ERRANDS* THEY WANT RUN. WHAT DO YOU NEED?
I'VE GOT A FRIEND WHOSE GRANDDAUGHTER WENT MISSING IN BROOKLYN. SHE ASKED ME TO LOOK INTO IT.
OBVIOUSLY IT'S NOT THE SORT OF CASE I'M *SUPPOSED* TO BE WORKING, BUT LIKE I SAID, IT'S A FRIEND.
OKAY, I'M IN. YOU THINK WE GOT A PRETTY DECENT CHANCE OF *FINDING* HER?
I SAVED THE WORLD, I FIGURE I CAN PROBABLY FIND A MISSING KID.
SAVED THE *WORLD,* HUH?
WORLD'S GREATEST UNCLE

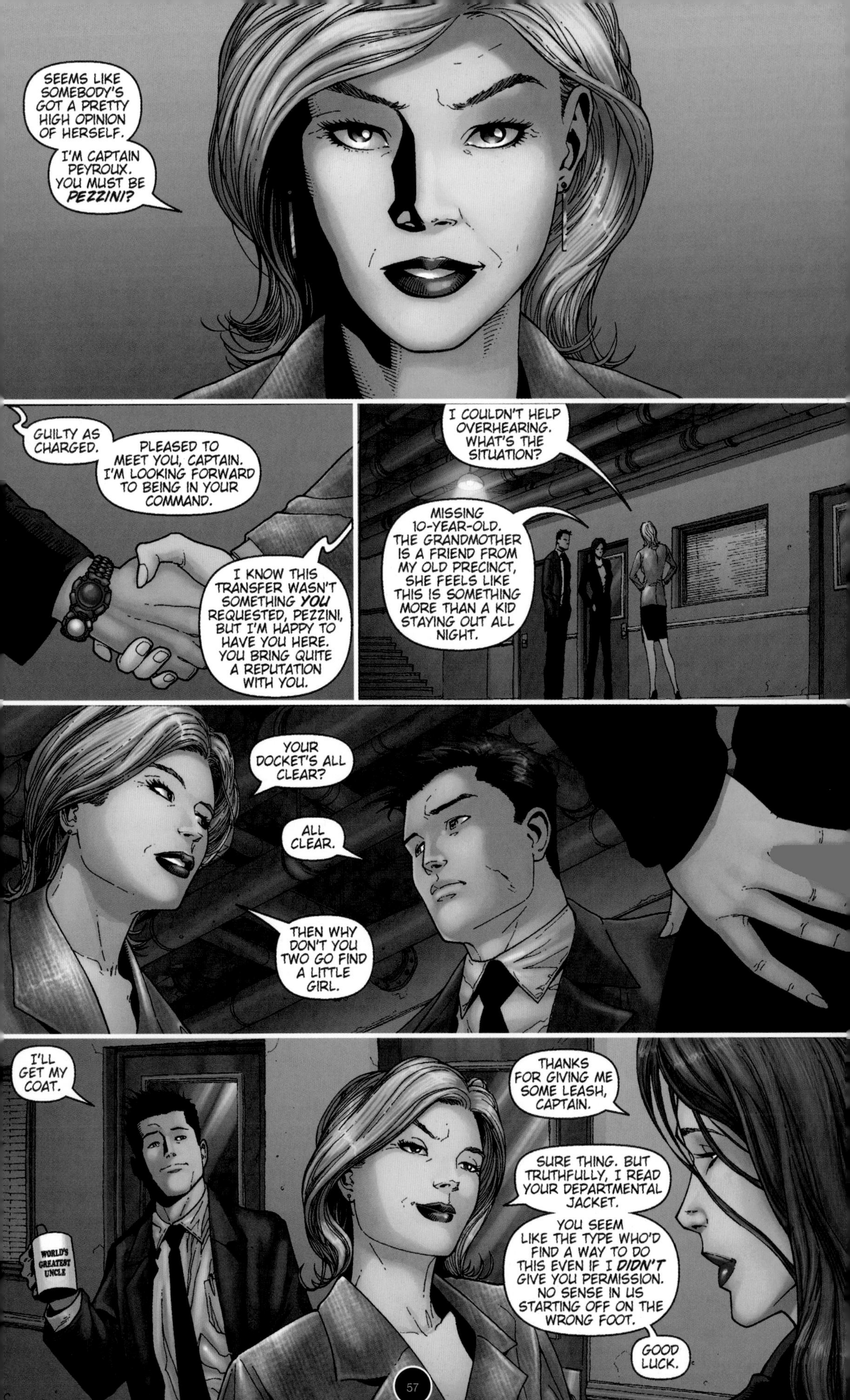
SEEMS LIKE SOMEBODY'S GOT A PRETTY HIGH OPINION OF HERSELF.
I'M CAPTAIN PEYROUX. YOU MUST BE **PEZZINI?**
GUILTY AS CHARGED.
PLEASED TO MEET YOU, CAPTAIN. I'M LOOKING FORWARD TO BEING IN YOUR COMMAND.
I KNOW THIS TRANSFER WASN'T SOMETHING ***YOU*** REQUESTED, PEZZINI, BUT I'M HAPPY TO HAVE YOU HERE. YOU BRING QUITE A REPUTATION WITH YOU.
I COULDN'T HELP OVERHEARING. WHAT'S THE SITUATION?
MISSING 10-YEAR-OLD. THE GRANDMOTHER IS A FRIEND FROM MY OLD PRECINCT, SHE FEELS LIKE THIS IS SOMETHING MORE THAN A KID STAYING OUT ALL NIGHT.
YOUR DOCKET'S ALL CLEAR?
ALL CLEAR.
THEN WHY DON'T YOU TWO GO FIND A LITTLE GIRL.
I'LL GET MY COAT.
WORLD'S GREATEST UNCLE
THANKS FOR GIVING ME SOME LEASH, CAPTAIN.
SURE THING. BUT TRUTHFULLY, I READ YOUR DEPARTMENTAL JACKET.
YOU SEEM LIKE THE TYPE WHO'D FIND A WAY TO DO THIS EVEN IF I ***DIDN'T*** GIVE YOU PERMISSION. NO SENSE IN US STARTING OFF ON THE WRONG FOOT.
GOOD LUCK.

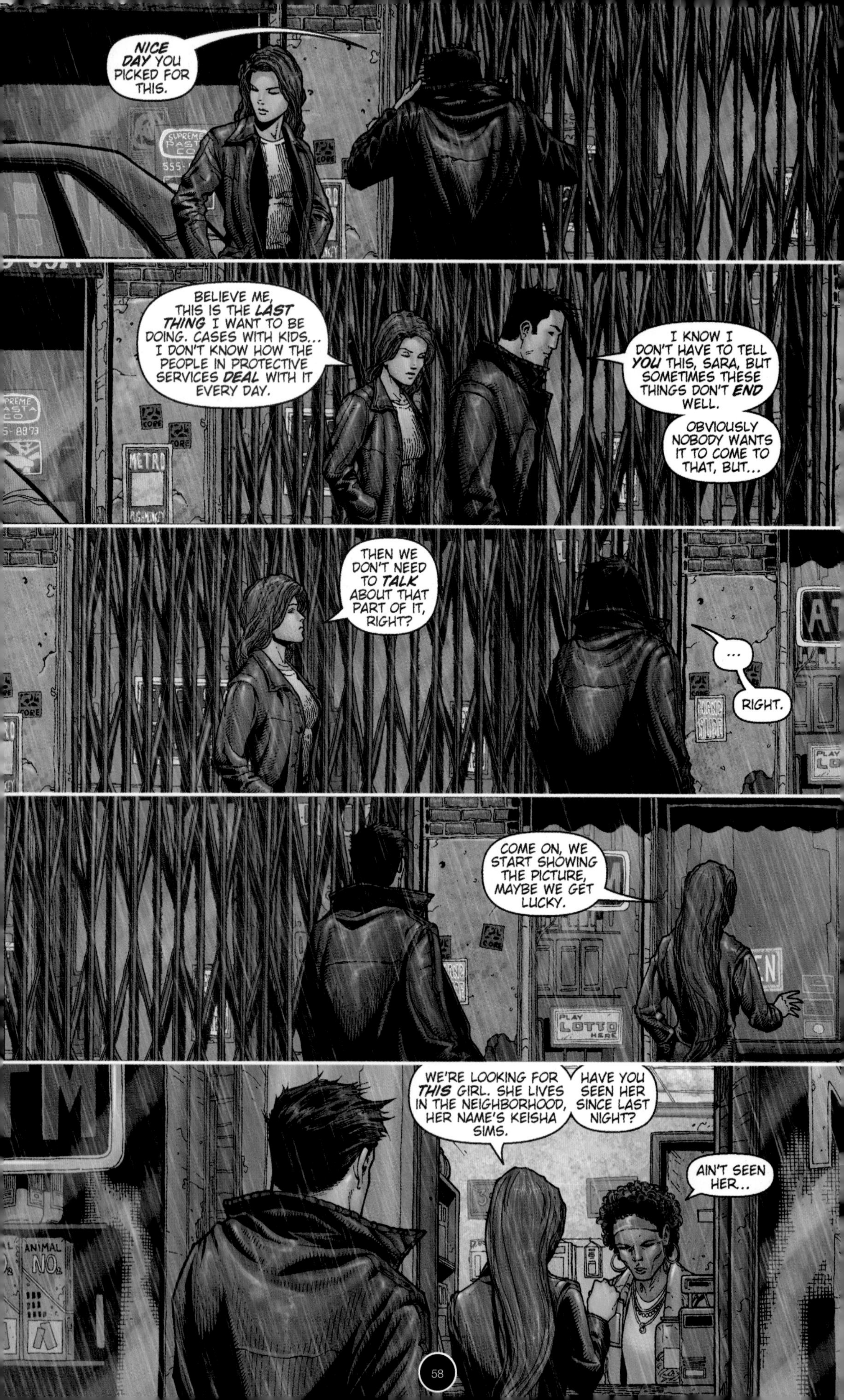
NICE DAY YOU PICKED FOR THIS.
BELIEVE ME, THIS IS THE LAST THING I WANT TO BE DOING. CASES WITH KIDS... I DON'T KNOW HOW THE PEOPLE IN PROTECTIVE SERVICES DEAL WITH IT EVERY DAY.
I KNOW I DON'T HAVE TO TELL YOU THIS, SARA, BUT SOMETIMES THESE THINGS DON'T END WELL.
OBVIOUSLY NOBODY WANTS IT TO COME TO THAT, BUT...
THEN WE DON'T NEED TO TALK ABOUT THAT PART OF IT, RIGHT?
...
RIGHT.
COME ON, WE START SHOWING THE PICTURE, MAYBE WE GET LUCKY.
PLAY LOTTO HERE
WE'RE LOOKING FOR THIS GIRL. SHE LIVES IN THE NEIGHBORHOOD, HER NAME'S KEISHA SIMS.
HAVE YOU SEEN HER SINCE LAST NIGHT?
AIN'T SEEN HER..
ANIMAL NO₂

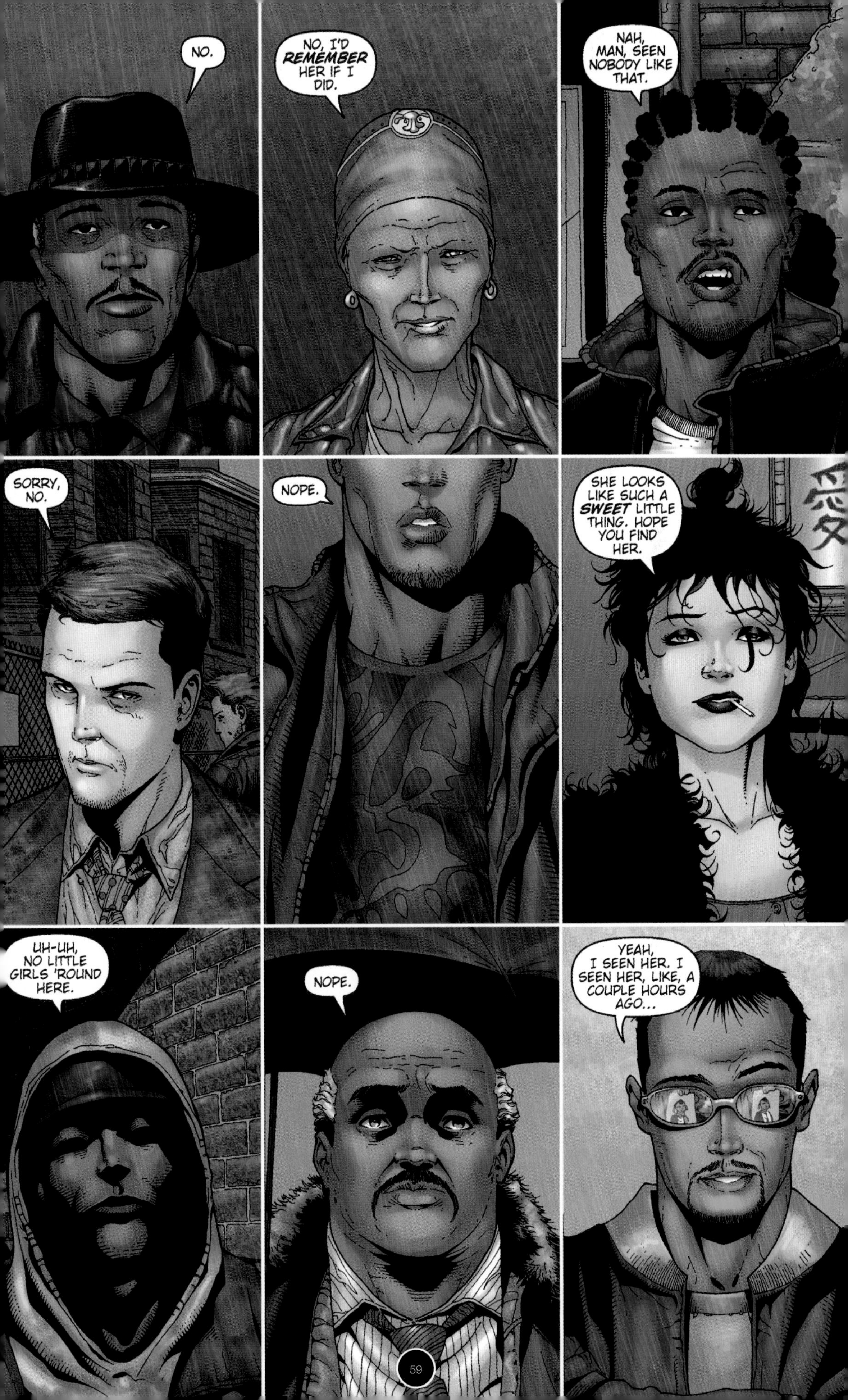
NO.
NO, I'D REMEMBER HER IF I DID.
NAH, MAN, SEEN NOBODY LIKE THAT.
SORRY, NO.
NOPE.
SHE LOOKS LIKE SUCH A SWEET LITTLE THING. HOPE YOU FIND HER.
UH-UH, NO LITTLE GIRLS 'ROUND HERE.
NOPE.
YEAH, I SEEN HER. I SEEN HER, LIKE, A COUPLE HOURS AGO...

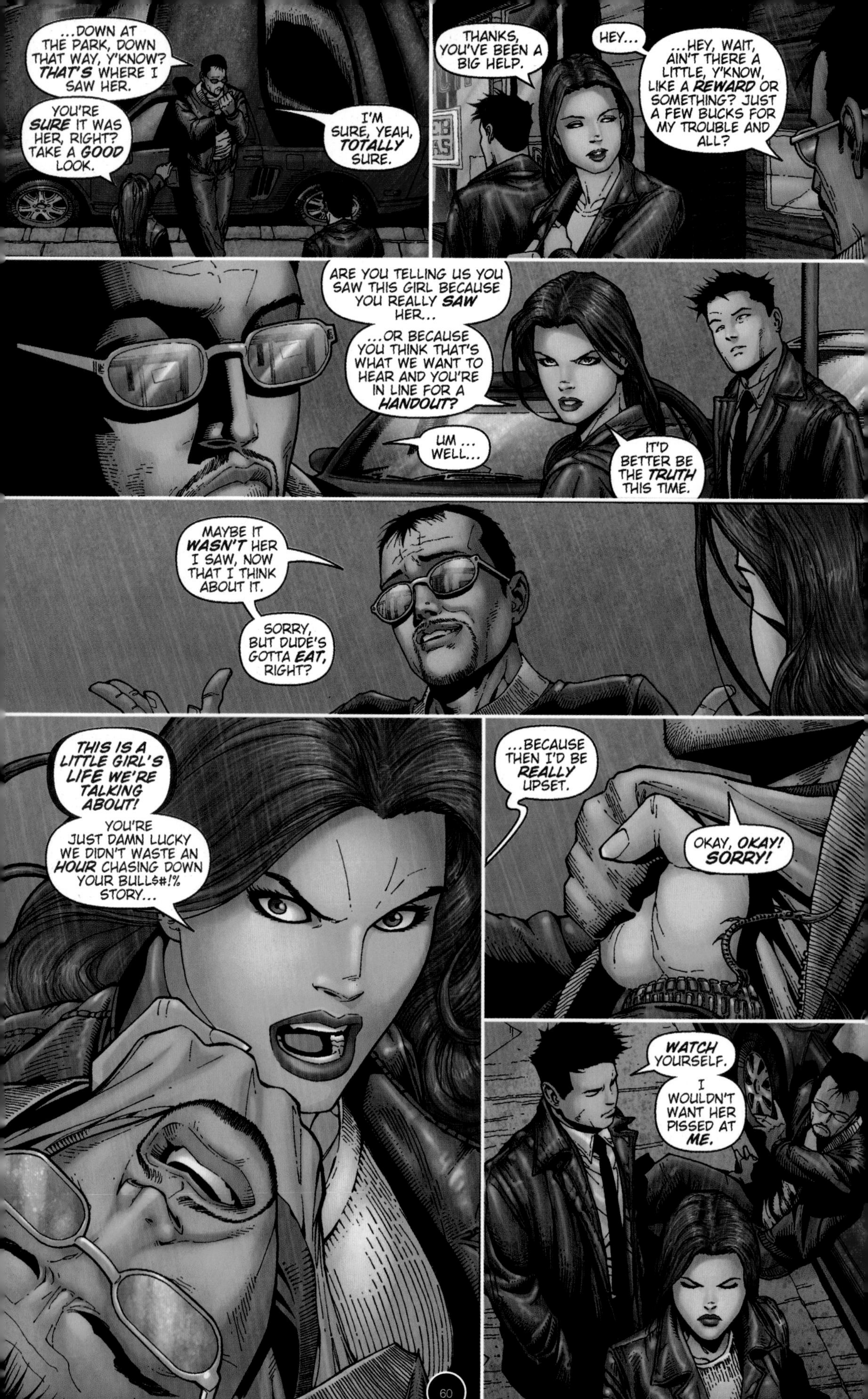
...DOWN AT THE PARK, DOWN THAT WAY, Y'KNOW? THAT'S WHERE I SAW HER.
YOU'RE SURE IT WAS HER, RIGHT? TAKE A GOOD LOOK.
I'M SURE, YEAH, TOTALLY SURE.
THANKS, YOU'VE BEEN A BIG HELP.
HEY...
...HEY, WAIT, AIN'T THERE A LITTLE, Y'KNOW, LIKE A REWARD OR SOMETHING? JUST A FEW BUCKS FOR MY TROUBLE AND ALL?
ARE YOU TELLING US YOU SAW THIS GIRL BECAUSE YOU REALLY SAW HER...
...OR BECAUSE YOU THINK THAT'S WHAT WE WANT TO HEAR AND YOU'RE IN LINE FOR A HANDOUT?
UM ... WELL...
IT'D BETTER BE THE TRUTH THIS TIME.
MAYBE IT WASN'T HER I SAW, NOW THAT I THINK ABOUT IT.
SORRY, BUT DUDE'S GOTTA EAT, RIGHT?
THIS IS A LITTLE GIRL'S LIFE WE'RE TALKING ABOUT!
YOU'RE JUST DAMN LUCKY WE DIDN'T WASTE AN HOUR CHASING DOWN YOUR BULL$#!% STORY...
...BECAUSE THEN I'D BE REALLY UPSET.
OKAY, OKAY! SORRY!
WATCH YOURSELF.
I WOULDN'T WANT HER PISSED AT ME.

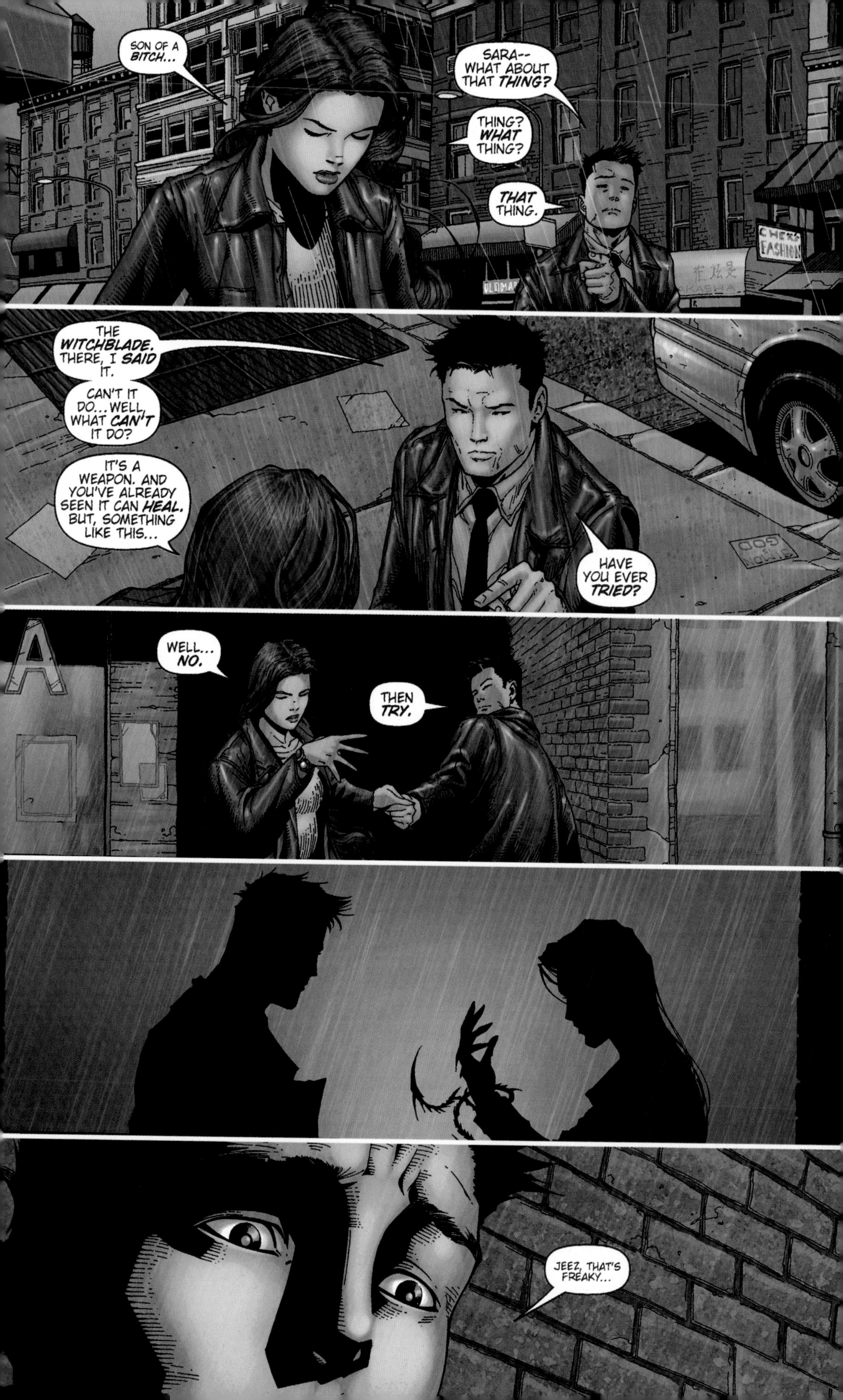

SON OF A BITCH...
SARA-- WHAT ABOUT THAT THING?
THING? WHAT THING?
THAT THING.
CHEN'S FASHION
THE WITCHBLADE. THERE, I SAID IT.
CAN'T IT DO... WELL, WHAT CAN'T IT DO?
IT'S A WEAPON. AND YOU'VE ALREADY SEEN IT CAN HEAL. BUT, SOMETHING LIKE THIS...
HAVE YOU EVER TRIED?
WELL... NO.
THEN TRY.
JEEZ, THAT'S FREAKY...

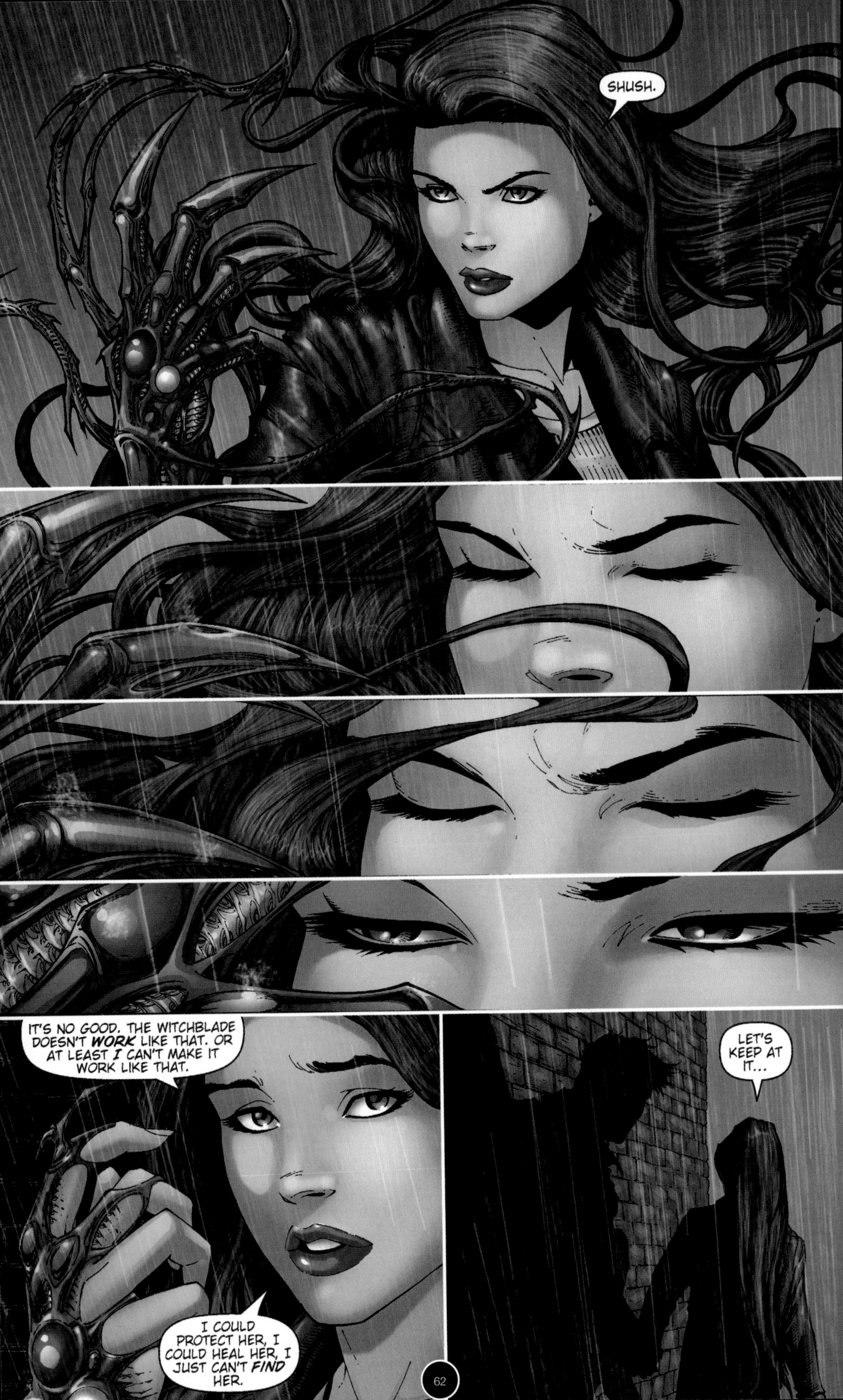
SHUSH.
IT'S NO GOOD. THE WITCHBLADE DOESN'T WORK LIKE THAT. OR AT LEAST I CAN'T MAKE IT WORK LIKE THAT.
I COULD PROTECT HER, I COULD HEAL HER, I JUST CAN'T FIND HER.
LET'S KEEP AT IT...

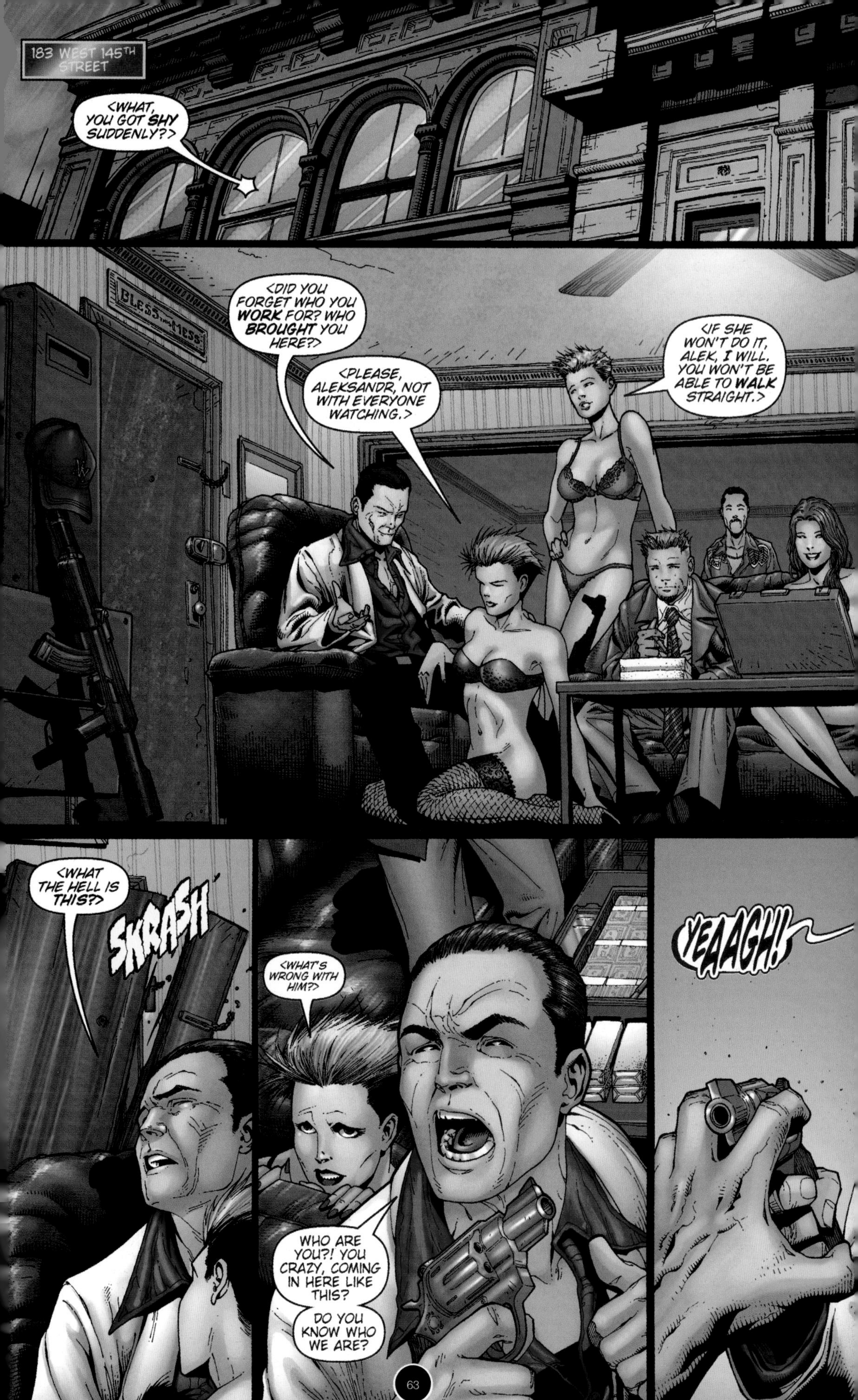
183 WEST 145TH STREET
<WHAT, YOU GOT SHY SUDDENLY?>
<DID YOU FORGET WHO YOU WORK FOR? WHO BROUGHT YOU HERE?>
<PLEASE, ALEKSANDR, NOT WITH EVERYONE WATCHING.>
<IF SHE WON'T DO IT, ALEK, I WILL. YOU WON'T BE ABLE TO WALK STRAIGHT.>
BLESS THIS MESS
<WHAT THE HELL IS THIS?>
SKRASH
<WHAT'S WRONG WITH HIM?>
WHO ARE YOU?! YOU CRAZY, COMING IN HERE LIKE THIS?
DO YOU KNOW WHO WE ARE?
YEAAGH!

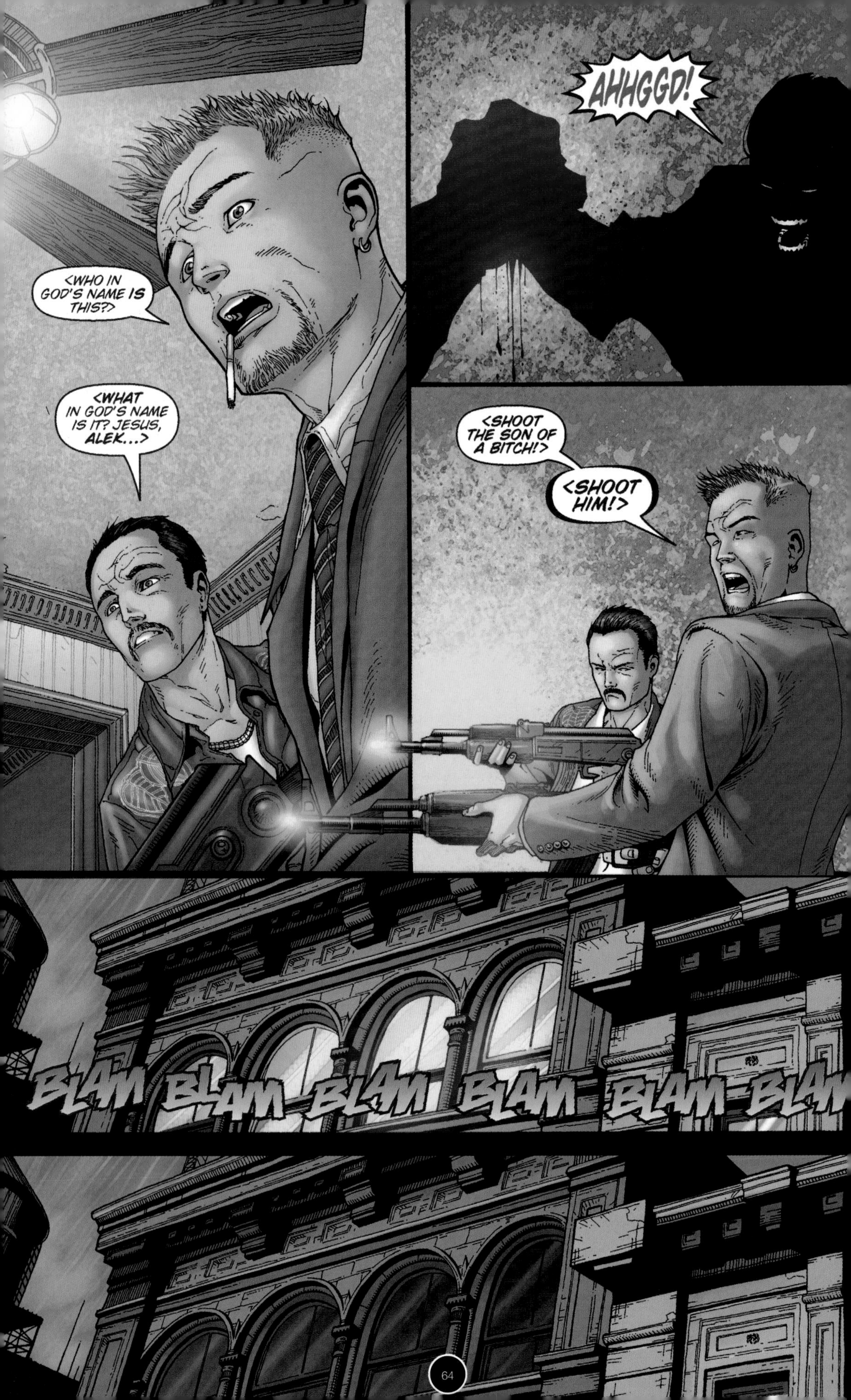
<WHO IN GOD'S NAME IS THIS?>
<WHAT IN GOD'S NAME IS IT? JESUS, ALEK...>
AHHGGD!
<SHOOT THE SON OF A BITCH!>
<SHOOT HIM!>
BLAM BLAM BLAM BLAM BLAM BLAM

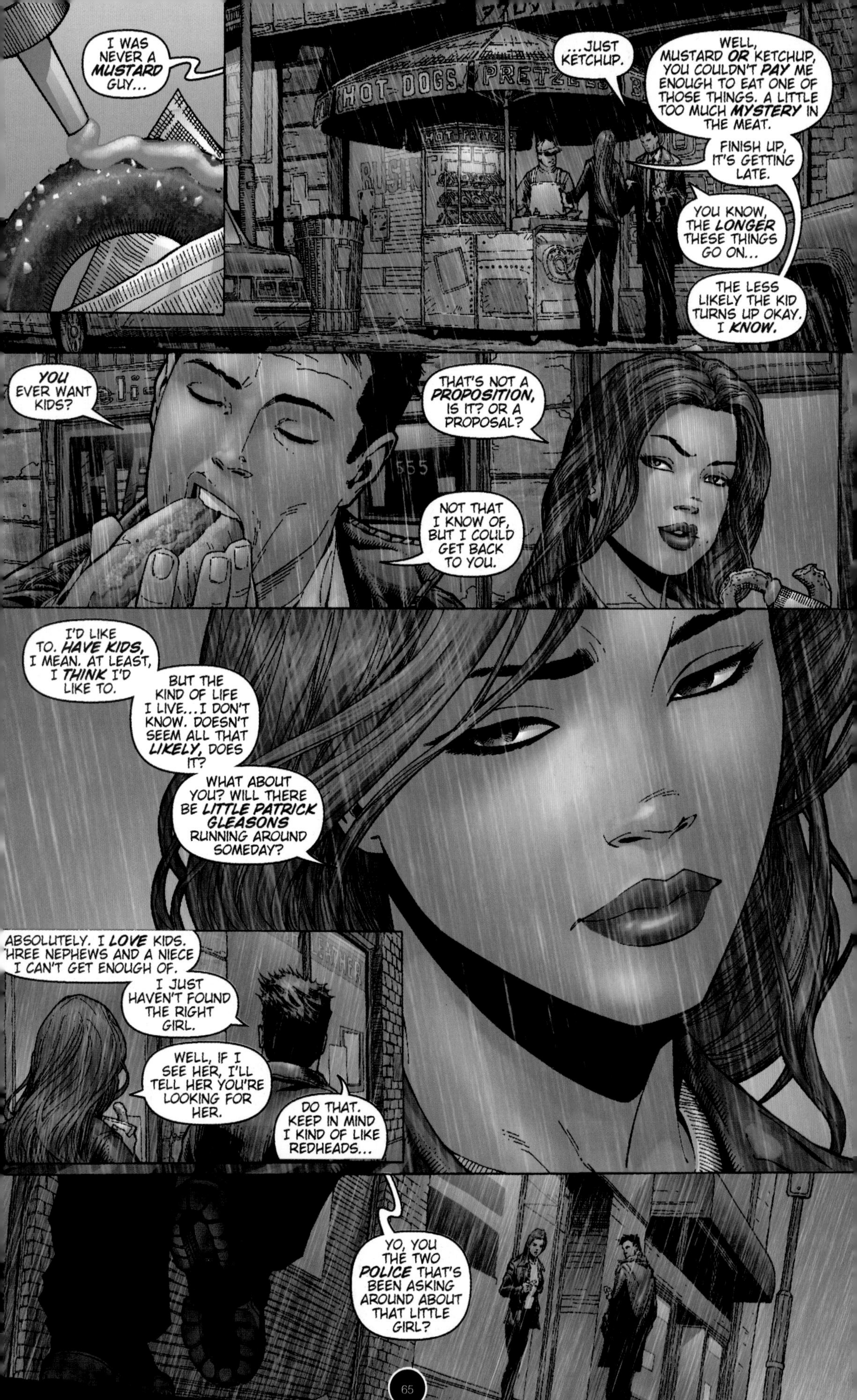
I WAS NEVER A MUSTARD GUY...
...JUST KETCHUP.
WELL, MUSTARD OR KETCHUP, YOU COULDN'T PAY ME ENOUGH TO EAT ONE OF THOSE THINGS. A LITTLE TOO MUCH MYSTERY IN THE MEAT.
FINISH UP, IT'S GETTING LATE.
YOU KNOW, THE LONGER THESE THINGS GO ON...
THE LESS LIKELY THE KID TURNS UP OKAY. I KNOW.
HOT DOGS
PRETZELS
YOU EVER WANT KIDS?
THAT'S NOT A PROPOSITION, IS IT? OR A PROPOSAL?
NOT THAT I KNOW OF, BUT I COULD GET BACK TO YOU.
I'D LIKE TO. HAVE KIDS, I MEAN. AT LEAST, I THINK I'D LIKE TO.
BUT THE KIND OF LIFE I LIVE...I DON'T KNOW. DOESN'T SEEM ALL THAT LIKELY, DOES IT?
WHAT ABOUT YOU? WILL THERE BE LITTLE PATRICK GLEASONS RUNNING AROUND SOMEDAY?
ABSOLUTELY. I LOVE KIDS. THREE NEPHEWS AND A NIECE I CAN'T GET ENOUGH OF.
I JUST HAVEN'T FOUND THE RIGHT GIRL.
WELL, IF I SEE HER, I'LL TELL HER YOU'RE LOOKING FOR HER.
DO THAT. KEEP IN MIND I KIND OF LIKE REDHEADS...
YO, YOU THE TWO POLICE THAT'S BEEN ASKING AROUND ABOUT THAT LITTLE GIRL?

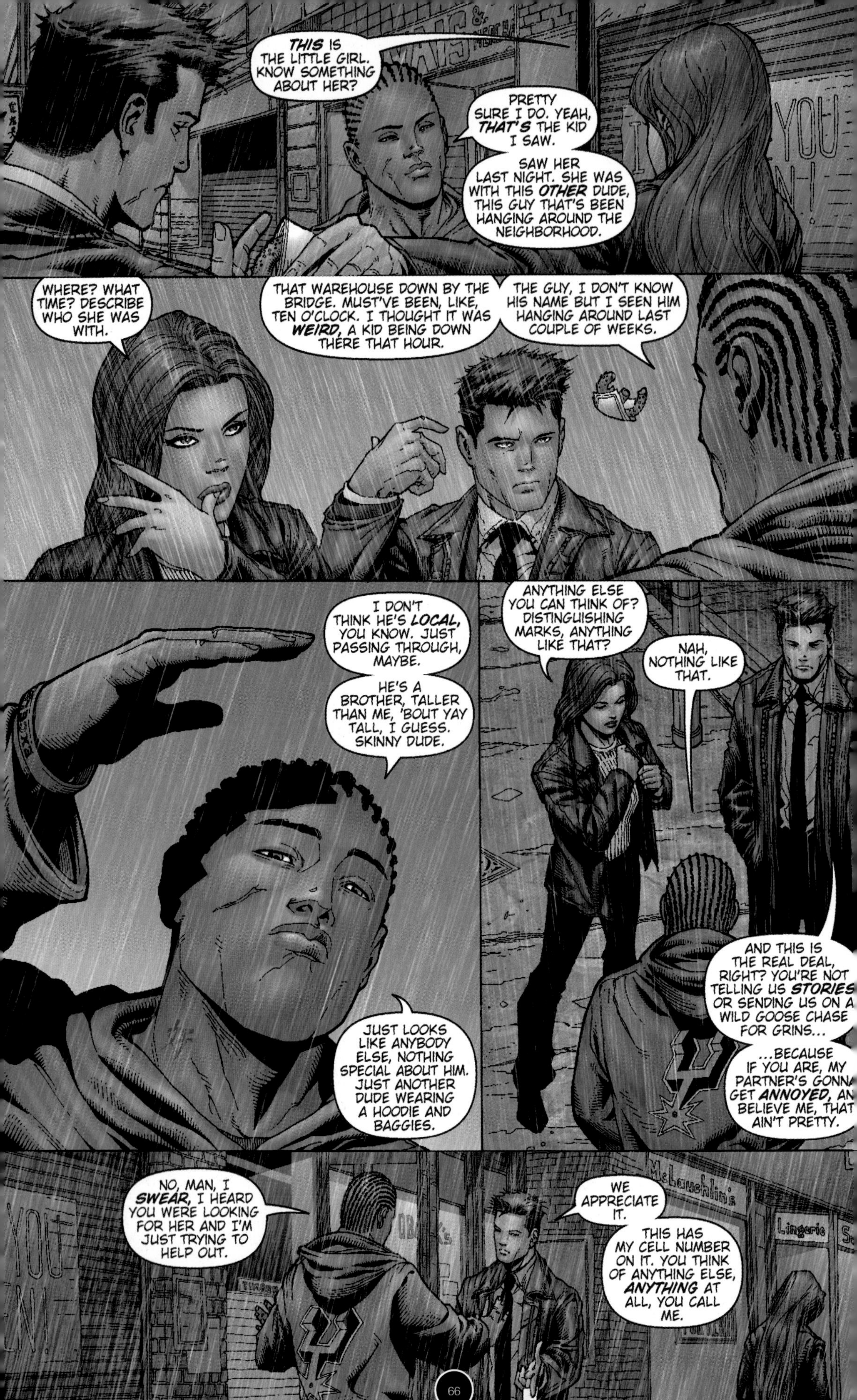
THIS IS THE LITTLE GIRL. KNOW SOMETHING ABOUT HER?
PRETTY SURE I DO. YEAH, THAT'S THE KID I SAW.
SAW HER LAST NIGHT. SHE WAS WITH THIS OTHER DUDE, THIS GUY THAT'S BEEN HANGING AROUND THE NEIGHBORHOOD.
WHERE? WHAT TIME? DESCRIBE WHO SHE WAS WITH.
THAT WAREHOUSE DOWN BY THE BRIDGE. MUST'VE BEEN, LIKE, TEN O'CLOCK. I THOUGHT IT WAS WEIRD, A KID BEING DOWN THERE THAT HOUR.
THE GUY, I DON'T KNOW HIS NAME BUT I SEEN HIM HANGING AROUND LAST COUPLE OF WEEKS.
I DON'T THINK HE'S LOCAL, YOU KNOW. JUST PASSING THROUGH, MAYBE.
HE'S A BROTHER, TALLER THAN ME, 'BOUT YAY TALL, I GUESS. SKINNY DUDE.
JUST LOOKS LIKE ANYBODY ELSE, NOTHING SPECIAL ABOUT HIM. JUST ANOTHER DUDE WEARING A HOODIE AND BAGGIES.
ANYTHING ELSE YOU CAN THINK OF? DISTINGUISHING MARKS, ANYTHING LIKE THAT?
NAH, NOTHING LIKE THAT.
AND THIS IS THE REAL DEAL, RIGHT? YOU'RE NOT TELLING US STORIES OR SENDING US ON A WILD GOOSE CHASE FOR GRINS...
...BECAUSE IF YOU ARE, MY PARTNER'S GONNA GET ANNOYED, AN BELIEVE ME, THAT AIN'T PRETTY.
NO, MAN, I SWEAR, I HEARD YOU WERE LOOKING FOR HER AND I'M JUST TRYING TO HELP OUT.
WE APPRECIATE IT.
THIS HAS MY CELL NUMBER ON IT. YOU THINK OF ANYTHING ELSE, ANYTHING AT ALL, YOU CALL ME.
McLaughlin's
Lingerie

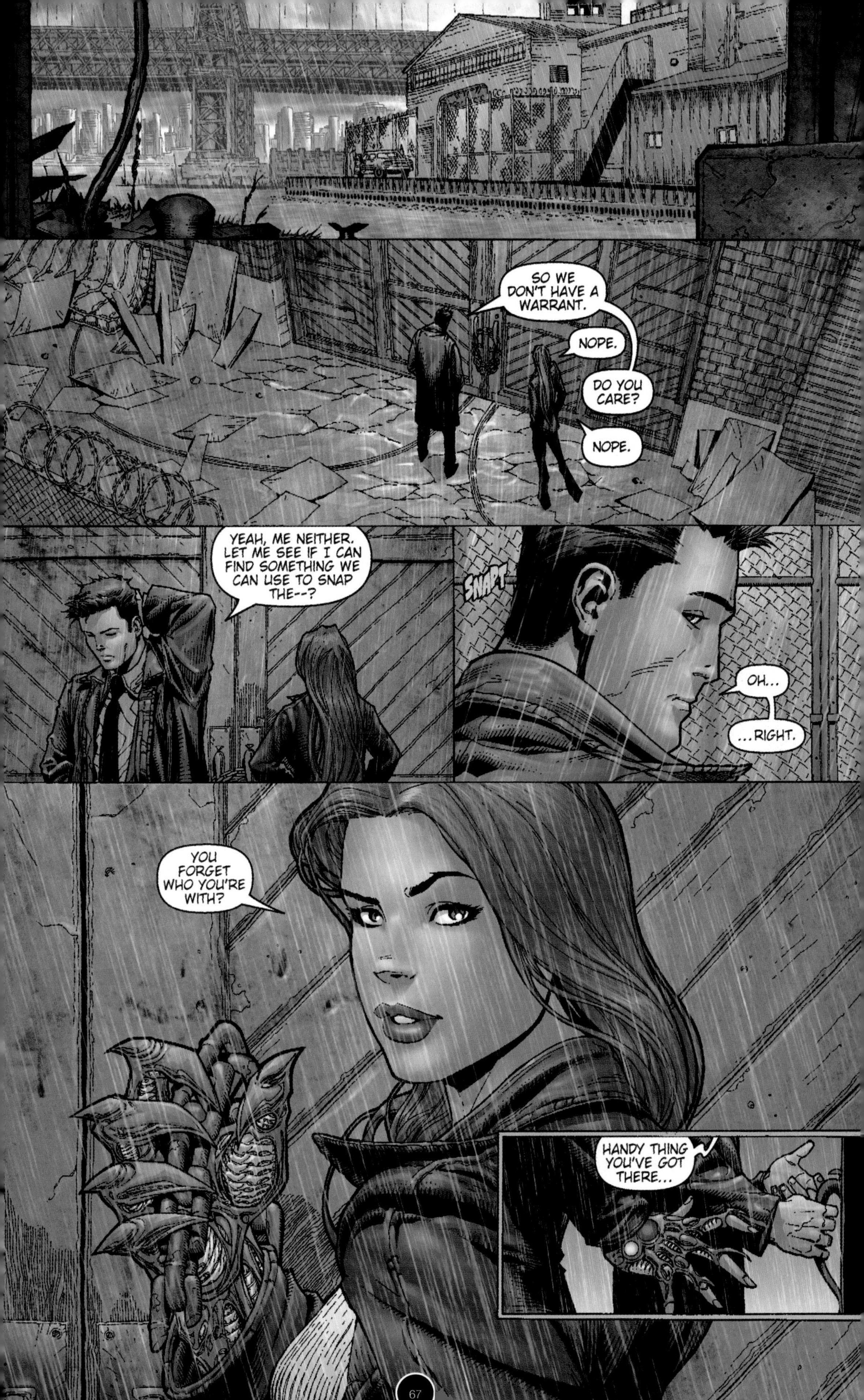
SO WE DON'T HAVE A WARRANT.
NOPE.
DO YOU CARE?
NOPE.
YEAH, ME NEITHER. LET ME SEE IF I CAN FIND SOMETHING WE CAN USE TO SNAP THE--?
SNAP!
OH...
...RIGHT.
YOU FORGET WHO YOU'RE WITH?
HANDY THING YOU'VE GOT THERE...

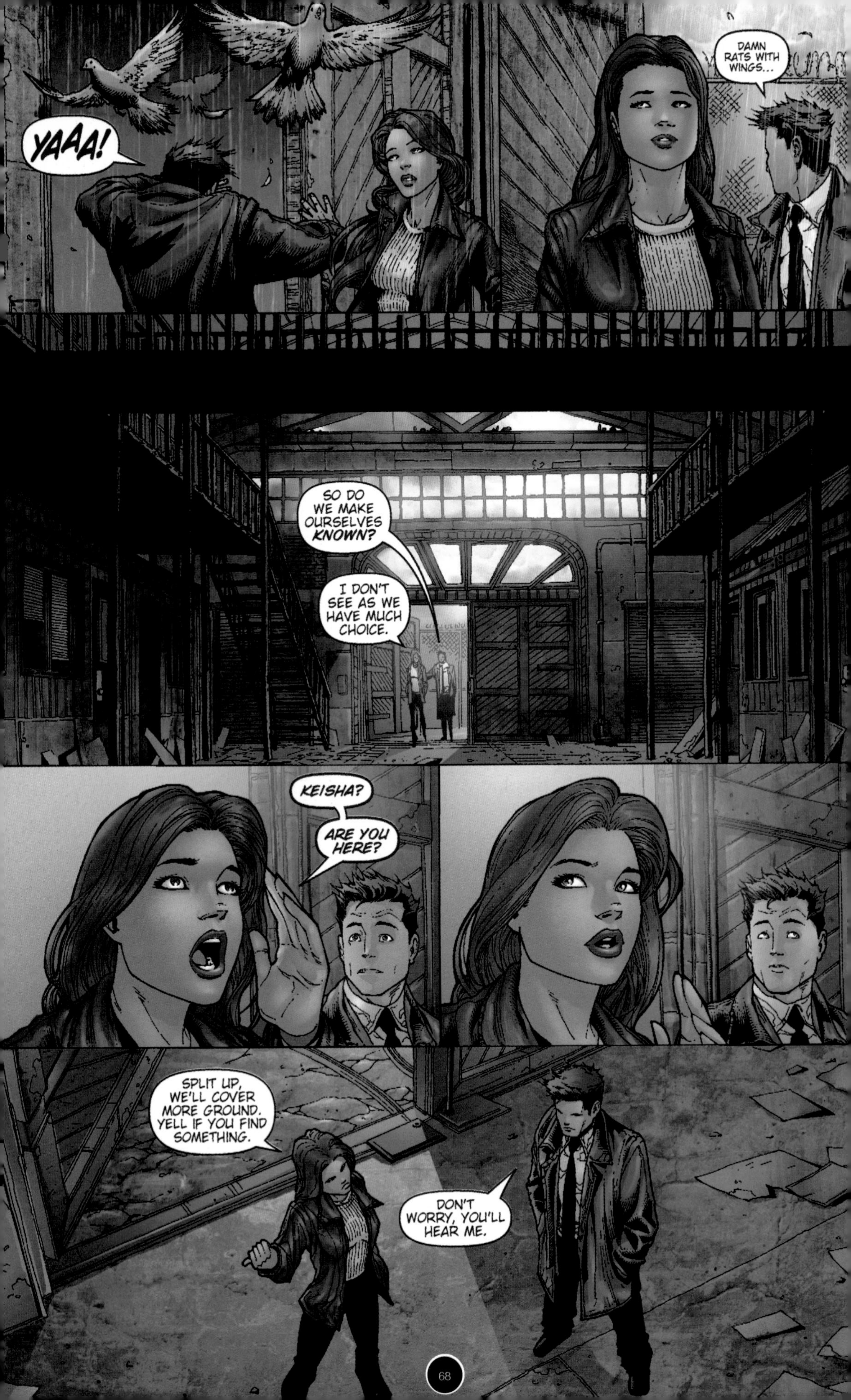
YAAA!
DAMN RATS WITH WINGS...
SO DO WE MAKE OURSELVES KNOWN?
I DON'T SEE AS WE HAVE MUCH CHOICE.
KEISHA?
ARE YOU HERE?
SPLIT UP, WE'LL COVER MORE GROUND. YELL IF YOU FIND SOMETHING.
DON'T WORRY, YOU'LL HEAR ME.

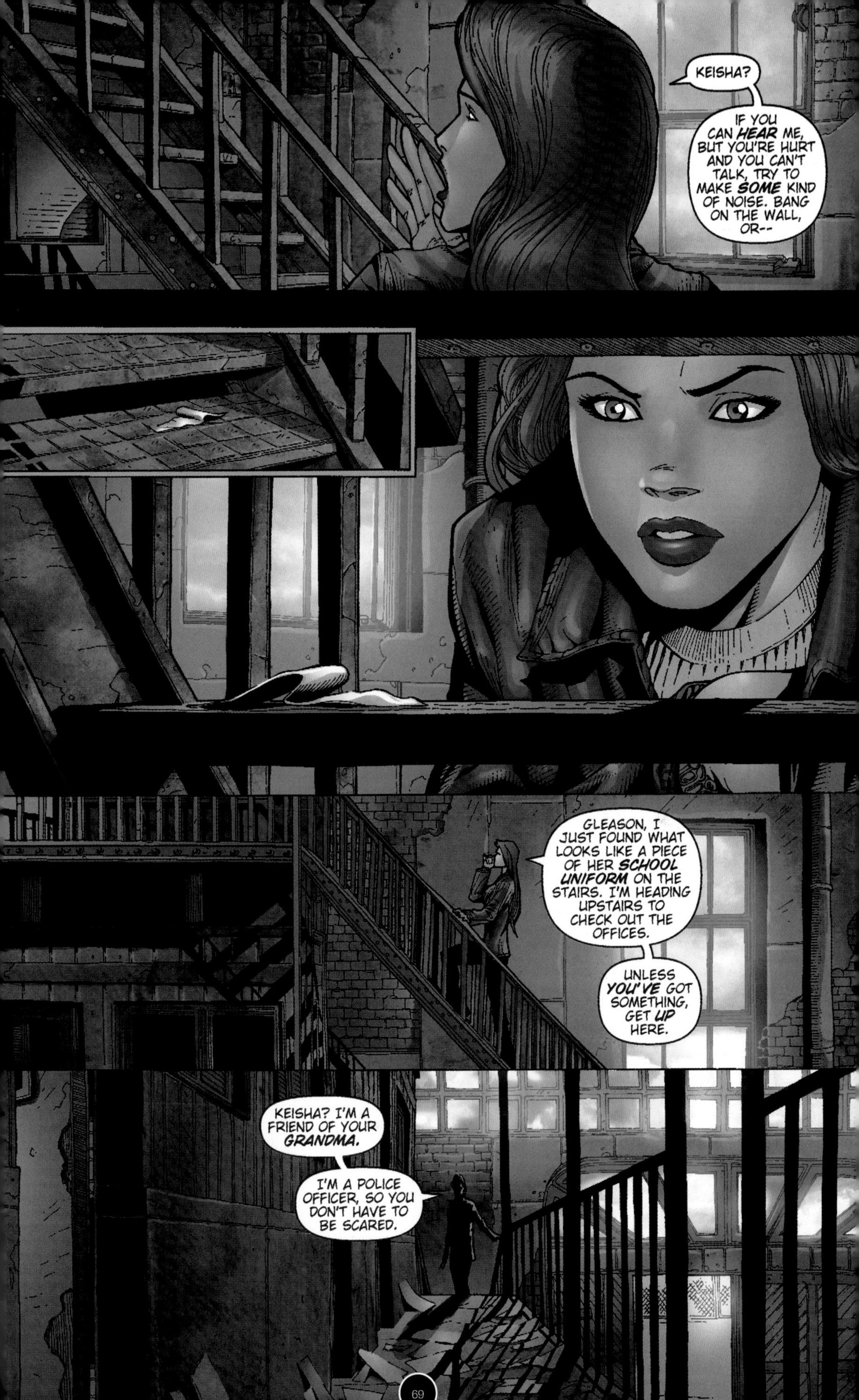
KEISHA?
IF YOU CAN HEAR ME, BUT YOU'RE HURT AND YOU CAN'T TALK, TRY TO MAKE SOME KIND OF NOISE. BANG ON THE WALL, OR--
GLEASON, I JUST FOUND WHAT LOOKS LIKE A PIECE OF HER SCHOOL UNIFORM ON THE STAIRS. I'M HEADING UPSTAIRS TO CHECK OUT THE OFFICES.
UNLESS YOU'VE GOT SOMETHING, GET UP HERE.
KEISHA? I'M A FRIEND OF YOUR GRANDMA.
I'M A POLICE OFFICER, SO YOU DON'T HAVE TO BE SCARED.

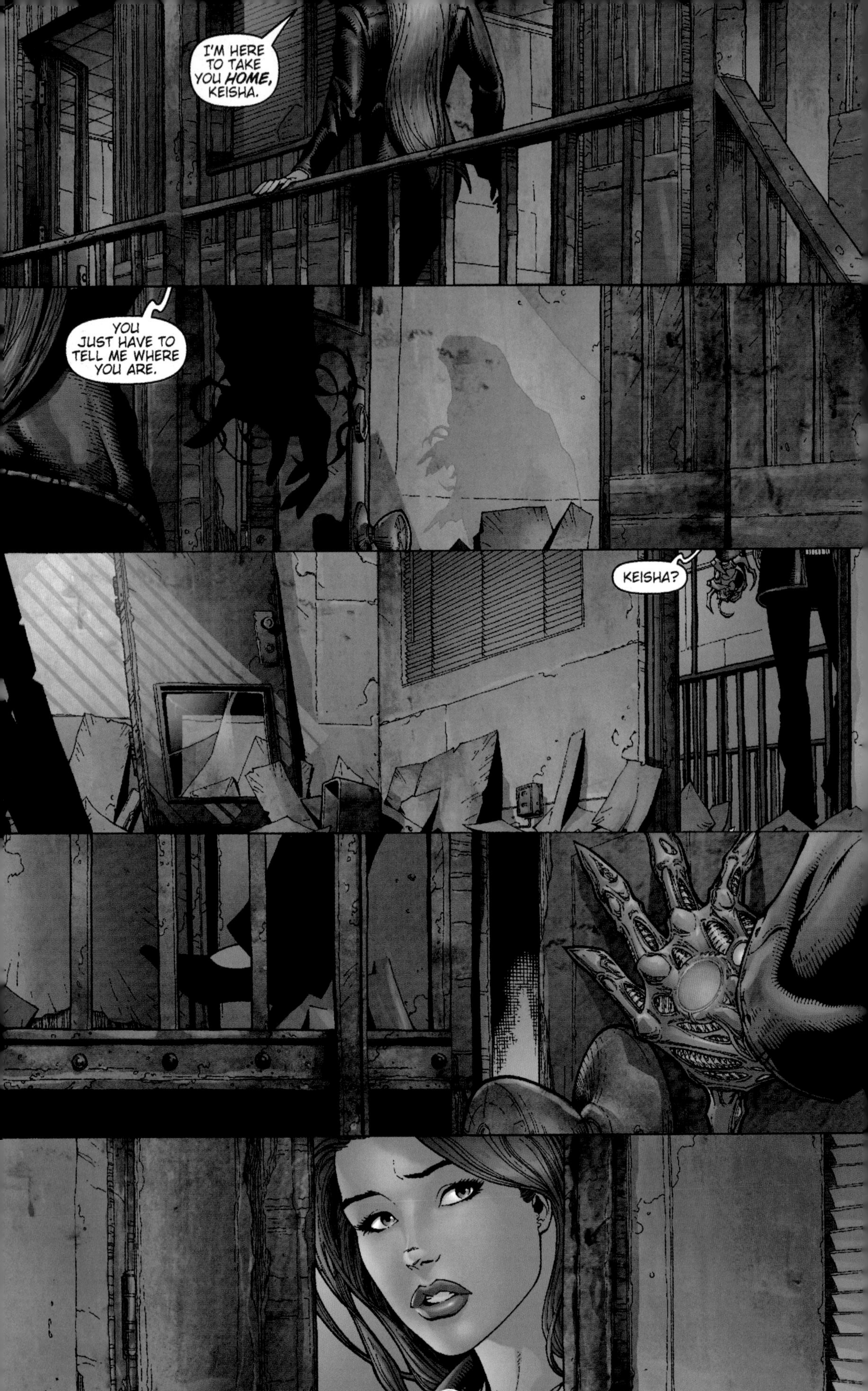
I'M HERE TO TAKE YOU HOME, KEISHA.
YOU JUST HAVE TO TELL ME WHERE YOU ARE.
KEISHA?

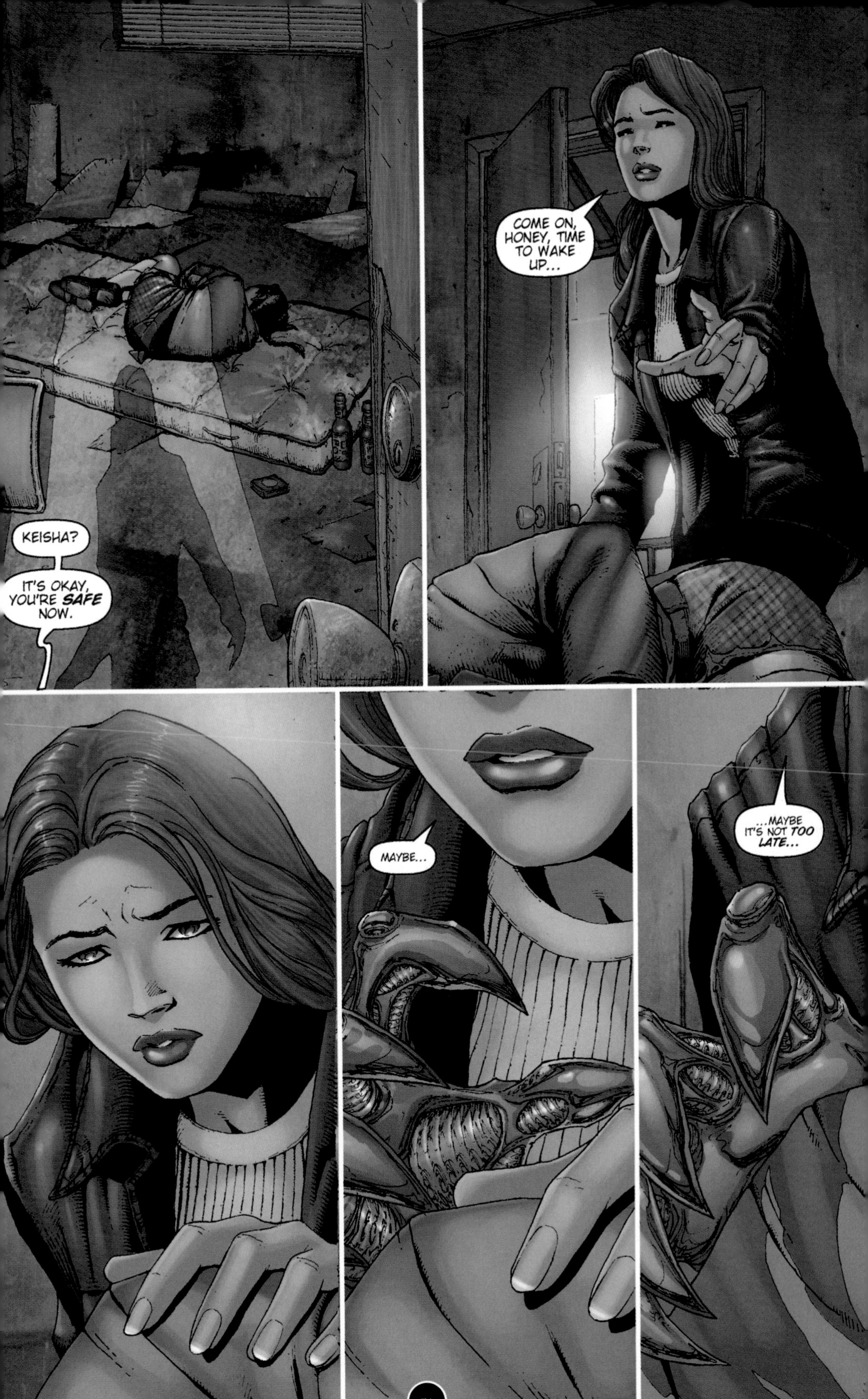
KEISHA?
IT'S OKAY, YOU'RE SAFE NOW.
COME ON, HONEY, TIME TO WAKE UP...
MAYBE...
...MAYBE IT'S NOT TOO LATE...

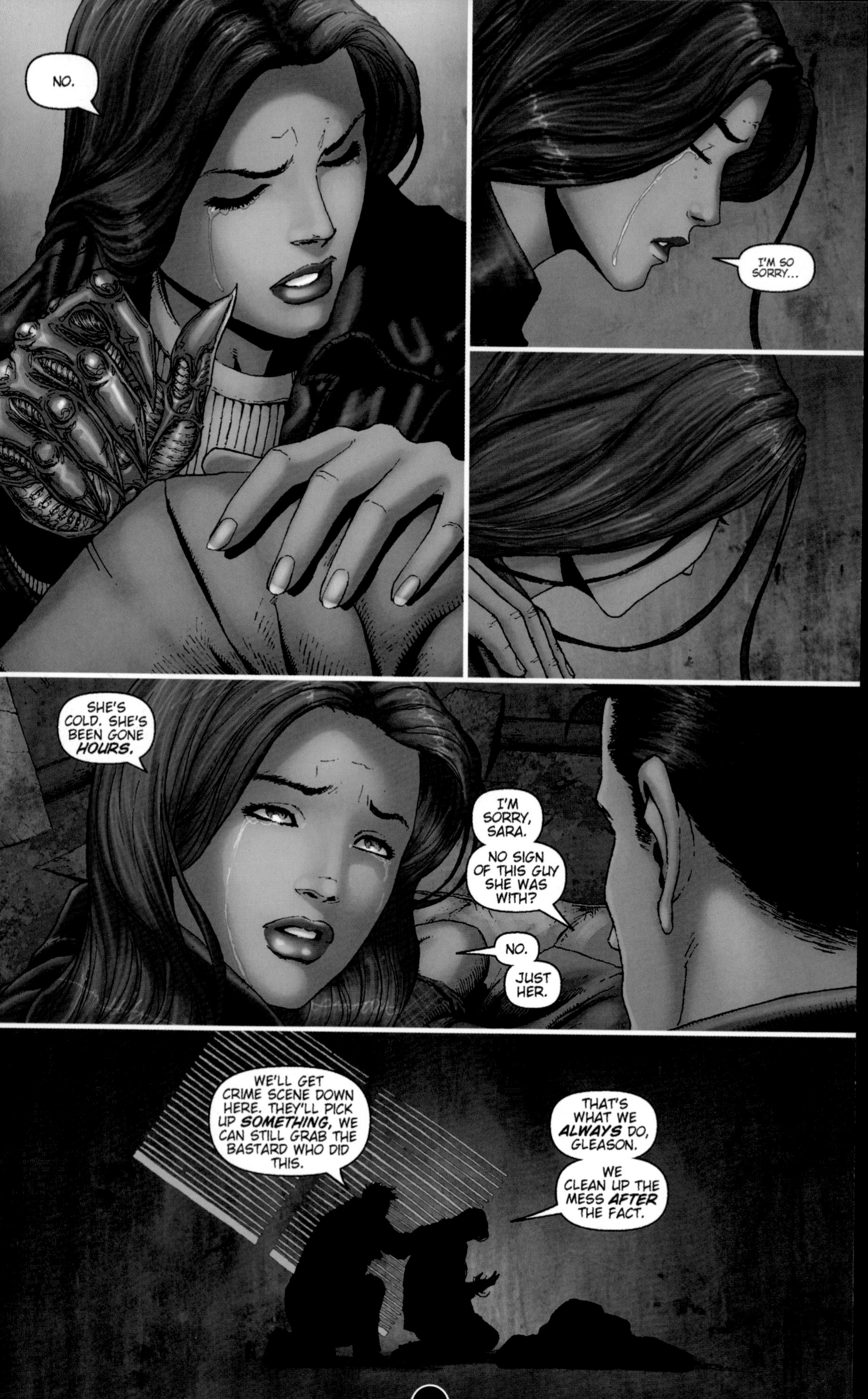
NO.
I'M SO SORRY...
SHE'S COLD. SHE'S BEEN GONE HOURS.
I'M SORRY, SARA.
NO SIGN OF THIS GUY SHE WAS WITH?
NO.
JUST HER.
WE'LL GET CRIME SCENE DOWN HERE. THEY'LL PICK UP SOMETHING, WE CAN STILL GRAB THE BASTARD WHO DID THIS.
THAT'S WHAT WE ALWAYS DO, GLEASON.
WE CLEAN UP THE MESS AFTER THE FACT.

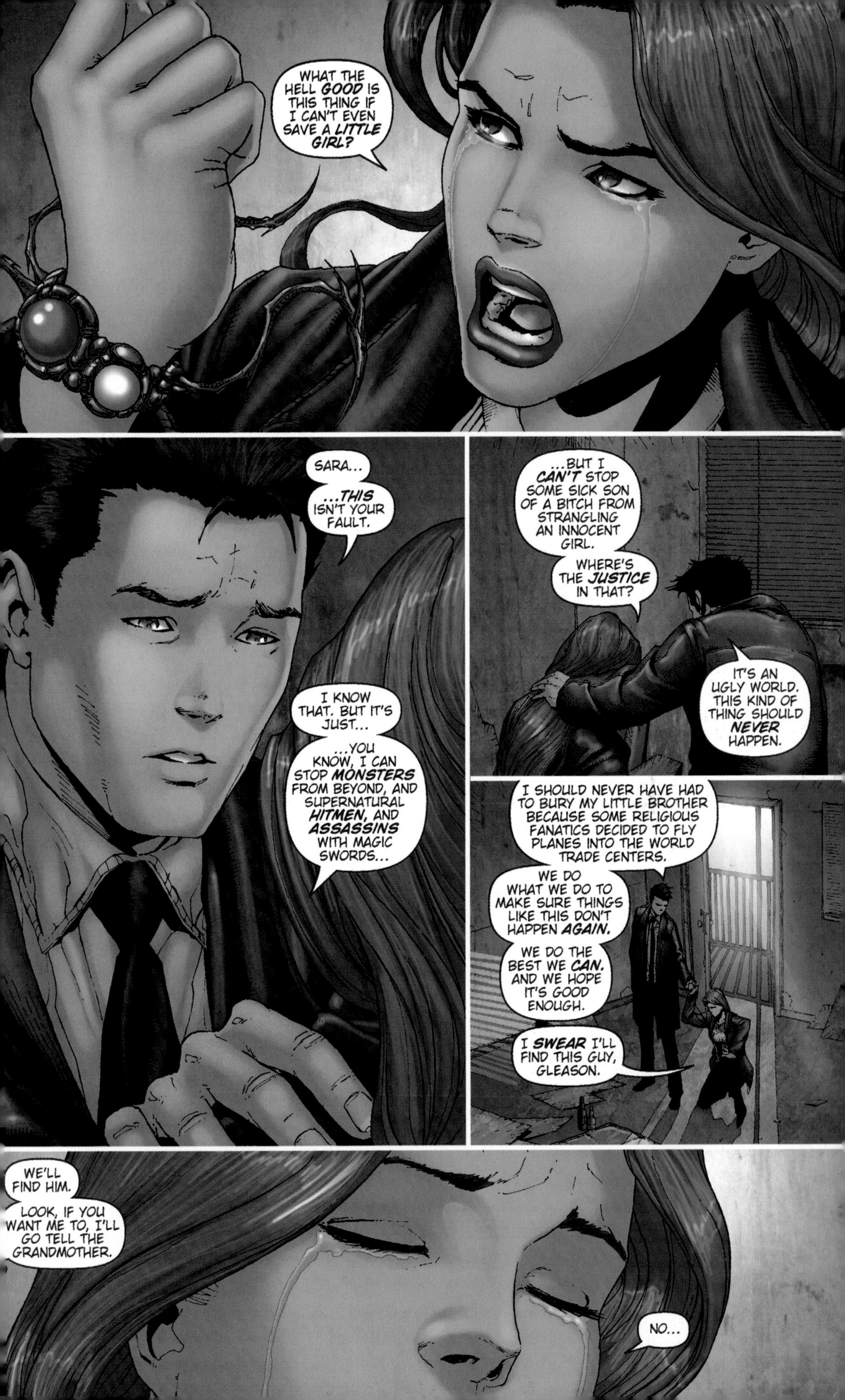
WHAT THE HELL GOOD IS THIS THING IF I CAN'T EVEN SAVE A LITTLE GIRL?
SARA...
...THIS ISN'T YOUR FAULT.
I KNOW THAT. BUT IT'S JUST...
...YOU KNOW, I CAN STOP MONSTERS FROM BEYOND, AND SUPERNATURAL HITMEN, AND ASSASSINS WITH MAGIC SWORDS...
...BUT I CAN'T STOP SOME SICK SON OF A BITCH FROM STRANGLING AN INNOCENT GIRL.
WHERE'S THE JUSTICE IN THAT?
IT'S AN UGLY WORLD. THIS KIND OF THING SHOULD NEVER HAPPEN.
I SHOULD NEVER HAVE HAD TO BURY MY LITTLE BROTHER BECAUSE SOME RELIGIOUS FANATICS DECIDED TO FLY PLANES INTO THE WORLD TRADE CENTERS.
WE DO WHAT WE DO TO MAKE SURE THINGS LIKE THIS DON'T HAPPEN AGAIN.
WE DO THE BEST WE CAN. AND WE HOPE IT'S GOOD ENOUGH.
I SWEAR I'LL FIND THIS GUY, GLEASON.
WE'LL FIND HIM.
LOOK, IF YOU WANT ME TO, I'LL GO TELL THE GRANDMOTHER.
NO...

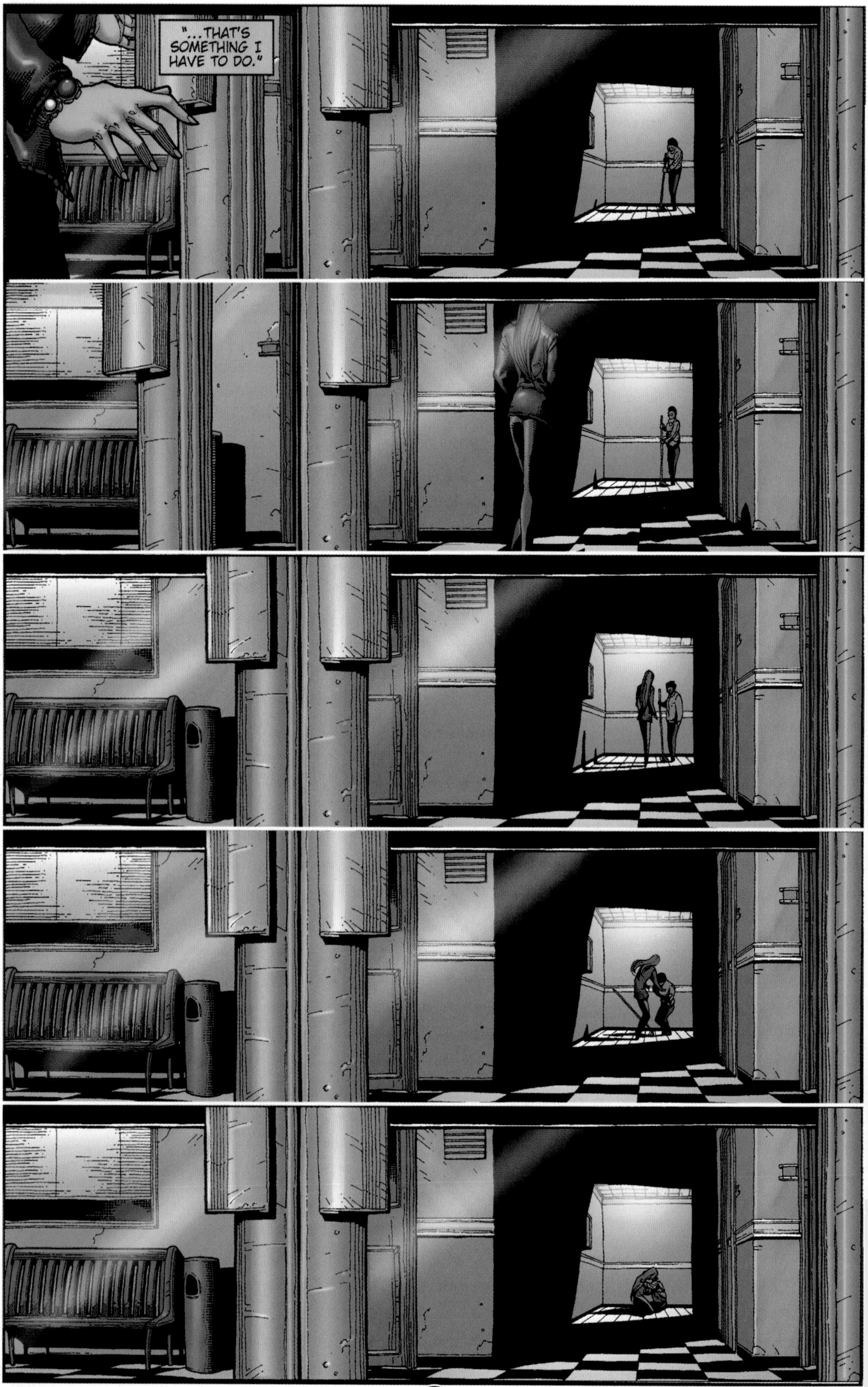
"...THAT'S SOMETHING I HAVE TO DO."

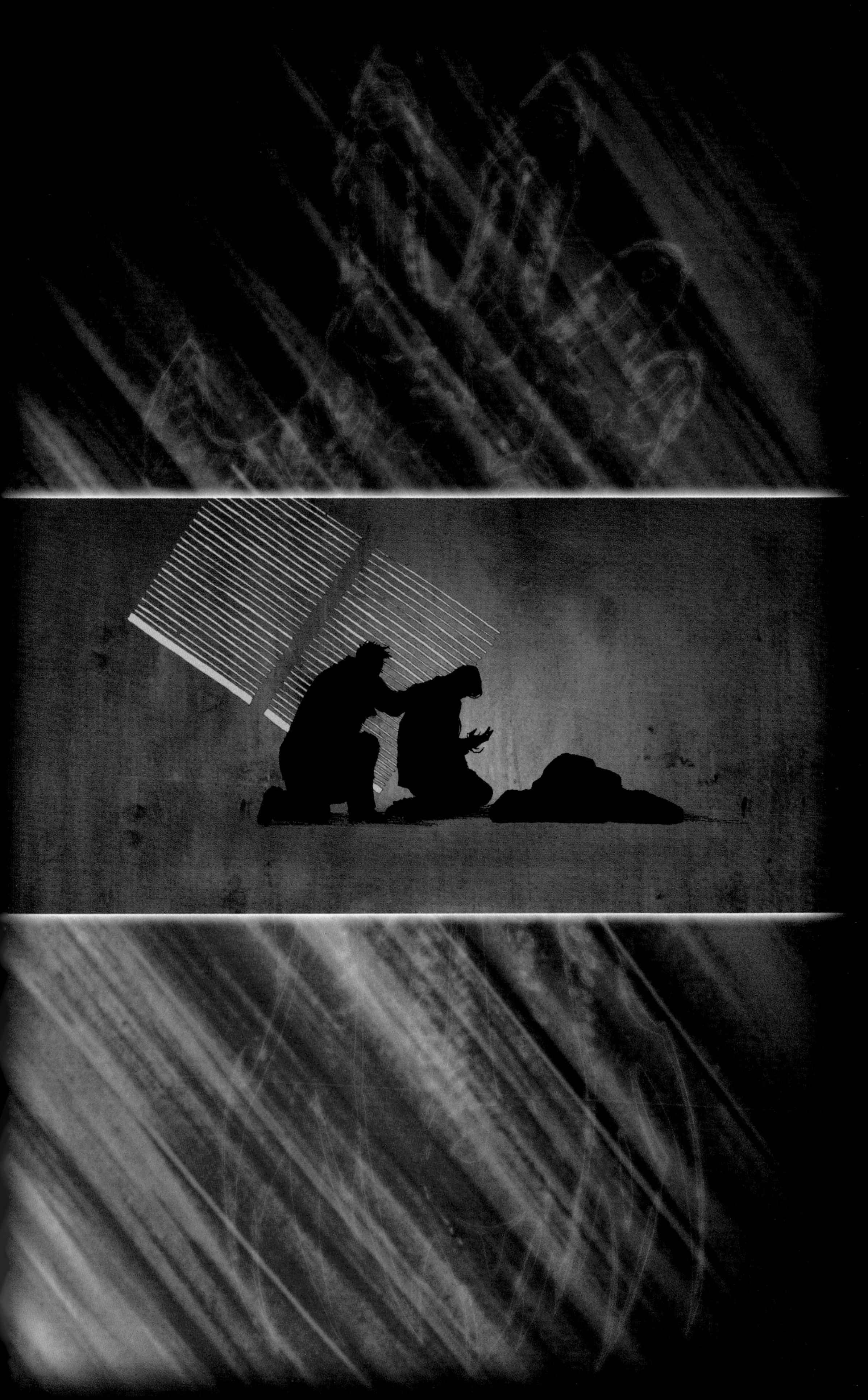

Witchblade

issues #89-#91

written by: **Ron Marz**

pencils by: **Michael Choi**

inks by: **Sal Regla**

and **Michael Choi** inks in issue #91

pages 1, 3-5 and 8-9

colors by: **Brian Buccellato**

and **Tyson Wengler** issue #89

letters by: **Troy Peteri**

"Fugitive"

parts 1-3

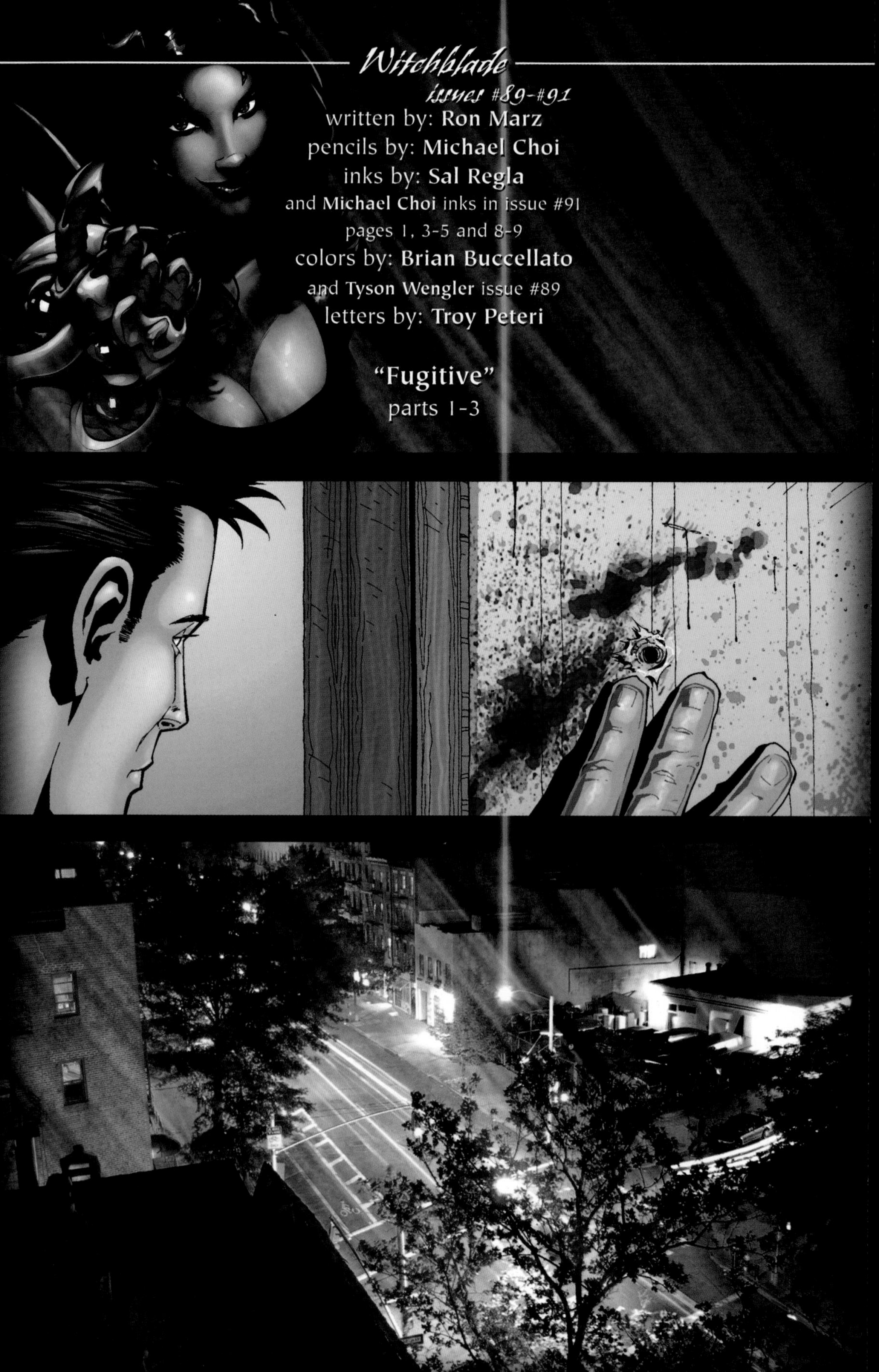

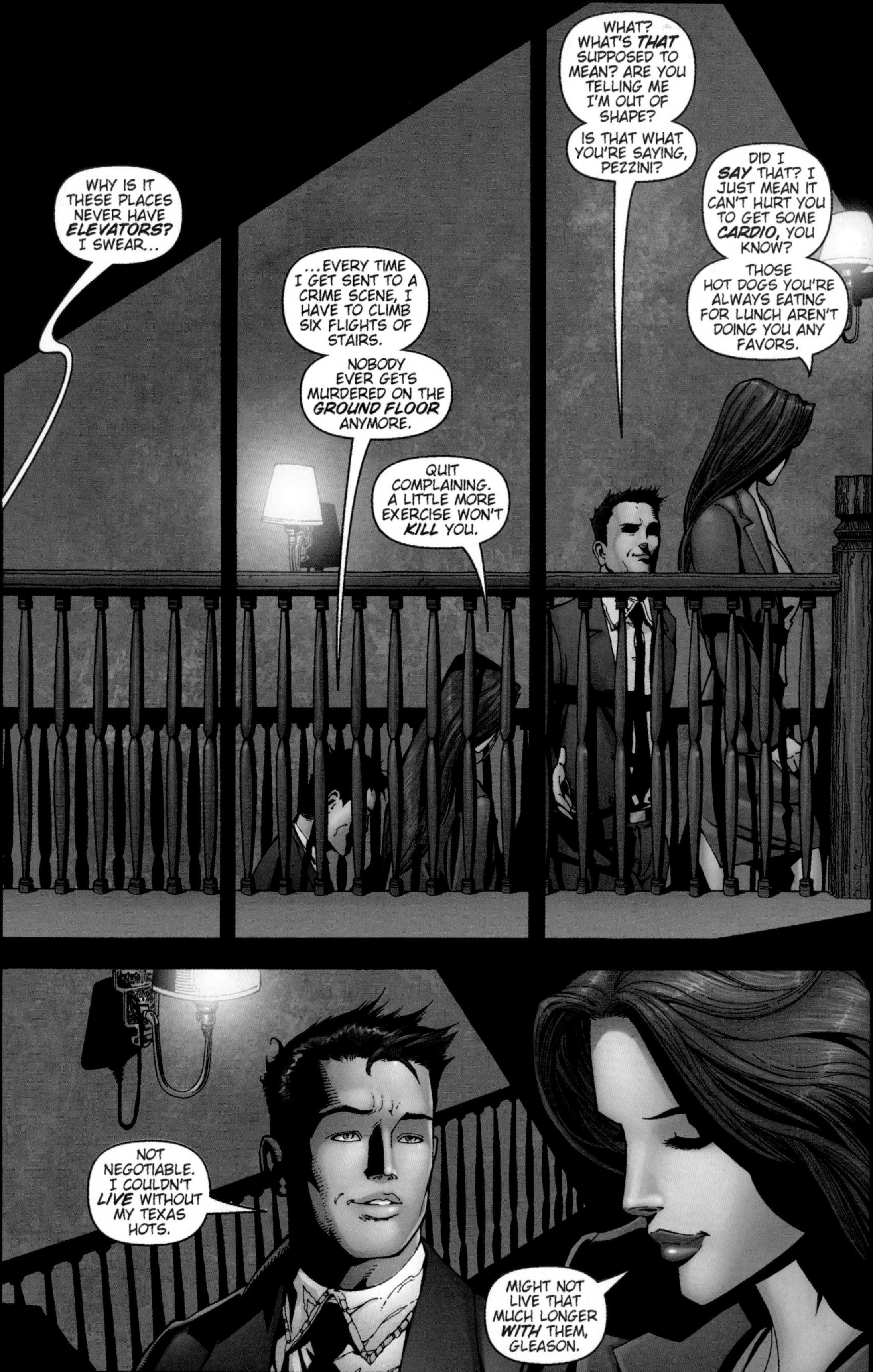

WHY IS IT THESE PLACES NEVER HAVE ELEVATORS? I SWEAR...
...EVERY TIME I GET SENT TO A CRIME SCENE, I HAVE TO CLIMB SIX FLIGHTS OF STAIRS.
NOBODY EVER GETS MURDERED ON THE GROUND FLOOR ANYMORE.
QUIT COMPLAINING. A LITTLE MORE EXERCISE WON'T KILL YOU.
WHAT? WHAT'S THAT SUPPOSED TO MEAN? ARE YOU TELLING ME I'M OUT OF SHAPE?
IS THAT WHAT YOU'RE SAYING, PEZZINI?
DID I SAY THAT? I JUST MEAN IT CAN'T HURT YOU TO GET SOME CARDIO, YOU KNOW?
THOSE HOT DOGS YOU'RE ALWAYS EATING FOR LUNCH AREN'T DOING YOU ANY FAVORS.
NOT NEGOTIABLE. I COULDN'T LIVE WITHOUT MY TEXAS HOTS.
MIGHT NOT LIVE THAT MUCH LONGER WITH THEM, GLEASON.

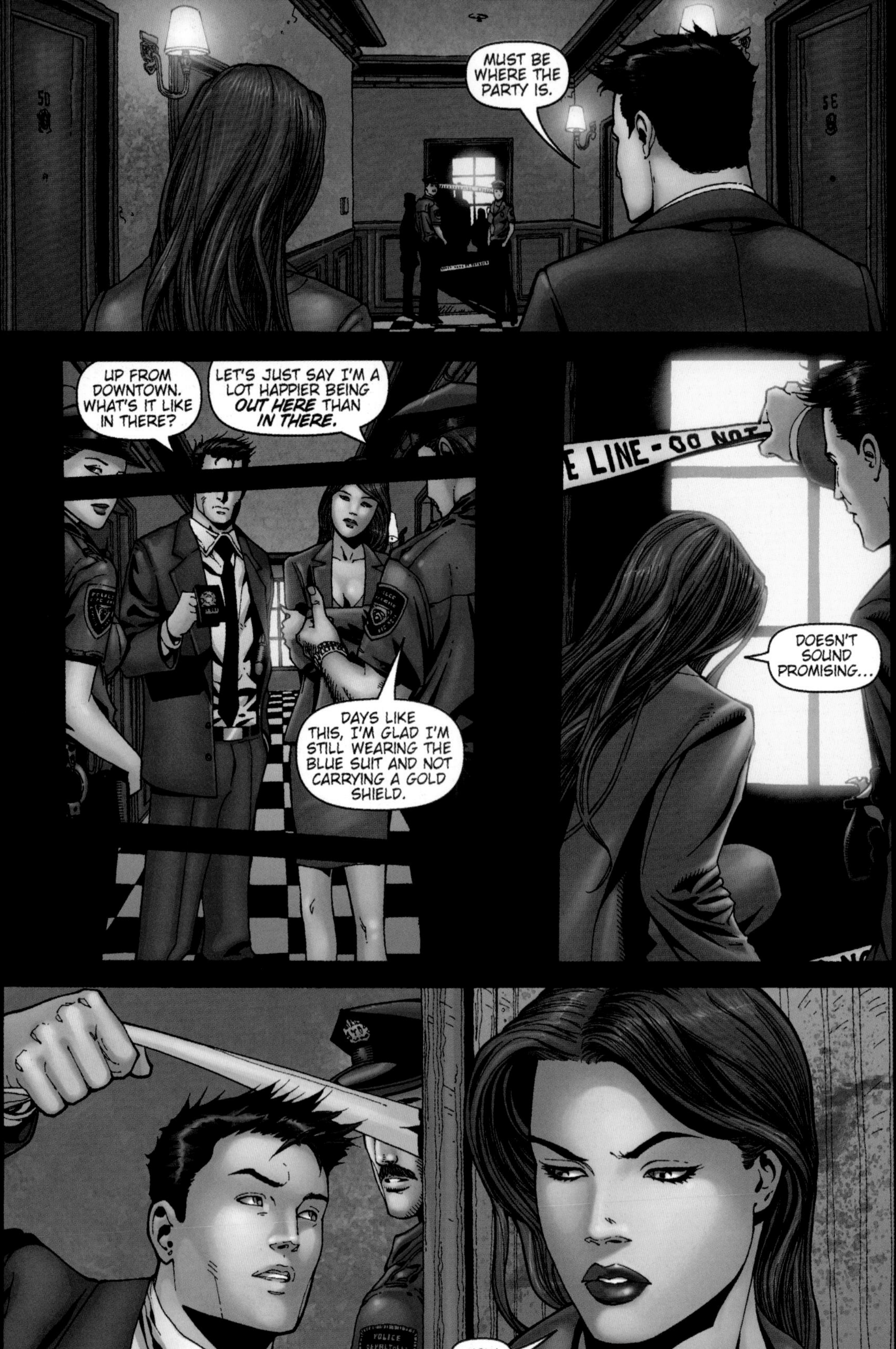
MUST BE WHERE THE PARTY IS.
UP FROM DOWNTOWN. WHAT'S IT LIKE IN THERE?
LET'S JUST SAY I'M A LOT HAPPIER BEING *OUT HERE* THAN *IN THERE.*
DAYS LIKE THIS, I'M GLAD I'M STILL WEARING THE BLUE SUIT AND NOT CARRYING A GOLD SHIELD.
DOESN'T SOUND PROMISING...
HOLY JEEZ...

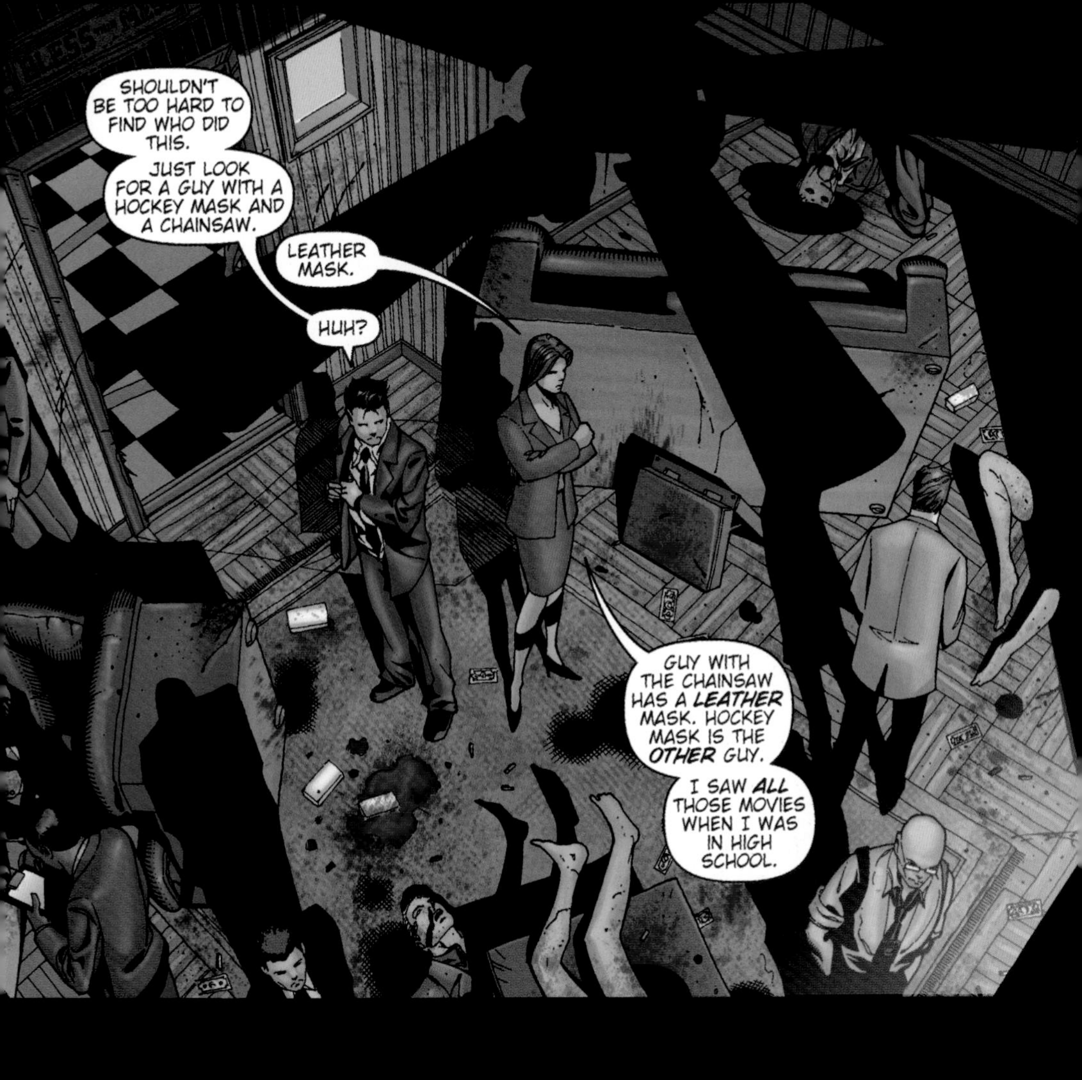
SHOULDN'T BE TOO HARD TO FIND WHO DID THIS.
JUST LOOK FOR A GUY WITH A HOCKEY MASK AND A CHAINSAW.
LEATHER MASK.
HUH?
GUY WITH THE CHAINSAW HAS A **LEATHER** MASK. HOCKEY MASK IS THE **OTHER** GUY.
I SAW **ALL** THOSE MOVIES WHEN I WAS IN HIGH SCHOOL.

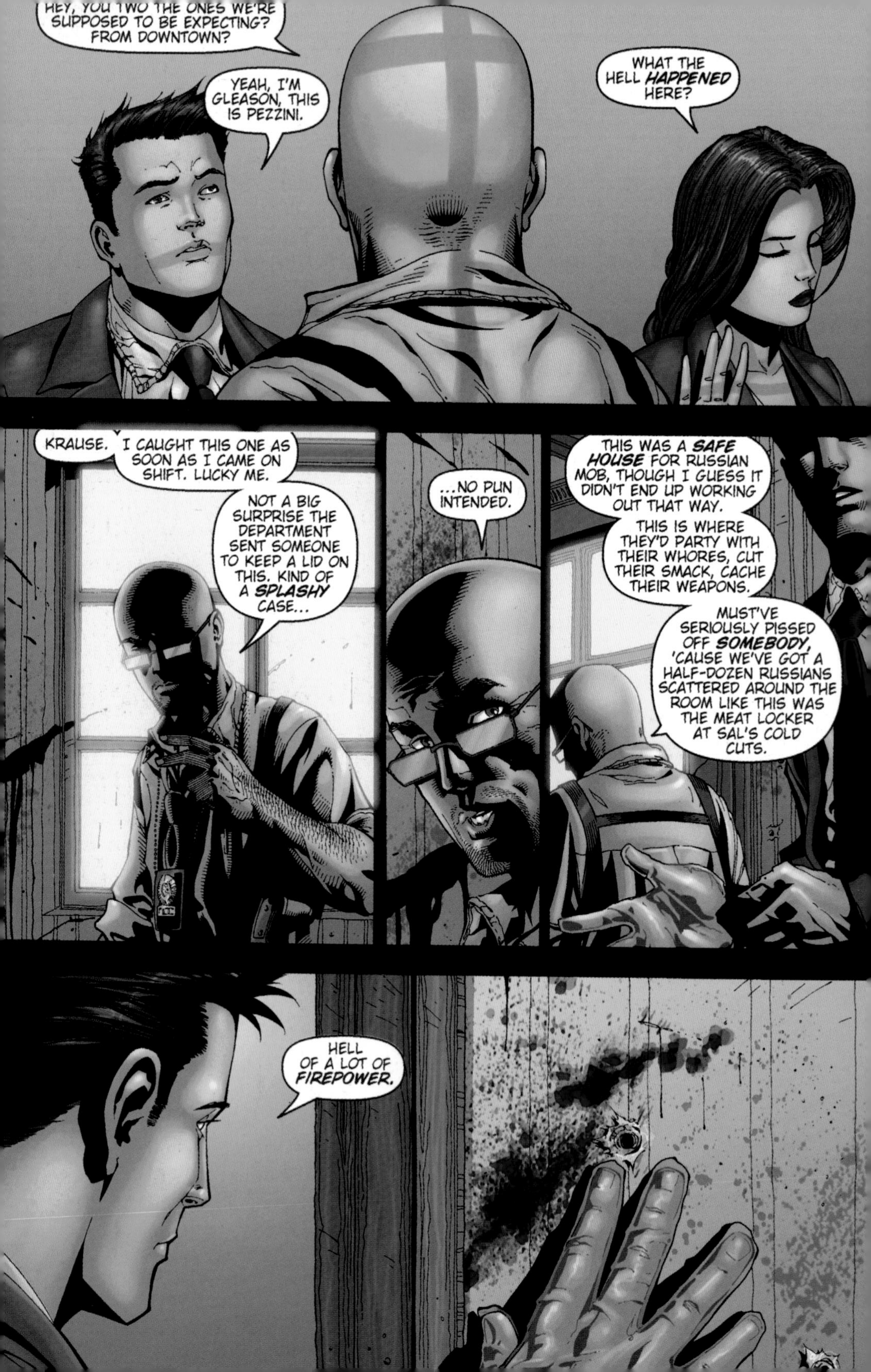
HEY, YOU TWO THE ONES WE'RE SUPPOSED TO BE EXPECTING? FROM DOWNTOWN?
YEAH, I'M GLEASON, THIS IS PEZZINI.
WHAT THE HELL *HAPPENED* HERE?
KRAUSE.
I CAUGHT THIS ONE AS SOON AS I CAME ON SHIFT. LUCKY ME.
NOT A BIG SURPRISE THE DEPARTMENT SENT SOMEONE TO KEEP A LID ON THIS. KIND OF A *SPLASHY* CASE...
...NO PUN INTENDED.
THIS WAS A *SAFE HOUSE* FOR RUSSIAN MOB, THOUGH I GUESS IT DIDN'T END UP WORKING OUT THAT WAY.
THIS IS WHERE THEY'D PARTY WITH THEIR WHORES, CUT THEIR SMACK, CACHE THEIR WEAPONS.
MUST'VE SERIOUSLY PISSED OFF *SOMEBODY,* 'CAUSE WE'VE GOT A HALF-DOZEN RUSSIANS SCATTERED AROUND THE ROOM LIKE THIS WAS THE MEAT LOCKER AT SAL'S COLD CUTS.
HELL OF A LOT OF *FIREPOWER.*

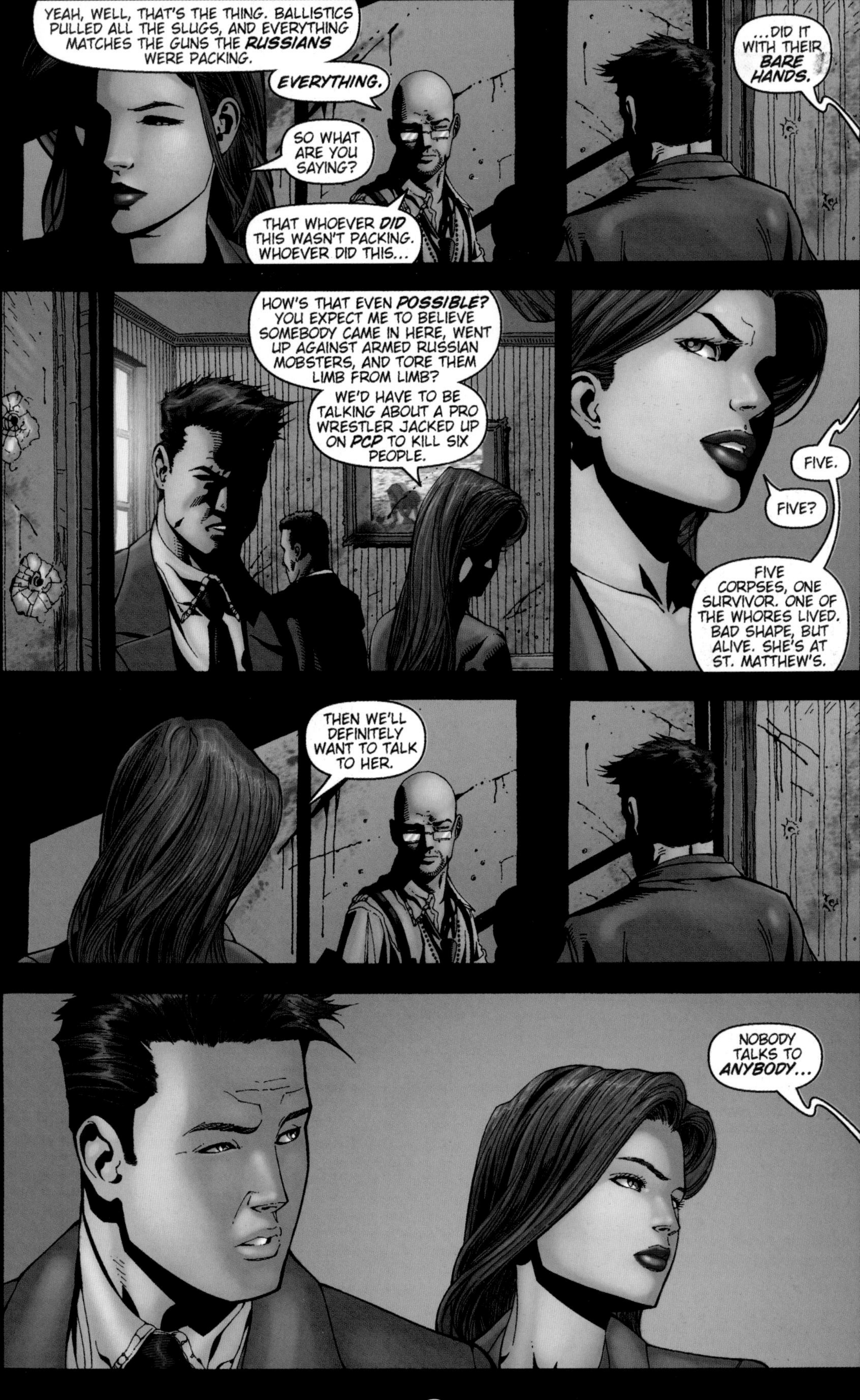
YEAH, WELL, THAT'S THE THING. BALLISTICS PULLED ALL THE SLUGS, AND EVERYTHING MATCHES THE GUNS THE RUSSIANS WERE PACKING.
EVERYTHING.
SO WHAT ARE YOU SAYING?
THAT WHOEVER DID THIS WASN'T PACKING. WHOEVER DID THIS...
...DID IT WITH THEIR BARE HANDS.
HOW'S THAT EVEN POSSIBLE? YOU EXPECT ME TO BELIEVE SOMEBODY CAME IN HERE, WENT UP AGAINST ARMED RUSSIAN MOBSTERS, AND TORE THEM LIMB FROM LIMB?
WE'D HAVE TO BE TALKING ABOUT A PRO WRESTLER JACKED UP ON PCP TO KILL SIX PEOPLE.
FIVE.
FIVE?
FIVE CORPSES, ONE SURVIVOR. ONE OF THE WHORES LIVED. BAD SHAPE, BUT ALIVE. SHE'S AT ST. MATTHEW'S.
THEN WE'LL DEFINITELY WANT TO TALK TO HER.
NOBODY TALKS TO ANYBODY...

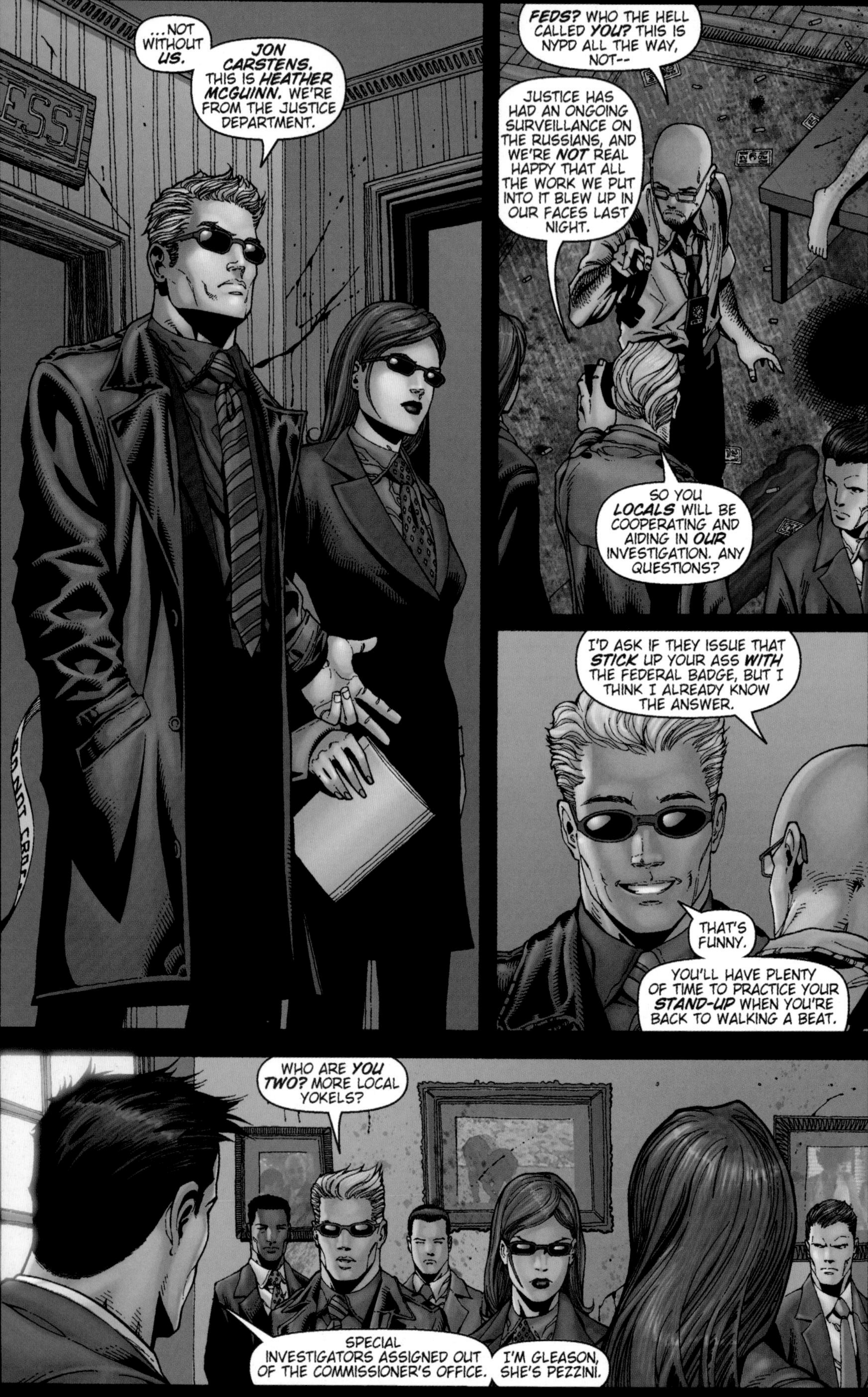

...NOT WITHOUT US.
JON CARSTENS. THIS IS HEATHER MCGUINN. WE'RE FROM THE JUSTICE DEPARTMENT.
FEDS? WHO THE HELL CALLED YOU? THIS IS NYPD ALL THE WAY, NOT--
JUSTICE HAS HAD AN ONGOING SURVEILLANCE ON THE RUSSIANS, AND WE'RE NOT REAL HAPPY THAT ALL THE WORK WE PUT INTO IT BLEW UP IN OUR FACES LAST NIGHT.
SO YOU LOCALS WILL BE COOPERATING AND AIDING IN OUR INVESTIGATION. ANY QUESTIONS?
I'D ASK IF THEY ISSUE THAT STICK UP YOUR ASS WITH THE FEDERAL BADGE, BUT I THINK I ALREADY KNOW THE ANSWER.
THAT'S FUNNY.
YOU'LL HAVE PLENTY OF TIME TO PRACTICE YOUR STAND-UP WHEN YOU'RE BACK TO WALKING A BEAT.
WHO ARE YOU TWO? MORE LOCAL YOKELS?
SPECIAL INVESTIGATORS ASSIGNED OUT OF THE COMMISSIONER'S OFFICE.
I'M GLEASON, SHE'S PEZZINI.

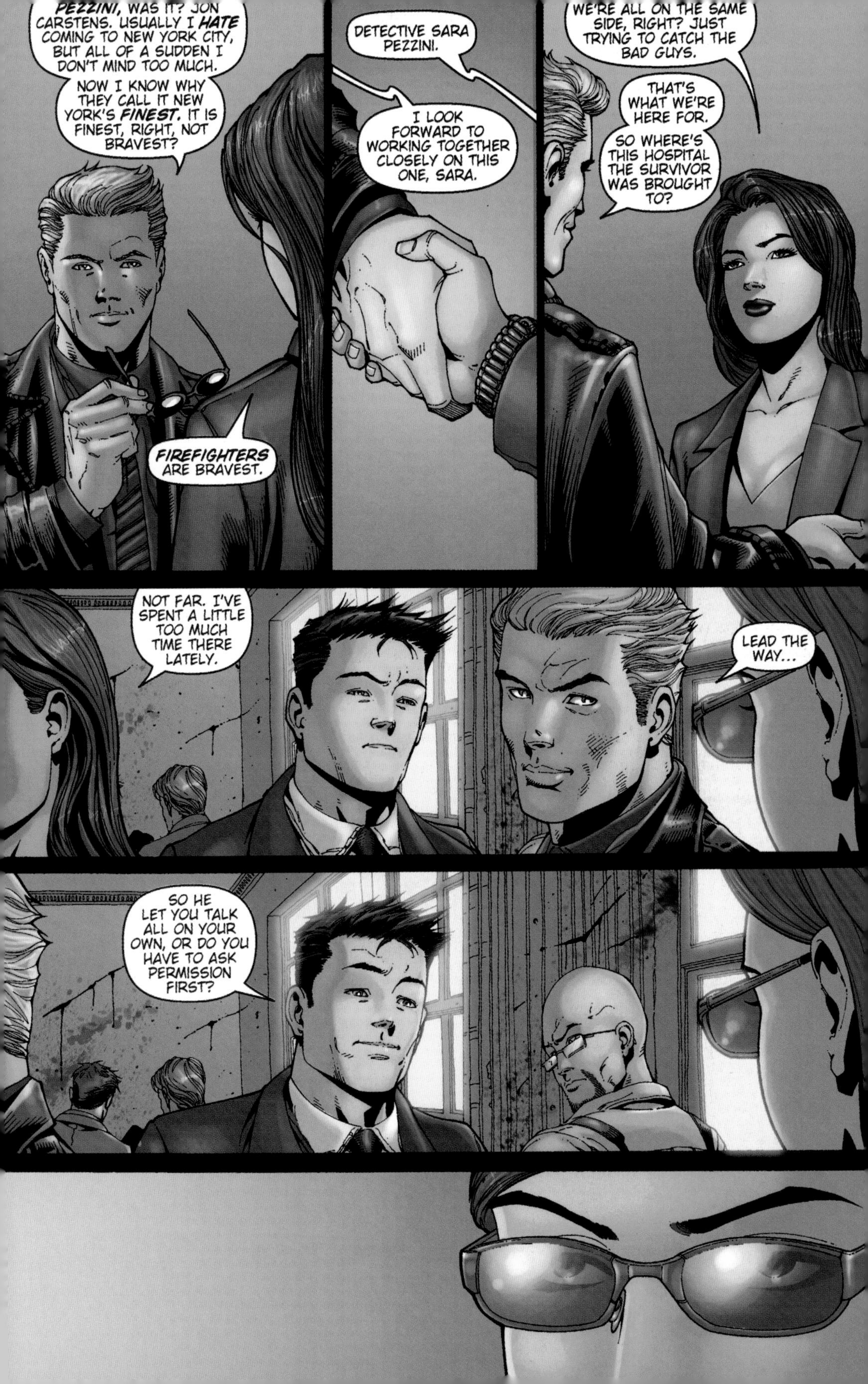

PEZZINI, WAS IT? JON CARSTENS. USUALLY I HATE COMING TO NEW YORK CITY, BUT ALL OF A SUDDEN I DON'T MIND TOO MUCH.
NOW I KNOW WHY THEY CALL IT NEW YORK'S FINEST. IT IS FINEST, RIGHT, NOT BRAVEST?
FIREFIGHTERS ARE BRAVEST.
DETECTIVE SARA PEZZINI.
I LOOK FORWARD TO WORKING TOGETHER CLOSELY ON THIS ONE, SARA.
WE'RE ALL ON THE SAME SIDE, RIGHT? JUST TRYING TO CATCH THE BAD GUYS.
THAT'S WHAT WE'RE HERE FOR.
SO WHERE'S THIS HOSPITAL THE SURVIVOR WAS BROUGHT TO?
NOT FAR. I'VE SPENT A LITTLE TOO MUCH TIME THERE LATELY.
LEAD THE WAY...
SO HE LET YOU TALK ALL ON YOUR OWN, OR DO YOU HAVE TO ASK PERMISSION FIRST?

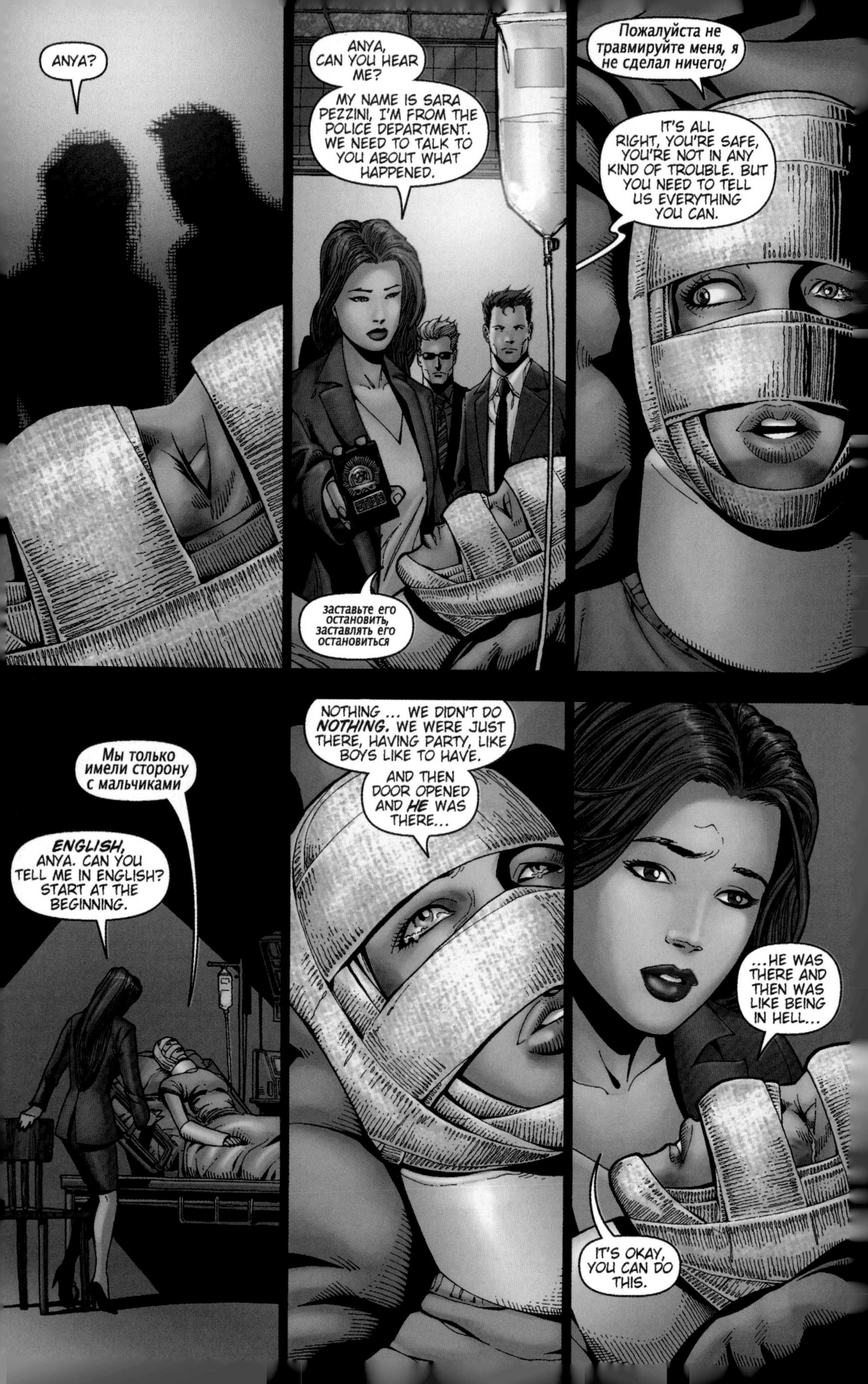
ANYA?
ANYA, CAN YOU HEAR ME?
MY NAME IS SARA PEZZINI, I'M FROM THE POLICE DEPARTMENT. WE NEED TO TALK TO YOU ABOUT WHAT HAPPENED.
заставьте его остановить, заставлять его остановиться
Пожалуйста не травмируйте меня, я не сделал ничего!
IT'S ALL RIGHT, YOU'RE SAFE, YOU'RE NOT IN ANY KIND OF TROUBLE. BUT YOU NEED TO TELL US EVERYTHING YOU CAN.
Мы только имели сторону с мальчиками
ENGLISH, ANYA. CAN YOU TELL ME IN ENGLISH? START AT THE BEGINNING.
NOTHING ... WE DIDN'T DO NOTHING. WE WERE JUST THERE, HAVING PARTY, LIKE BOYS LIKE TO HAVE.
AND THEN DOOR OPENED AND HE WAS THERE...
...HE WAS THERE AND THEN WAS LIKE BEING IN HELL...
IT'S OKAY, YOU CAN DO THIS.

BOYS TOLD HIM *GO,* WARNED HIM, BUT HE DIDN'T GO. HE GRABBED ALEK AND *BROKE* HIM.

THEN EVERYONE'S GUNS WAS SHOOTING, AND THERE WAS BLOOD AND SMOKE EVERYWHERE...

...AND HE STARTED *HURTING* EVERYONE...

WHO, ANYA?

WHO DID THIS?

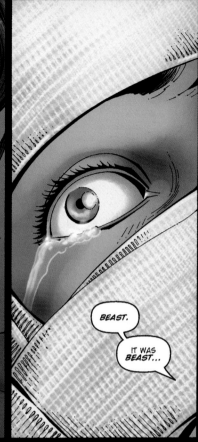

BEAST.

IT WAS *BEAST...*

...HORRIBLE, HORRIBLE THING!

SHHH, IT'S ALL RIGHT. THANK YOU, ANYA, YOU DID GREAT.

Животное в коже человека...

...Я должен был умереть также...

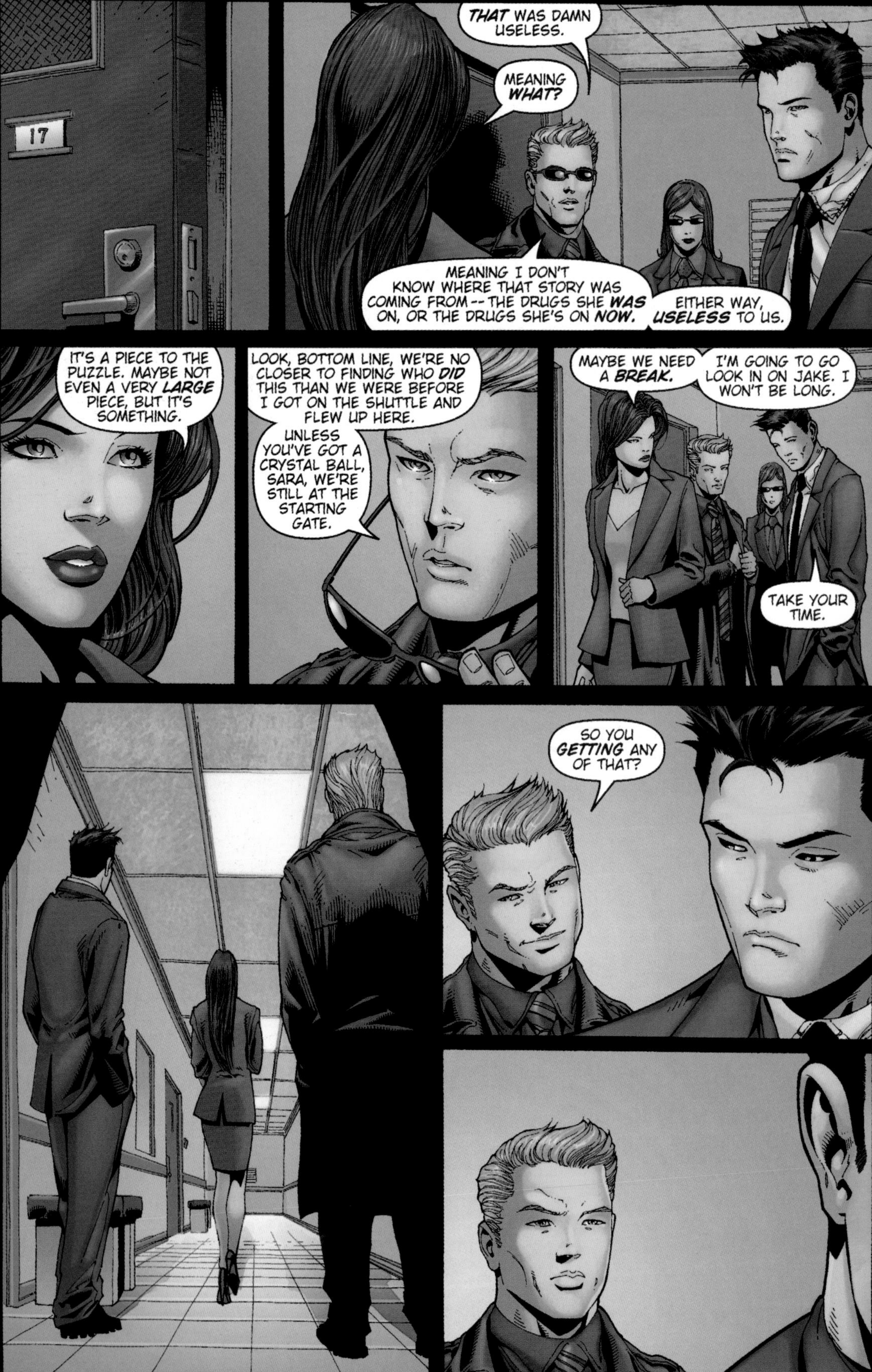
17
THAT WAS DAMN USELESS.
MEANING WHAT?
MEANING I DON'T KNOW WHERE THAT STORY WAS COMING FROM -- THE DRUGS SHE WAS ON, OR THE DRUGS SHE'S ON NOW.
EITHER WAY, USELESS TO US.
IT'S A PIECE TO THE PUZZLE. MAYBE NOT EVEN A VERY LARGE PIECE, BUT IT'S SOMETHING.
LOOK, BOTTOM LINE, WE'RE NO CLOSER TO FINDING WHO DID THIS THAN WE WERE BEFORE I GOT ON THE SHUTTLE AND FLEW UP HERE.
UNLESS YOU'VE GOT A CRYSTAL BALL, SARA, WE'RE STILL AT THE STARTING GATE.
MAYBE WE NEED A BREAK.
I'M GOING TO GO LOOK IN ON JAKE. I WON'T BE LONG.
TAKE YOUR TIME.
SO YOU GETTING ANY OF THAT?

HI, JAKE.

HOPE YOU DON'T MIND ME STOPPING IN.

HAD TO BE HERE BECAUSE OF A CASE. SOMEBODY SPLATTERED A BUNCH OF RUSSIANS ALL OVER ONE OF THEIR UPTOWN SAFE HOUSES.

REMEMBER THAT TIME WE HAD TO GO OVER TO LITTLE ODESSA AND ROUND UP A FEW OF THEM?

ANYWAY, WON'T BE MANY TEARS SHED FOR THIS BUNCH, BUT I FEEL SORRY FOR THE STREETWALKERS WHO GOT CAUGHT IN THE MIDDLE OF IT.

THE ONE WHO SURVIVED IS HERE, BUT SHE'S IN PRETTY ROUGH SHAPE.

I GUESS THAT'S *RELATIVE*, THOUGH.

SO HOW ARE *YOU* DOING?

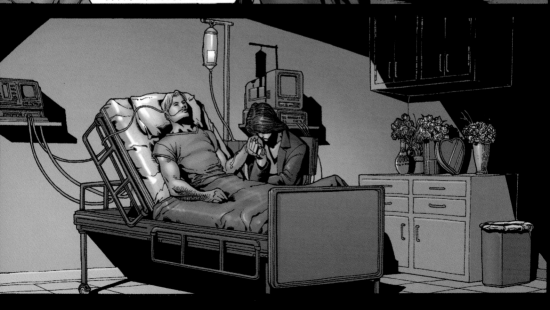

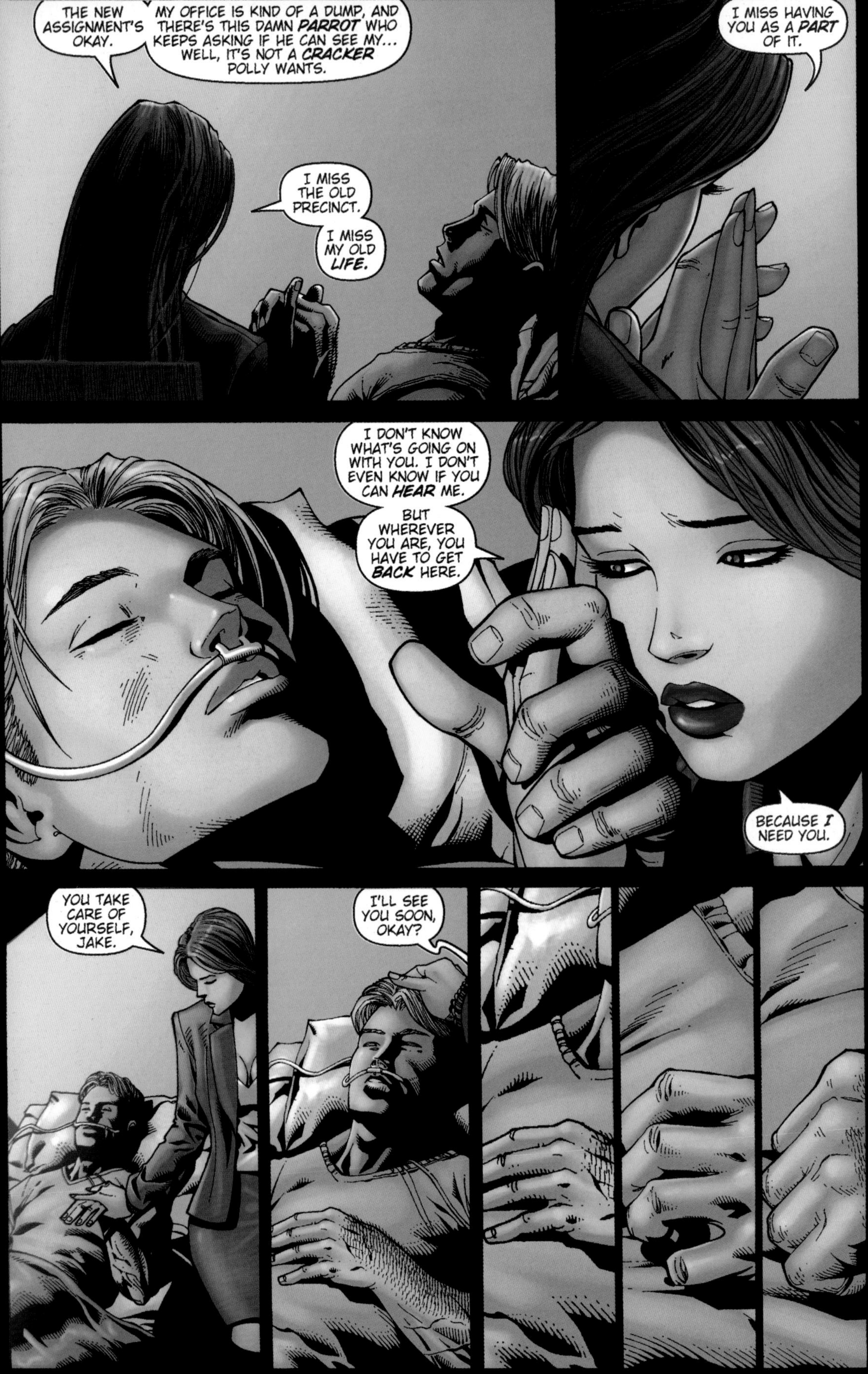
THE NEW ASSIGNMENT'S OKAY.
MY OFFICE IS KIND OF A DUMP, AND THERE'S THIS DAMN PARROT WHO KEEPS ASKING IF HE CAN SEE MY... WELL, IT'S NOT A CRACKER POLLY WANTS.
I MISS THE OLD PRECINCT.
I MISS MY OLD LIFE.
I MISS HAVING YOU AS A PART OF IT.
I DON'T KNOW WHAT'S GOING ON WITH YOU. I DON'T EVEN KNOW IF YOU CAN HEAR ME.
BUT WHEREVER YOU ARE, YOU HAVE TO GET BACK HERE.
BECAUSE I NEED YOU.
YOU TAKE CARE OF YOURSELF, JAKE.
I'LL SEE YOU SOON, OKAY?

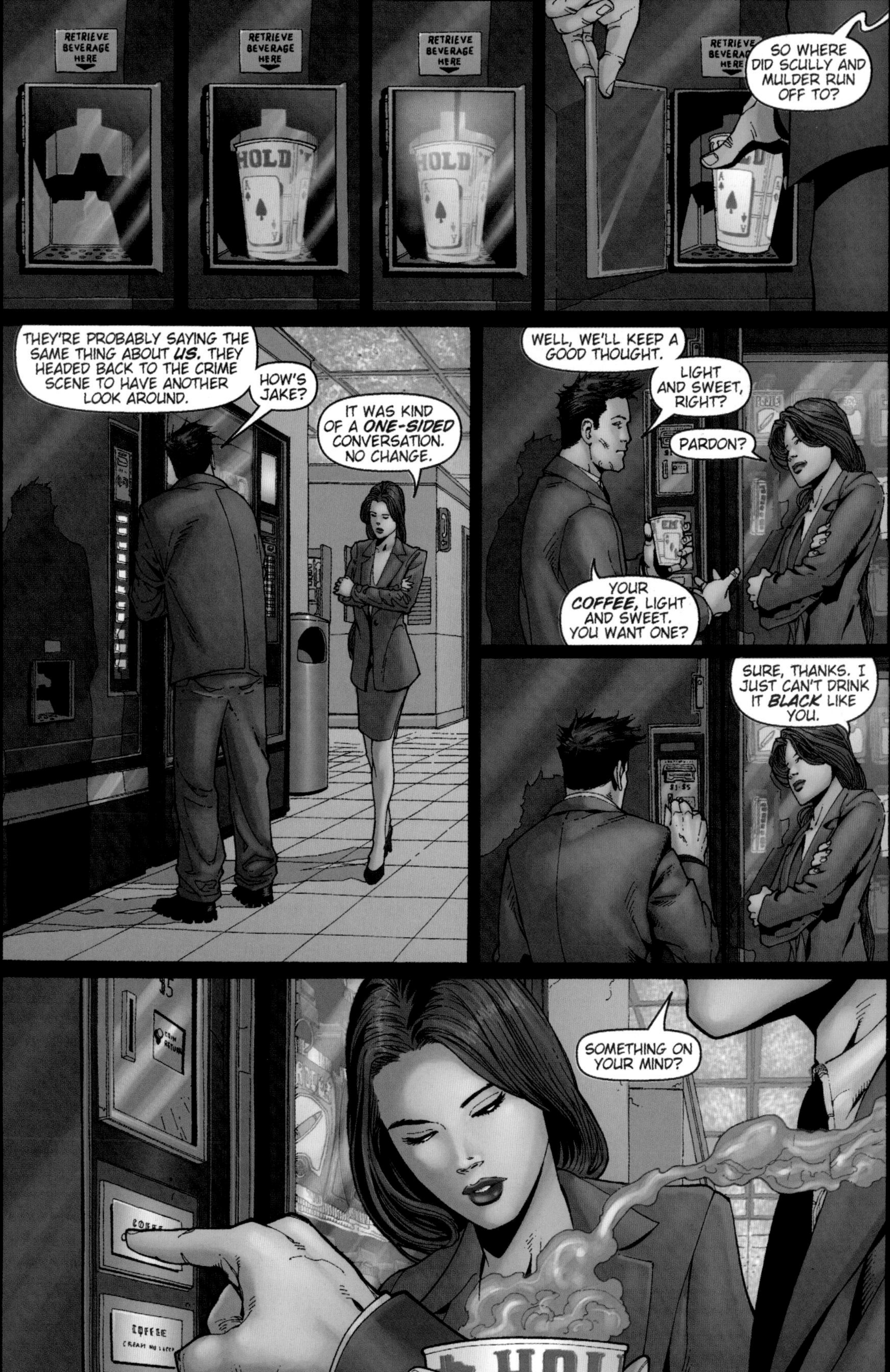
RETRIEVE BEVERAGE HERE
RETRIEVE BEVERAGE HERE
RETRIEVE BEVERAGE HERE
RETRIEVE BEVERAGE HERE
SO WHERE DID SCULLY AND MULDER RUN OFF TO?
THEY'RE PROBABLY SAYING THE SAME THING ABOUT ***US.*** THEY HEADED BACK TO THE CRIME SCENE TO HAVE ANOTHER LOOK AROUND.
HOW'S JAKE?
IT WAS KIND OF A ***ONE-SIDED*** CONVERSATION. NO CHANGE.
WELL, WE'LL KEEP A GOOD THOUGHT.
LIGHT AND SWEET, RIGHT?
PARDON?
YOUR ***COFFEE,*** LIGHT AND SWEET. YOU WANT ONE?
SURE, THANKS. I JUST CAN'T DRINK IT ***BLACK*** LIKE YOU.
SOMETHING ON YOUR MIND?

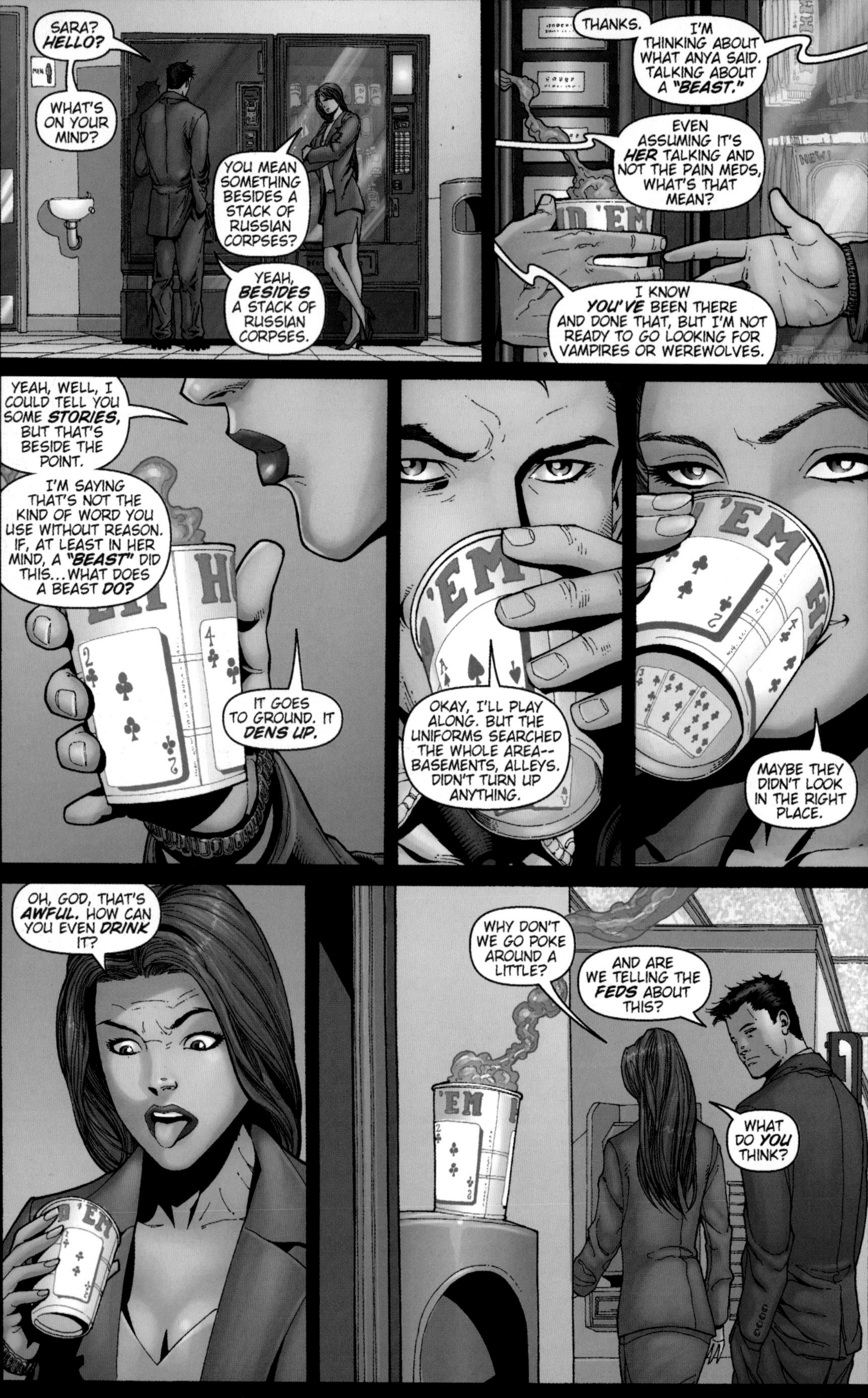
SARA? HELLO?
WHAT'S ON YOUR MIND?
MEN
YOU MEAN SOMETHING BESIDES A STACK OF RUSSIAN CORPSES?
YEAH, BESIDES A STACK OF RUSSIAN CORPSES.
THANKS.
I'M THINKING ABOUT WHAT ANYA SAID. TALKING ABOUT A "BEAST."
EVEN ASSUMING IT'S HER TALKING AND NOT THE PAIN MEDS, WHAT'S THAT MEAN?
I KNOW YOU'VE BEEN THERE AND DONE THAT, BUT I'M NOT READY TO GO LOOKING FOR VAMPIRES OR WEREWOLVES.
YEAH, WELL, I COULD TELL YOU SOME STORIES, BUT THAT'S BESIDE THE POINT.
I'M SAYING THAT'S NOT THE KIND OF WORD YOU USE WITHOUT REASON. IF, AT LEAST IN HER MIND, A "BEAST" DID THIS...WHAT DOES A BEAST DO?
IT GOES TO GROUND. IT DENS UP.
OKAY, I'LL PLAY ALONG. BUT THE UNIFORMS SEARCHED THE WHOLE AREA--BASEMENTS, ALLEYS. DIDN'T TURN UP ANYTHING.
MAYBE THEY DIDN'T LOOK IN THE RIGHT PLACE.
OH, GOD, THAT'S AWFUL. HOW CAN YOU EVEN DRINK IT?
WHY DON'T WE GO POKE AROUND A LITTLE?
AND ARE WE TELLING THE FEDS ABOUT THIS?
WHAT DO YOU THINK?

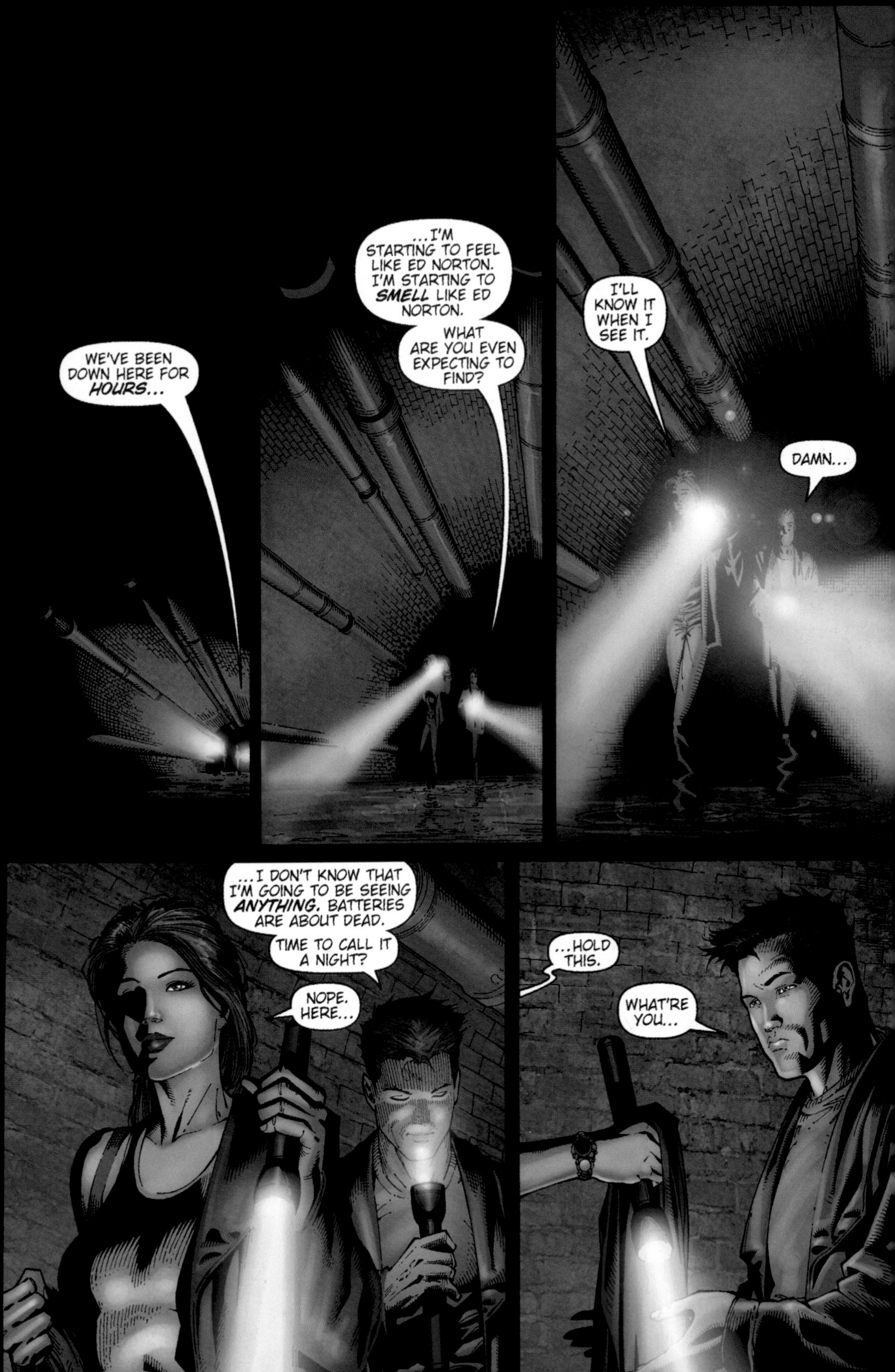
WE'VE BEEN DOWN HERE FOR *HOURS...*
...I'M STARTING TO FEEL LIKE ED NORTON. I'M STARTING TO *SMELL* LIKE ED NORTON.
WHAT ARE YOU EVEN EXPECTING TO FIND?
I'LL KNOW IT WHEN I SEE IT.
DAMN...
...I DON'T KNOW THAT I'M GOING TO BE SEEING *ANYTHING.* BATTERIES ARE ABOUT DEAD.
TIME TO CALL IT A NIGHT?
NOPE. HERE...
...HOLD THIS.
WHAT'RE YOU...

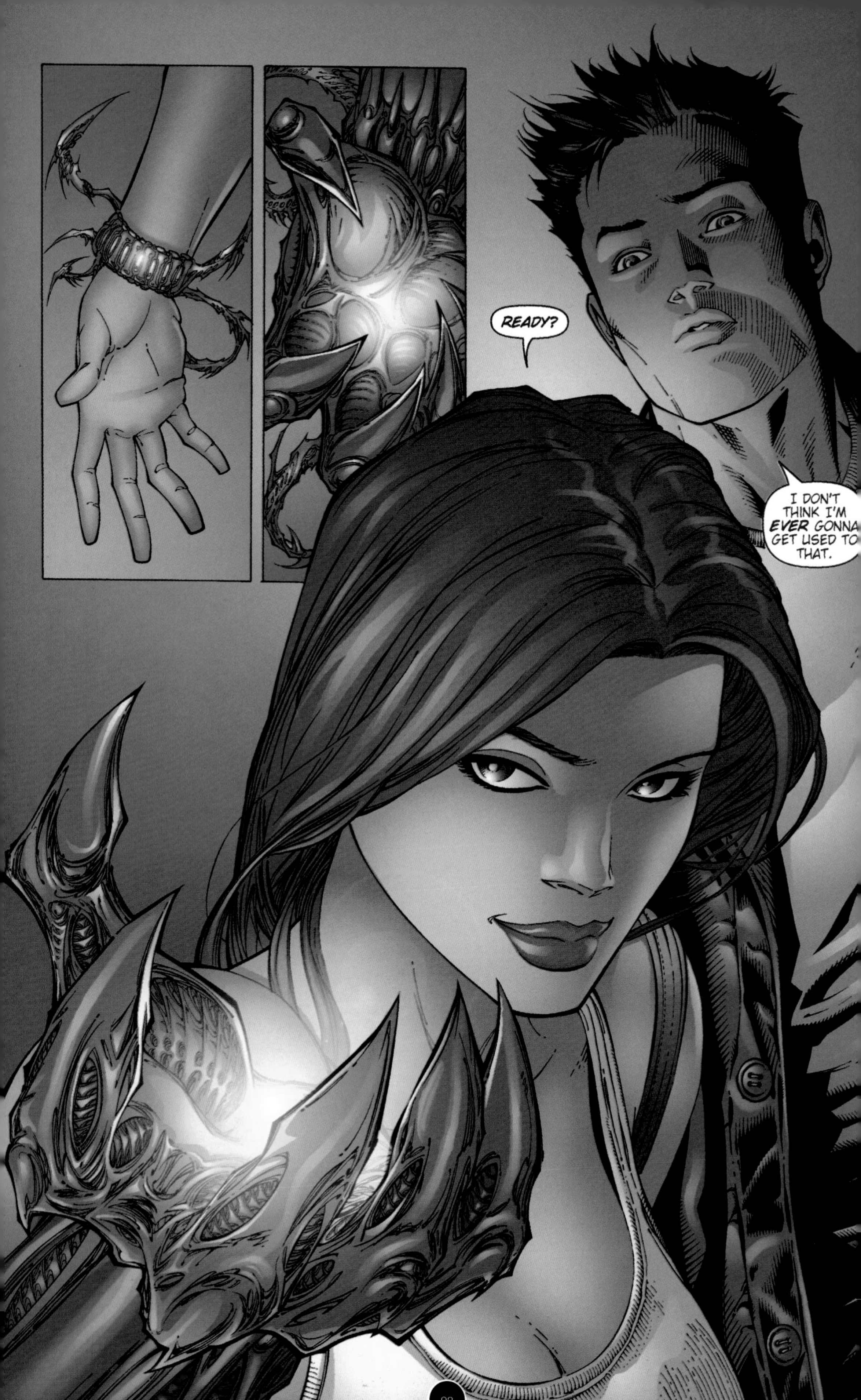
READY?
I DON'T THINK I'M EVER GONNA GET USED TO THAT.

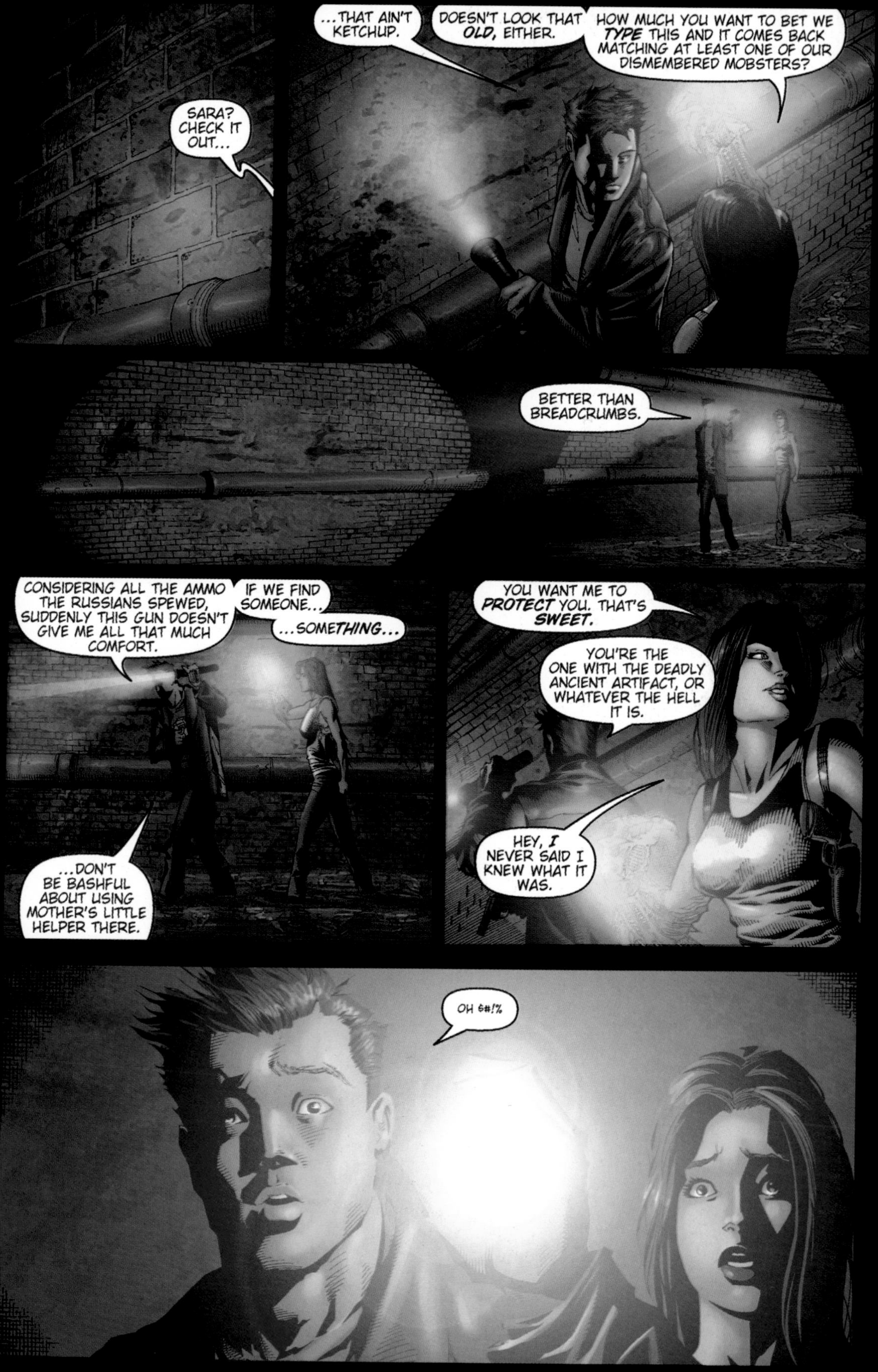
SARA? CHECK IT OUT...
...THAT AIN'T KETCHUP.
DOESN'T LOOK THAT OLD, EITHER.
HOW MUCH YOU WANT TO BET WE TYPE THIS AND IT COMES BACK MATCHING AT LEAST ONE OF OUR DISMEMBERED MOBSTERS?
BETTER THAN BREADCRUMBS.
CONSIDERING ALL THE AMMO THE RUSSIANS SPEWED, SUDDENLY THIS GUN DOESN'T GIVE ME ALL THAT MUCH COMFORT.
IF WE FIND SOMEONE...
...SOMETHING...
...DON'T BE BASHFUL ABOUT USING MOTHER'S LITTLE HELPER THERE.
YOU WANT ME TO PROTECT YOU. THAT'S SWEET.
YOU'RE THE ONE WITH THE DEADLY ANCIENT ARTIFACT, OR WHATEVER THE HELL IT IS.
HEY, I NEVER SAID I KNEW WHAT IT WAS.
OH $#!%

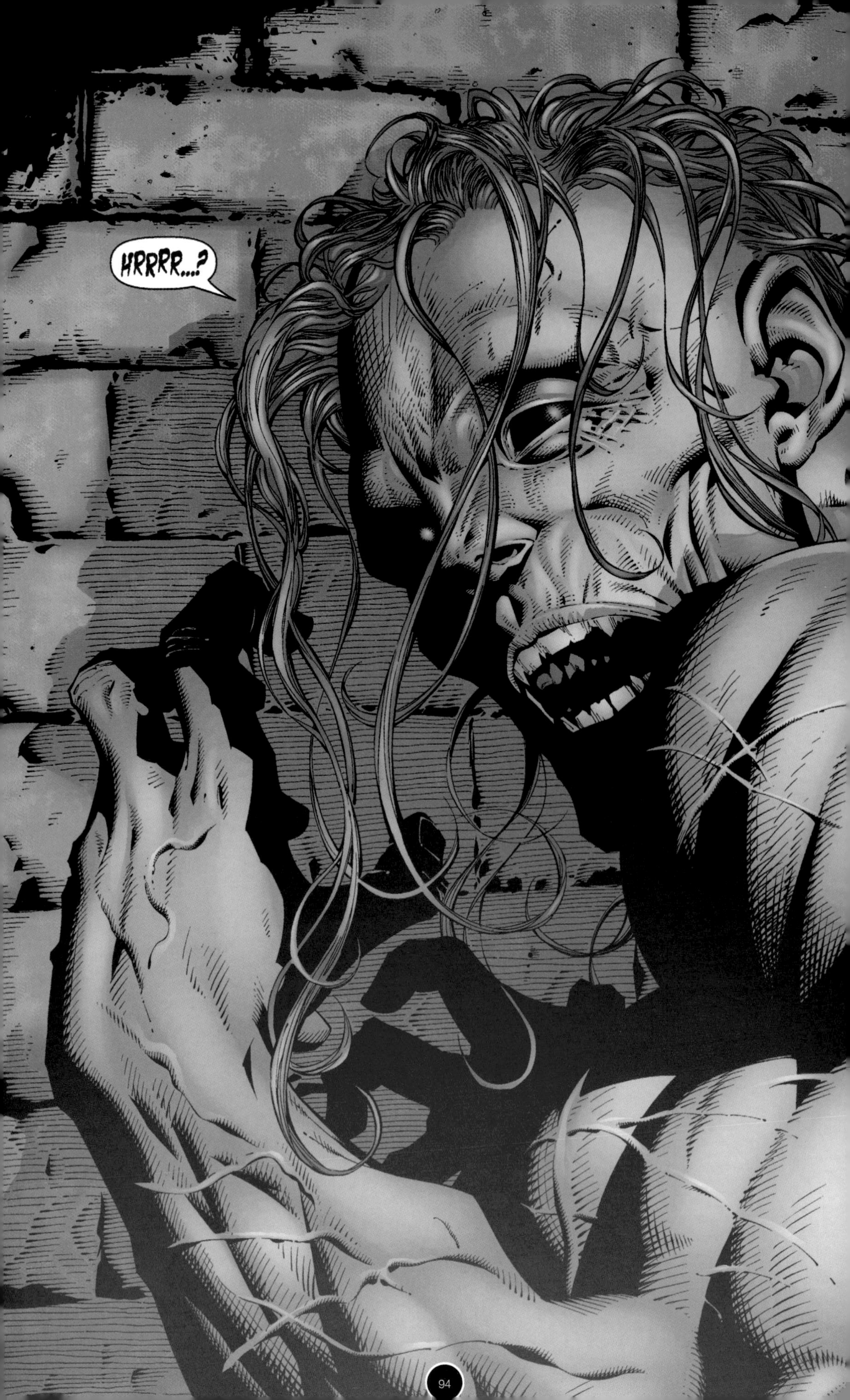
HRRRR...?

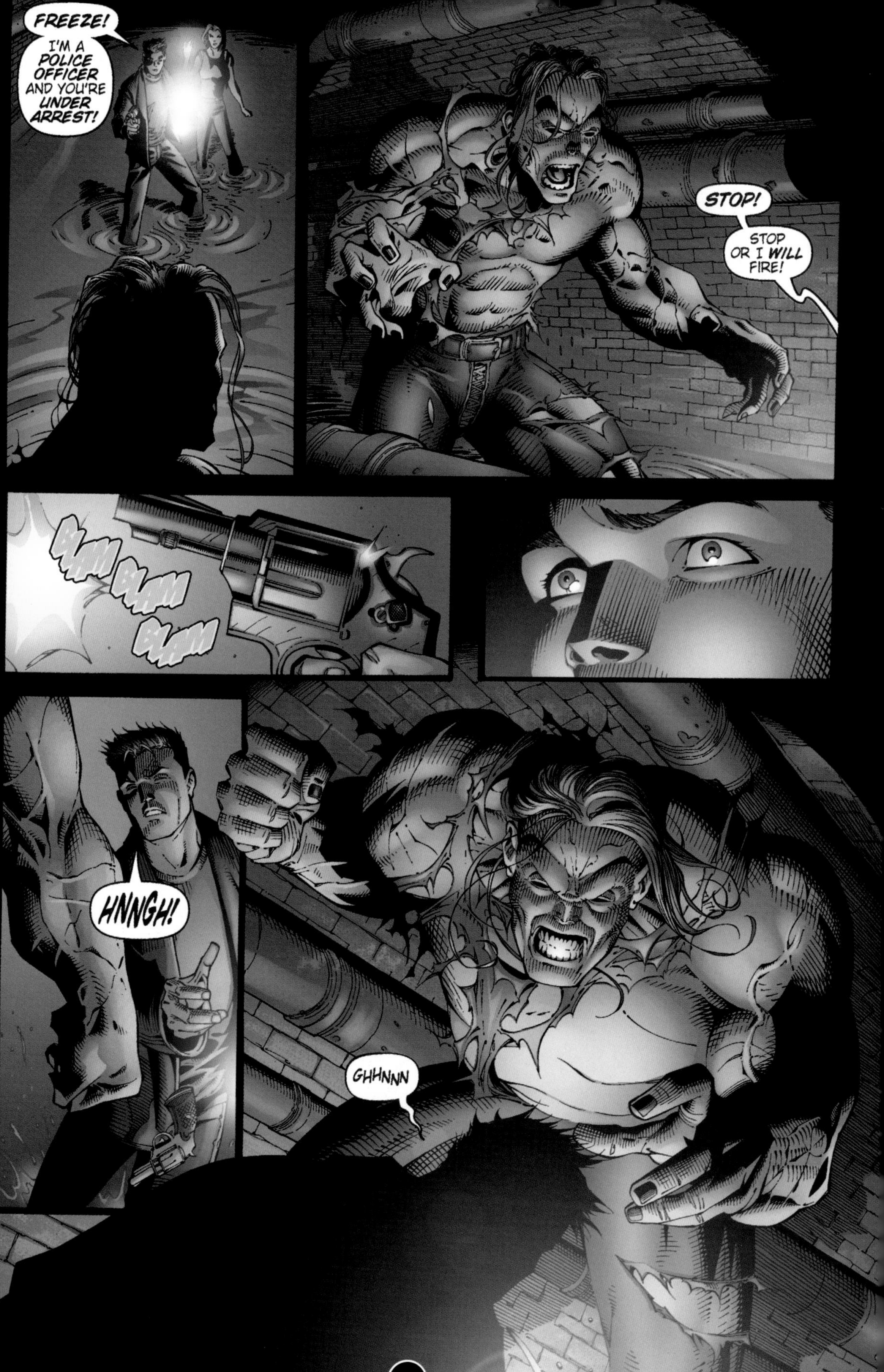
FREEZE!
I'M A POLICE OFFICER AND YOU'RE UNDER ARREST!
STOP!
STOP OR I WILL FIRE!
BLAM BLAM BLAM
HNNGH!
GHHNNN

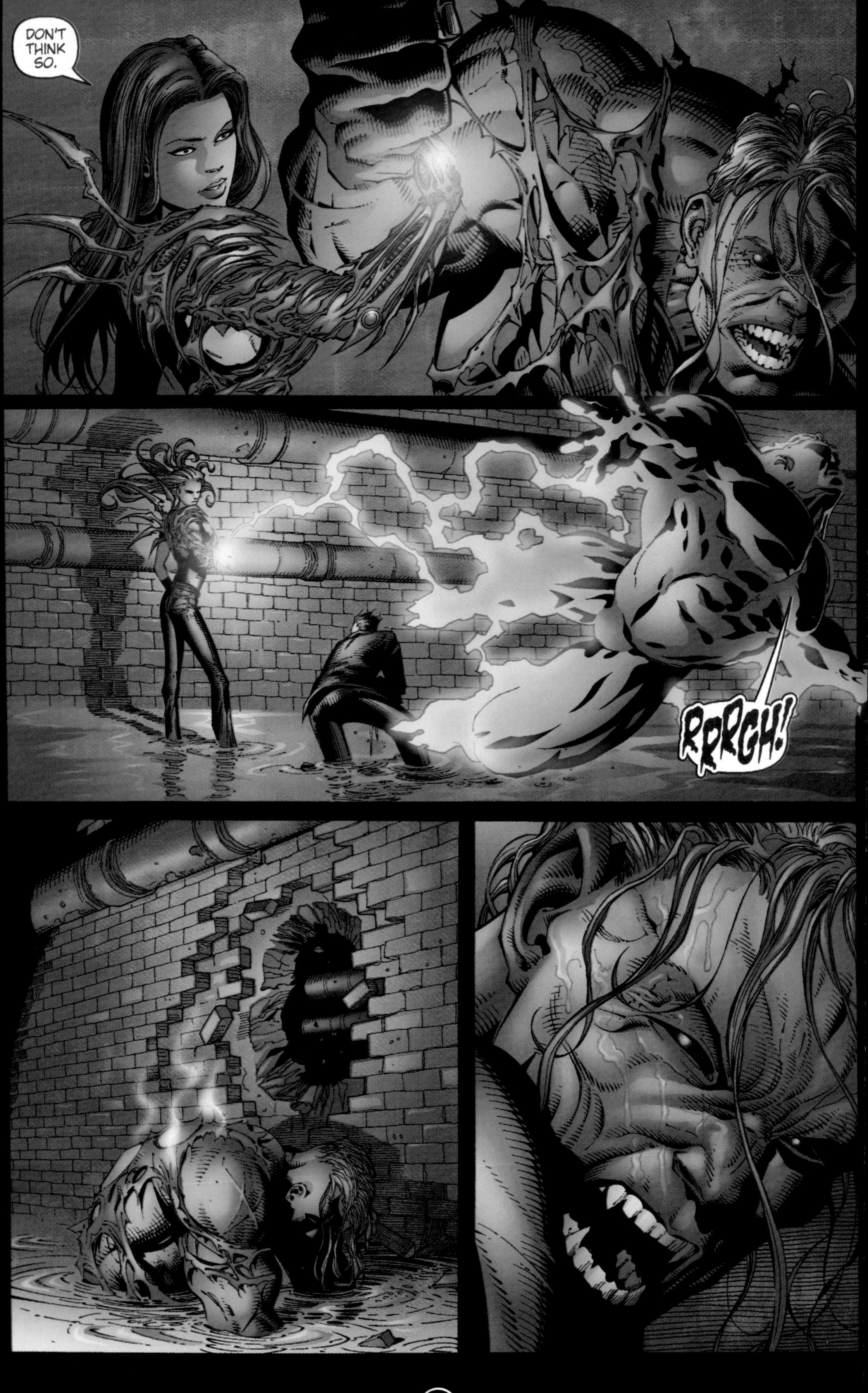
DON'T THINK SO.
RRRGH!

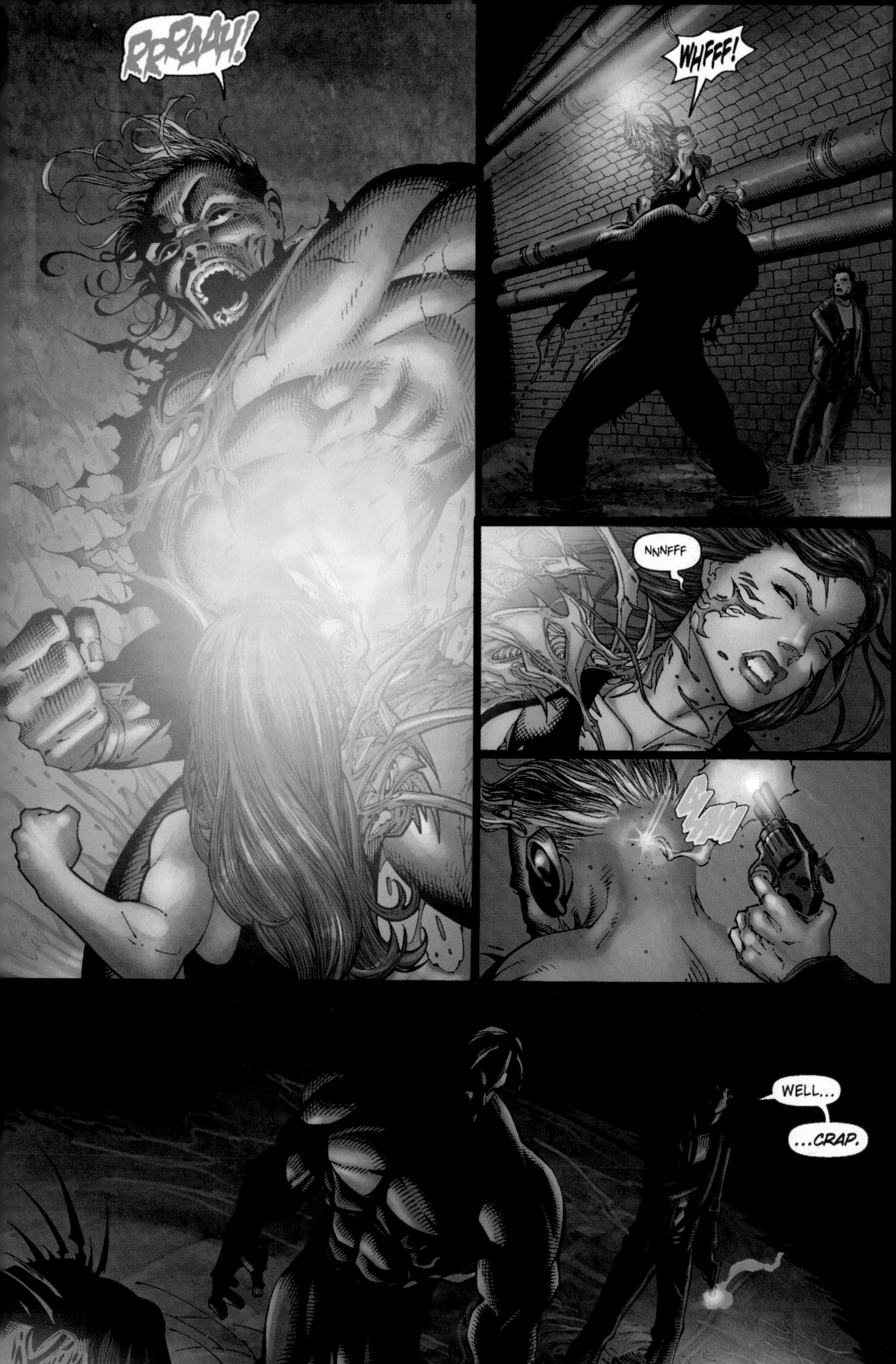
RRRAAH!
WHFFF!
NNNFFF
BLAM
WELL...
...CRAP.

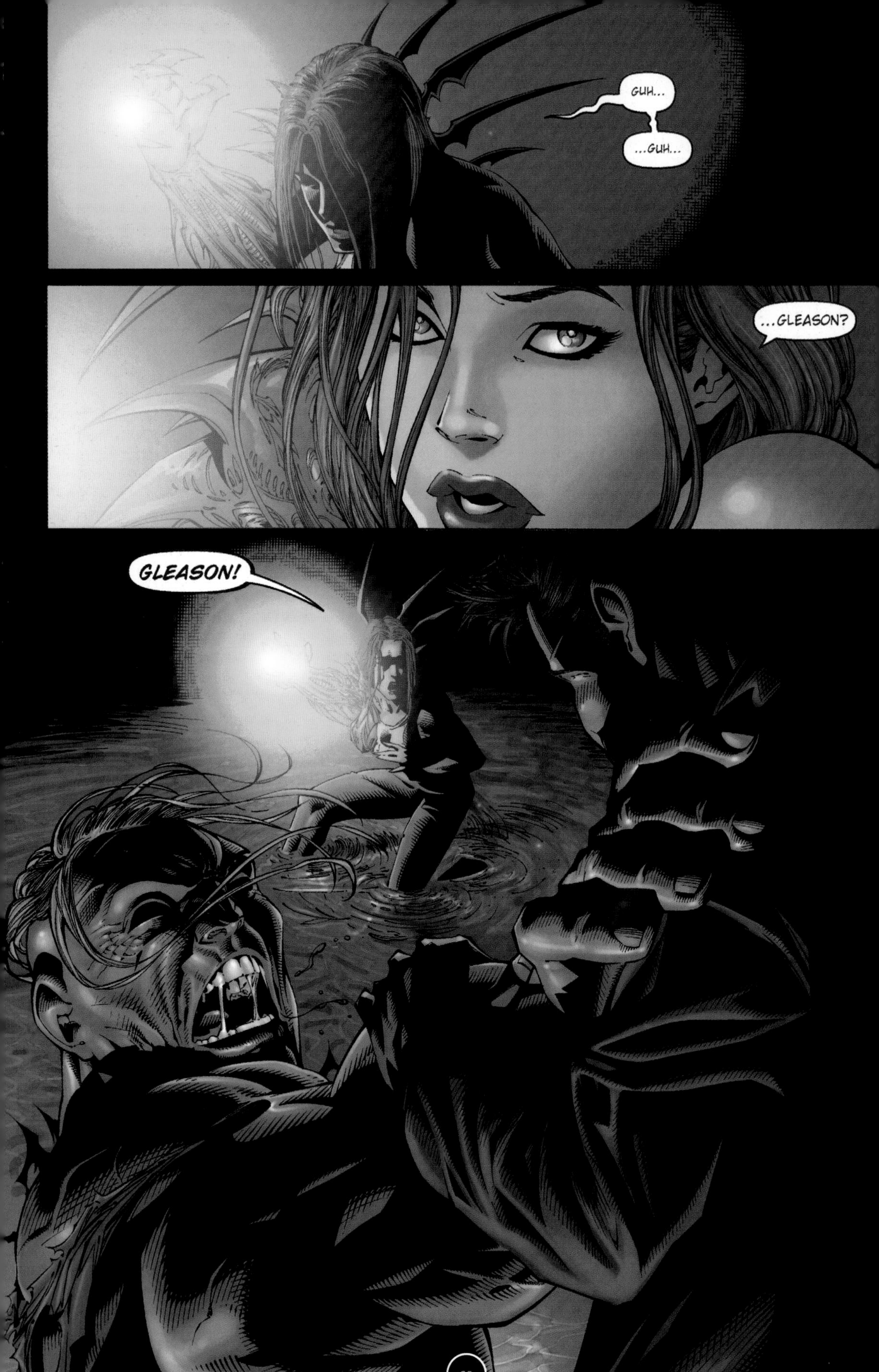
GUH...
...GUH...
...GLEASON?
GLEASON!

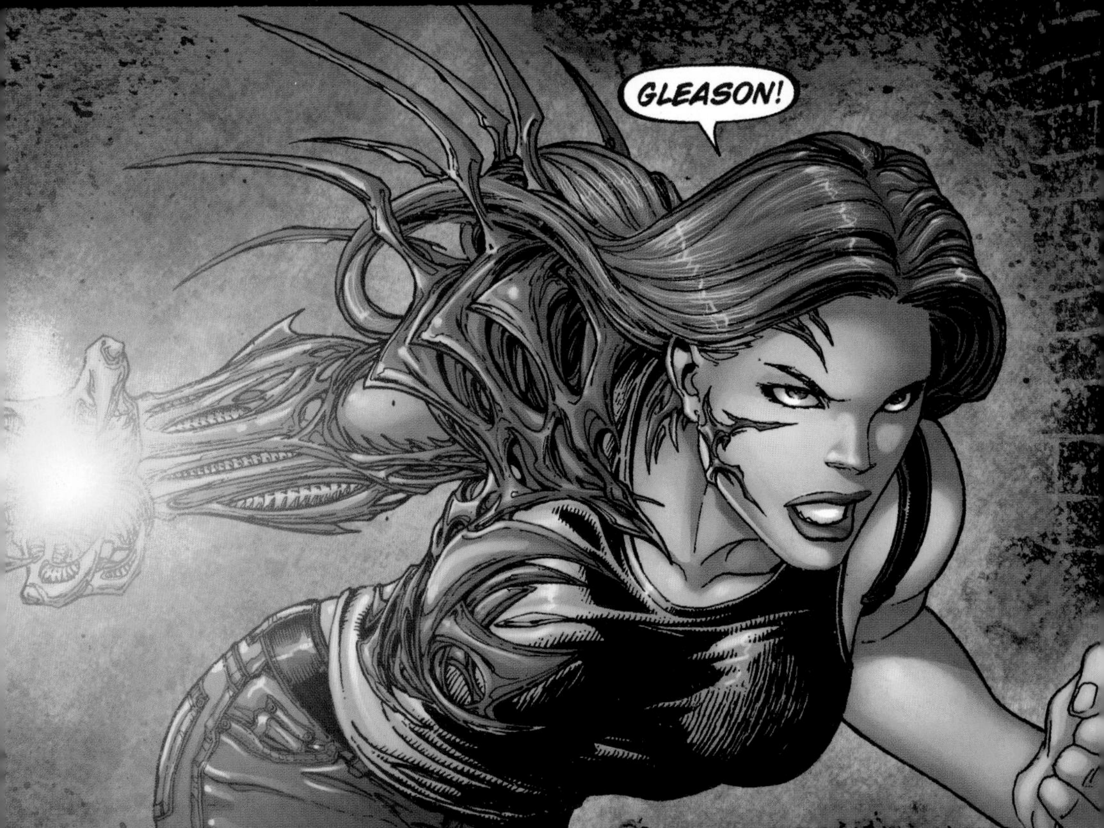
GLEASON!

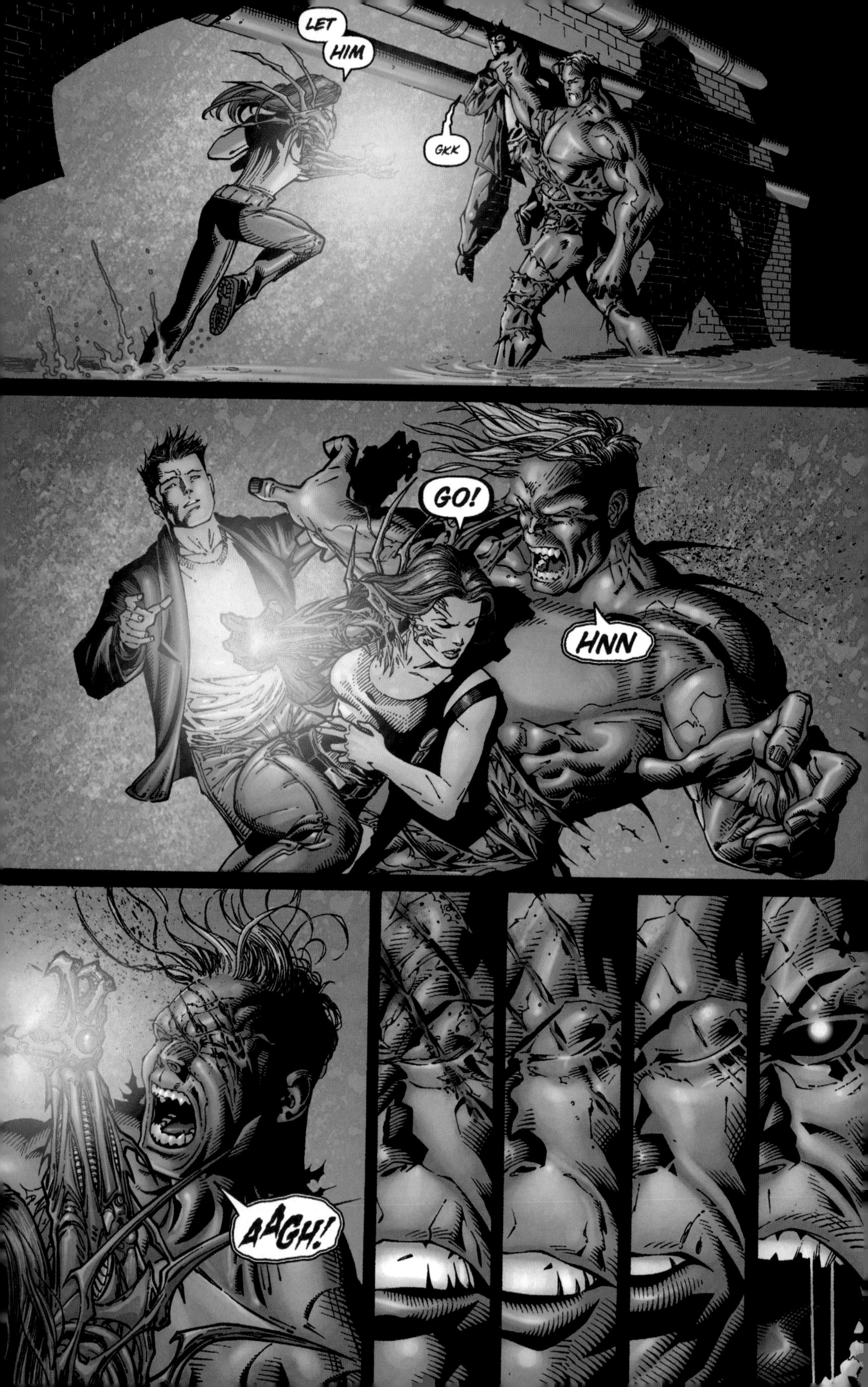
LET HIM
GKK
GO!
HNN
AAGH!

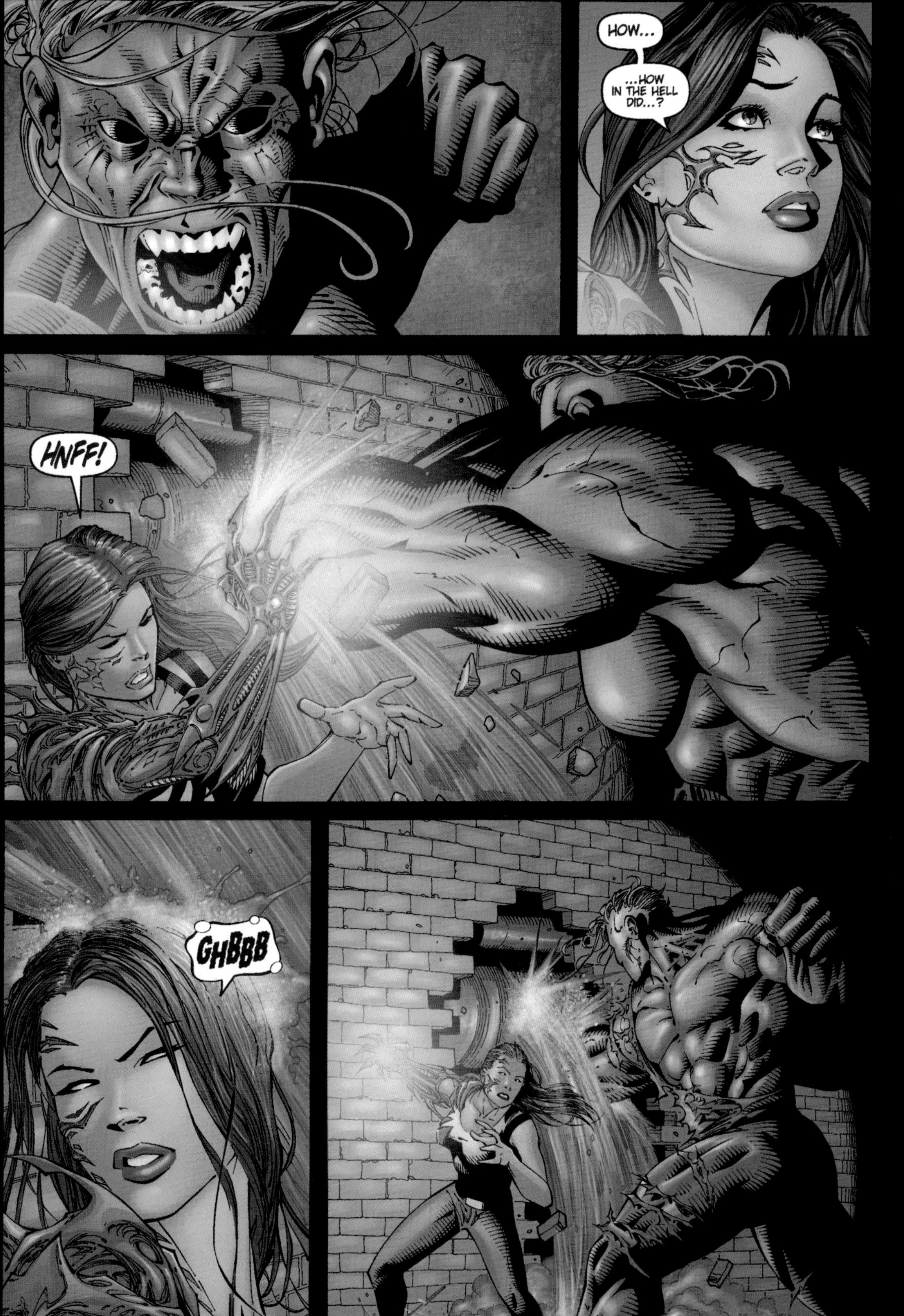
HOW...
...HOW IN THE HELL DID...?
HNFF!
GHBBB

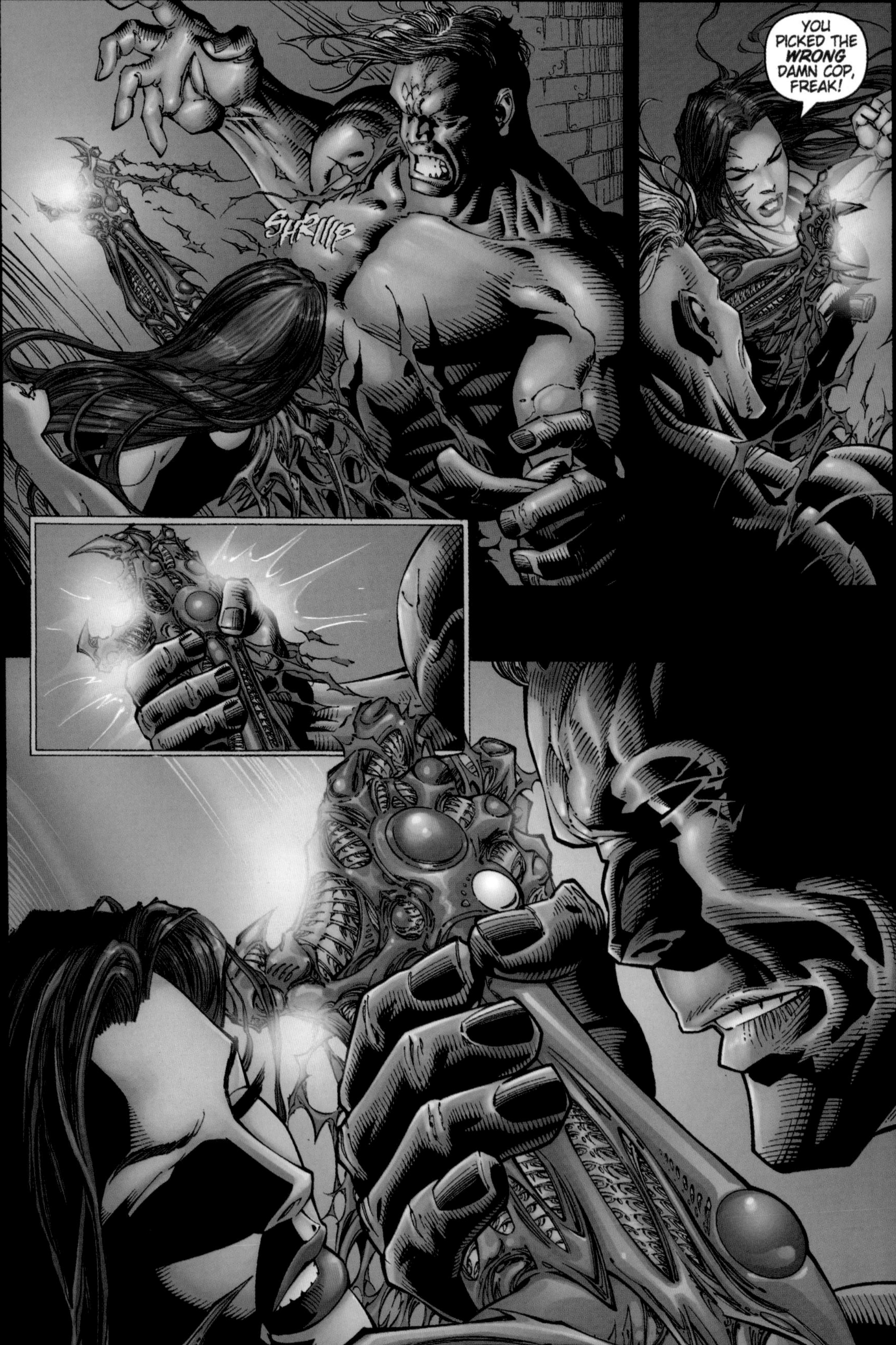
SHRIIIP
YOU PICKED THE WRONG DAMN COP, FREAK!

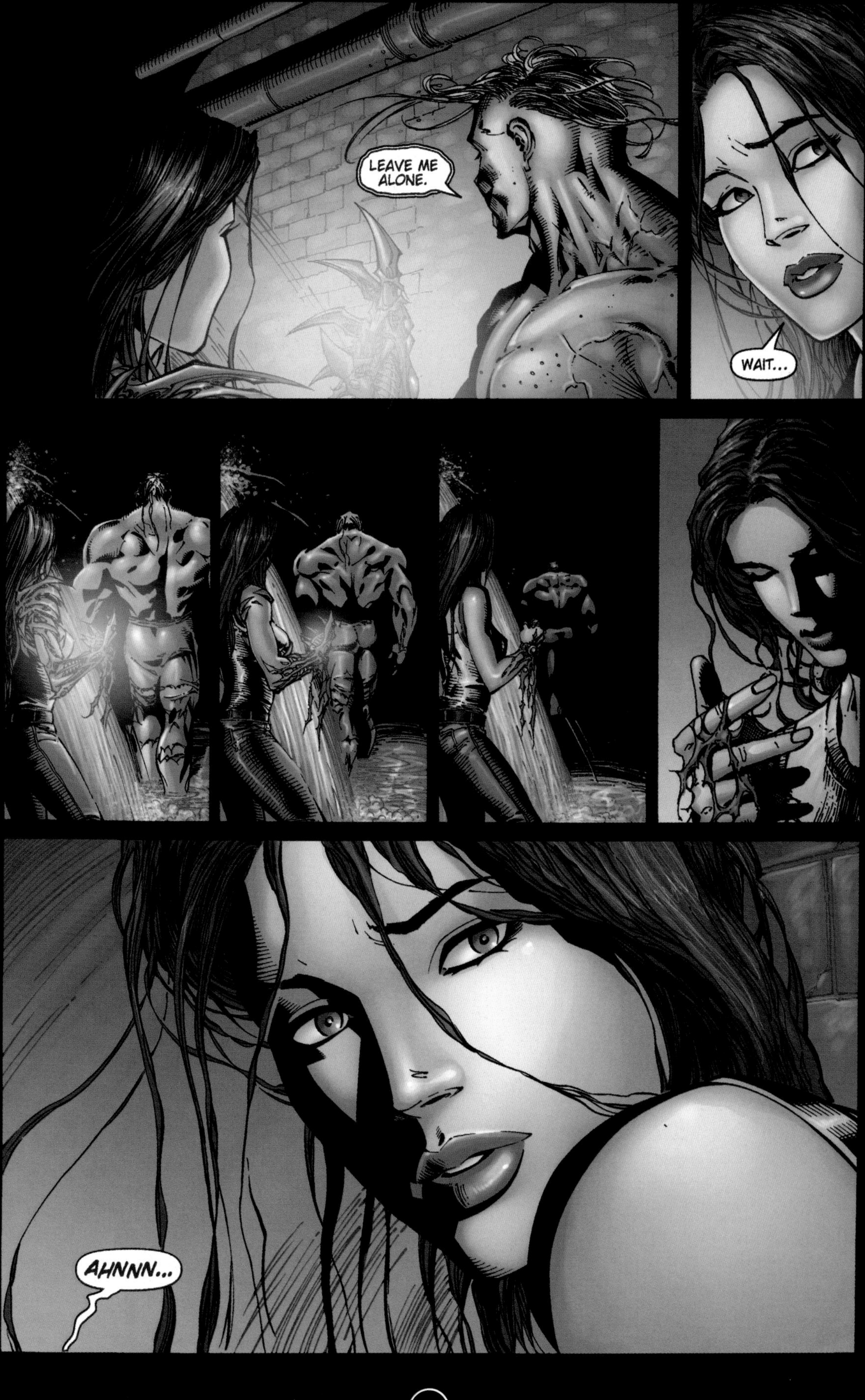
LEAVE ME ALONE.
WAIT...
AHNNN...

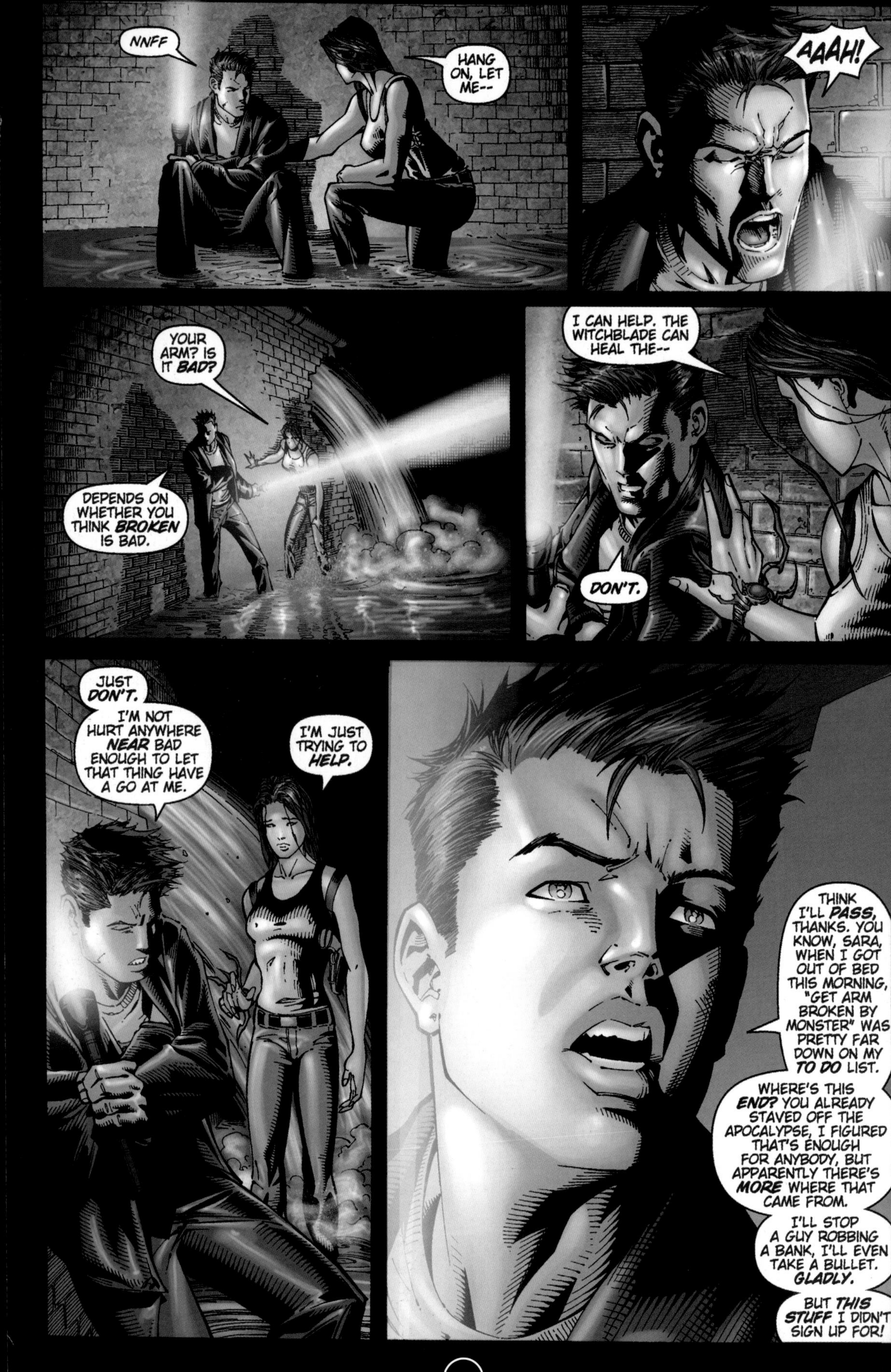
NNFF
HANG ON, LET ME--
AAAH!
YOUR ARM? IS IT BAD?
DEPENDS ON WHETHER YOU THINK BROKEN IS BAD.
I CAN HELP. THE WITCHBLADE CAN HEAL THE--
DON'T.
JUST DON'T.
I'M NOT HURT ANYWHERE NEAR BAD ENOUGH TO LET THAT THING HAVE A GO AT ME.
I'M JUST TRYING TO HELP.
THINK I'LL PASS, THANKS. YOU KNOW, SARA, WHEN I GOT OUT OF BED THIS MORNING, "GET ARM BROKEN BY MONSTER" WAS PRETTY FAR DOWN ON MY TO DO LIST.
WHERE'S THIS END? YOU ALREADY STAVED OFF THE APOCALYPSE, I FIGURED THAT'S ENOUGH FOR ANYBODY, BUT APPARENTLY THERE'S MORE WHERE THAT CAME FROM.
I'LL STOP A GUY ROBBING A BANK, I'LL EVEN TAKE A BULLET. GLADLY.
BUT THIS STUFF I DIDN'T SIGN UP FOR!

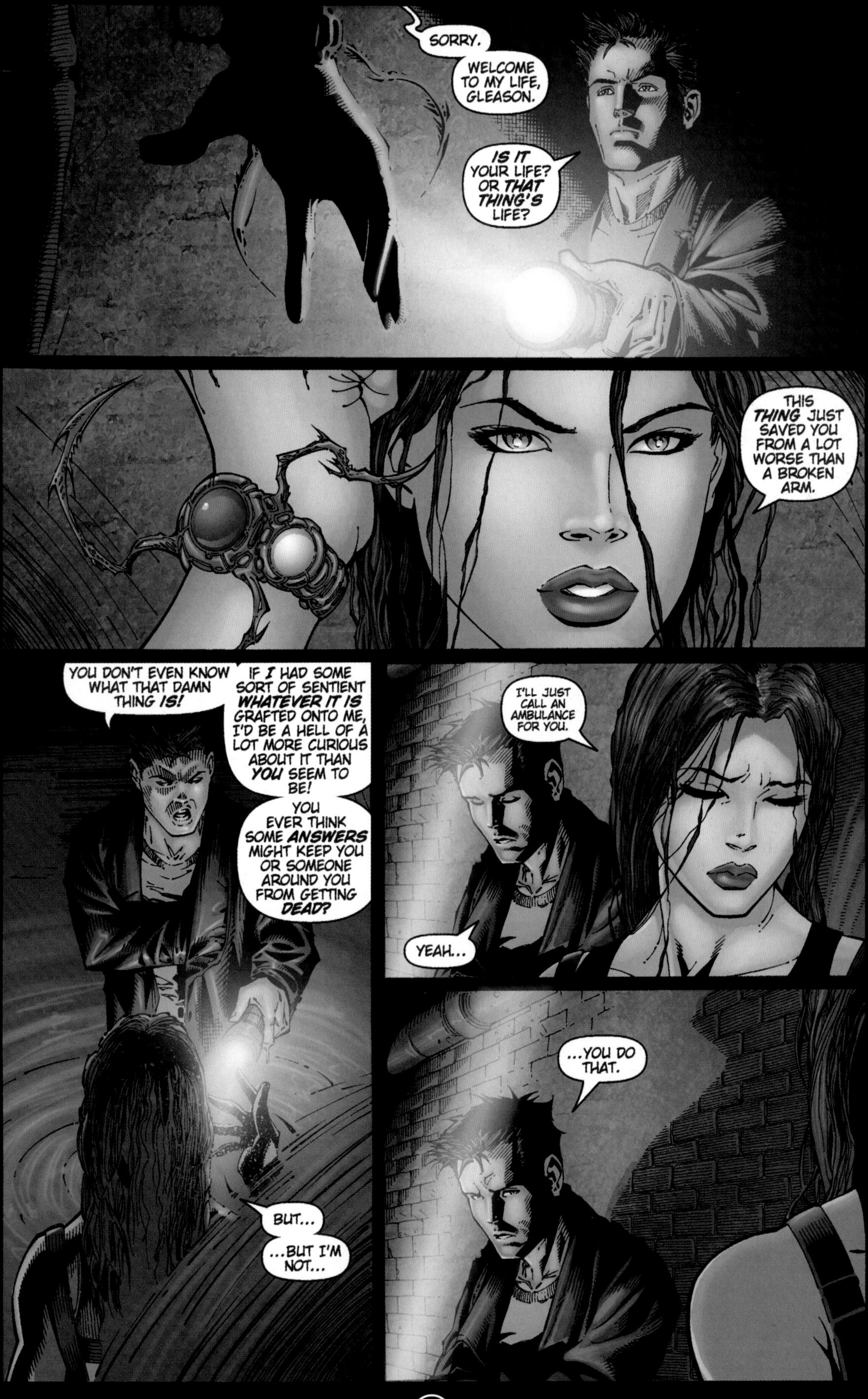
SORRY.
WELCOME TO MY LIFE, GLEASON.
IS IT YOUR LIFE? OR THAT THING'S LIFE?
THIS THING JUST SAVED YOU FROM A LOT WORSE THAN A BROKEN ARM.
YOU DON'T EVEN KNOW WHAT THAT DAMN THING IS!
IF I HAD SOME SORT OF SENTIENT WHATEVER IT IS GRAFTED ONTO ME, I'D BE A HELL OF A LOT MORE CURIOUS ABOUT IT THAN YOU SEEM TO BE!
YOU EVER THINK SOME ANSWERS MIGHT KEEP YOU OR SOMEONE AROUND YOU FROM GETTING DEAD?
BUT...
...BUT I'M NOT...
I'LL JUST CALL AN AMBULANCE FOR YOU.
YEAH...
...YOU DO THAT.

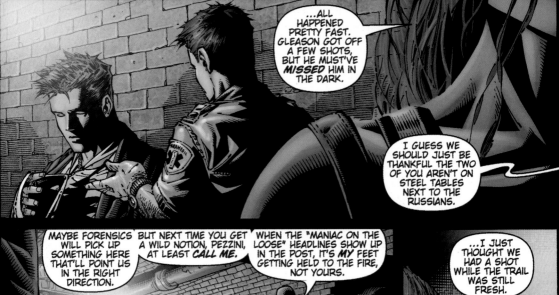

...ALL HAPPENED PRETTY FAST. GLEASON GOT OFF A FEW SHOTS, BUT HE MUST'VE *MISSED* HIM IN THE DARK.

I GUESS WE SHOULD JUST BE THANKFUL THE TWO OF YOU AREN'T ON STEEL TABLES NEXT TO THE RUSSIANS.

MAYBE FORENSICS WILL PICK UP SOMETHING HERE THAT'LL POINT US IN THE RIGHT DIRECTION.

BUT NEXT TIME YOU GET A WILD NOTION, PEZZINI, AT LEAST *CALL ME.*

WHEN THE "MANIAC ON THE LOOSE" HEADLINES SHOW UP IN THE POST, IT'S *MY* FEET GETTING HELD TO THE FIRE, NOT YOURS.

MY BAD, KRAUSE. I WASN'T TRYING TO GO AROUND YOU...

...I JUST THOUGHT WE HAD A SHOT WHILE THE TRAIL WAS STILL FRESH.

AW, CRIPES...

LOOKS LIKE YOU GUYS HAD A PARTY AND DIDN'T INVITE US. I'M *HURT.*

IT WAS *MY* PARTY, CARSTENS.

YOU FEEL LIKE NAILING SOMEBODY'S HIDE TO THE WALL, YOU CAN MAKE IT *MINE.*

WELL, MAYBE NOT *QUITE* WHAT I WAS THINKING OF.

I THOUGHT WE WERE GOING TO WORK TOGETHER ON THIS, SARA. I SCRATCH YOUR BACK, YOU SCRATCH MINE.

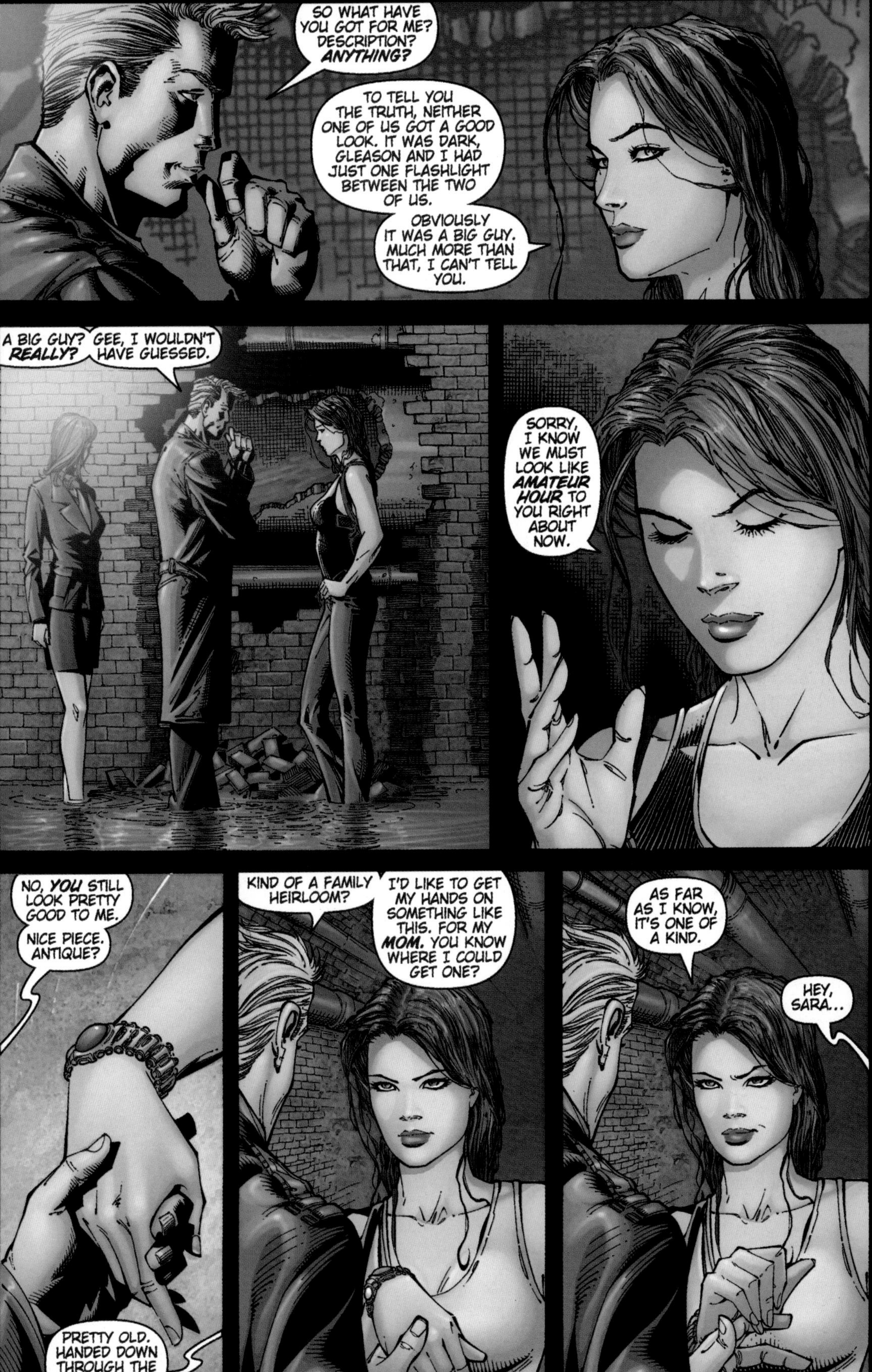

SO WHAT HAVE YOU GOT FOR ME? DESCRIPTION? *ANYTHING?*
TO TELL YOU THE TRUTH, NEITHER ONE OF US GOT A GOOD LOOK. IT WAS DARK, GLEASON AND I HAD JUST ONE FLASHLIGHT BETWEEN THE TWO OF US.
OBVIOUSLY IT WAS A BIG GUY. MUCH MORE THAN THAT, I CAN'T TELL YOU.
A BIG GUY? *REALLY?*
GEE, I WOULDN'T HAVE GUESSED.
SORRY, I KNOW WE MUST LOOK LIKE *AMATEUR HOUR* TO YOU RIGHT ABOUT NOW.
NO, *YOU* STILL LOOK PRETTY GOOD TO ME.
NICE PIECE. ANTIQUE?
PRETTY OLD. HANDED DOWN THROUGH THE GENERATIONS.
KIND OF A FAMILY HEIRLOOM?
I'D LIKE TO GET MY HANDS ON SOMETHING LIKE THIS. FOR MY *MOM.* YOU KNOW WHERE I COULD GET ONE?
AS FAR AS I KNOW, IT'S ONE OF A KIND.
HEY, SARA...

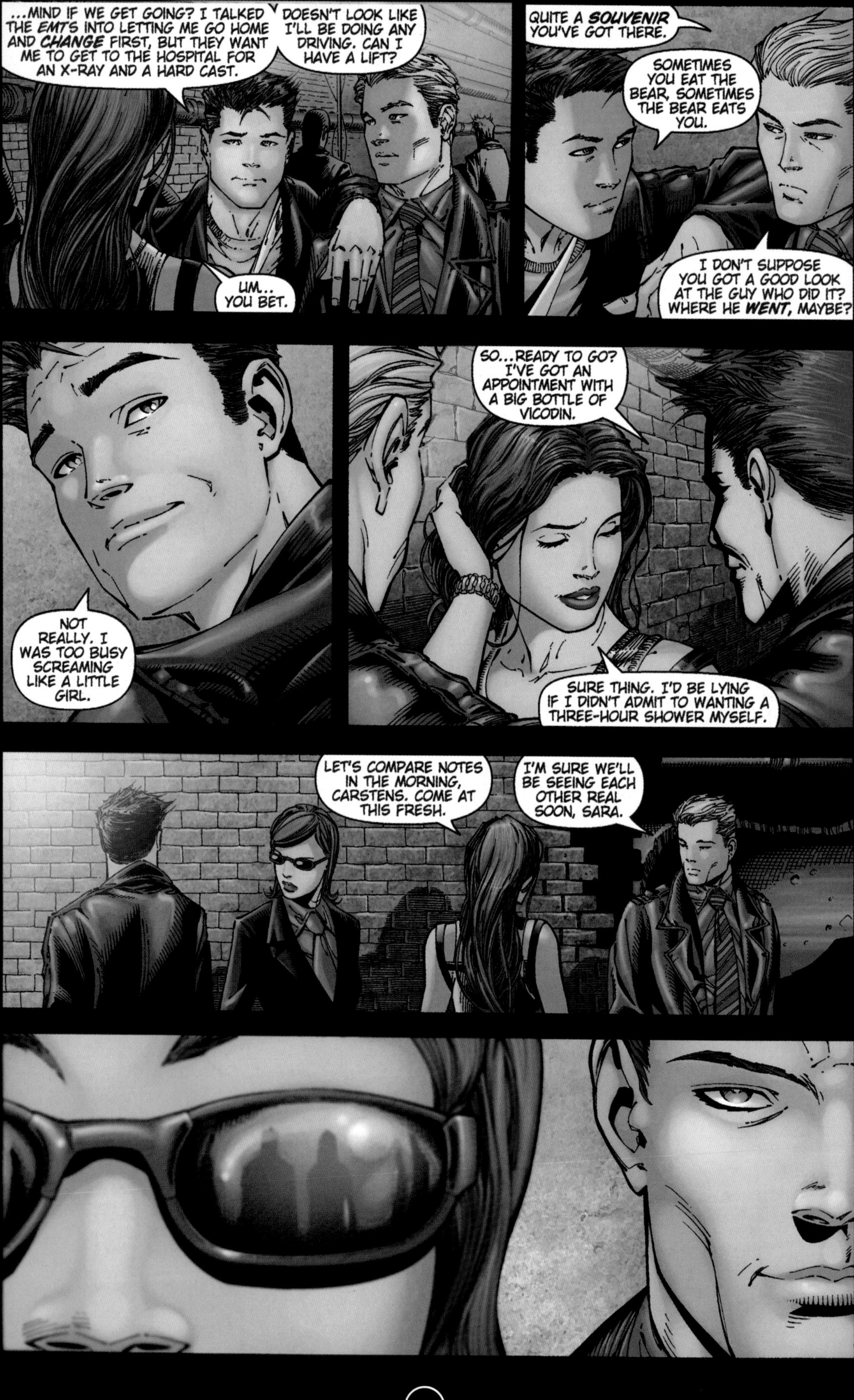
...MIND IF WE GET GOING? I TALKED THE EMT'S INTO LETTING ME GO HOME AND CHANGE FIRST, BUT THEY WANT ME TO GET TO THE HOSPITAL FOR AN X-RAY AND A HARD CAST.
DOESN'T LOOK LIKE I'LL BE DOING ANY DRIVING. CAN I HAVE A LIFT?
UM.. YOU BET.
QUITE A SOUVENIR YOU'VE GOT THERE.
SOMETIMES YOU EAT THE BEAR, SOMETIMES THE BEAR EATS YOU.
I DON'T SUPPOSE YOU GOT A GOOD LOOK AT THE GUY WHO DID IT? WHERE HE WENT, MAYBE?
NOT REALLY. I WAS TOO BUSY SCREAMING LIKE A LITTLE GIRL.
SO...READY TO GO? I'VE GOT AN APPOINTMENT WITH A BIG BOTTLE OF VICODIN.
SURE THING. I'D BE LYING IF I DIDN'T ADMIT TO WANTING A THREE-HOUR SHOWER MYSELF.
LET'S COMPARE NOTES IN THE MORNING, CARSTENS. COME AT THIS FRESH.
I'M SURE WE'LL BE SEEING EACH OTHER REAL SOON, SARA.

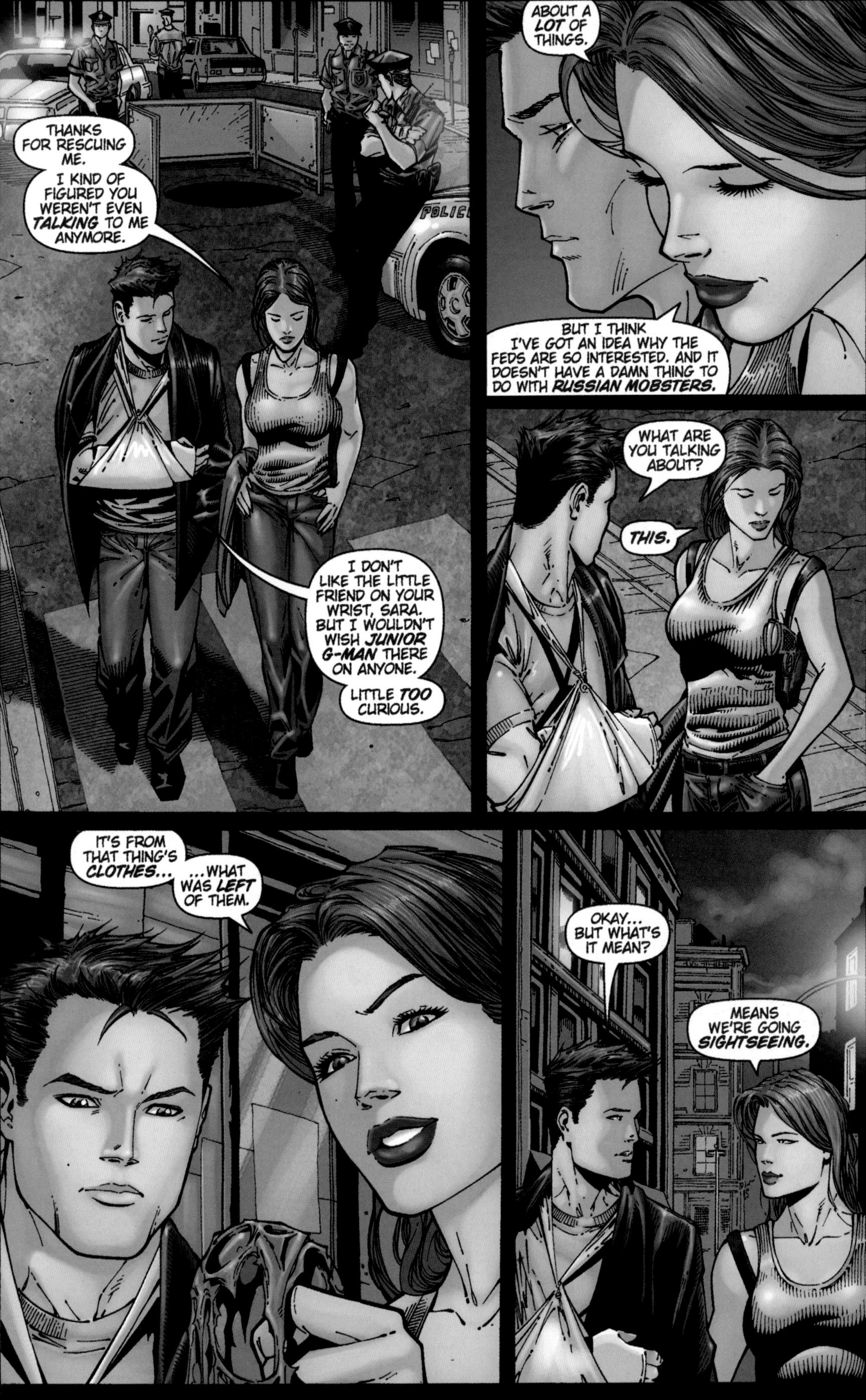
THANKS FOR RESCUING ME.
I KIND OF FIGURED YOU WEREN'T EVEN TALKING TO ME ANYMORE.
POLICE
I DON'T LIKE THE LITTLE FRIEND ON YOUR WRIST, SARA. BUT I WOULDN'T WISH JUNIOR G-MAN THERE ON ANYONE.
LITTLE TOO CURIOUS.
ABOUT A LOT OF THINGS.
BUT I THINK I'VE GOT AN IDEA WHY THE FEDS ARE SO INTERESTED. AND IT DOESN'T HAVE A DAMN THING TO DO WITH RUSSIAN MOBSTERS.
WHAT ARE YOU TALKING ABOUT?
THIS.
IT'S FROM THAT THING'S CLOTHES...
...WHAT WAS LEFT OF THEM.
OKAY... BUT WHAT'S IT MEAN?
MEANS WE'RE GOING SIGHTSEEING.

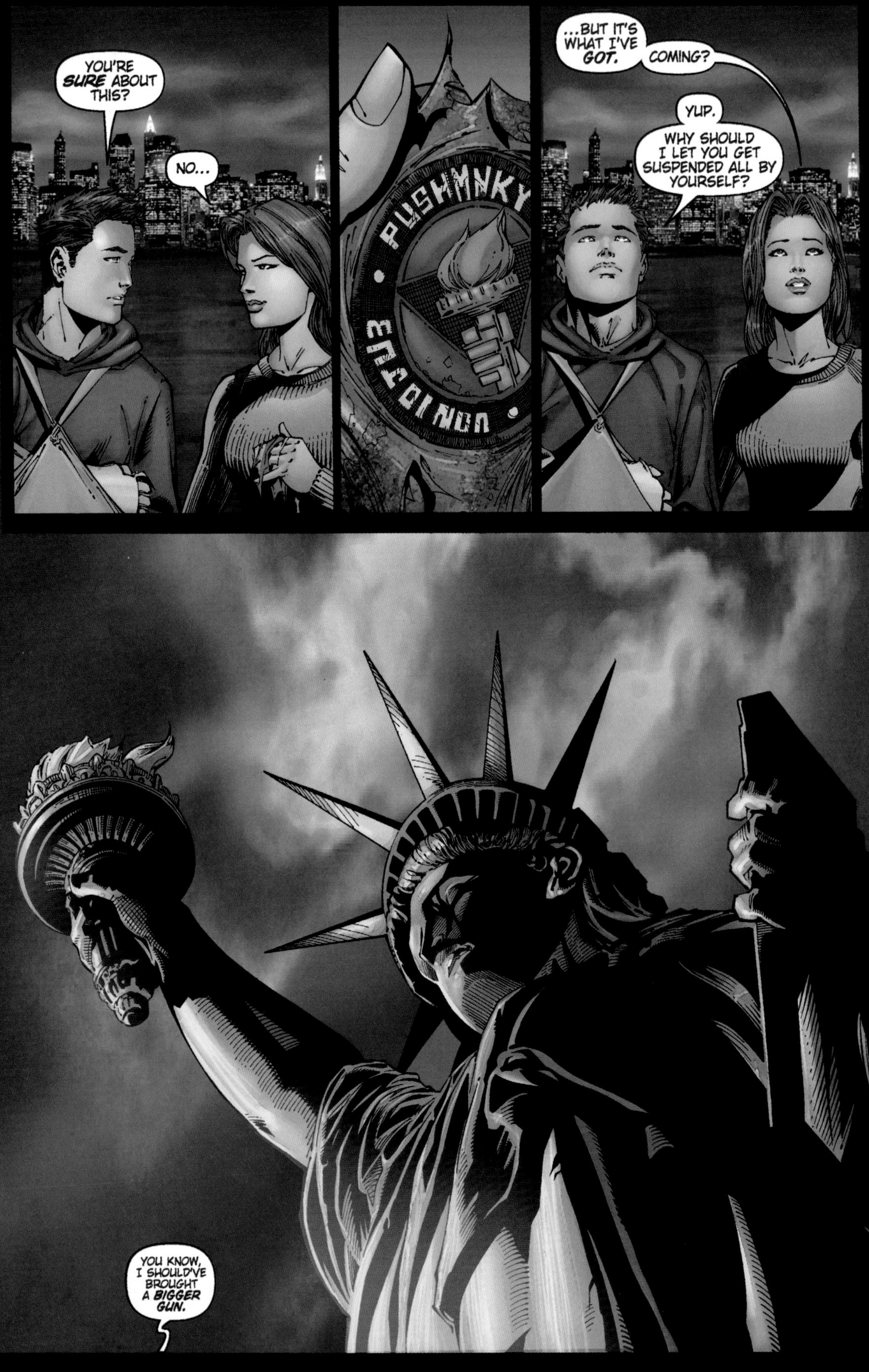

YOU'RE SURE ABOUT THIS?
NO...
PUSHMNKY
...BUT IT'S WHAT I'VE GOT.
COMING?
YUP.
WHY SHOULD I LET YOU GET SUSPENDED ALL BY YOURSELF?
YOU KNOW, I SHOULD'VE BROUGHT A BIGGER GUN.

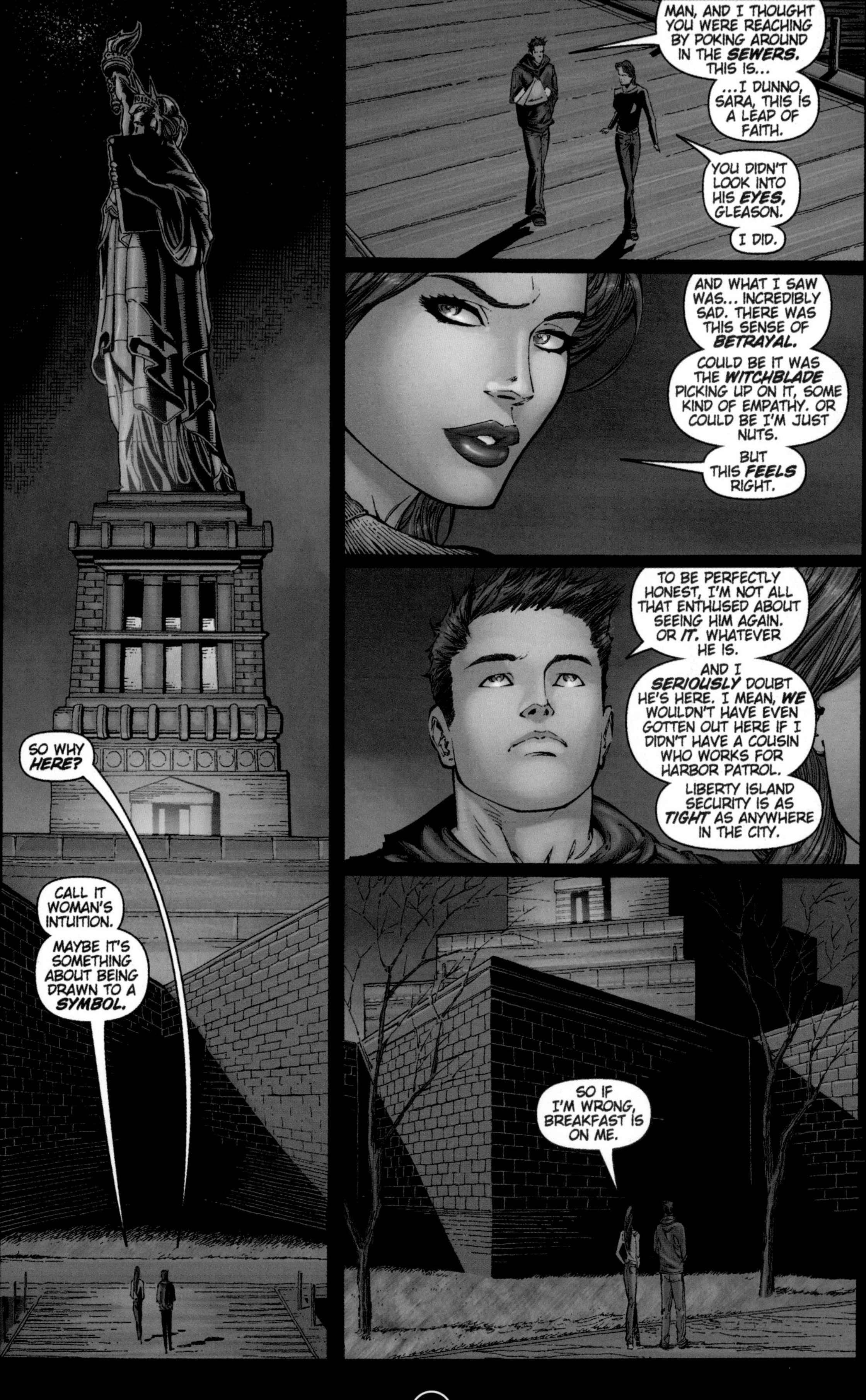
MAN, AND I THOUGHT YOU WERE REACHING BY POKING AROUND IN THE SEWERS. THIS IS...
...I DUNNO, SARA, THIS IS A LEAP OF FAITH.
YOU DIDN'T LOOK INTO HIS EYES, GLEASON.
I DID.
AND WHAT I SAW WAS... INCREDIBLY SAD. THERE WAS THIS SENSE OF BETRAYAL.
COULD BE IT WAS THE WITCHBLADE PICKING UP ON IT, SOME KIND OF EMPATHY. OR COULD BE I'M JUST NUTS.
BUT THIS FEELS RIGHT.
TO BE PERFECTLY HONEST, I'M NOT ALL THAT ENTHUSED ABOUT SEEING HIM AGAIN. OR IT. WHATEVER HE IS.
AND I SERIOUSLY DOUBT HE'S HERE. I MEAN, WE WOULDN'T HAVE EVEN GOTTEN OUT HERE IF I DIDN'T HAVE A COUSIN WHO WORKS FOR HARBOR PATROL.
LIBERTY ISLAND SECURITY IS AS TIGHT AS ANYWHERE IN THE CITY.
SO WHY HERE?
CALL IT WOMAN'S INTUITION.
MAYBE IT'S SOMETHING ABOUT BEING DRAWN TO A SYMBOL.
SO IF I'M WRONG, BREAKFAST IS ON ME.

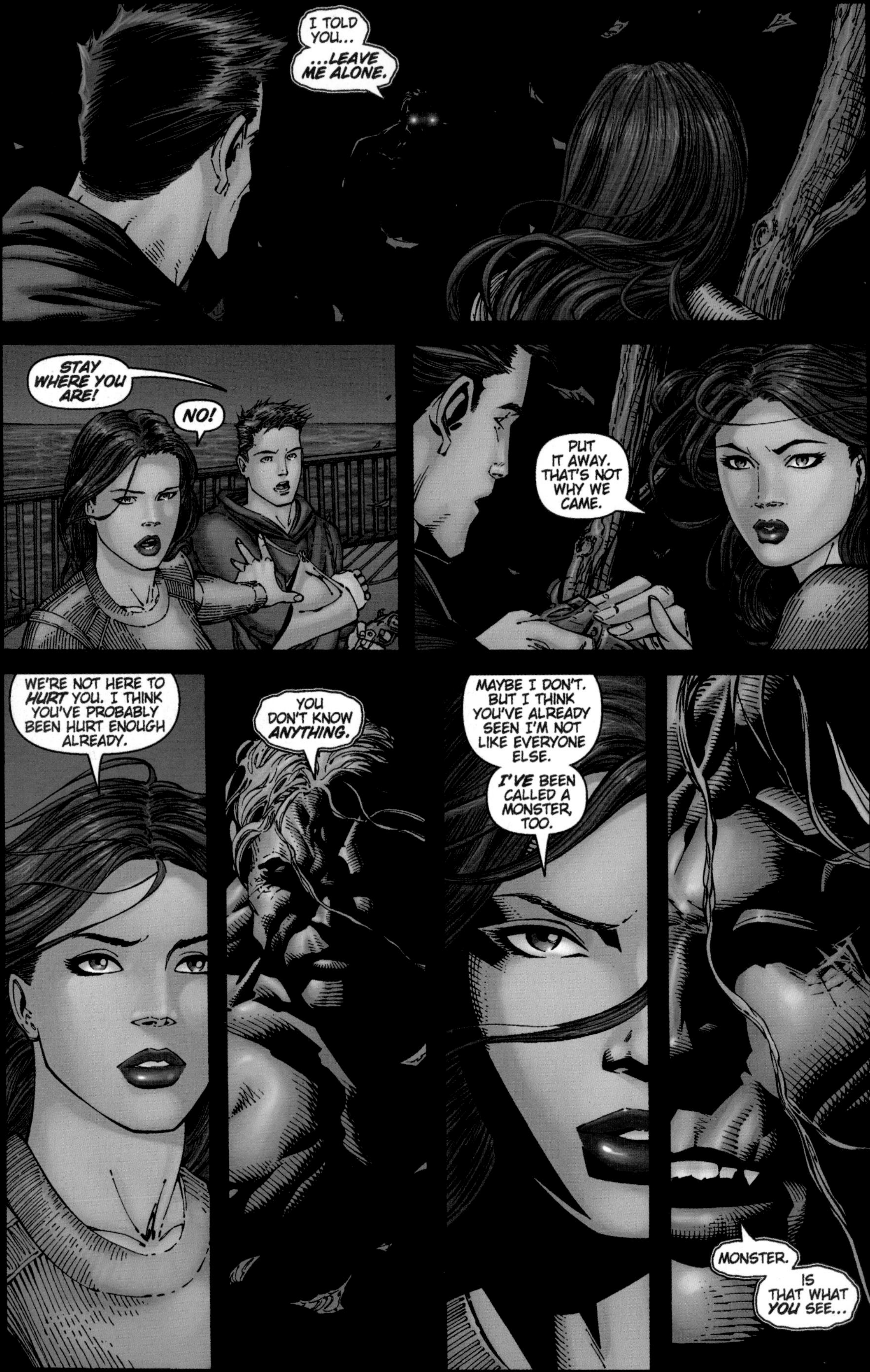
I TOLD YOU...
...LEAVE ME ALONE.
STAY WHERE YOU ARE!
NO!
PUT IT AWAY. THAT'S NOT WHY WE CAME.
WE'RE NOT HERE TO HURT YOU. I THINK YOU'VE PROBABLY BEEN HURT ENOUGH ALREADY.
YOU DON'T KNOW ANYTHING.
MAYBE I DON'T. BUT I THINK YOU'VE ALREADY SEEN I'M NOT LIKE EVERYONE ELSE.
I'VE BEEN CALLED A MONSTER, TOO.
MONSTER.
IS THAT WHAT YOU SEE...

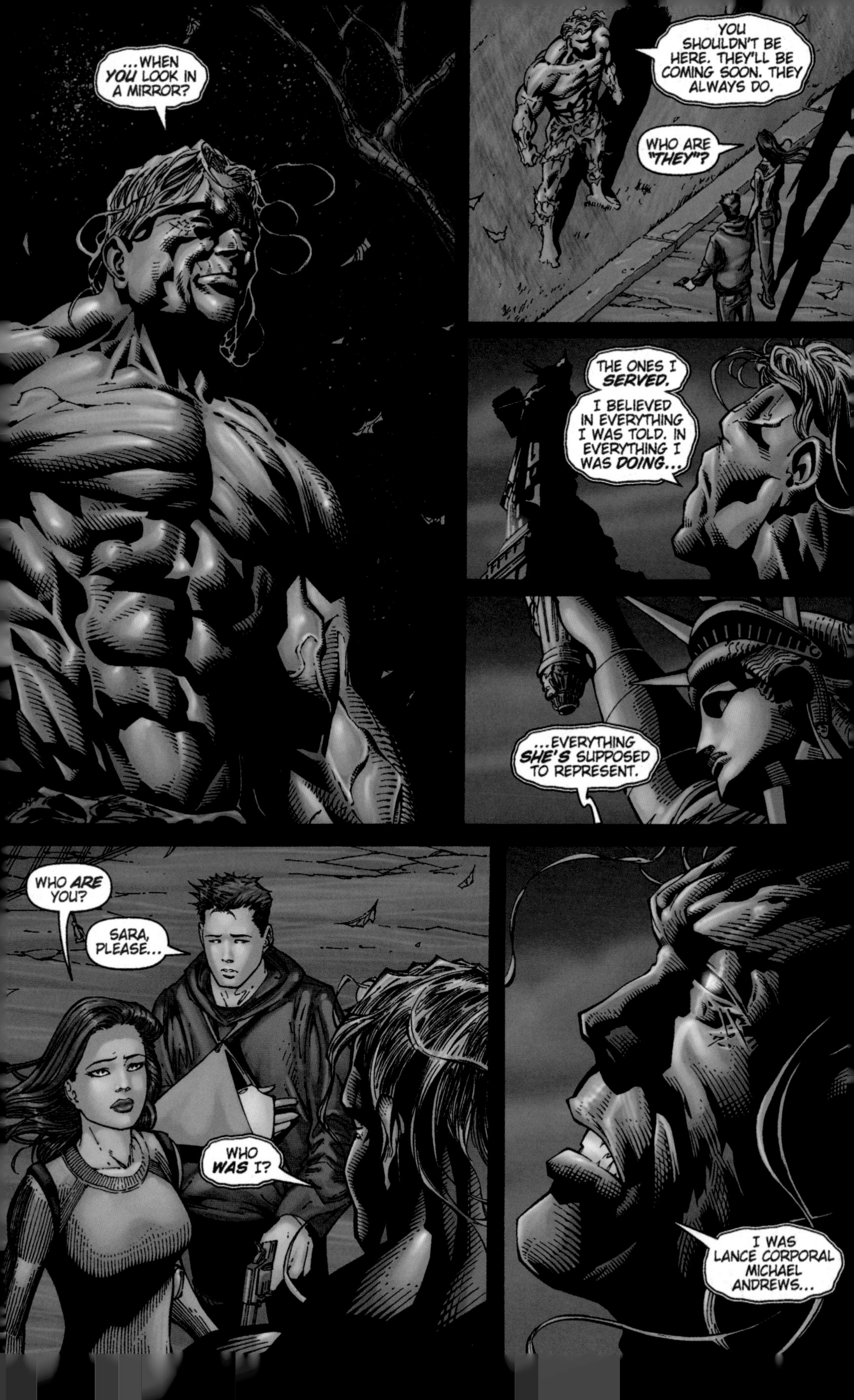
...WHEN YOU LOOK IN A MIRROR?
YOU SHOULDN'T BE HERE. THEY'LL BE COMING SOON. THEY ALWAYS DO.
WHO ARE "THEY"?
THE ONES I SERVED.
I BELIEVED IN EVERYTHING I WAS TOLD. IN EVERYTHING I WAS DOING...
...EVERYTHING SHE'S SUPPOSED TO REPRESENT.
WHO ARE YOU?
SARA, PLEASE...
WHO WAS I?
I WAS LANCE CORPORAL MICHAEL ANDREWS...

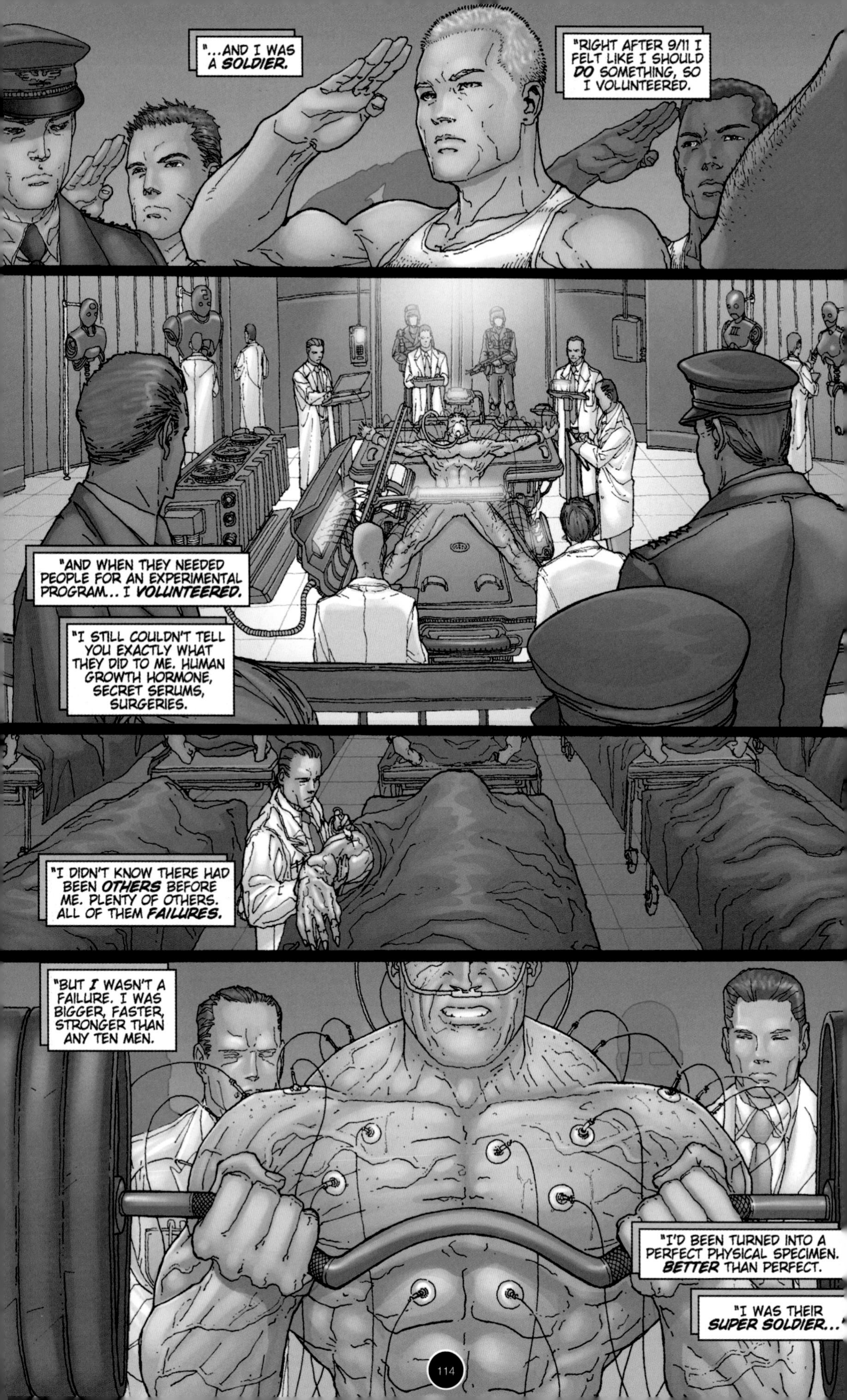
"...AND I WAS A **SOLDIER.**
"RIGHT AFTER 9/11 I FELT LIKE I SHOULD **DO** SOMETHING, SO I VOLUNTEERED.
"AND WHEN THEY NEEDED PEOPLE FOR AN EXPERIMENTAL PROGRAM... I **VOLUNTEERED.**
"I STILL COULDN'T TELL YOU EXACTLY WHAT THEY DID TO ME. HUMAN GROWTH HORMONE, SECRET SERUMS, SURGERIES.
"I DIDN'T KNOW THERE HAD BEEN **OTHERS** BEFORE ME. PLENTY OF OTHERS. ALL OF THEM **FAILURES.**
"BUT **I** WASN'T A FAILURE. I WAS BIGGER, FASTER, STRONGER THAN ANY TEN MEN.
"I'D BEEN TURNED INTO A PERFECT PHYSICAL SPECIMEN. **BETTER** THAN PERFECT.
"I WAS THEIR **SUPER SOLDIER...**"

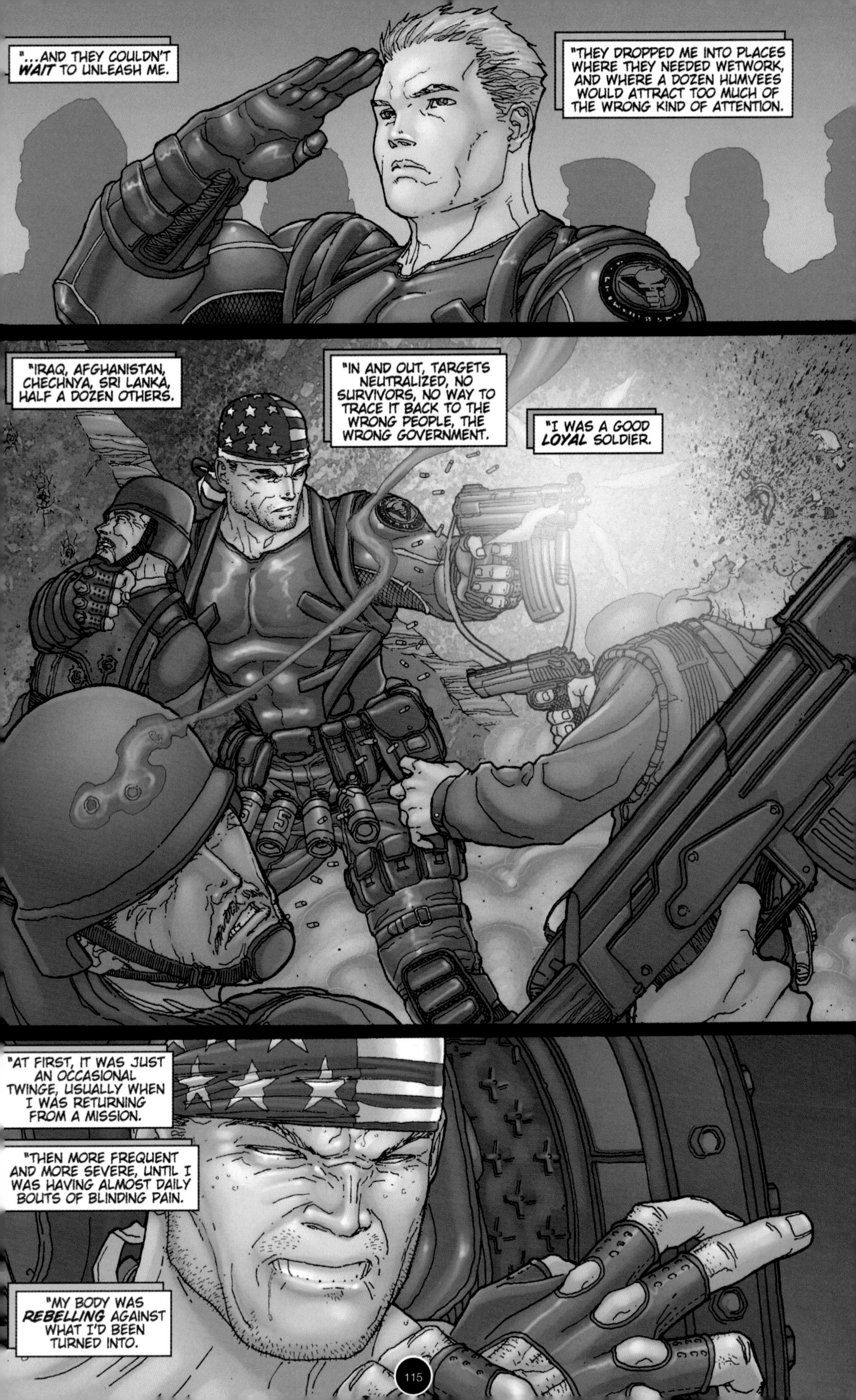
"...AND THEY COULDN'T WAIT TO UNLEASH ME.
"THEY DROPPED ME INTO PLACES WHERE THEY NEEDED WETWORK, AND WHERE A DOZEN HUMVEES WOULD ATTRACT TOO MUCH OF THE WRONG KIND OF ATTENTION.
"IRAQ, AFGHANISTAN, CHECHNYA, SRI LANKA, HALF A DOZEN OTHERS.
"IN AND OUT, TARGETS NEUTRALIZED, NO SURVIVORS, NO WAY TO TRACE IT BACK TO THE WRONG PEOPLE, THE WRONG GOVERNMENT.
"I WAS A GOOD LOYAL SOLDIER.
"AT FIRST, IT WAS JUST AN OCCASIONAL TWINGE, USUALLY WHEN I WAS RETURNING FROM A MISSION.
"THEN MORE FREQUENT AND MORE SEVERE, UNTIL I WAS HAVING ALMOST DAILY BOUTS OF BLINDING PAIN.
"MY BODY WAS REBELLING AGAINST WHAT I'D BEEN TURNED INTO.

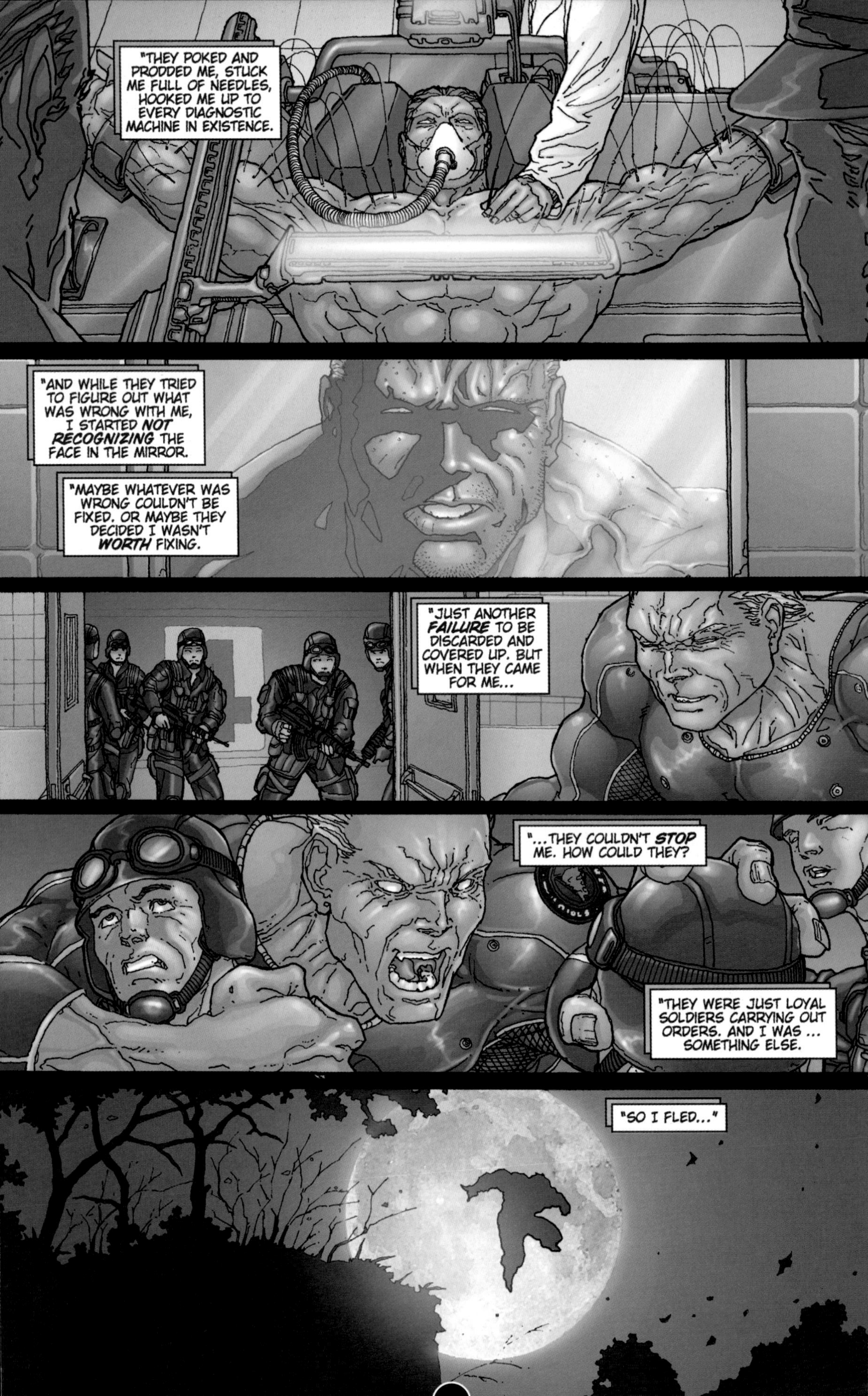
"THEY POKED AND PRODDED ME, STUCK ME FULL OF NEEDLES, HOOKED ME UP TO EVERY DIAGNOSTIC MACHINE IN EXISTENCE.
"AND WHILE THEY TRIED TO FIGURE OUT WHAT WAS WRONG WITH ME, I STARTED NOT RECOGNIZING THE FACE IN THE MIRROR.
"MAYBE WHATEVER WAS WRONG COULDN'T BE FIXED. OR MAYBE THEY DECIDED I WASN'T WORTH FIXING.
"JUST ANOTHER FAILURE TO BE DISCARDED AND COVERED UP. BUT WHEN THEY CAME FOR ME...
"...THEY COULDN'T STOP ME. HOW COULD THEY?
"THEY WERE JUST LOYAL SOLDIERS CARRYING OUT ORDERS. AND I WAS ... SOMETHING ELSE.
"SO I FLED..."

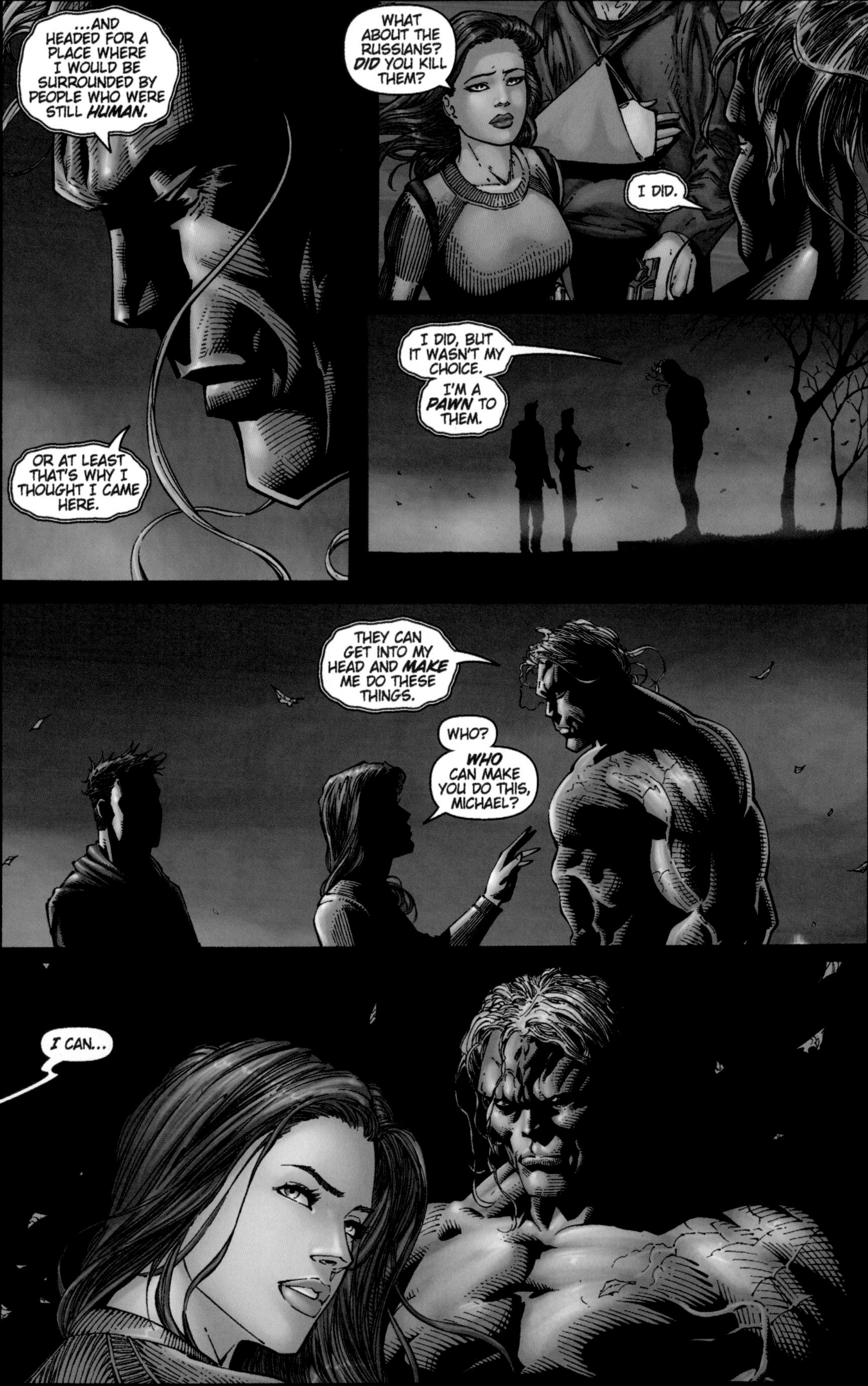
...AND HEADED FOR A PLACE WHERE I WOULD BE SURROUNDED BY PEOPLE WHO WERE STILL HUMAN.
OR AT LEAST THAT'S WHY I THOUGHT I CAME HERE.
WHAT ABOUT THE RUSSIANS? DID YOU KILL THEM?
I DID.
I DID, BUT IT WASN'T MY CHOICE.
I'M A PAWN TO THEM.
THEY CAN GET INTO MY HEAD AND MAKE ME DO THESE THINGS.
WHO? WHO CAN MAKE YOU DO THIS, MICHAEL?
I CAN...

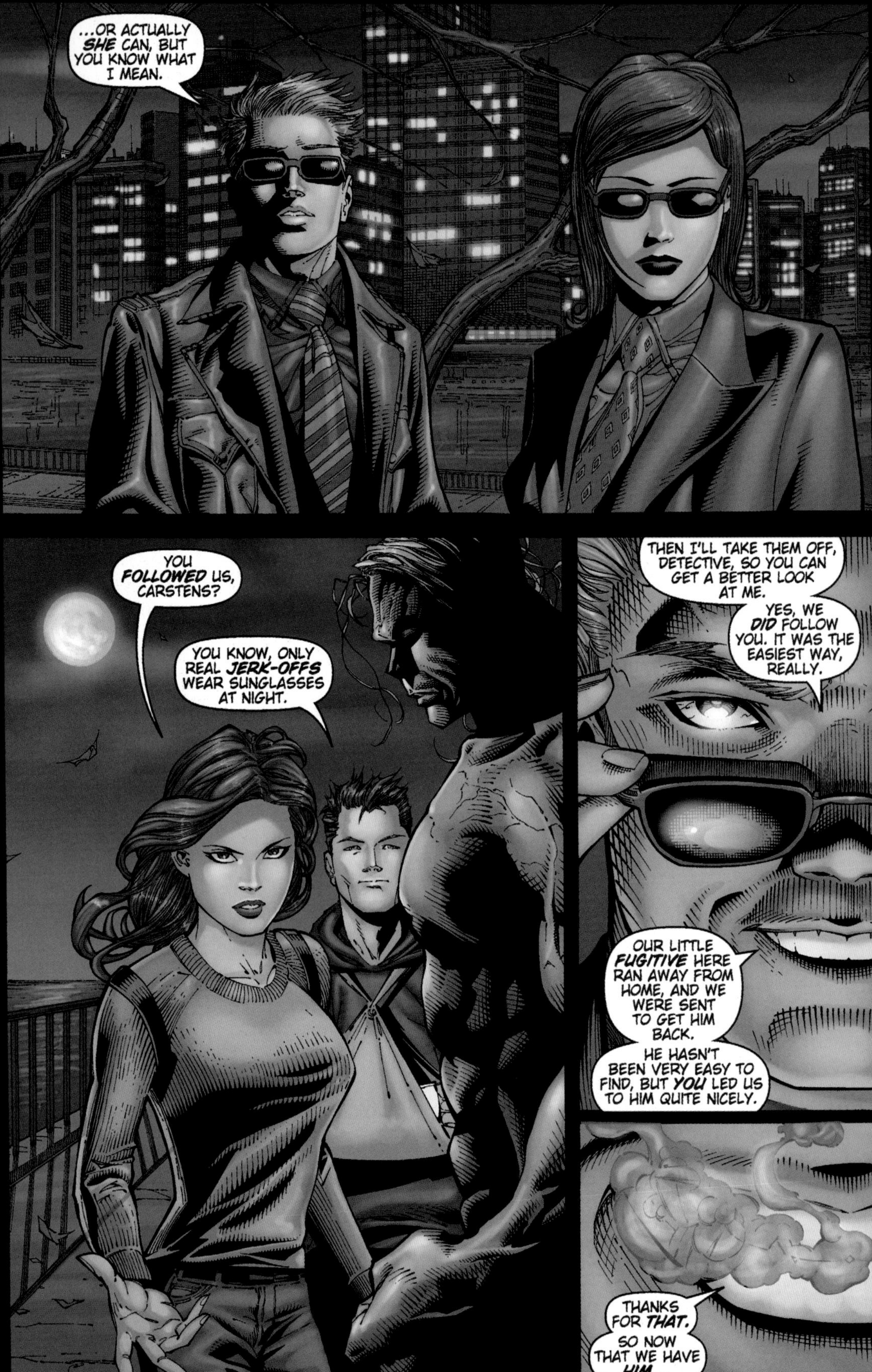
...OR ACTUALLY SHE CAN, BUT YOU KNOW WHAT I MEAN.
YOU FOLLOWED US, CARSTENS?
YOU KNOW, ONLY REAL JERK-OFFS WEAR SUNGLASSES AT NIGHT.
THEN I'LL TAKE THEM OFF, DETECTIVE, SO YOU CAN GET A BETTER LOOK AT ME.
YES, WE DID FOLLOW YOU. IT WAS THE EASIEST WAY, REALLY.
OUR LITTLE FUGITIVE HERE RAN AWAY FROM HOME, AND WE WERE SENT TO GET HIM BACK.
HE HASN'T BEEN VERY EASY TO FIND, BUT YOU LED US TO HIM QUITE NICELY.
THANKS FOR THAT.
SO NOW THAT WE HAVE HIM...

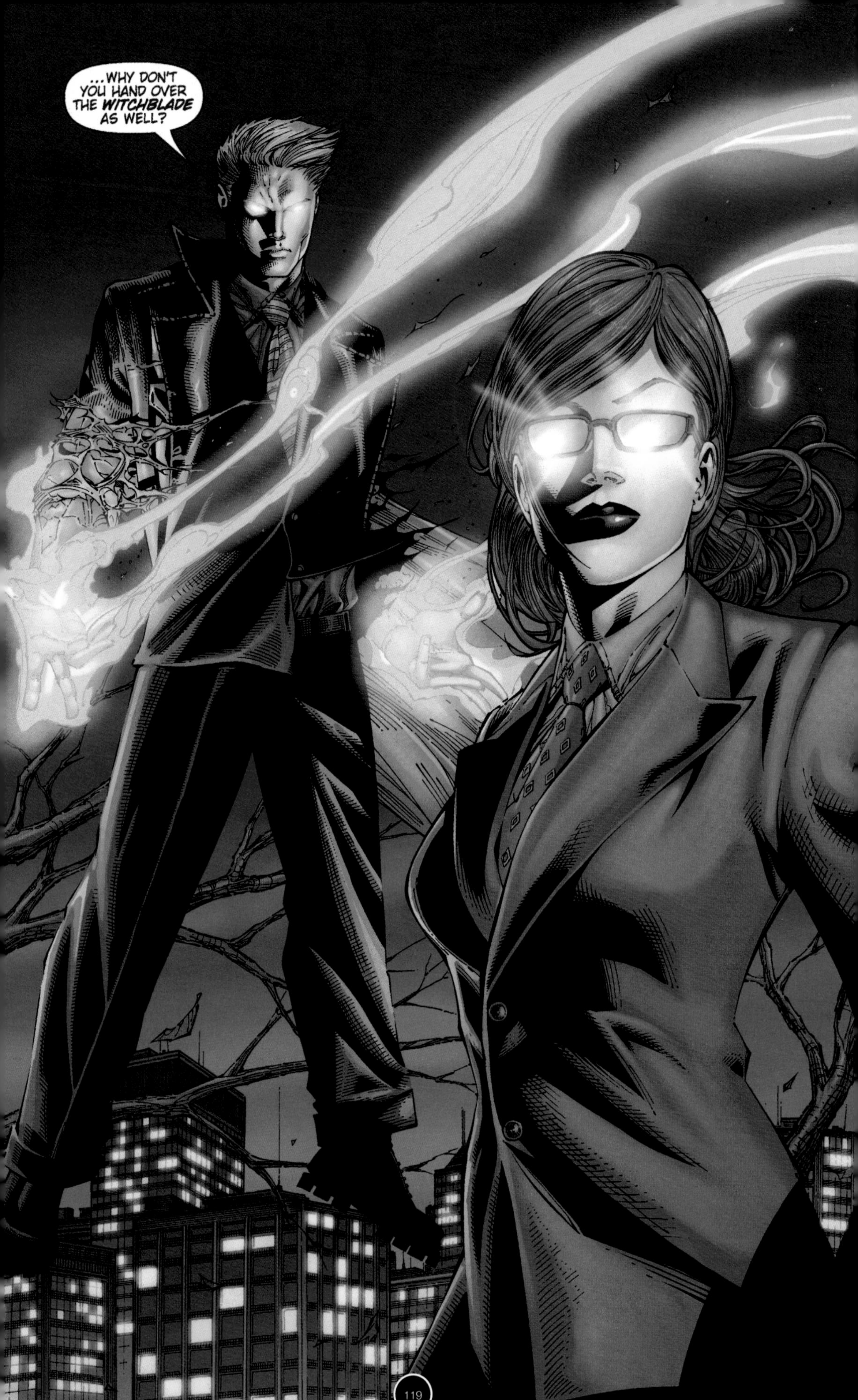
...WHY DON'T YOU HAND OVER THE *WITCHBLADE* AS WELL?

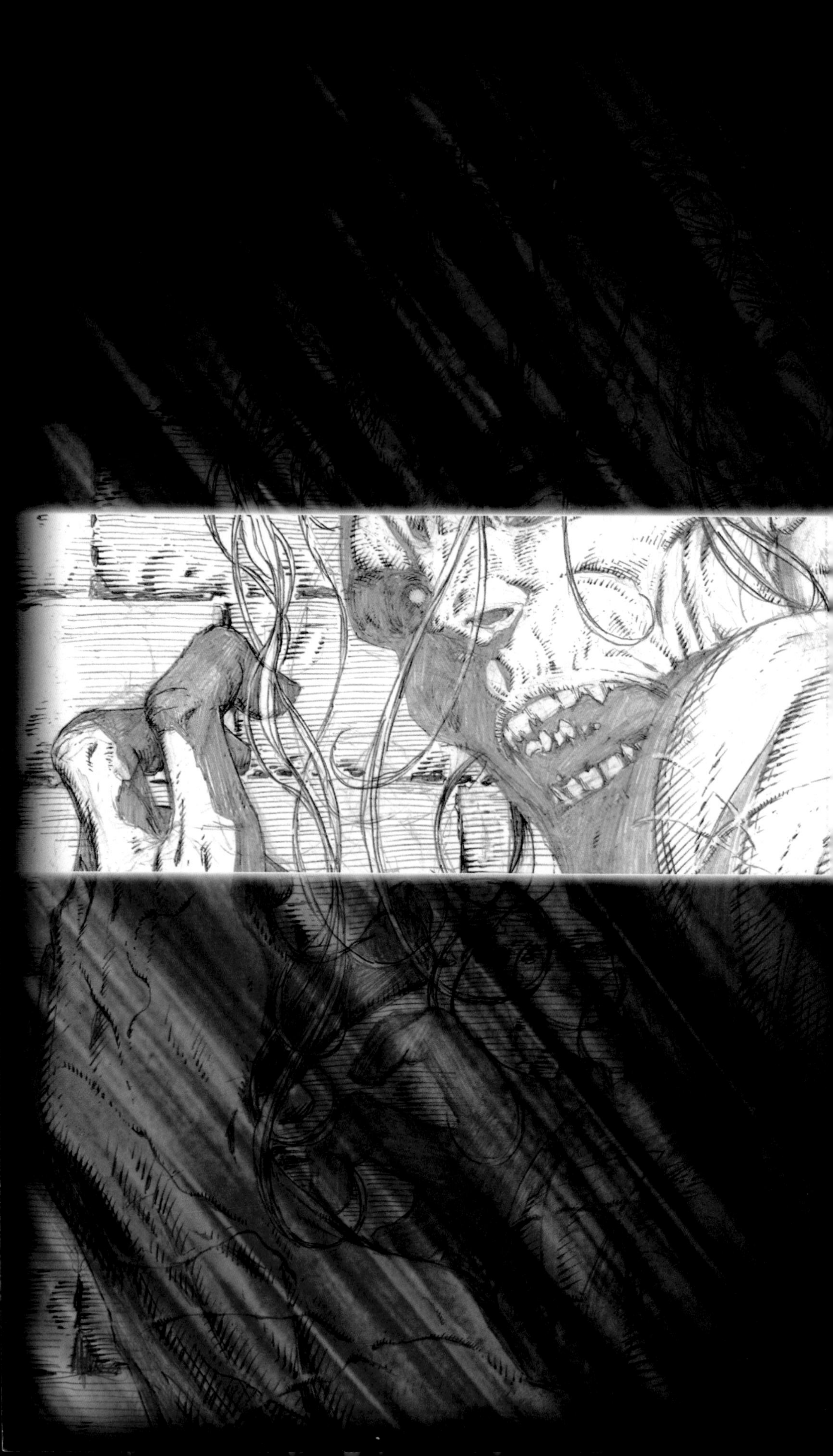

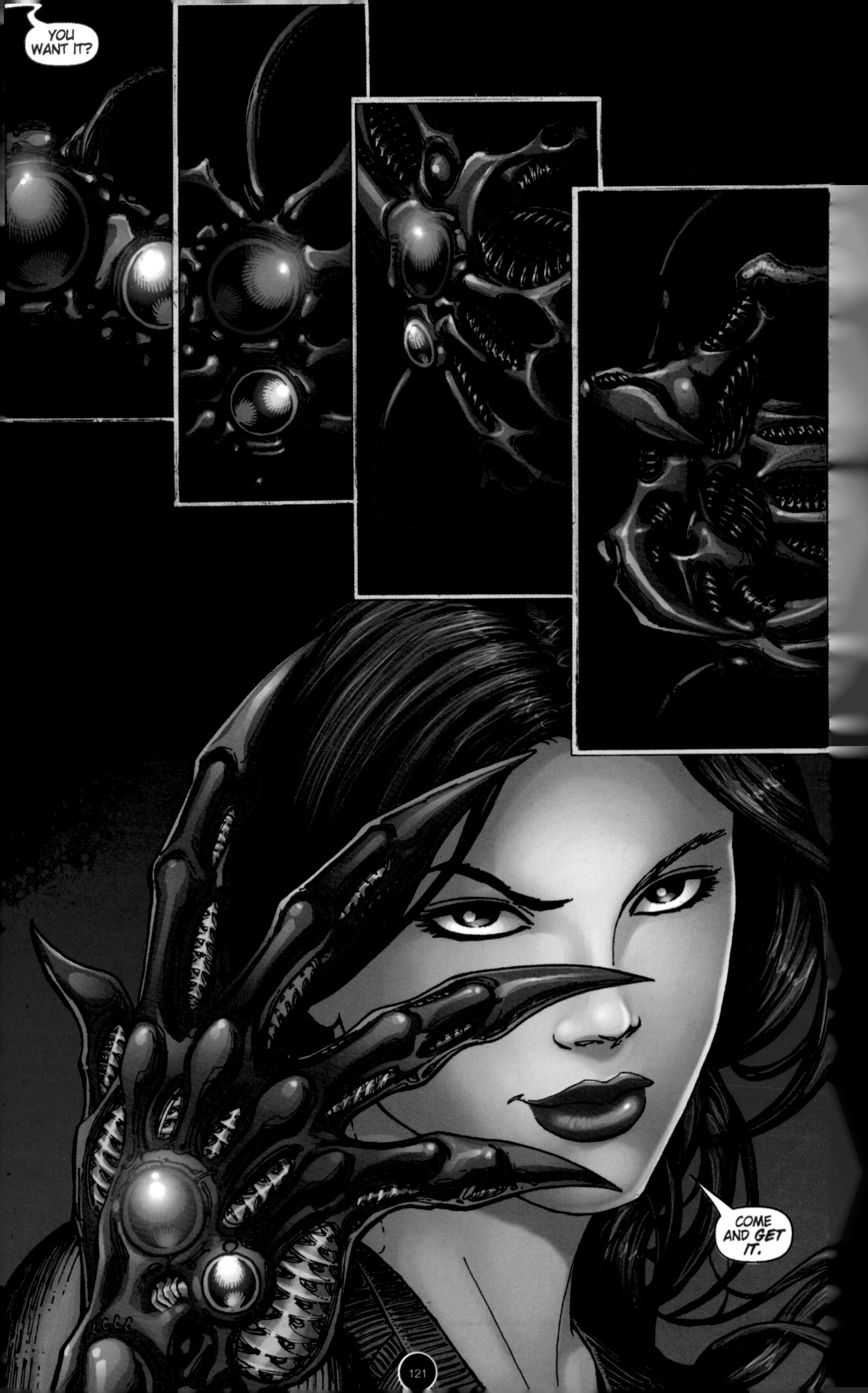
YOU WANT IT?
COME AND GET IT.

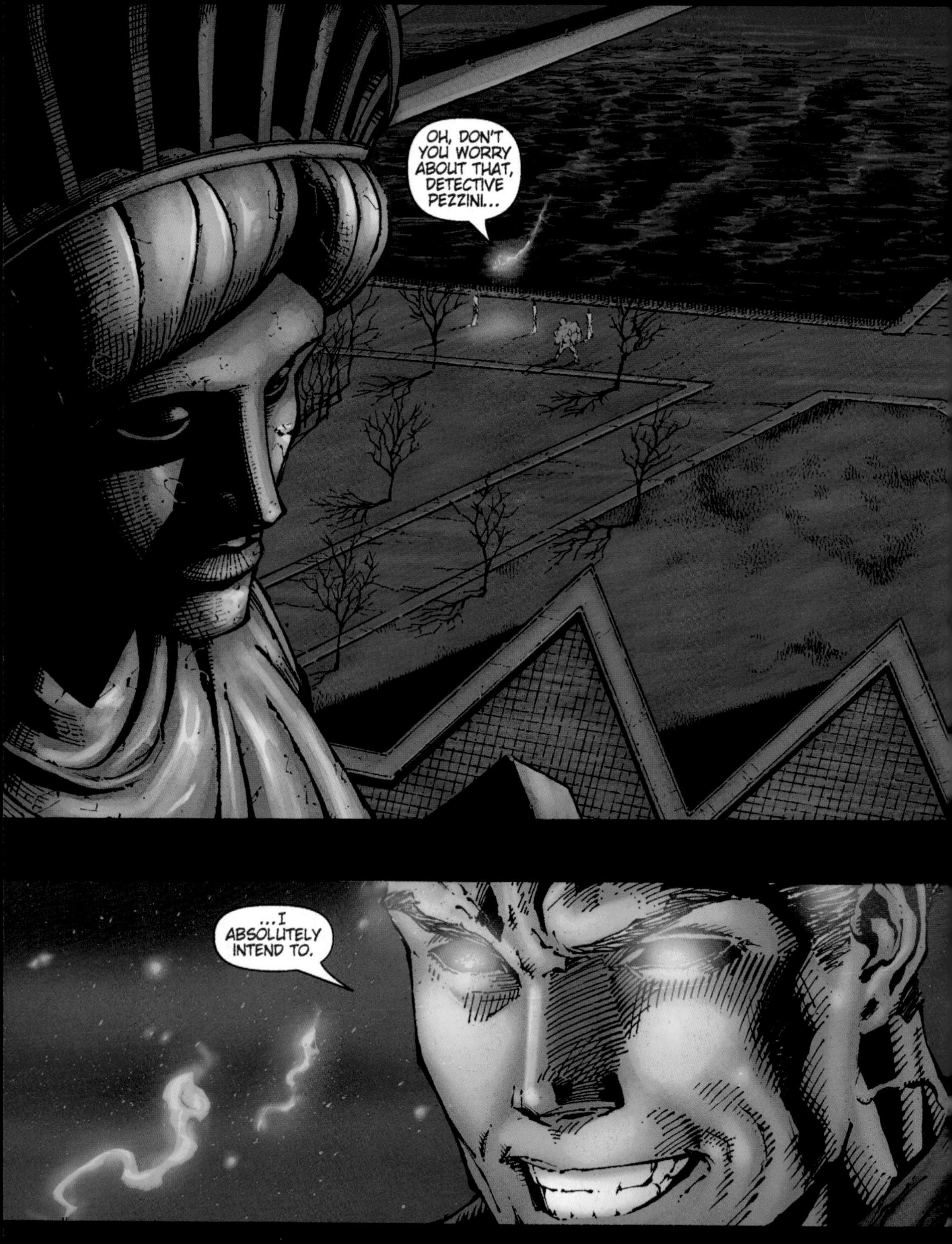
OH, DON'T YOU WORRY ABOUT THAT, DETECTIVE PEZZINI...
...I ABSOLUTELY INTEND TO.

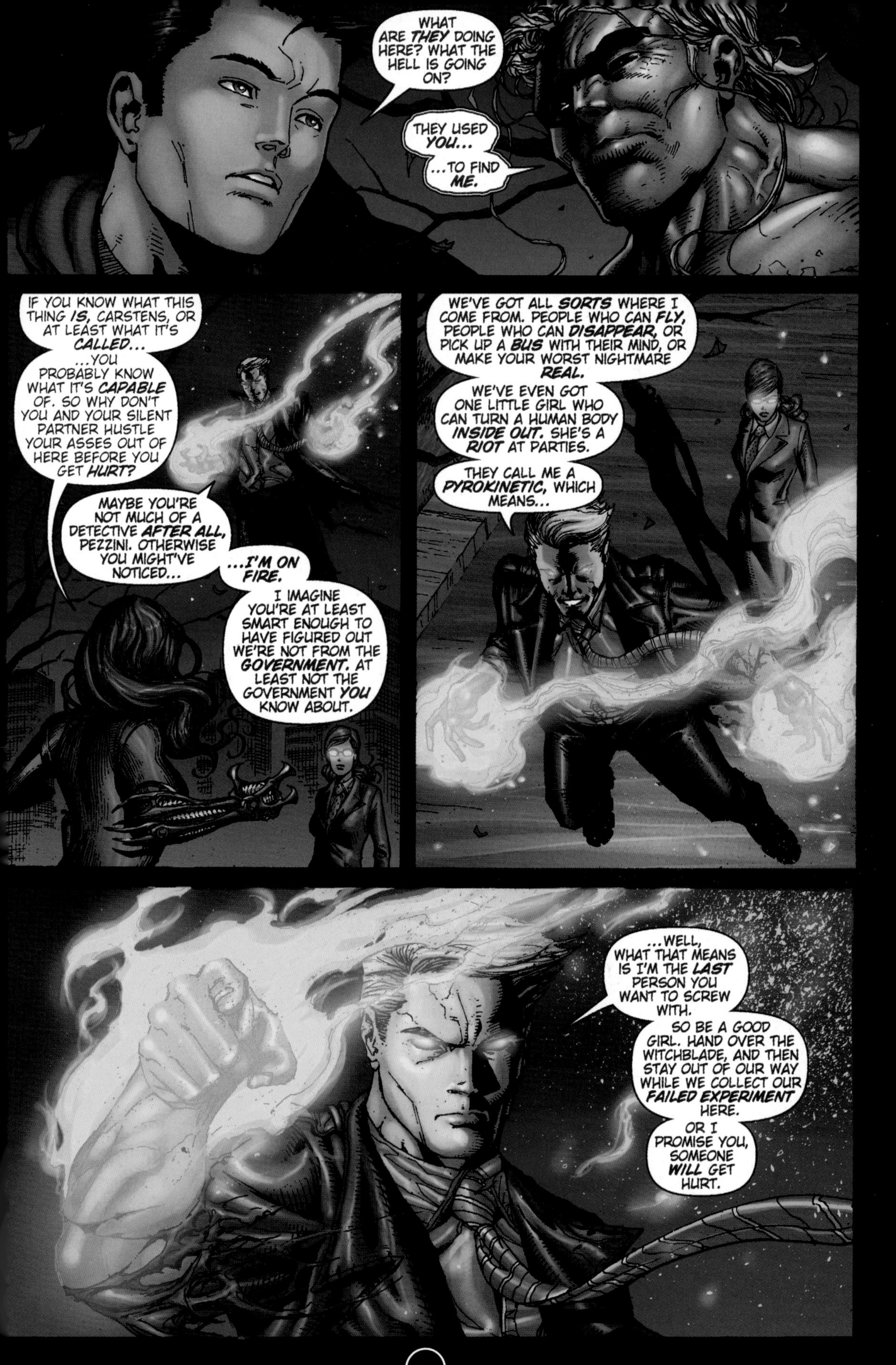
WHAT ARE THEY DOING HERE? WHAT THE HELL IS GOING ON?
THEY USED YOU...
...TO FIND ME.
IF YOU KNOW WHAT THIS THING IS, CARSTENS, OR AT LEAST WHAT IT'S CALLED...
...YOU PROBABLY KNOW WHAT IT'S CAPABLE OF. SO WHY DON'T YOU AND YOUR SILENT PARTNER HUSTLE YOUR ASSES OUT OF HERE BEFORE YOU GET HURT?
MAYBE YOU'RE NOT MUCH OF A DETECTIVE AFTER ALL, PEZZINI. OTHERWISE YOU MIGHT'VE NOTICED...
...I'M ON FIRE.
I IMAGINE YOU'RE AT LEAST SMART ENOUGH TO HAVE FIGURED OUT WE'RE NOT FROM THE GOVERNMENT. AT LEAST NOT THE GOVERNMENT YOU KNOW ABOUT.
WE'VE GOT ALL SORTS WHERE I COME FROM. PEOPLE WHO CAN FLY, PEOPLE WHO CAN DISAPPEAR, OR PICK UP A BUS WITH THEIR MIND, OR MAKE YOUR WORST NIGHTMARE REAL.
WE'VE EVEN GOT ONE LITTLE GIRL WHO CAN TURN A HUMAN BODY INSIDE OUT. SHE'S A RIOT AT PARTIES.
THEY CALL ME A PYROKINETIC, WHICH MEANS...
...WELL, WHAT THAT MEANS IS I'M THE LAST PERSON YOU WANT TO SCREW WITH.
SO BE A GOOD GIRL. HAND OVER THE WITCHBLADE, AND THEN STAY OUT OF OUR WAY WHILE WE COLLECT OUR FAILED EXPERIMENT HERE.
OR I PROMISE YOU, SOMEONE WILL GET HURT.

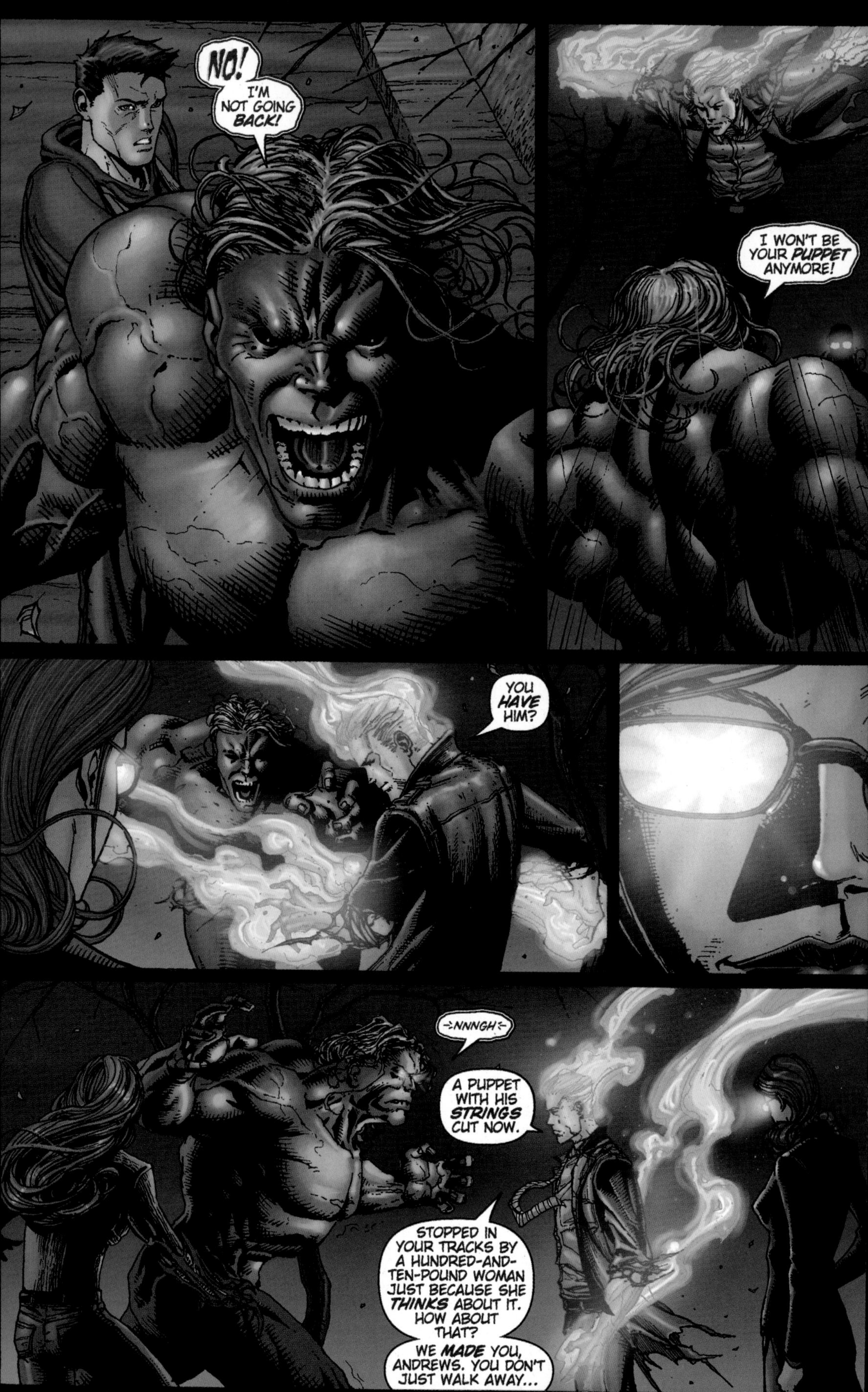
NO! I'M NOT GOING BACK!
I WON'T BE YOUR PUPPET ANYMORE!
YOU HAVE HIM?
-NNNGH-
A PUPPET WITH HIS STRINGS CUT NOW.
STOPPED IN YOUR TRACKS BY A HUNDRED-AND-TEN-POUND WOMAN JUST BECAUSE SHE THINKS ABOUT IT. HOW ABOUT THAT?
WE MADE YOU, ANDREWS. YOU DON'T JUST WALK AWAY...

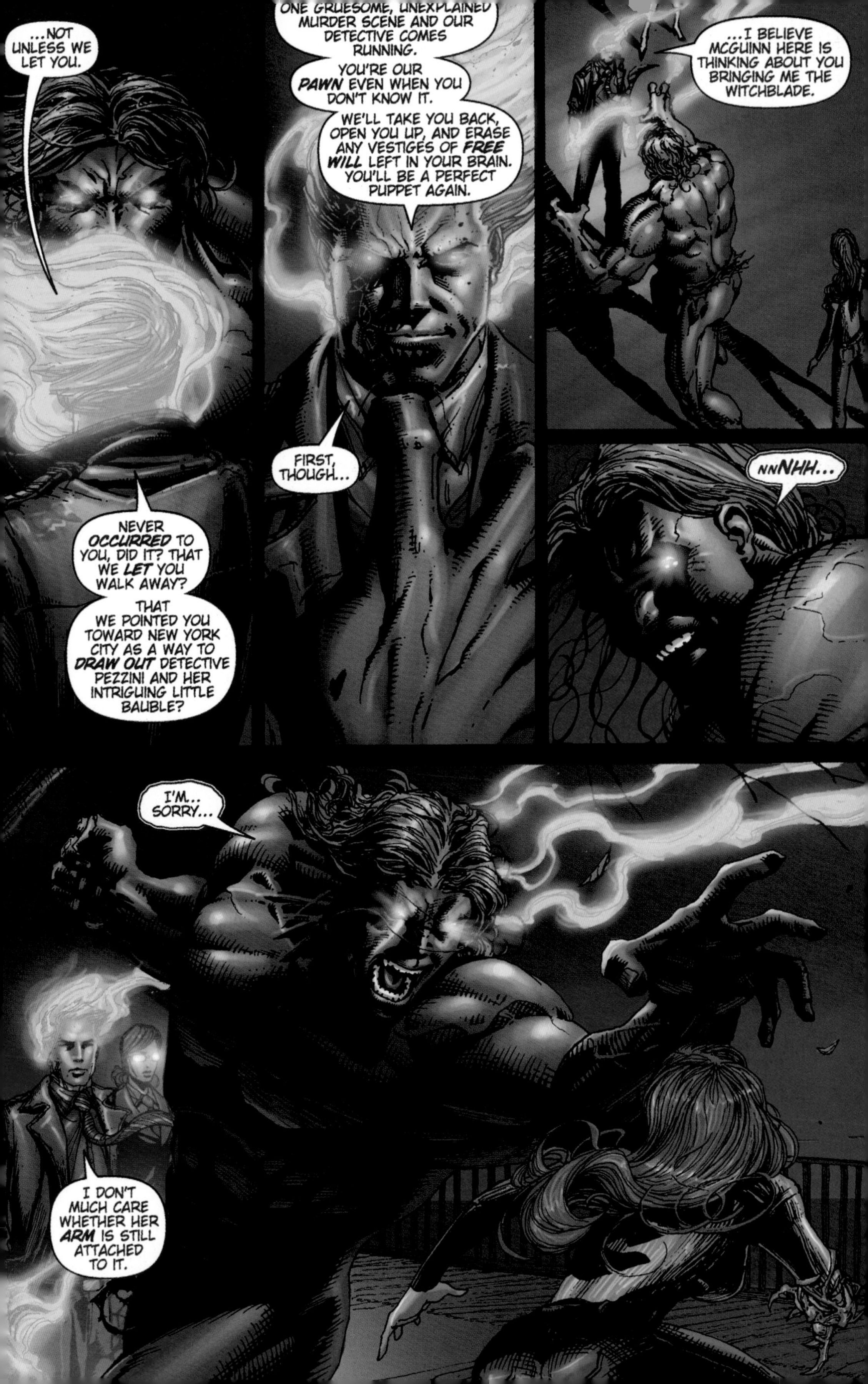
...NOT UNLESS WE LET YOU.
ONE GRUESOME, UNEXPLAINED MURDER SCENE AND OUR DETECTIVE COMES RUNNING.
YOU'RE OUR PAWN EVEN WHEN YOU DON'T KNOW IT.
WE'LL TAKE YOU BACK, OPEN YOU UP, AND ERASE ANY VESTIGES OF FREE WILL LEFT IN YOUR BRAIN. YOU'LL BE A PERFECT PUPPET AGAIN.
...I BELIEVE MCGUINN HERE IS THINKING ABOUT YOU BRINGING ME THE WITCHBLADE.
NEVER OCCURRED TO YOU, DID IT? THAT WE LET YOU WALK AWAY?
THAT WE POINTED YOU TOWARD NEW YORK CITY AS A WAY TO DRAW OUT DETECTIVE PEZZINI AND HER INTRIGUING LITTLE BAUBLE?
FIRST, THOUGH...
NNNHH...
I'M... SORRY...
I DON'T MUCH CARE WHETHER HER ARM IS STILL ATTACHED TO IT.

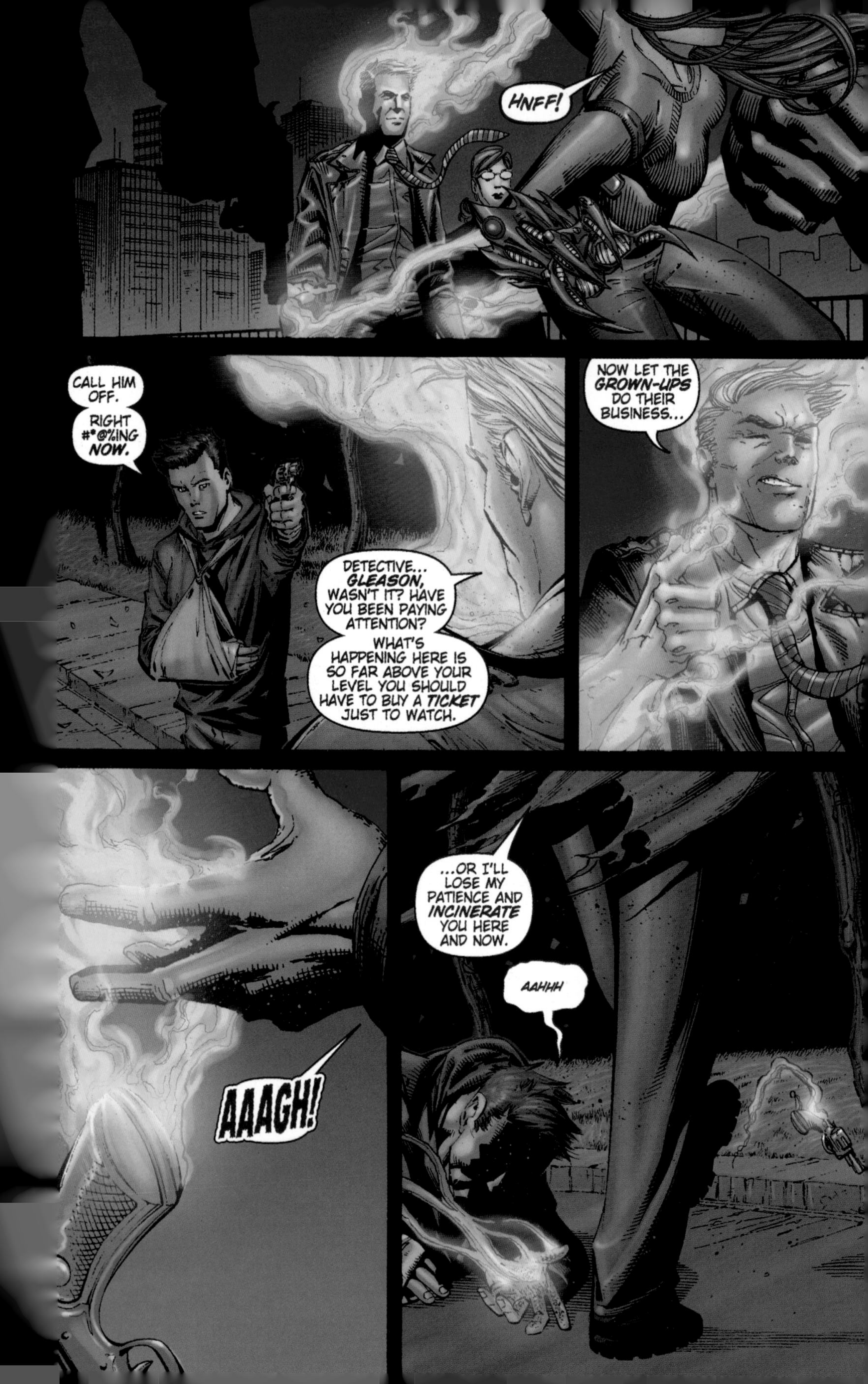
HNFF!
CALL HIM OFF.
RIGHT #*@%ING NOW.
DETECTIVE... GLEASON, WASN'T IT? HAVE YOU BEEN PAYING ATTENTION?
WHAT'S HAPPENING HERE IS SO FAR ABOVE YOUR LEVEL YOU SHOULD HAVE TO BUY A TICKET JUST TO WATCH.
NOW LET THE GROWN-UPS DO THEIR BUSINESS...
AAAGH!
...OR I'LL LOSE MY PATIENCE AND INCINERATE YOU HERE AND NOW.
AAHHH

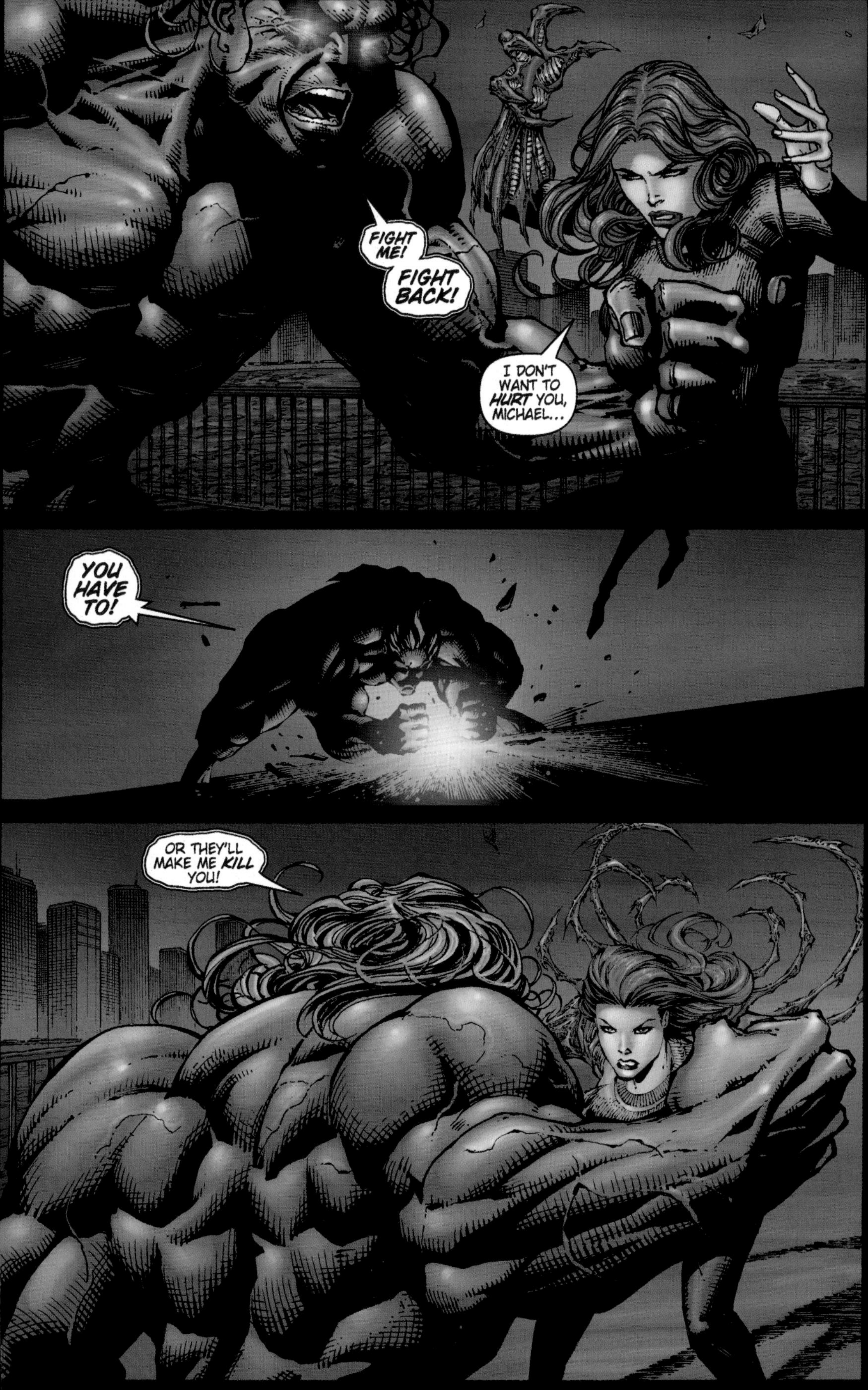
FIGHT ME!
FIGHT BACK!
I DON'T WANT TO HURT YOU, MICHAEL...
YOU HAVE TO!
OR THEY'LL MAKE ME KILL YOU!

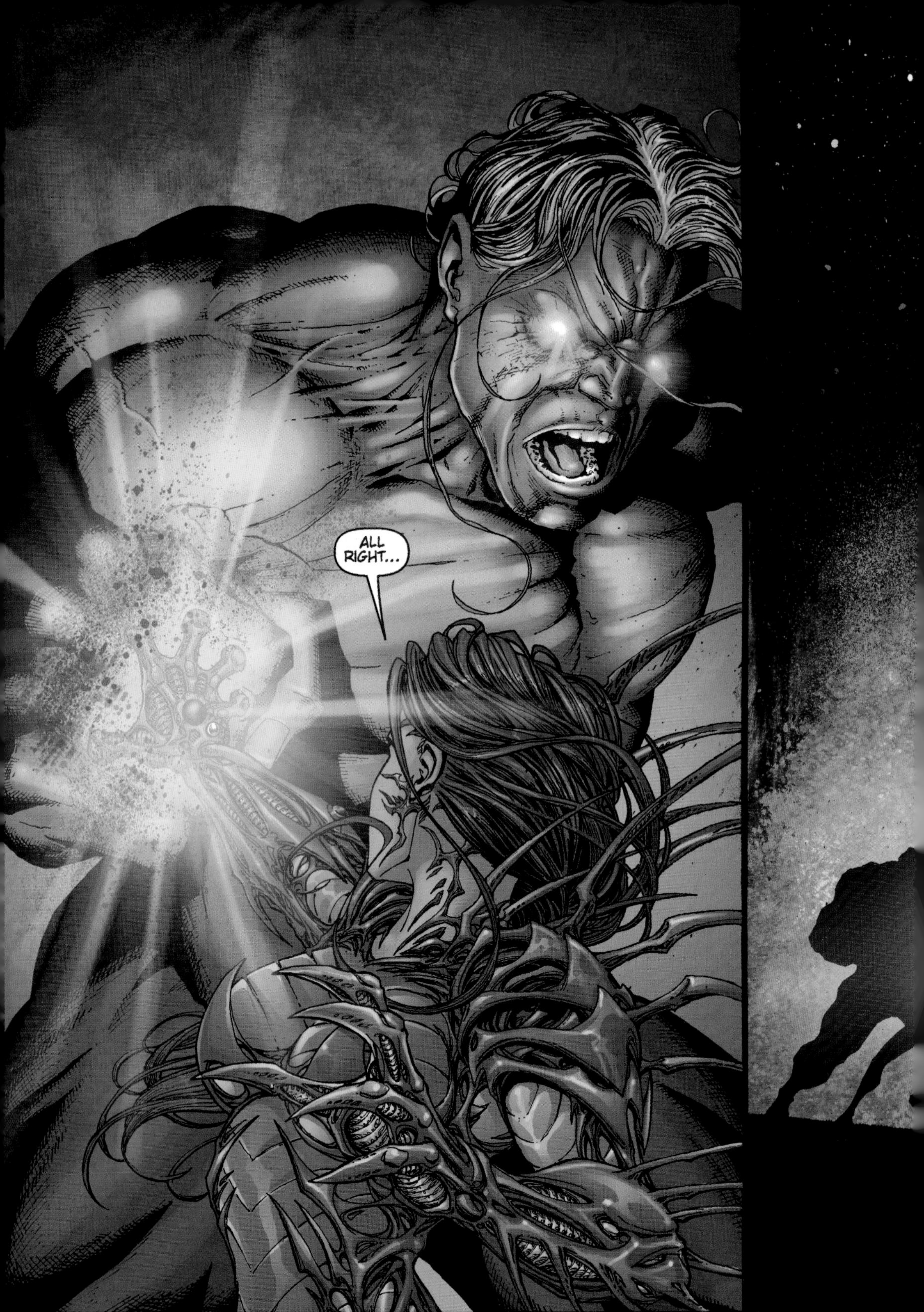
ALL RIGHT...

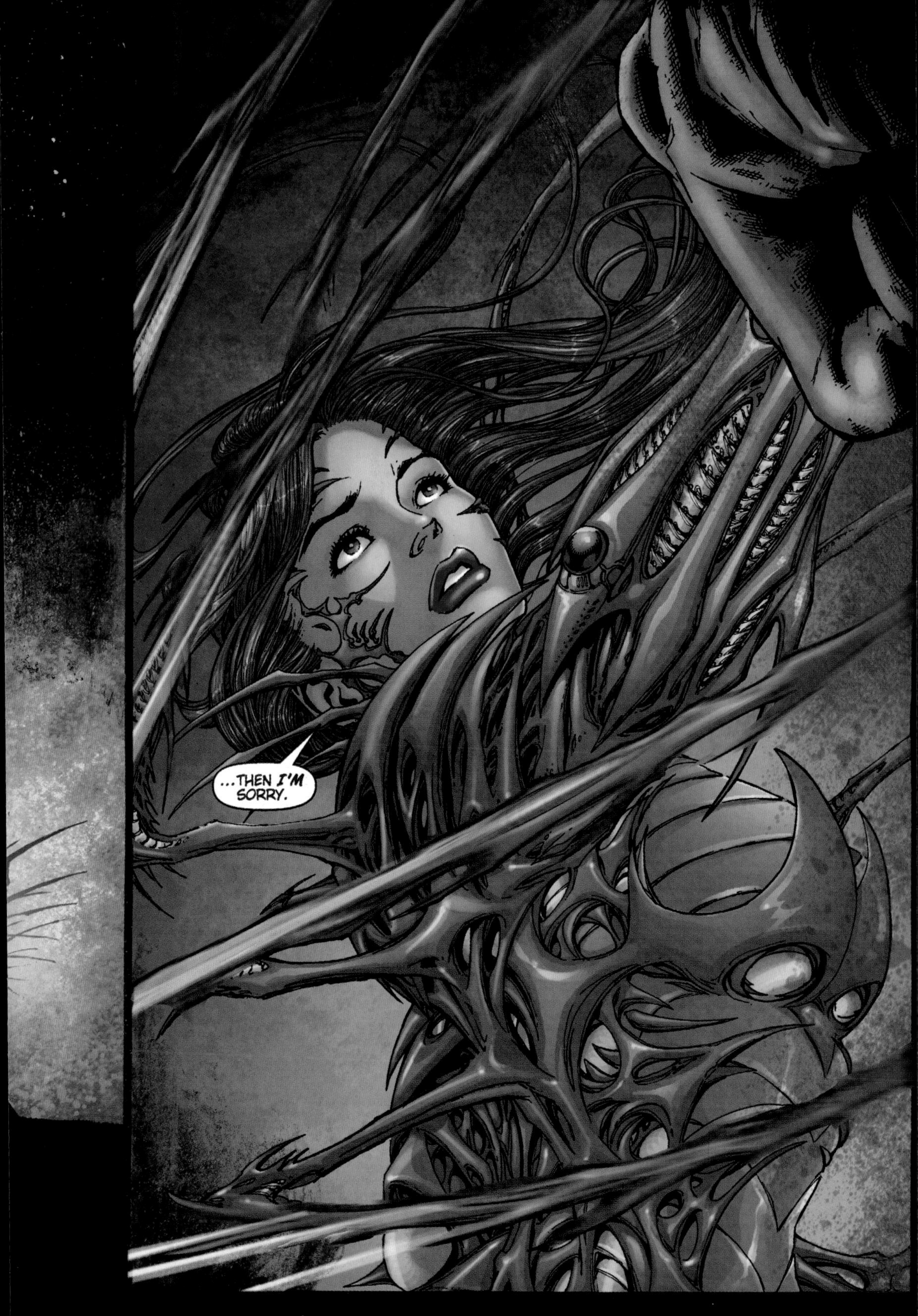
...THEN I'M SORRY.

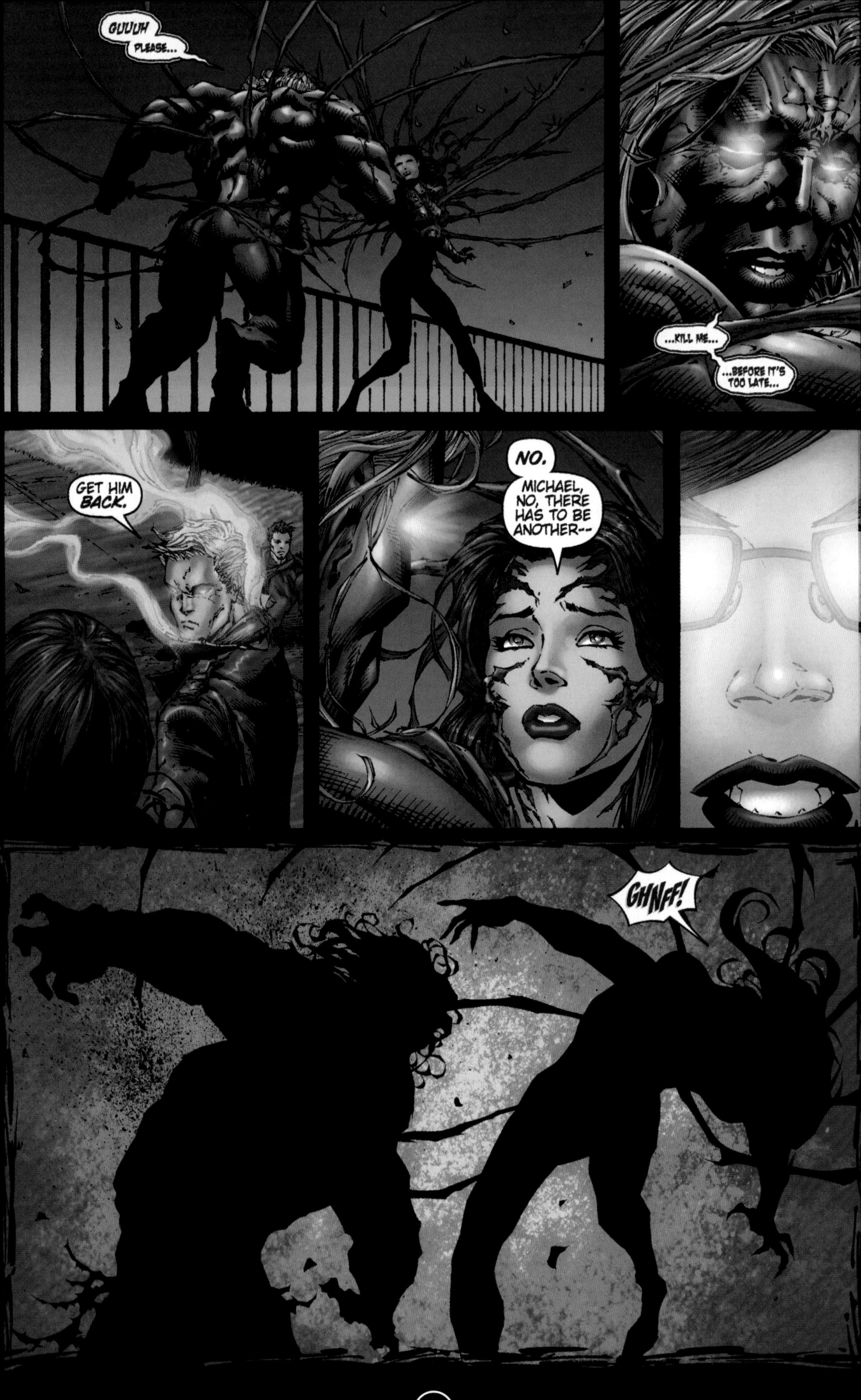
GUUUH
PLEASE...
...KILL ME...
...BEFORE IT'S TOO LATE...
GET HIM BACK.
NO.
MICHAEL, NO, THERE HAS TO BE ANOTHER--
GHNFF!

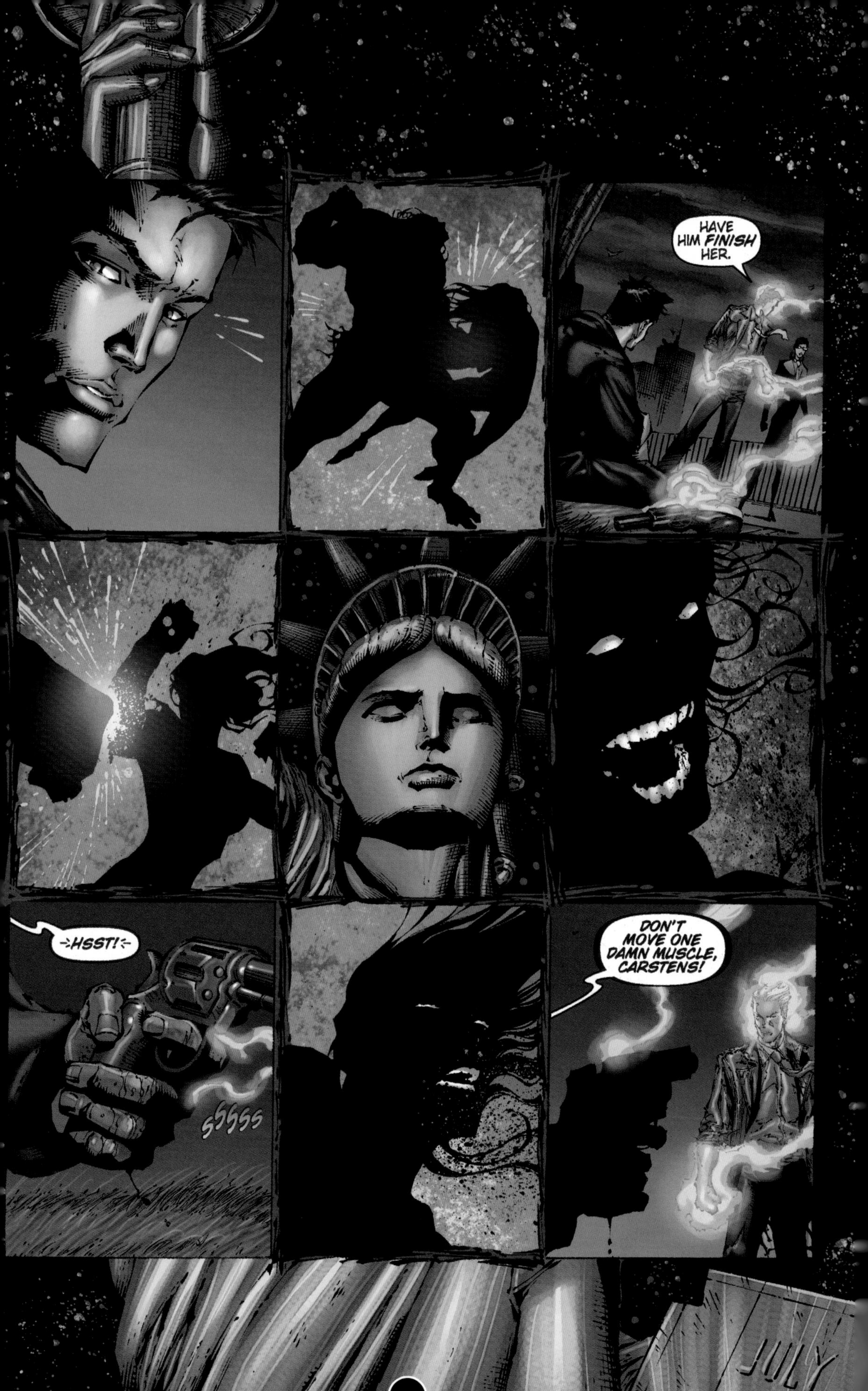
HAVE HIM FINISH HER.
-HSST!-
SSSSS
DON'T MOVE ONE DAMN MUSCLE, CARSTENS!
JULY

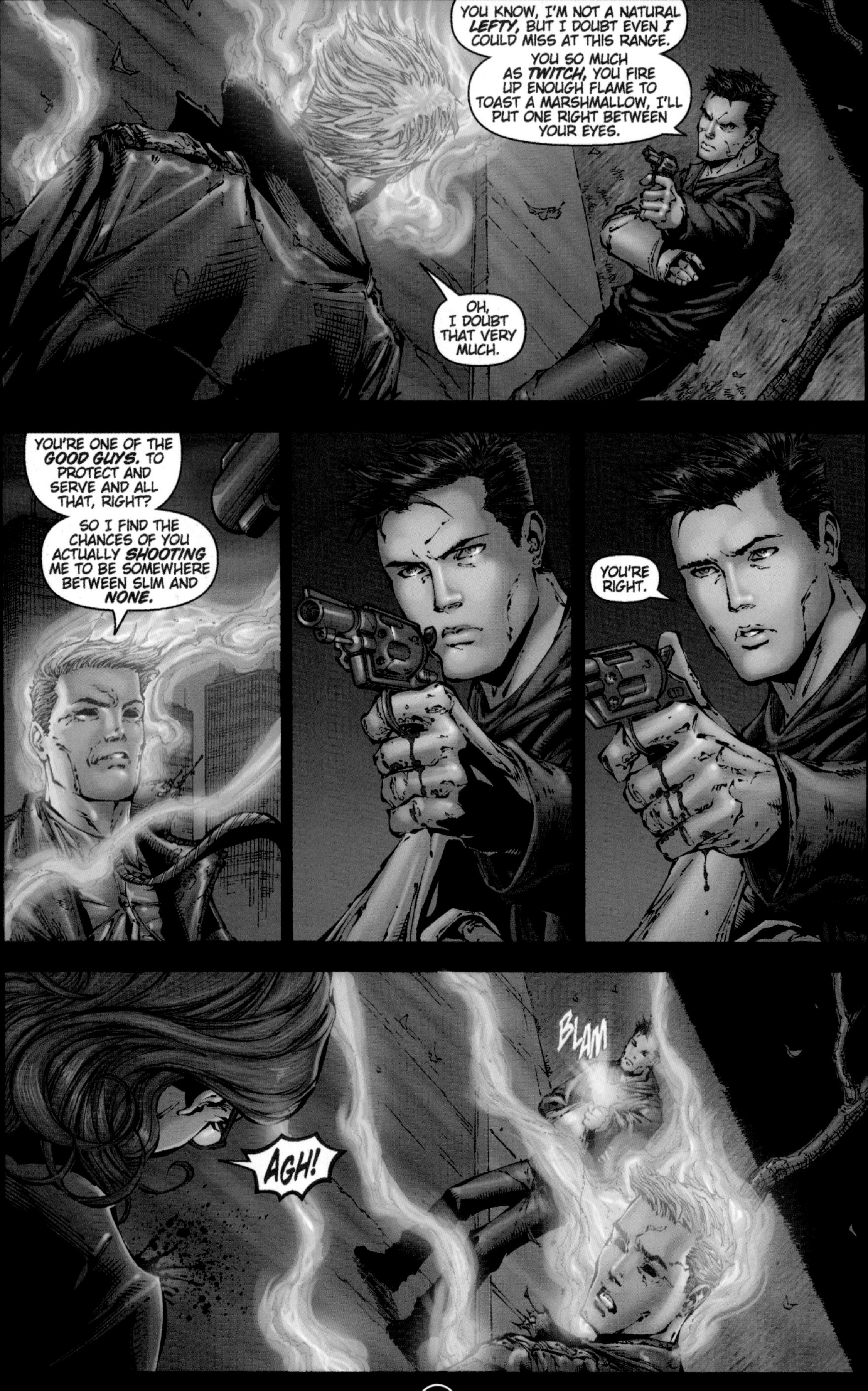
YOU KNOW, I'M NOT A NATURAL LEFTY, BUT I DOUBT EVEN I COULD MISS AT THIS RANGE.
YOU SO MUCH AS TWITCH, YOU FIRE UP ENOUGH FLAME TO TOAST A MARSHMALLOW, I'LL PUT ONE RIGHT BETWEEN YOUR EYES.
OH, I DOUBT THAT VERY MUCH.
YOU'RE ONE OF THE GOOD GUYS. TO PROTECT AND SERVE AND ALL THAT, RIGHT?
SO I FIND THE CHANCES OF YOU ACTUALLY SHOOTING ME TO BE SOMEWHERE BETWEEN SLIM AND NONE.
YOU'RE RIGHT.
BLAM
AGH!

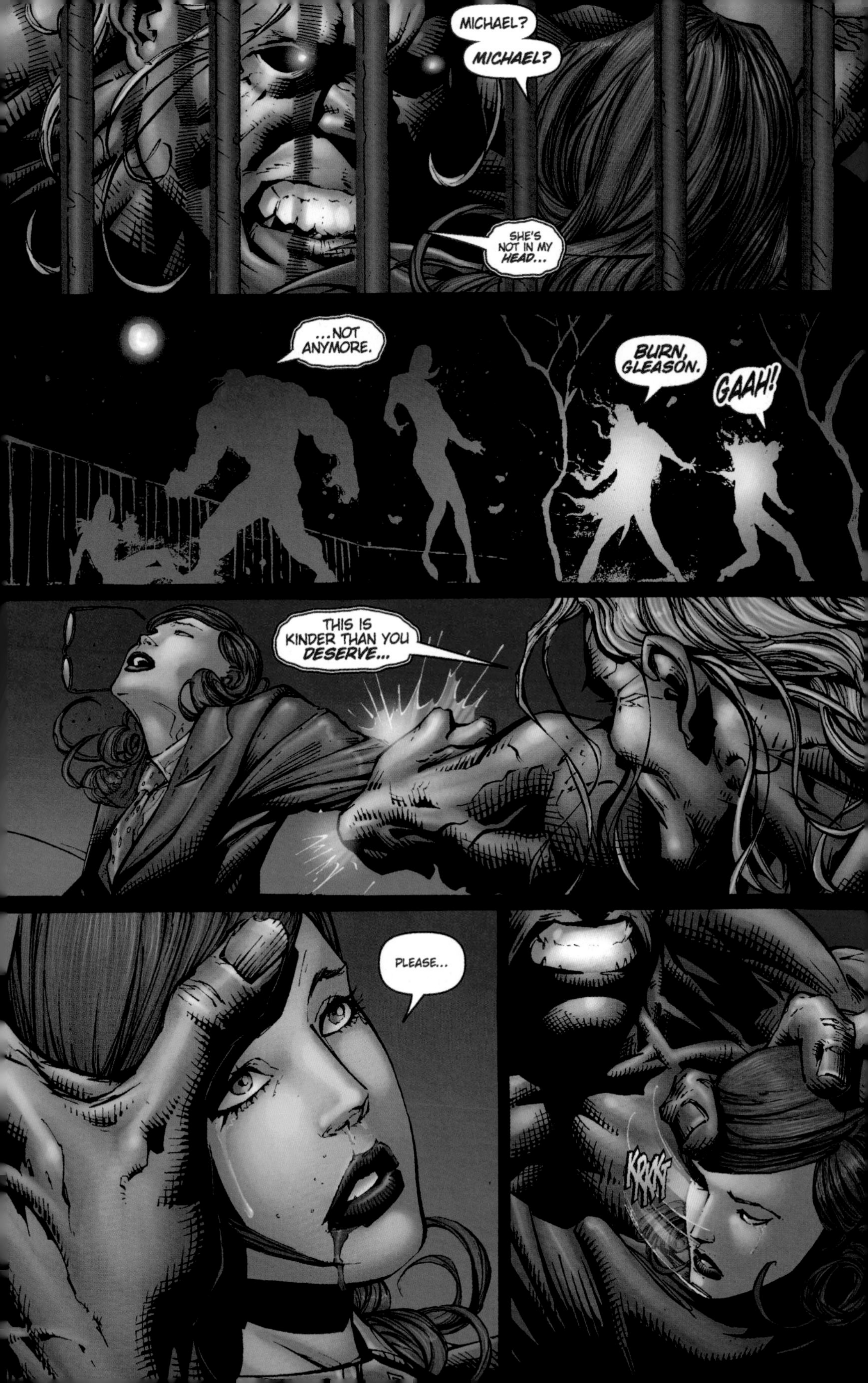

MICHAEL?
MICHAEL?
SHE'S NOT IN MY HEAD...
...NOT ANYMORE.
BURN, GLEASON.
GAAH!
THIS IS KINDER THAN YOU DESERVE...
PLEASE...
KRNNGT

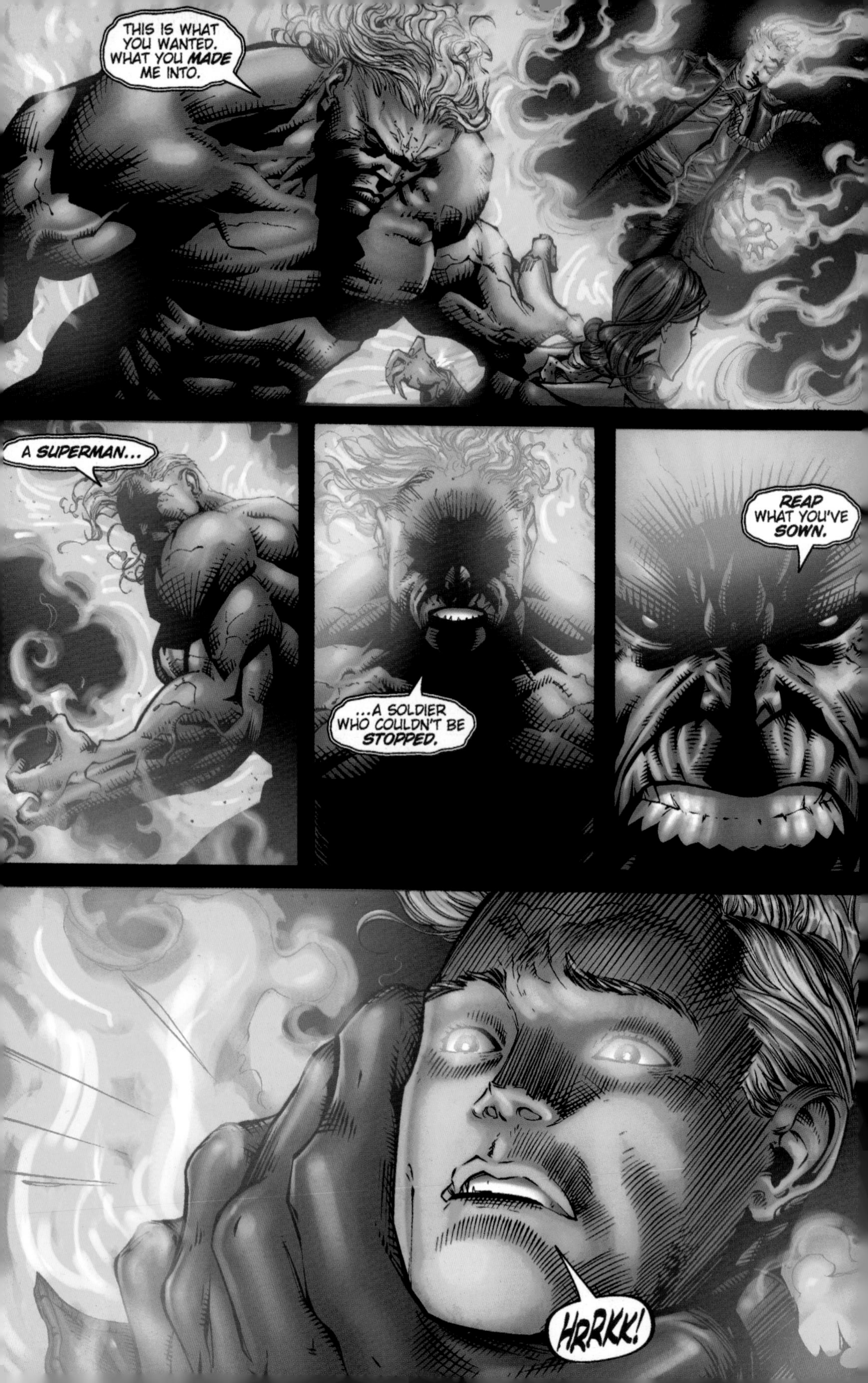
THIS IS WHAT YOU WANTED. WHAT YOU MADE ME INTO.
A SUPERMAN...
...A SOLDIER WHO COULDN'T BE STOPPED.
REAP WHAT YOU'VE SOWN.
HRRKK!

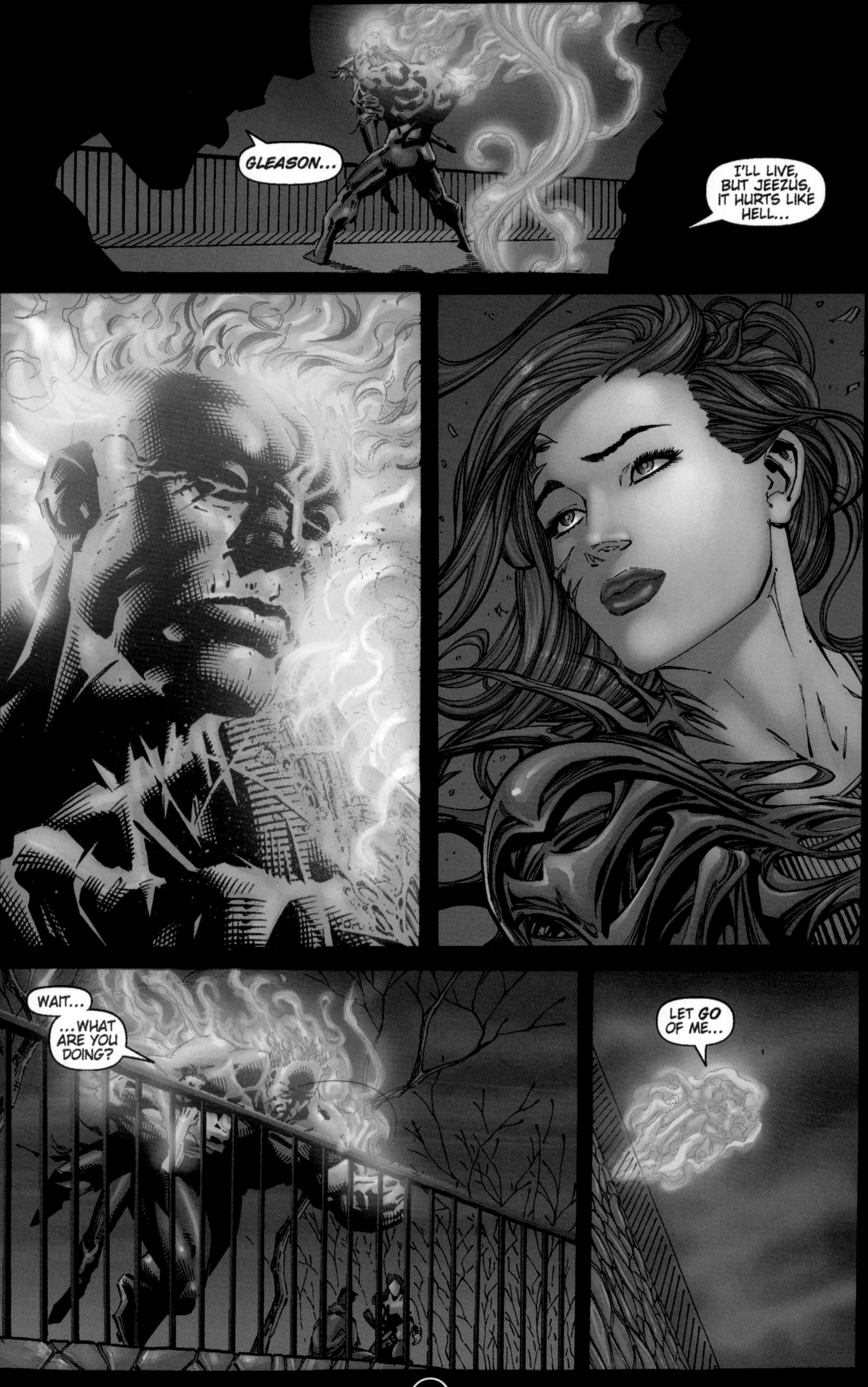
GLEASON...
I'LL LIVE, BUT JEEZUS, IT HURTS LIKE HELL...
WAIT...
...WHAT ARE YOU DOING?
LET GO OF ME...

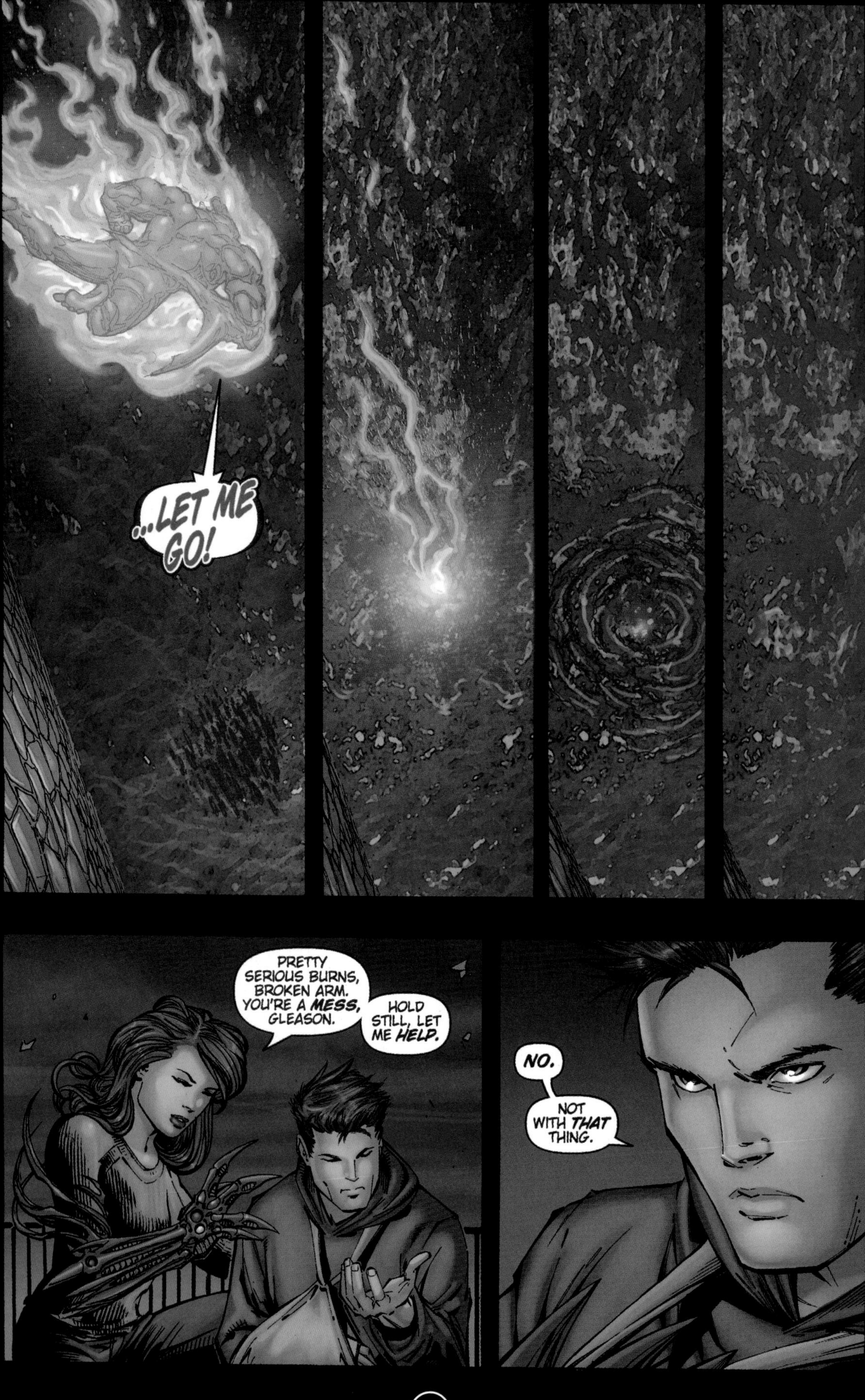
...LET ME GO!
PRETTY SERIOUS BURNS, BROKEN ARM. YOU'RE A **MESS,** GLEASON.
HOLD STILL, LET ME **HELP.**
NO.
NOT WITH **THAT** THING.

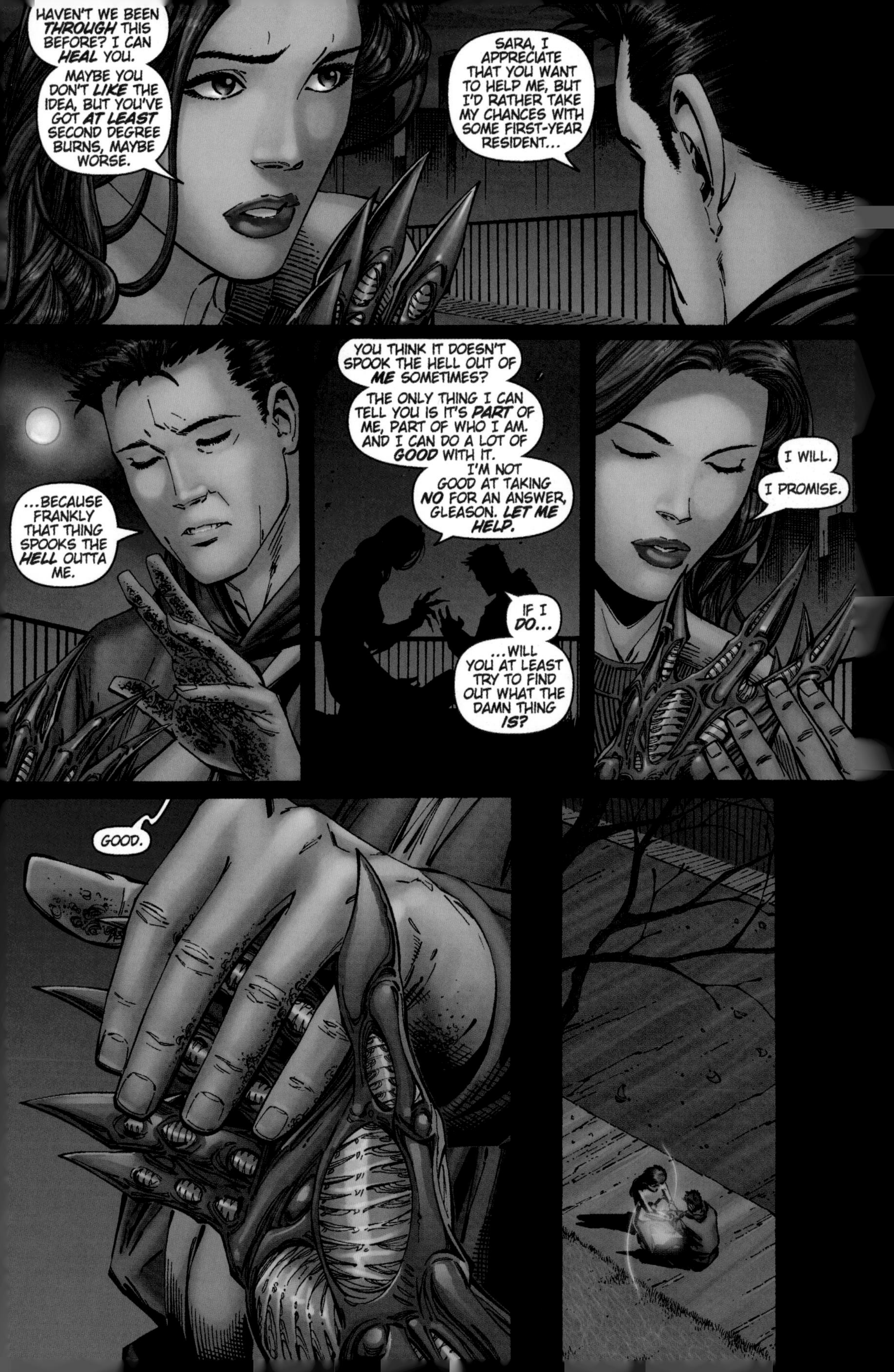
HAVEN'T WE BEEN THROUGH THIS BEFORE? I CAN HEAL YOU.
MAYBE YOU DON'T LIKE THE IDEA, BUT YOU'VE GOT AT LEAST SECOND DEGREE BURNS, MAYBE WORSE.
SARA, I APPRECIATE THAT YOU WANT TO HELP ME, BUT I'D RATHER TAKE MY CHANCES WITH SOME FIRST-YEAR RESIDENT...
...BECAUSE FRANKLY THAT THING SPOOKS THE HELL OUTTA ME.
YOU THINK IT DOESN'T SPOOK THE HELL OUT OF ME SOMETIMES?
THE ONLY THING I CAN TELL YOU IS IT'S PART OF ME, PART OF WHO I AM. AND I CAN DO A LOT OF GOOD WITH IT.
I'M NOT GOOD AT TAKING NO FOR AN ANSWER, GLEASON. LET ME HELP.
IF I DO...
...WILL YOU AT LEAST TRY TO FIND OUT WHAT THE DAMN THING IS?
I WILL.
I PROMISE.
GOOD.

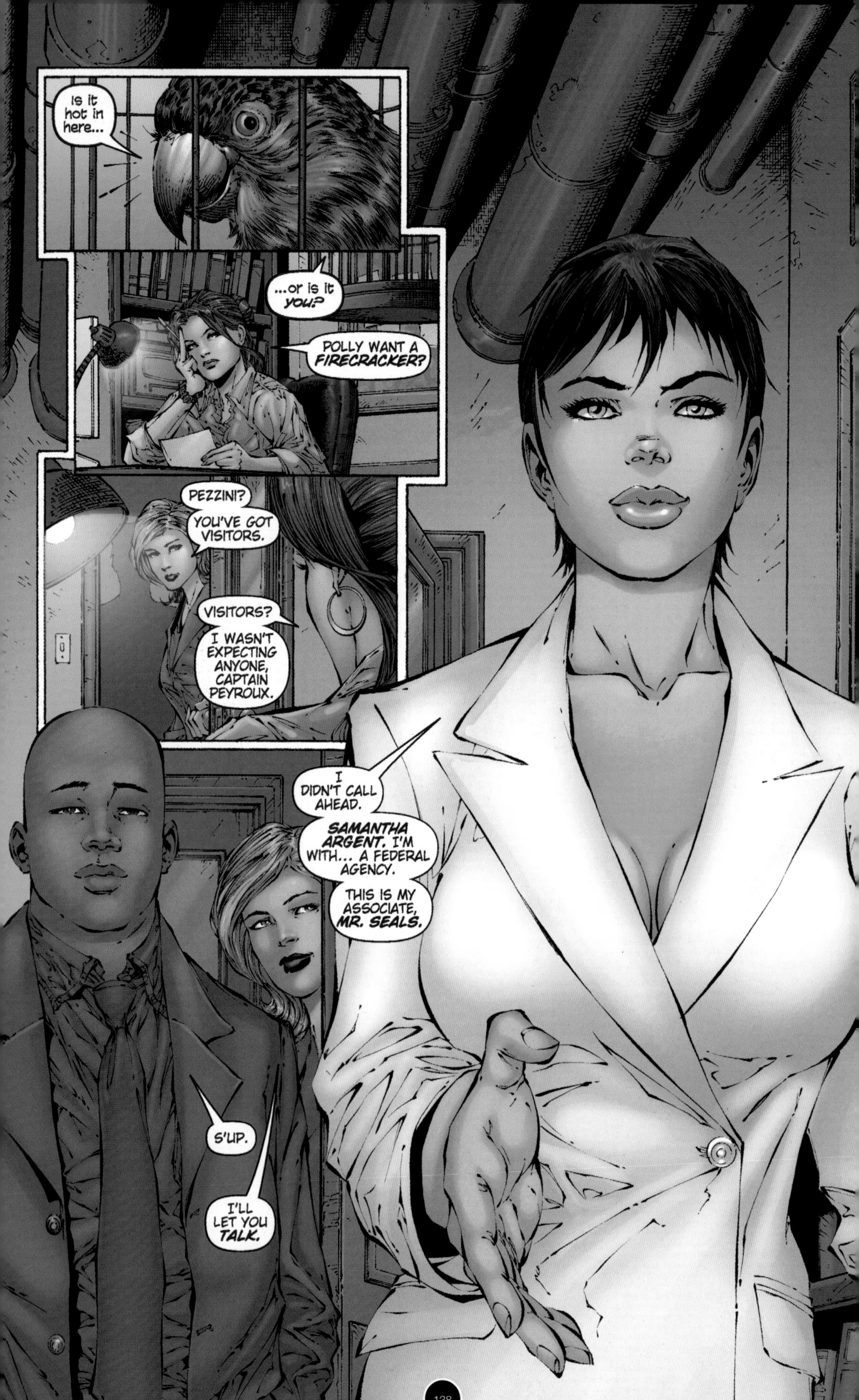
Is it hot in here...
...or is it you?
POLLY WANT A FIRECRACKER?
PEZZINI?
YOU'VE GOT VISITORS.
VISITORS?
I WASN'T EXPECTING ANYONE, CAPTAIN PEYROUX.
I DIDN'T CALL AHEAD.
SAMANTHA ARGENT. I'M WITH... A FEDERAL AGENCY.
THIS IS MY ASSOCIATE, MR. SEALS.
S'UP.
I'LL LET YOU TALK.

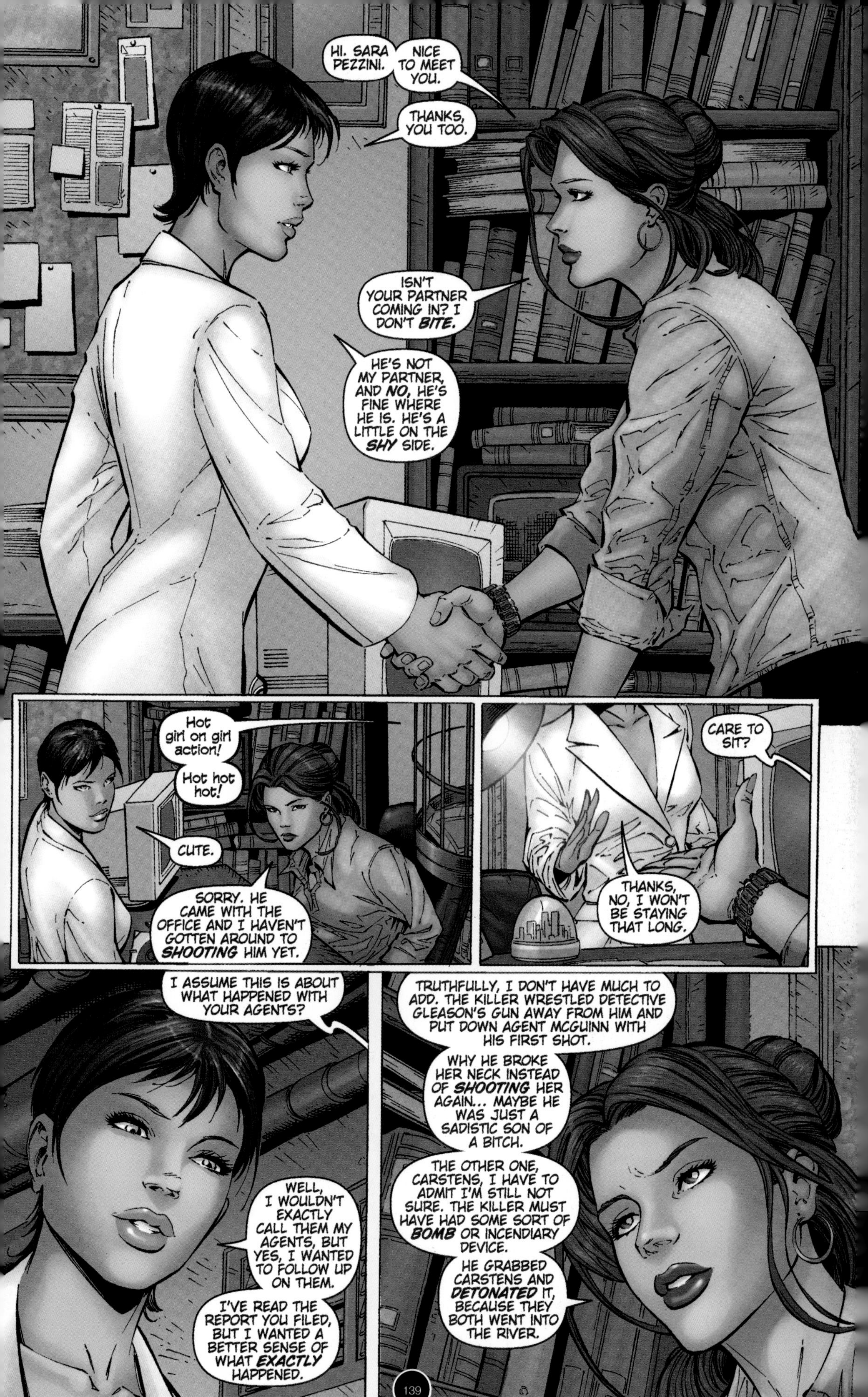
HI. SARA PEZZINI.
NICE TO MEET YOU.
THANKS, YOU TOO.
ISN'T YOUR PARTNER COMING IN? I DON'T BITE.
HE'S NOT MY PARTNER, AND NO, HE'S FINE WHERE HE IS. HE'S A LITTLE ON THE SHY SIDE.
Hot girl on girl action!
Hot hot hot!
CUTE.
SORRY. HE CAME WITH THE OFFICE AND I HAVEN'T GOTTEN AROUND TO SHOOTING HIM YET.
CARE TO SIT?
THANKS, NO, I WON'T BE STAYING THAT LONG.
I ASSUME THIS IS ABOUT WHAT HAPPENED WITH YOUR AGENTS?
WELL, I WOULDN'T EXACTLY CALL THEM MY AGENTS, BUT YES, I WANTED TO FOLLOW UP ON THEM.
I'VE READ THE REPORT YOU FILED, BUT I WANTED A BETTER SENSE OF WHAT EXACTLY HAPPENED.
TRUTHFULLY, I DON'T HAVE MUCH TO ADD. THE KILLER WRESTLED DETECTIVE GLEASON'S GUN AWAY FROM HIM AND PUT DOWN AGENT MCGUINN WITH HIS FIRST SHOT.
WHY HE BROKE HER NECK INSTEAD OF SHOOTING HER AGAIN... MAYBE HE WAS JUST A SADISTIC SON OF A BITCH.
THE OTHER ONE, CARSTENS, I HAVE TO ADMIT I'M STILL NOT SURE. THE KILLER MUST HAVE HAD SOME SORT OF BOMB OR INCENDIARY DEVICE.
HE GRABBED CARSTENS AND DETONATED IT, BECAUSE THEY BOTH WENT INTO THE RIVER.

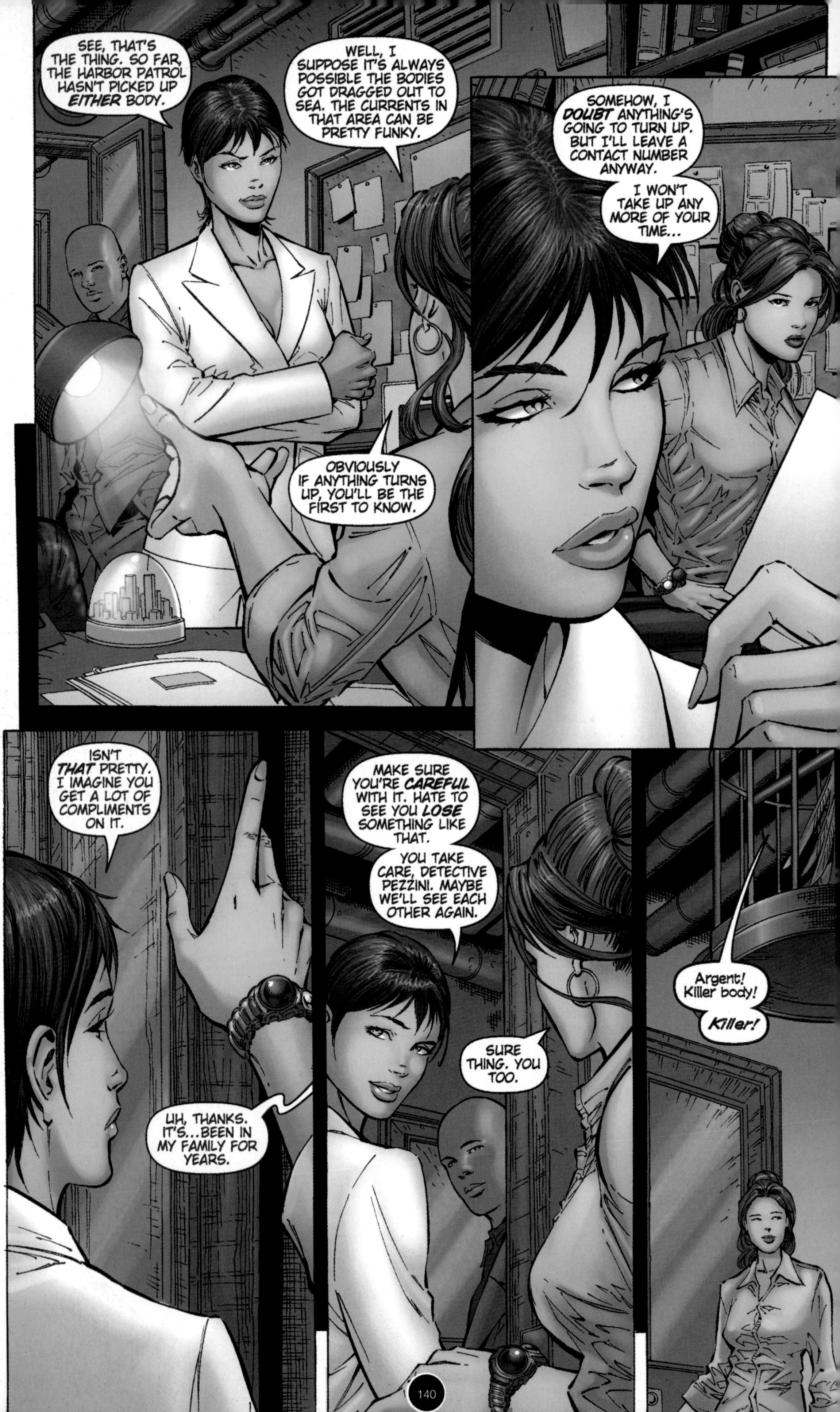

SEE, THAT'S THE THING. SO FAR, THE HARBOR PATROL HASN'T PICKED UP EITHER BODY.
WELL, I SUPPOSE IT'S ALWAYS POSSIBLE THE BODIES GOT DRAGGED OUT TO SEA. THE CURRENTS IN THAT AREA CAN BE PRETTY FUNKY.
OBVIOUSLY IF ANYTHING TURNS UP, YOU'LL BE THE FIRST TO KNOW.
SOMEHOW, I DOUBT ANYTHING'S GOING TO TURN UP. BUT I'LL LEAVE A CONTACT NUMBER ANYWAY.
I WON'T TAKE UP ANY MORE OF YOUR TIME...
ISN'T THAT PRETTY. I IMAGINE YOU GET A LOT OF COMPLIMENTS ON IT.
UH, THANKS. IT'S...BEEN IN MY FAMILY FOR YEARS.
MAKE SURE YOU'RE CAREFUL WITH IT. HATE TO SEE YOU LOSE SOMETHING LIKE THAT.
YOU TAKE CARE, DETECTIVE PEZZINI. MAYBE WE'LL SEE EACH OTHER AGAIN.
SURE THING. YOU TOO.
Argent! Killer body!
Killer!

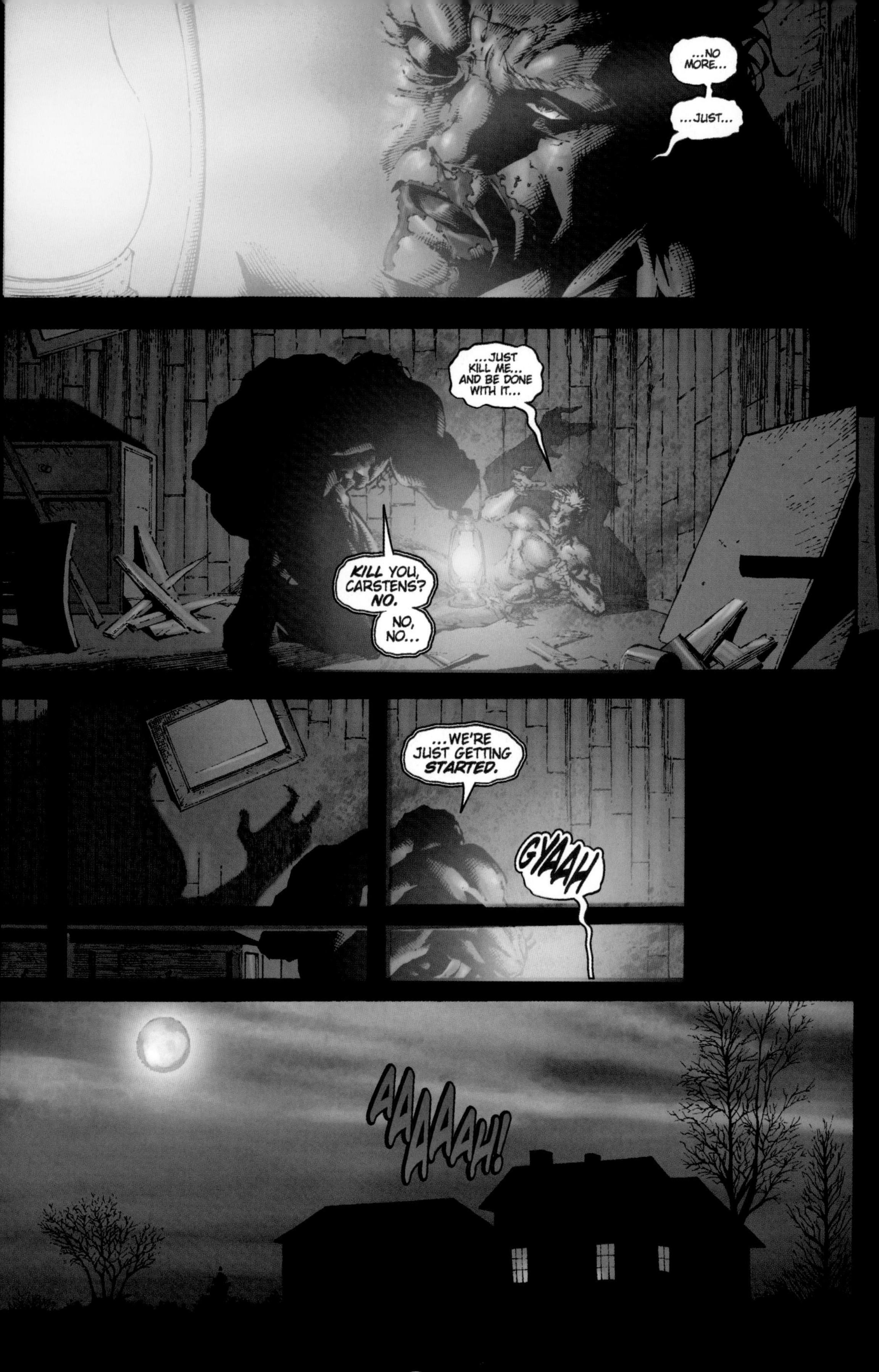
...NO MORE...
...JUST...
...JUST KILL ME... AND BE DONE WITH IT...
KILL YOU, CARSTENS? NO.
NO, NO...
...WE'RE JUST GETTING STARTED.
GYAAH
AAAAAH!

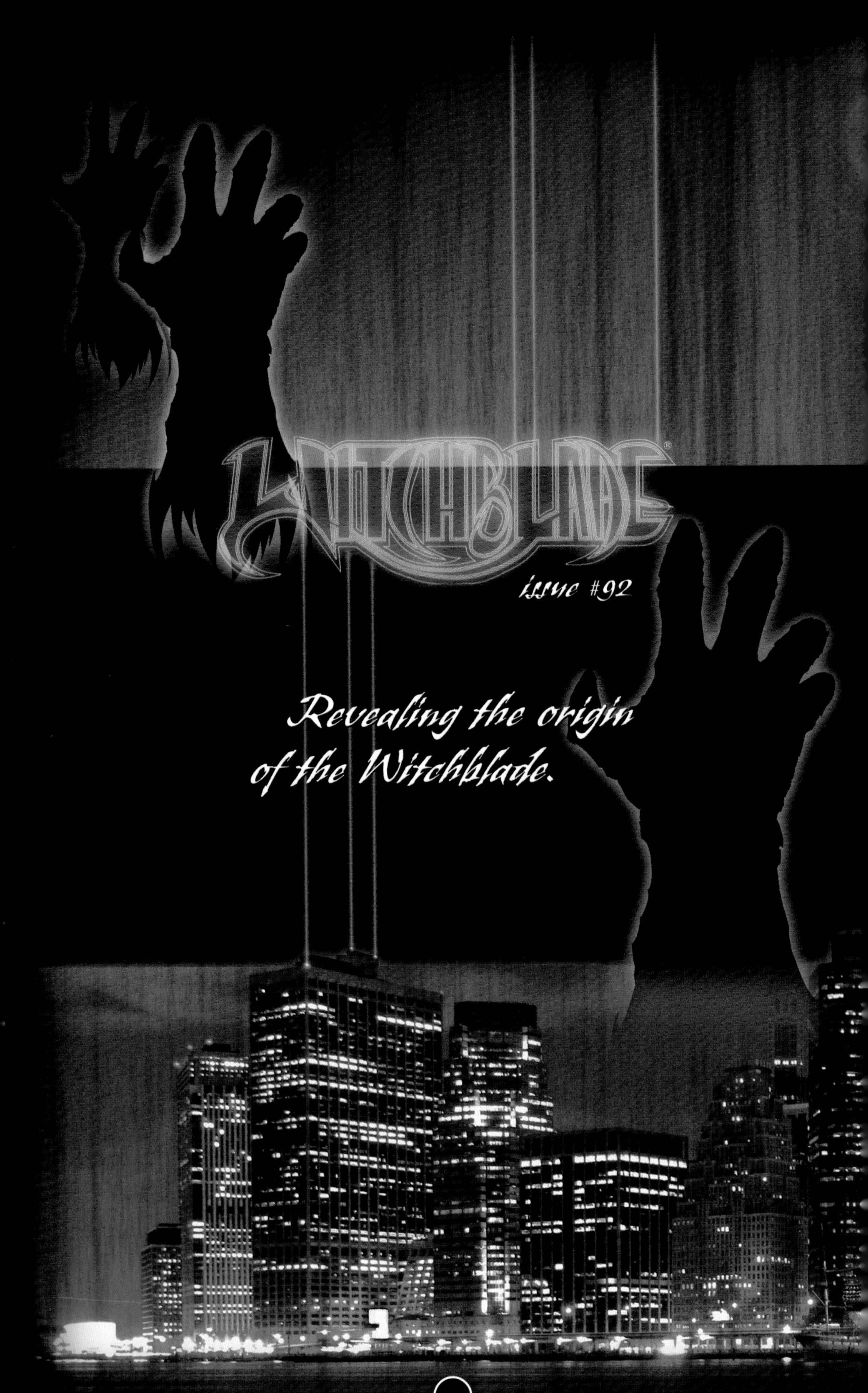
WITCHBLADE®
issue #92
Revealing the origin of the Witchblade.

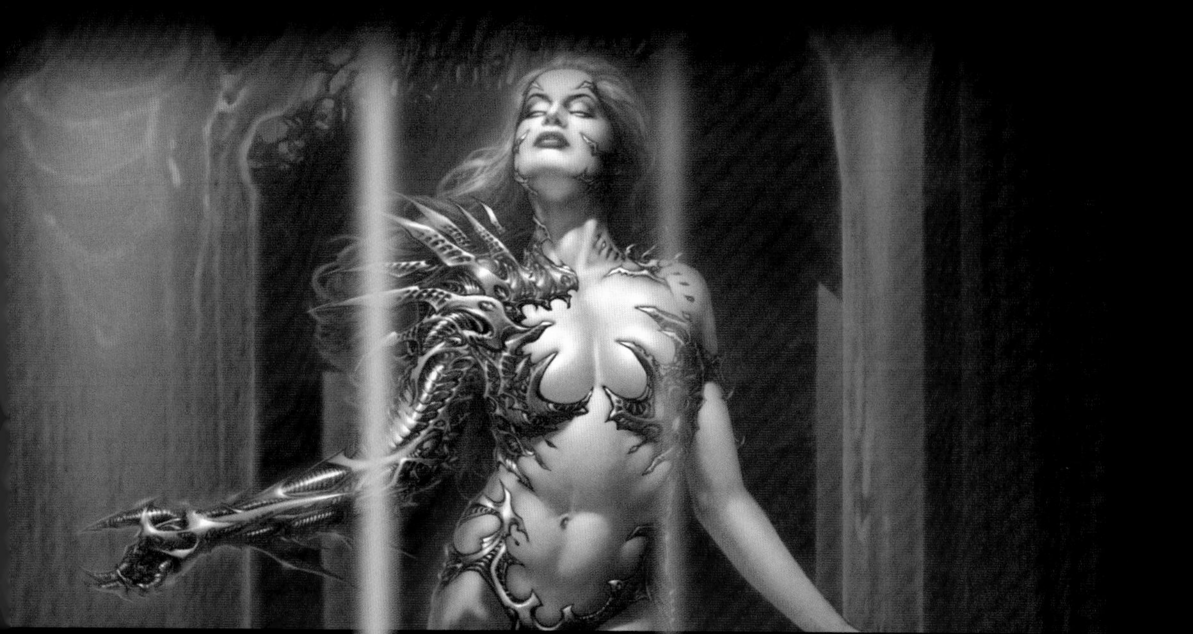

written by: Ron Marz

art by:

1-5: Michael Choi
6-7: Darwyn Cooke
8-9: Eric Basaldua
inks by: Jeff de los Santos
painted art 10-11: Keu Cha
12-13: Luke Ross
14-15: Francis Manapul
inks by: Kevin Conrad
16-17: Rodolfo Migliari
18-19: Brandon Peterson
20-21: Bart Sears
inks by: Andy Smith
22-23: Terry Dodson
inks by: Rachel Dodson

24-25: Chris Bachalo
inks by: Tim Townsend
colors by: Chris Bachalo
26-27: George Perez
inks by: Mike Perkins
28-29: Joseph Michael Linsner
colors by: Steve Firchow
30-31: Marc Silvestri
inks by: Joe Weems V and
Matt Banning
32-34: Michael Choi

colors on:
p.1-5, 8-9, 12-23,
26-27, 30-34
SONIA OBACK

letters by: Troy Peteri

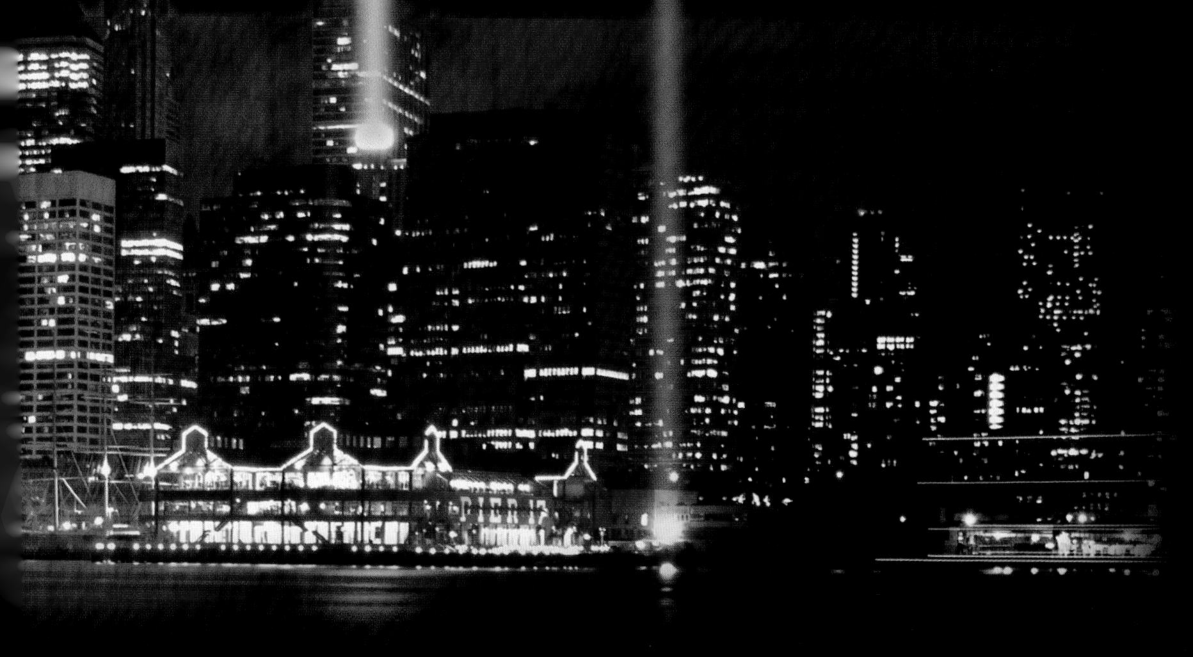

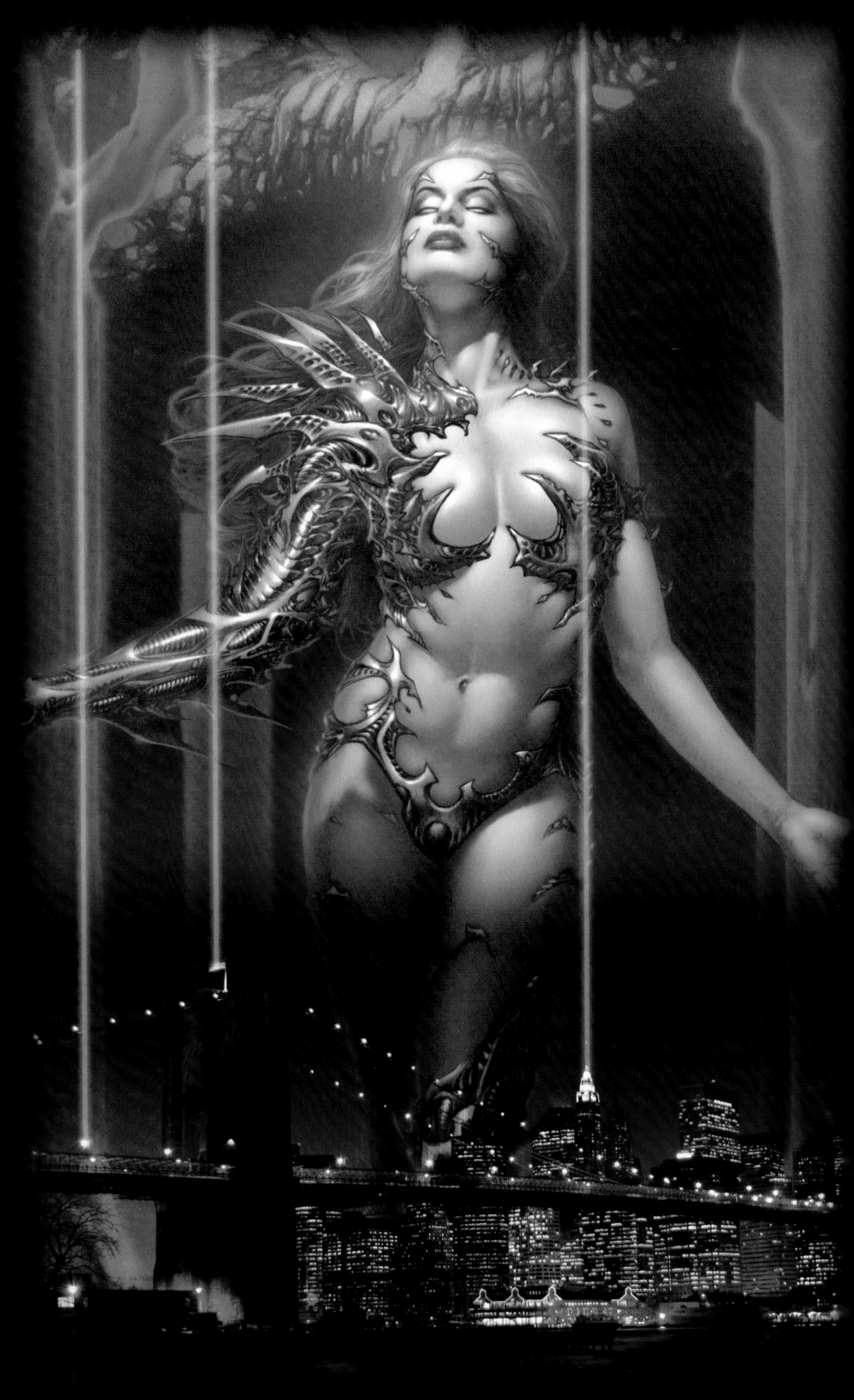

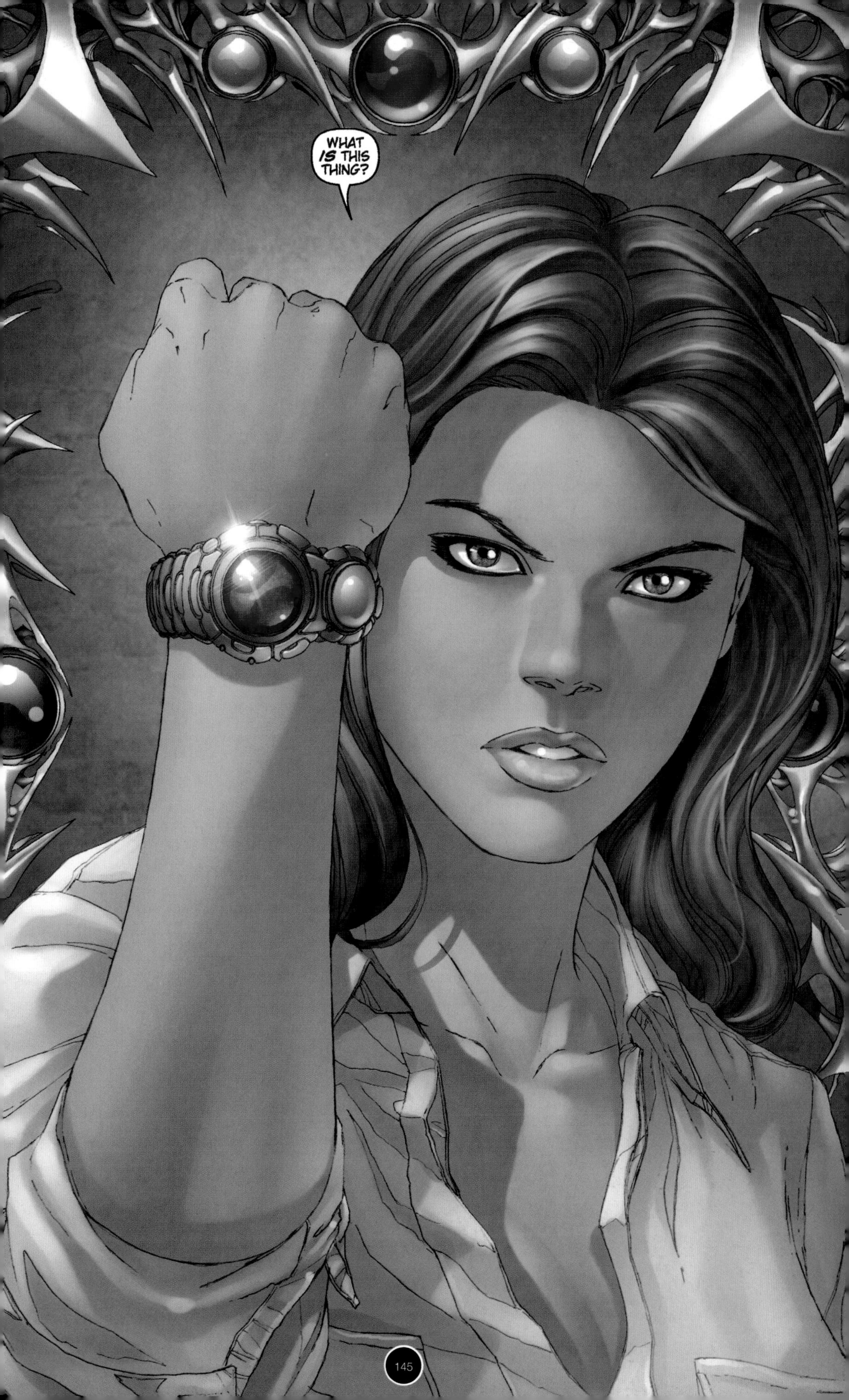
WHAT IS THIS THING?

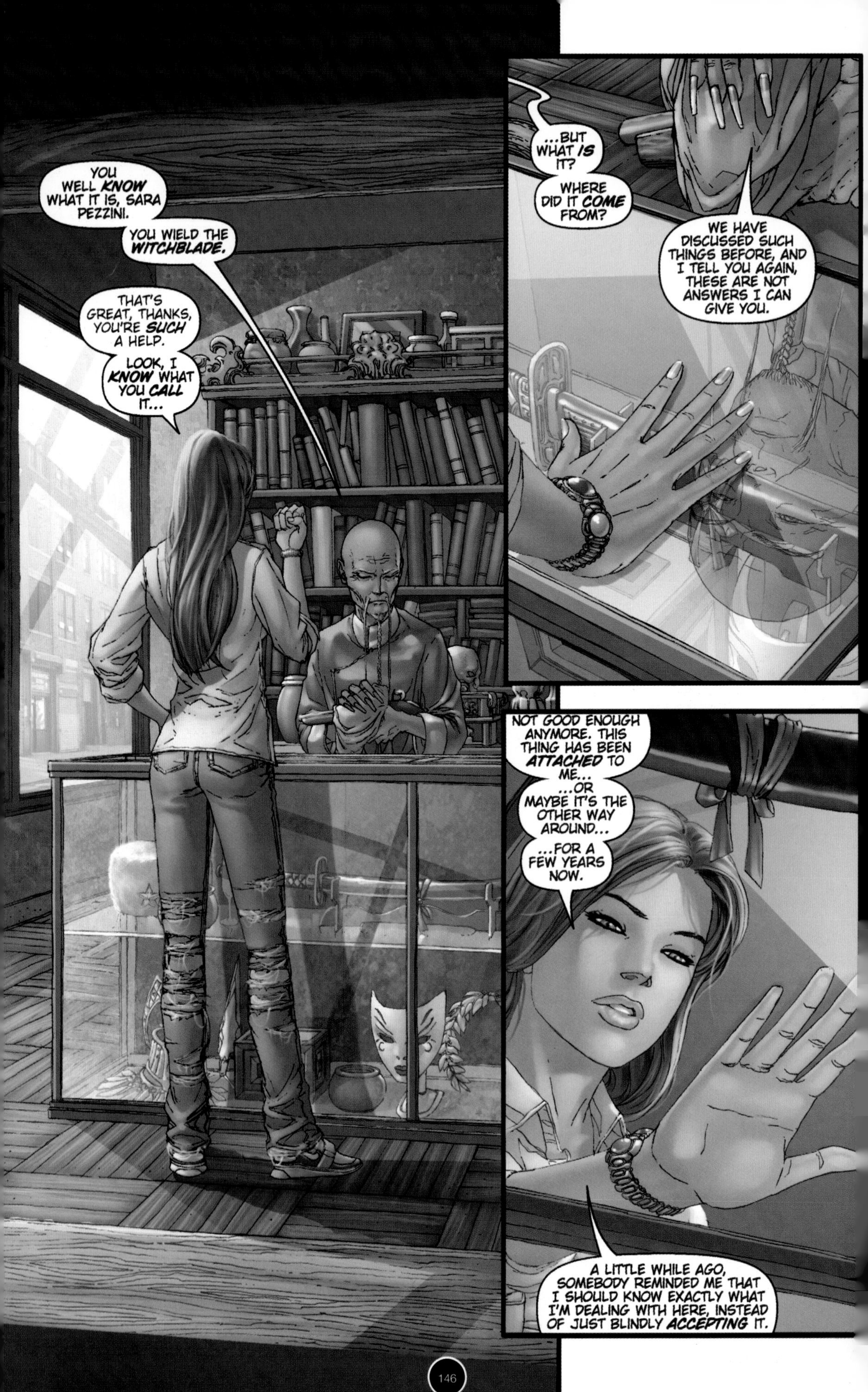
YOU WELL KNOW WHAT IT IS, SARA PEZZINI.
YOU WIELD THE WITCHBLADE.
THAT'S GREAT, THANKS, YOU'RE SUCH A HELP.
LOOK, I KNOW WHAT YOU CALL IT...
...BUT WHAT IS IT?
WHERE DID IT COME FROM?
WE HAVE DISCUSSED SUCH THINGS BEFORE, AND I TELL YOU AGAIN, THESE ARE NOT ANSWERS I CAN GIVE YOU.
NOT GOOD ENOUGH ANYMORE. THIS THING HAS BEEN ATTACHED TO ME...
...OR MAYBE IT'S THE OTHER WAY AROUND...
...FOR A FEW YEARS NOW.
A LITTLE WHILE AGO, SOMEBODY REMINDED ME THAT I SHOULD KNOW EXACTLY WHAT I'M DEALING WITH HERE, INSTEAD OF JUST BLINDLY ACCEPTING IT.

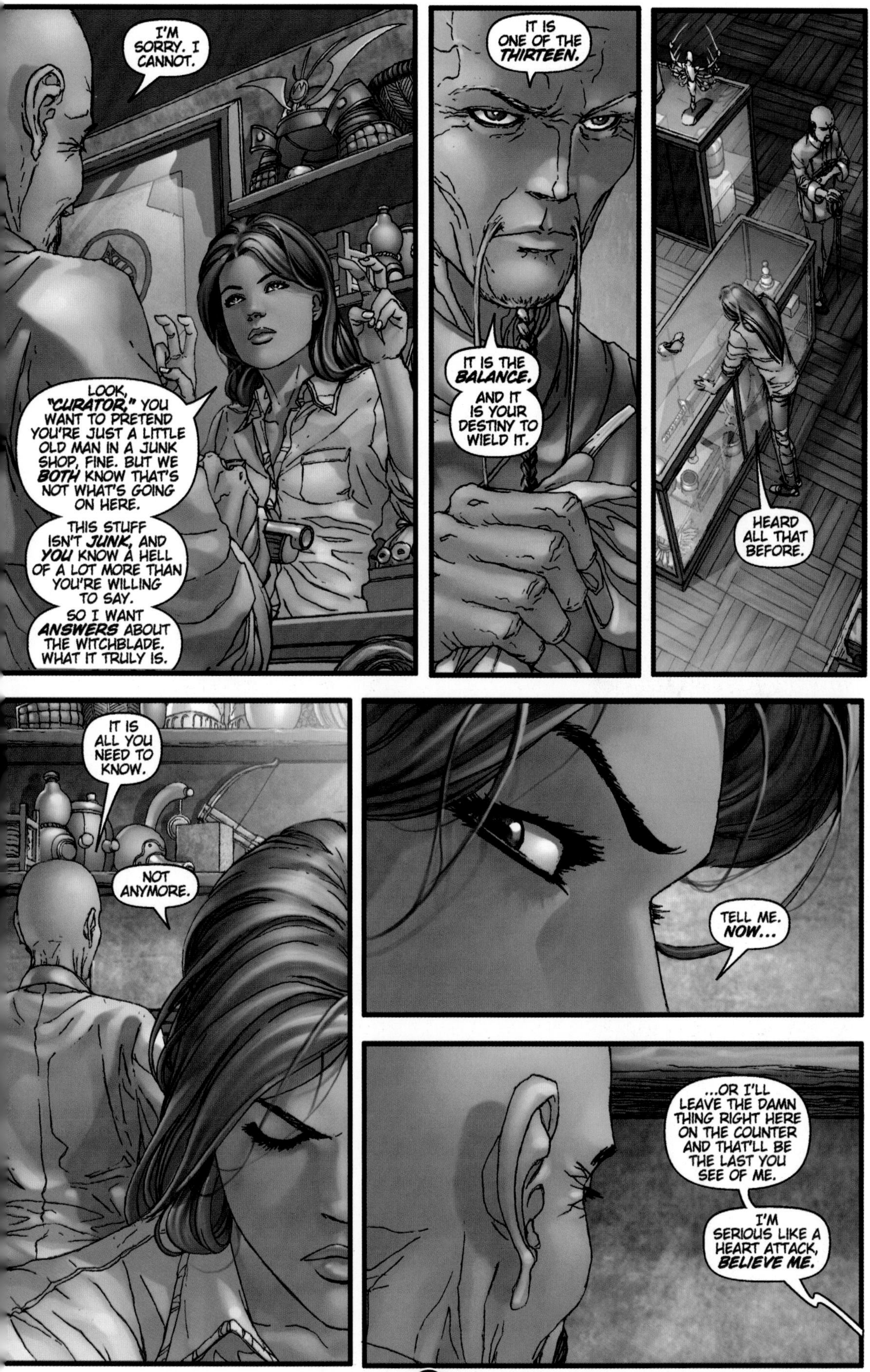
I'M SORRY. I CANNOT.
LOOK, "CURATOR," YOU WANT TO PRETEND YOU'RE JUST A LITTLE OLD MAN IN A JUNK SHOP, FINE. BUT WE BOTH KNOW THAT'S NOT WHAT'S GOING ON HERE.
THIS STUFF ISN'T JUNK, AND YOU KNOW A HELL OF A LOT MORE THAN YOU'RE WILLING TO SAY.
SO I WANT ANSWERS ABOUT THE WITCHBLADE. WHAT IT TRULY IS.
IT IS ONE OF THE THIRTEEN.
IT IS THE BALANCE.
AND IT IS YOUR DESTINY TO WIELD IT.
HEARD ALL THAT BEFORE.
IT IS ALL YOU NEED TO KNOW.
NOT ANYMORE.
TELL ME. NOW...
...OR I'LL LEAVE THE DAMN THING RIGHT HERE ON THE COUNTER AND THAT'LL BE THE LAST YOU SEE OF ME.
I'M SERIOUS LIKE A HEART ATTACK, BELIEVE ME.

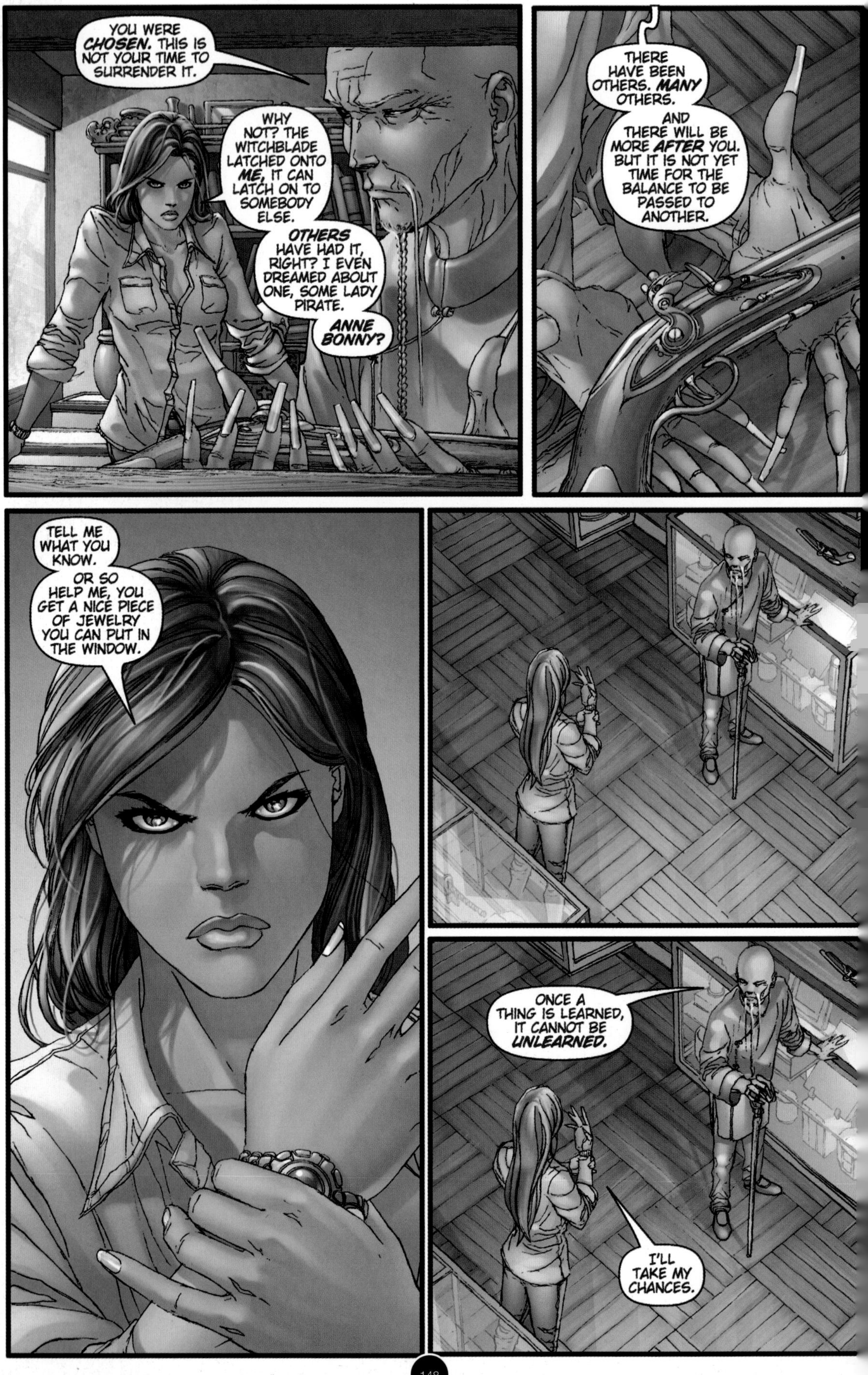
YOU WERE CHOSEN. THIS IS NOT YOUR TIME TO SURRENDER IT.
WHY NOT? THE WITCHBLADE LATCHED ONTO ME, IT CAN LATCH ON TO SOMEBODY ELSE.
OTHERS HAVE HAD IT, RIGHT? I EVEN DREAMED ABOUT ONE, SOME LADY PIRATE.
ANNE BONNY?
THERE HAVE BEEN OTHERS. MANY OTHERS.
AND THERE WILL BE MORE AFTER YOU. BUT IT IS NOT YET TIME FOR THE BALANCE TO BE PASSED TO ANOTHER.
TELL ME WHAT YOU KNOW.
OR SO HELP ME, YOU GET A NICE PIECE OF JEWELRY YOU CAN PUT IN THE WINDOW.
ONCE A THING IS LEARNED, IT CANNOT BE UNLEARNED.
I'LL TAKE MY CHANCES.

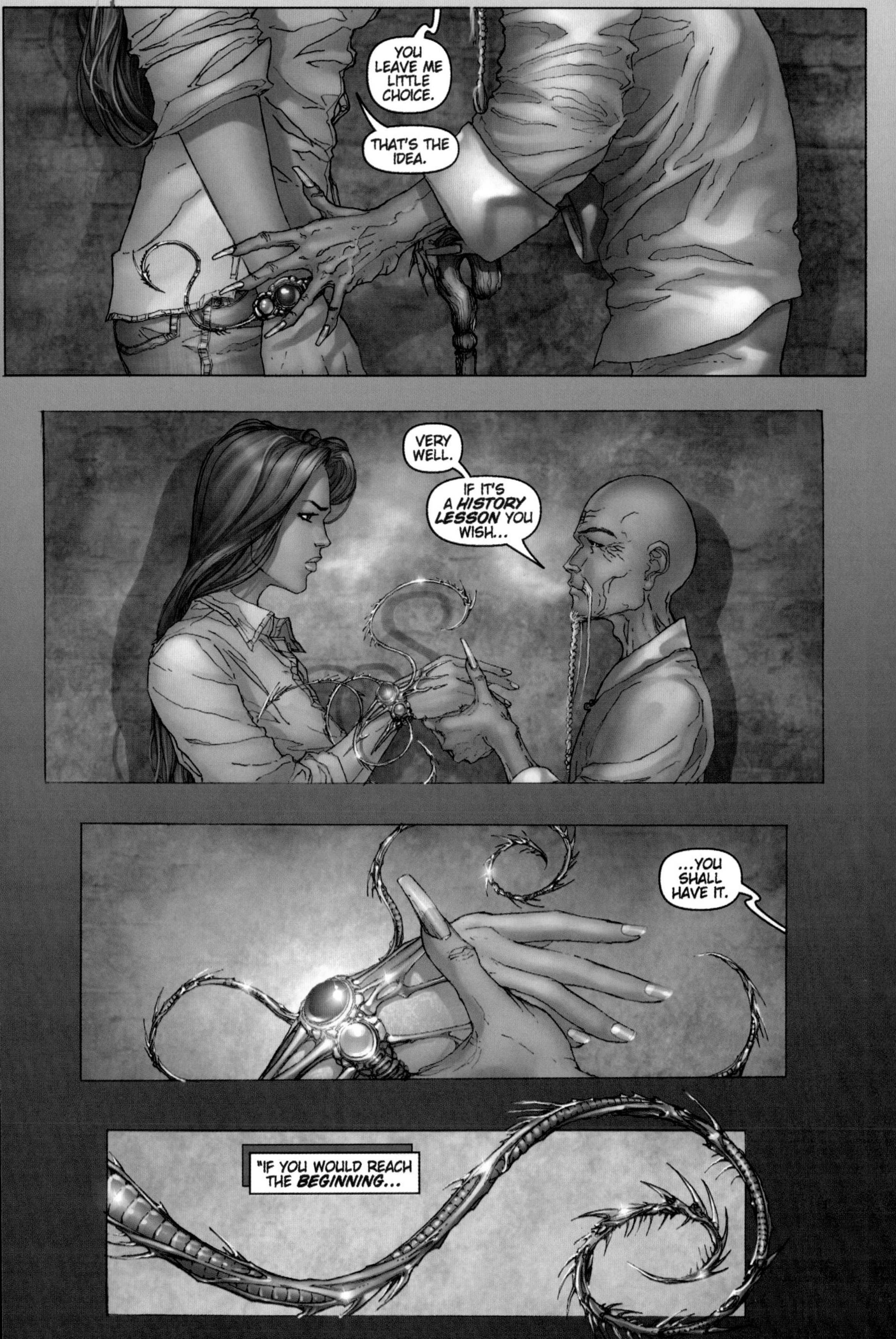
YOU LEAVE ME LITTLE CHOICE.
THAT'S THE IDEA.
VERY WELL.
IF IT'S A **HISTORY LESSON** YOU WISH...
...YOU SHALL HAVE IT.
"IF YOU WOULD REACH THE **BEGINNING**...

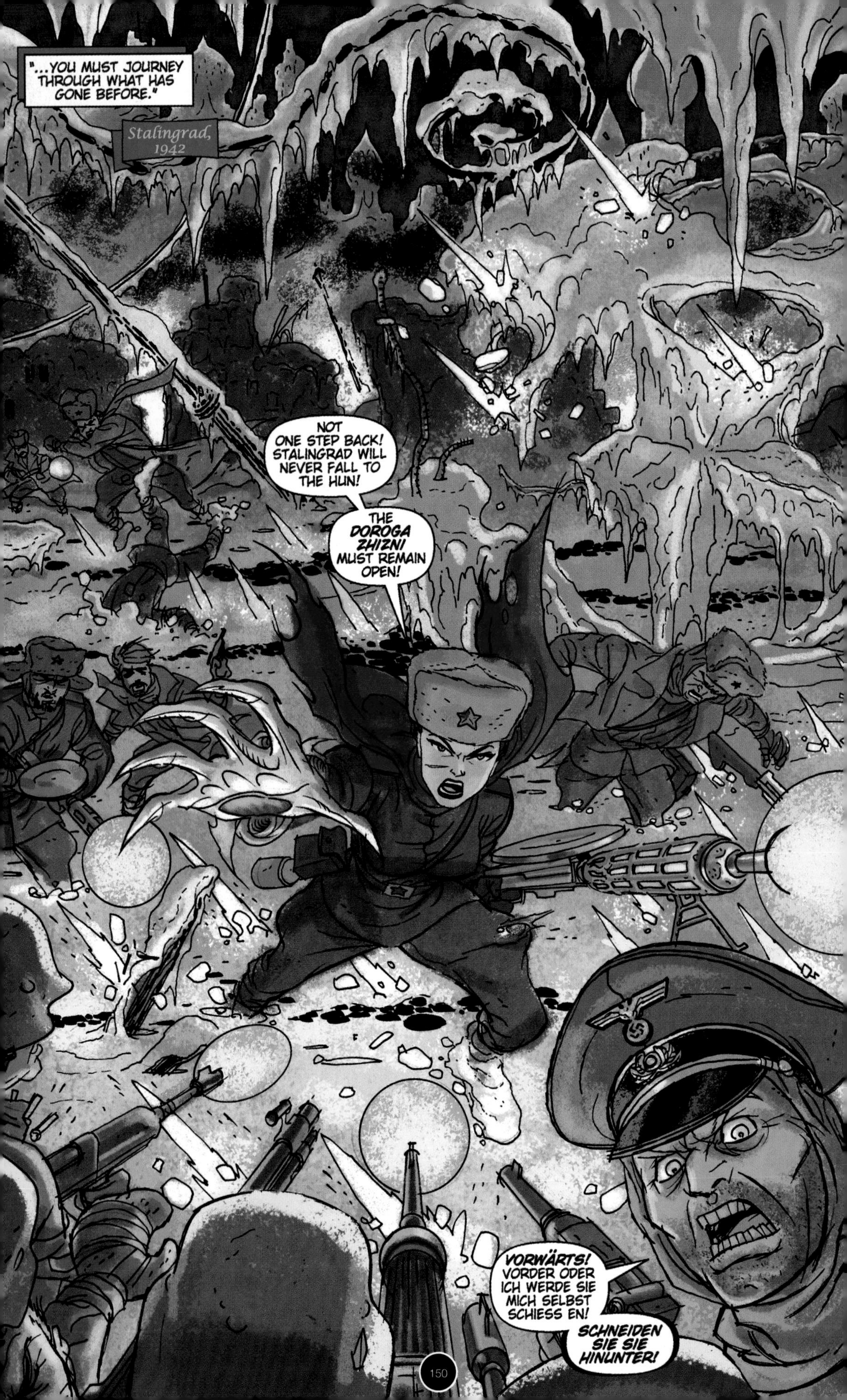
"...YOU MUST JOURNEY THROUGH WHAT HAS GONE BEFORE."
Stalingrad, 1942
NOT ONE STEP BACK! STALINGRAD WILL NEVER FALL TO THE HUN!
THE DOROGA ZHIZNI MUST REMAIN OPEN!
VORWÄRTS! VORDER ODER ICH WERDE SIE MICH SELBST SCHIESS EN!
SCHNEIDEN SIE SIE HINUNTER!

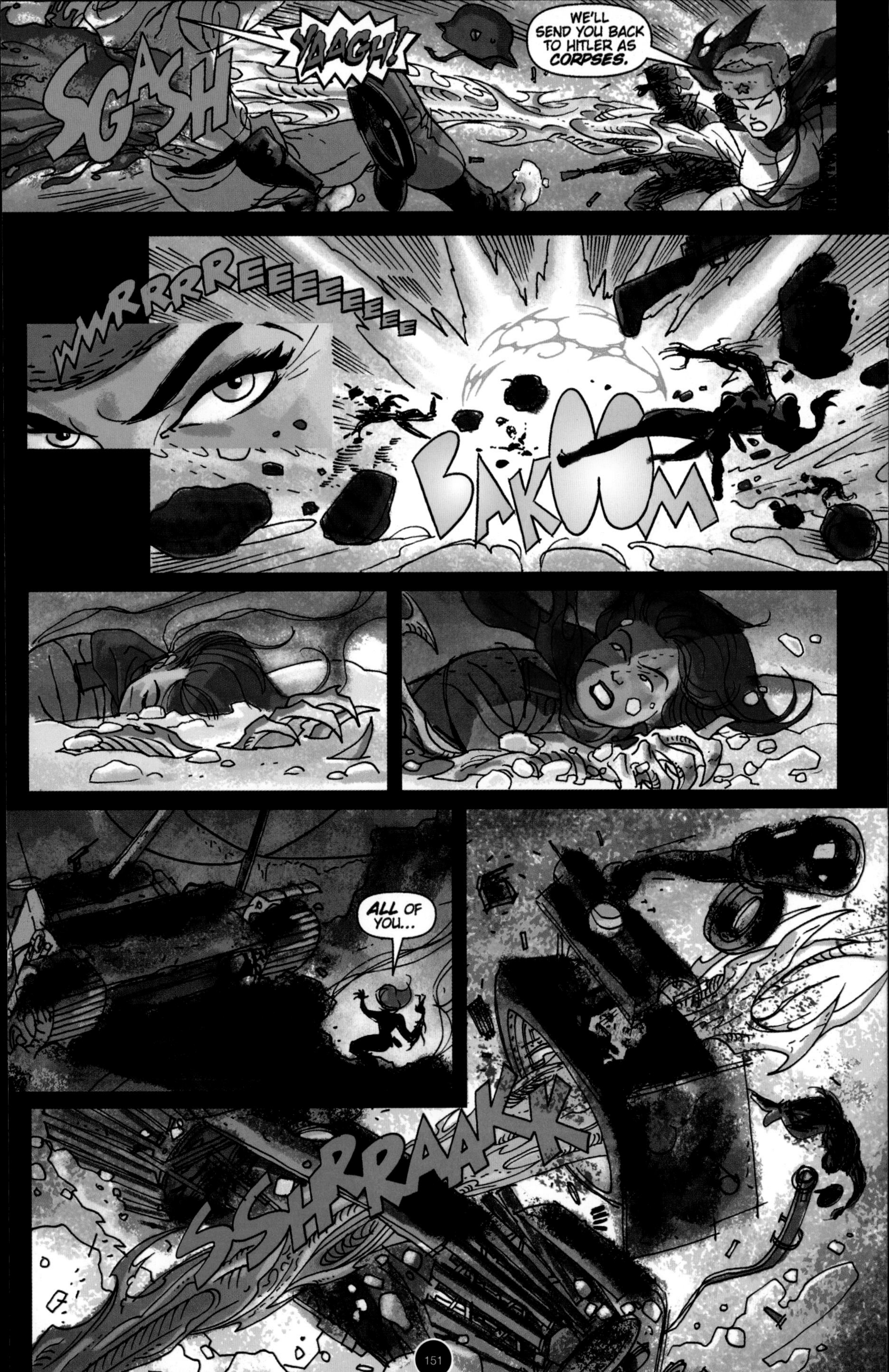
SGASH
YAAGH!
WE'LL SEND YOU BACK TO HITLER AS CORPSES.
WWRRRREEEEEEEEE
BAKOOM
ALL OF YOU...
SSHRRAAKK

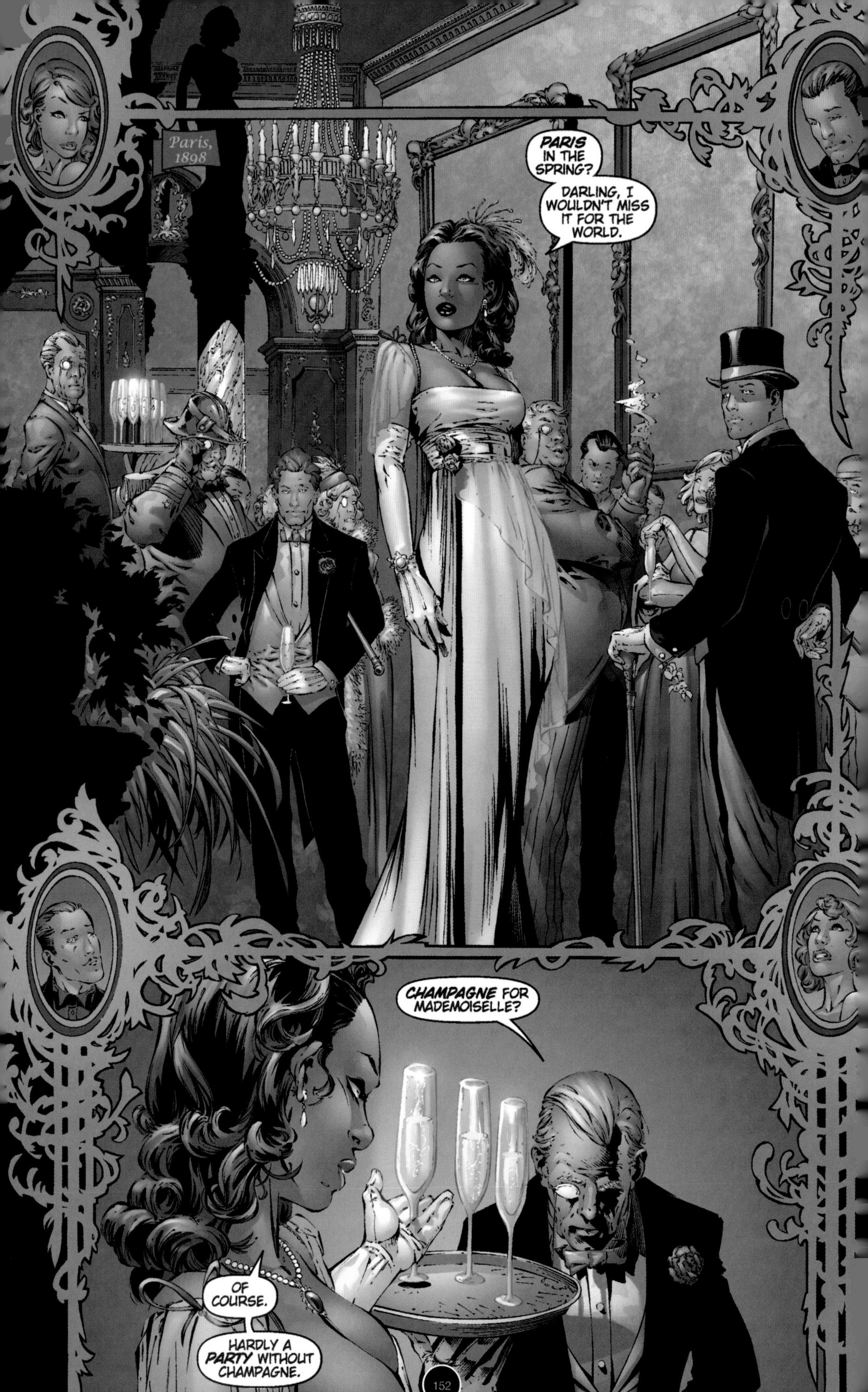
Paris, 1898
PARIS IN THE SPRING?
DARLING, I WOULDN'T MISS IT FOR THE WORLD.
CHAMPAGNE FOR MADEMOISELLE?
OF COURSE.
HARDLY A PARTY WITHOUT CHAMPAGNE.

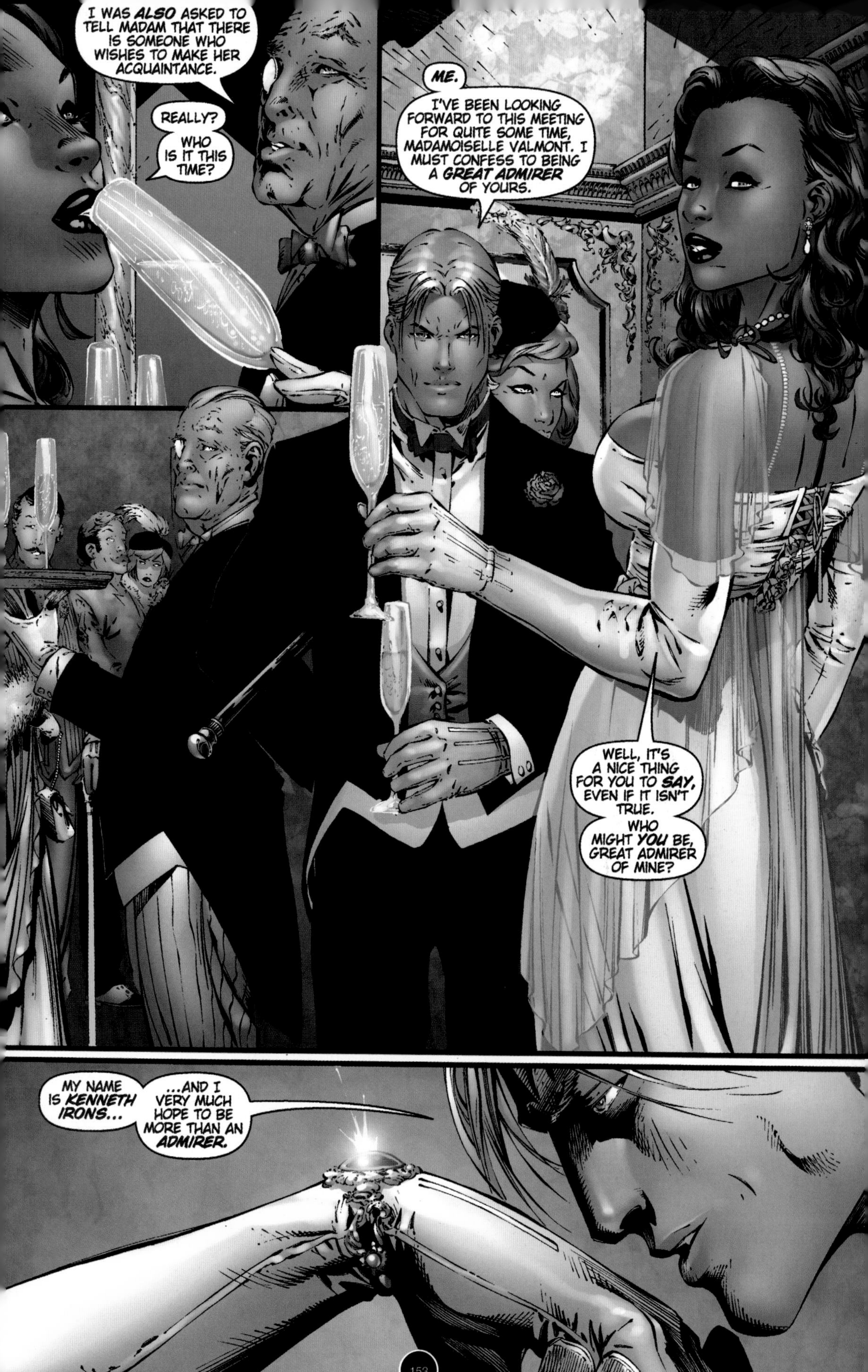
I WAS ALSO ASKED TO TELL MADAM THAT THERE IS SOMEONE WHO WISHES TO MAKE HER ACQUAINTANCE.
REALLY? WHO IS IT THIS TIME?
ME.
I'VE BEEN LOOKING FORWARD TO THIS MEETING FOR QUITE SOME TIME, MADAMOISELLE VALMONT. I MUST CONFESS TO BEING A GREAT ADMIRER OF YOURS.
WELL, IT'S A NICE THING FOR YOU TO SAY, EVEN IF IT ISN'T TRUE.
WHO MIGHT YOU BE, GREAT ADMIRER OF MINE?
MY NAME IS KENNETH IRONS...
...AND I VERY MUCH HOPE TO BE MORE THAN AN ADMIRER.

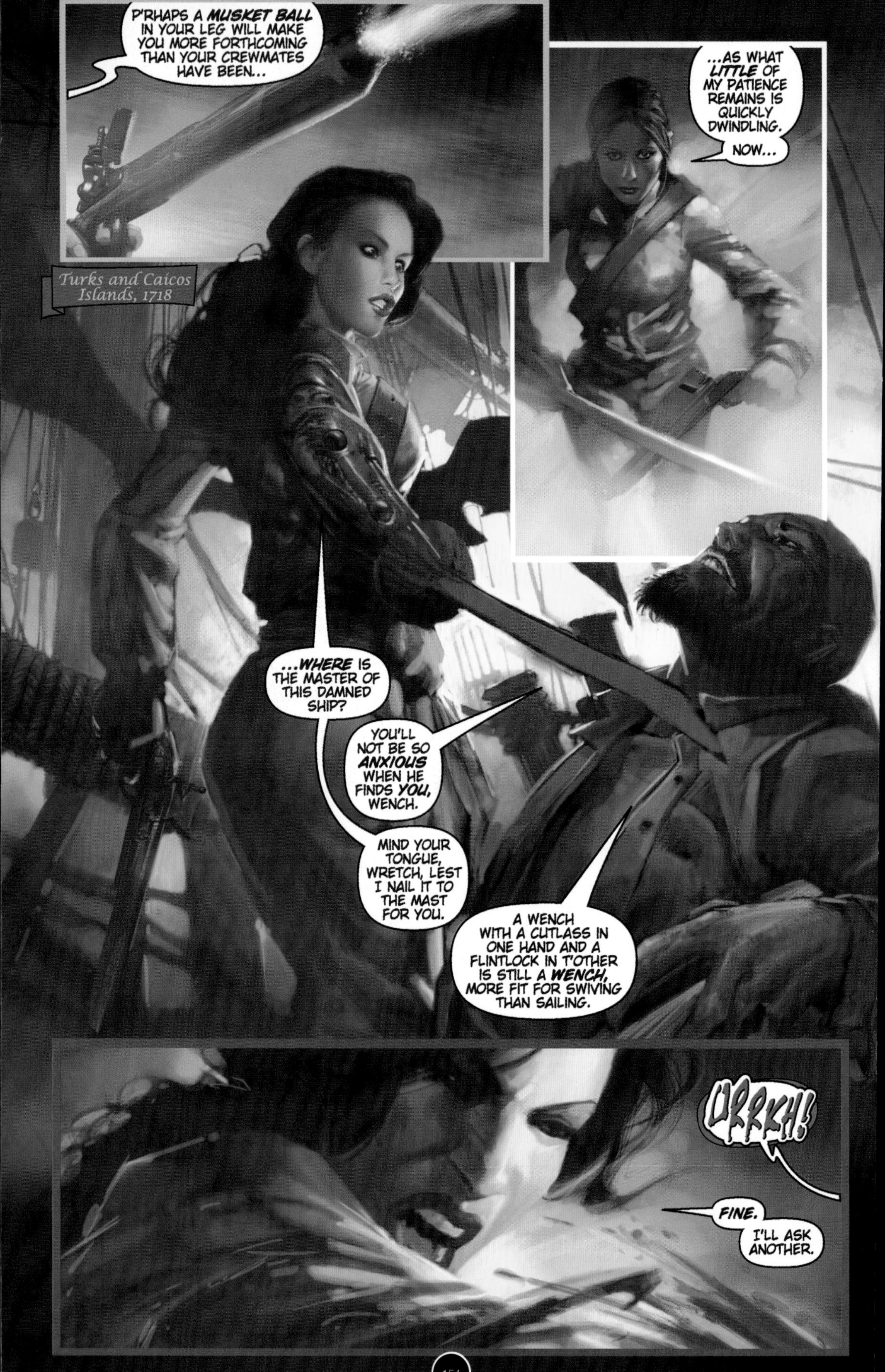
P'RHAPS A MUSKET BALL IN YOUR LEG WILL MAKE YOU MORE FORTHCOMING THAN YOUR CREWMATES HAVE BEEN...
...AS WHAT LITTLE OF MY PATIENCE REMAINS IS QUICKLY DWINDLING.
NOW...
Turks and Caicos Islands, 1718
...WHERE IS THE MASTER OF THIS DAMNED SHIP?
YOU'LL NOT BE SO ANXIOUS WHEN HE FINDS YOU, WENCH.
MIND YOUR TONGUE, WRETCH, LEST I NAIL IT TO THE MAST FOR YOU.
A WENCH WITH A CUTLASS IN ONE HAND AND A FLINTLOCK IN T'OTHER IS STILL A WENCH, MORE FIT FOR SWIVING THAN SAILING.
URRKH!
FINE.
I'LL ASK ANOTHER.

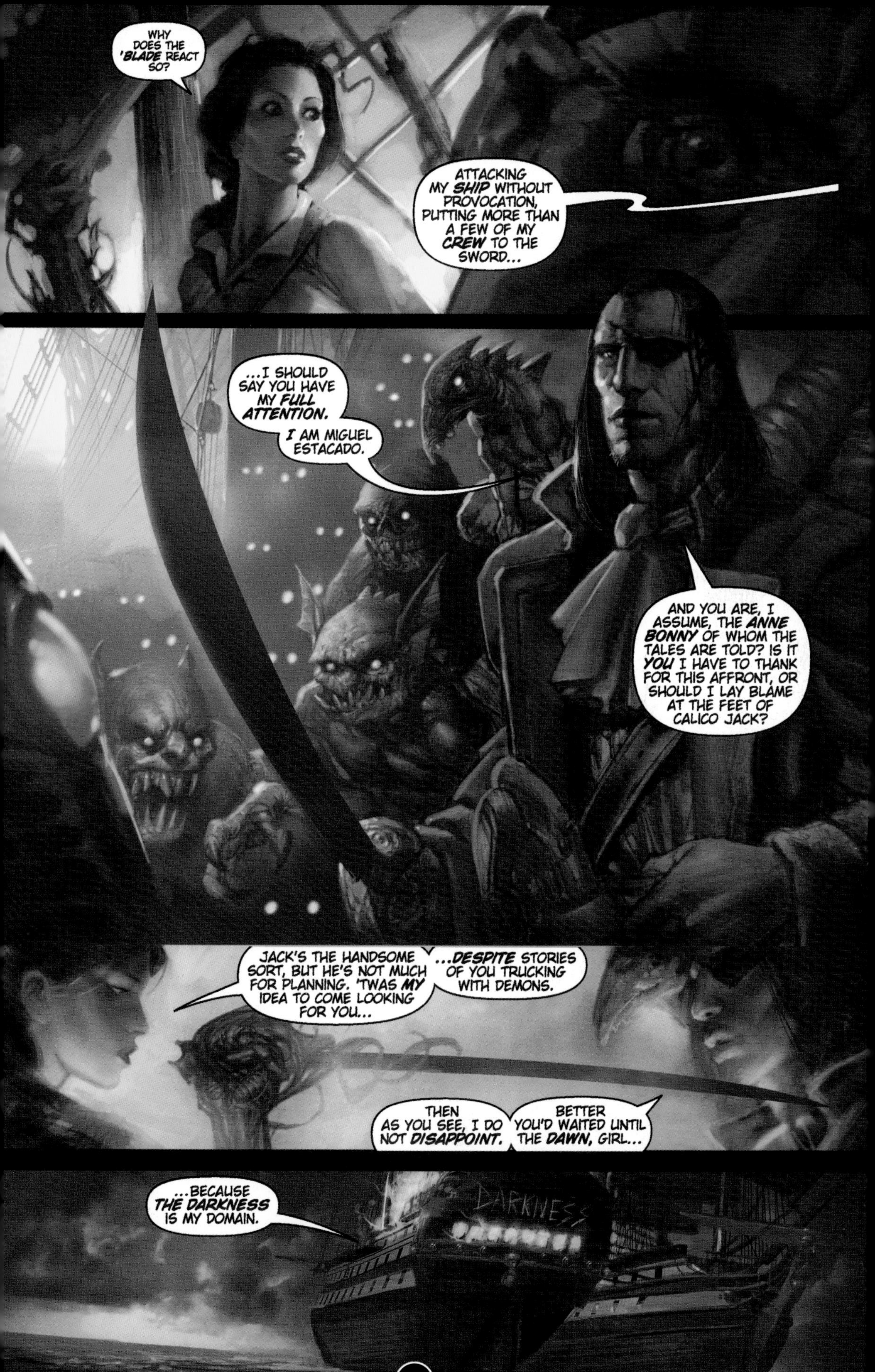
WHY DOES THE 'BLADE REACT SO?
ATTACKING MY SHIP WITHOUT PROVOCATION, PUTTING MORE THAN A FEW OF MY CREW TO THE SWORD...
...I SHOULD SAY YOU HAVE MY FULL ATTENTION.
I AM MIGUEL ESTACADO.
AND YOU ARE, I ASSUME, THE ANNE BONNY OF WHOM THE TALES ARE TOLD? IS IT YOU I HAVE TO THANK FOR THIS AFFRONT, OR SHOULD I LAY BLAME AT THE FEET OF CALICO JACK?
JACK'S THE HANDSOME SORT, BUT HE'S NOT MUCH FOR PLANNING. 'TWAS MY IDEA TO COME LOOKING FOR YOU...
...DESPITE STORIES OF YOU TRUCKING WITH DEMONS.
THEN AS YOU SEE, I DO NOT DISAPPOINT.
BETTER YOU'D WAITED UNTIL THE DAWN, GIRL...
...BECAUSE THE DARKNESS IS MY DOMAIN.
DARKNESS

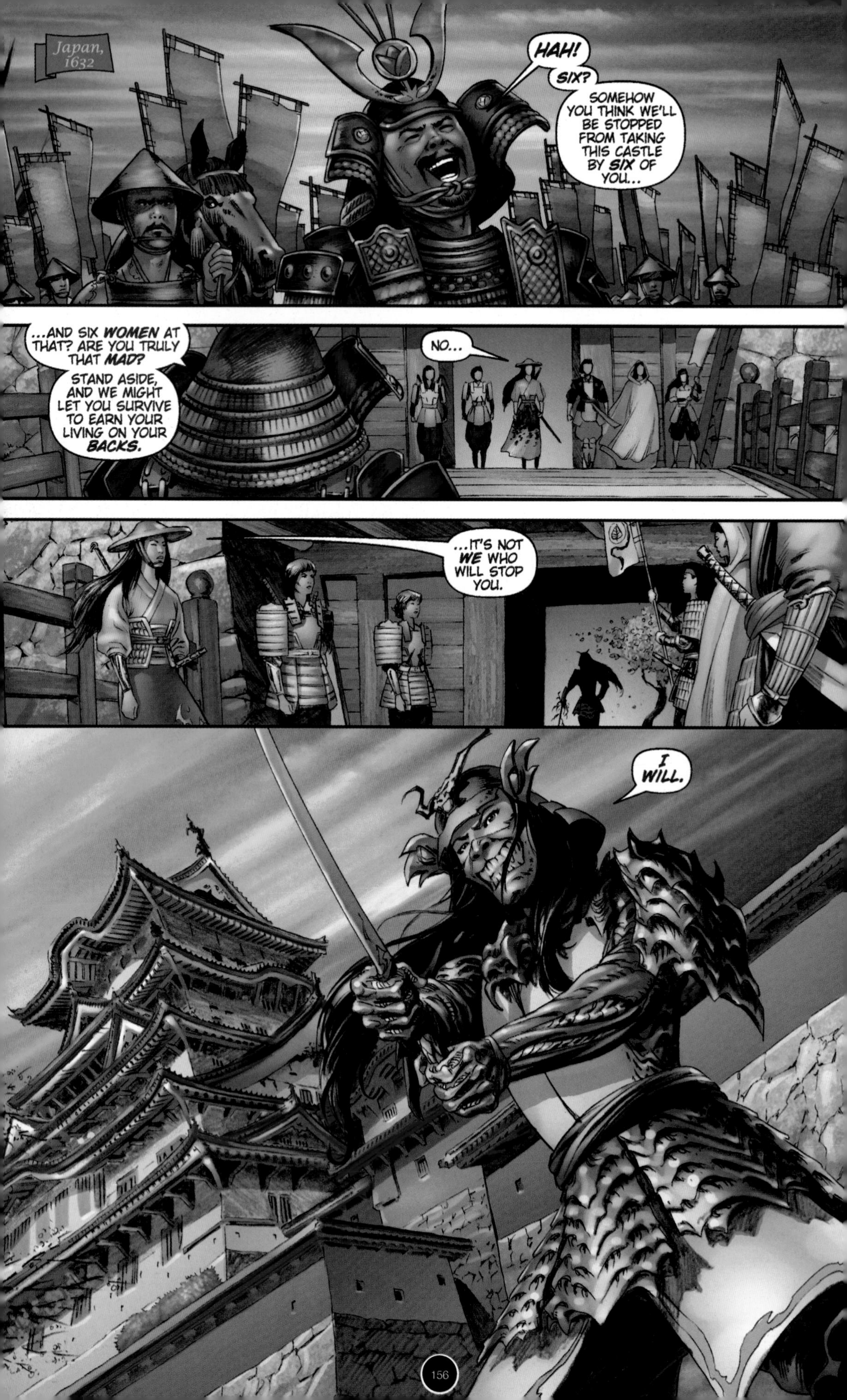
Japan, 1632
HAH!
SIX?
SOMEHOW YOU THINK WE'LL BE STOPPED FROM TAKING THIS CASTLE BY SIX OF YOU...
...AND SIX WOMEN AT THAT? ARE YOU TRULY THAT MAD?
STAND ASIDE, AND WE MIGHT LET YOU SURVIVE TO EARN YOUR LIVING ON YOUR BACKS.
NO...
...IT'S NOT WE WHO WILL STOP YOU.
I WILL.

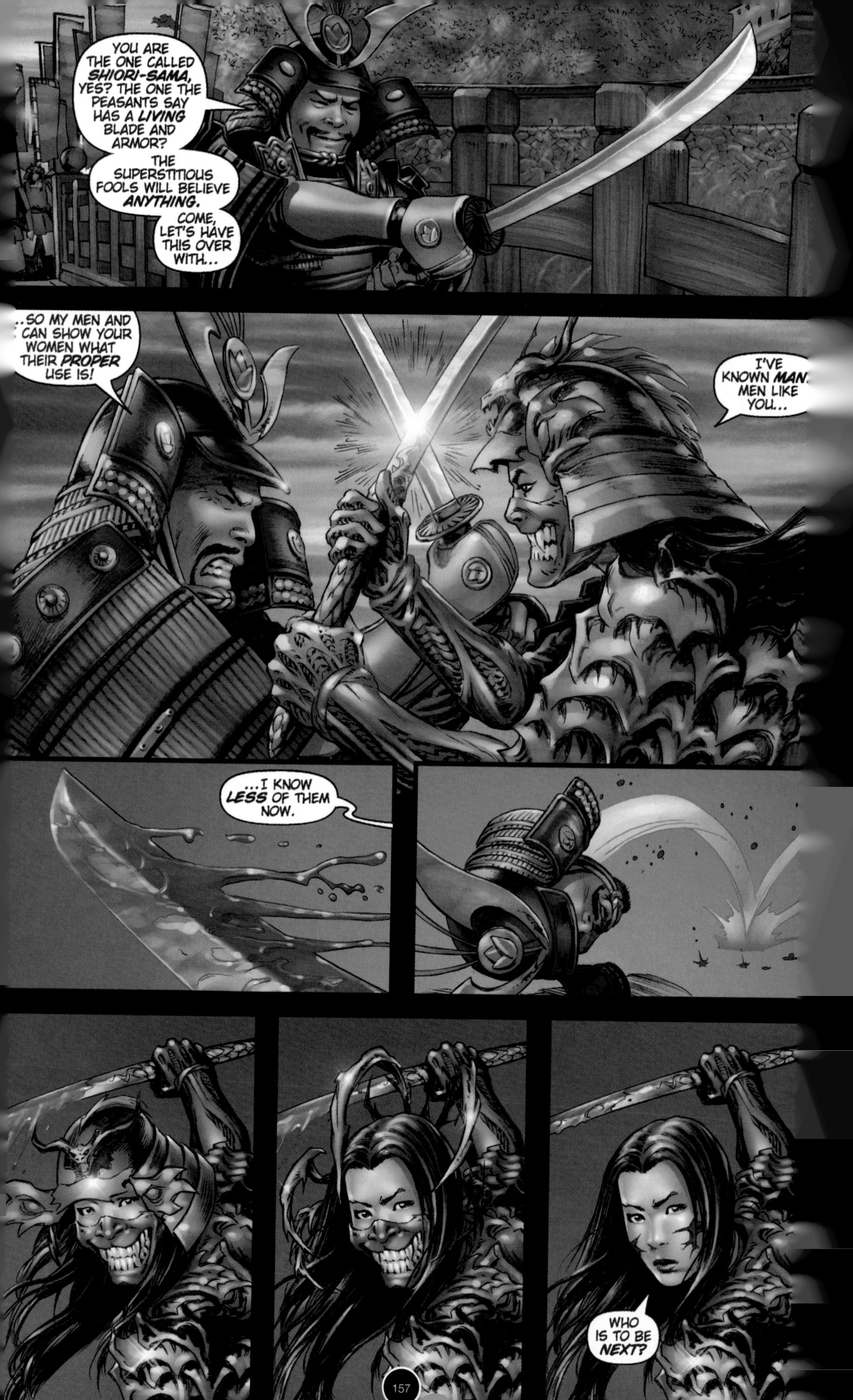
YOU ARE THE ONE CALLED SHIORI-SAMA, YES? THE ONE THE PEASANTS SAY HAS A LIVING BLADE AND ARMOR?
THE SUPERSTITIOUS FOOLS WILL BELIEVE ANYTHING.
COME, LET'S HAVE THIS OVER WITH...
..SO MY MEN AND I CAN SHOW YOUR WOMEN WHAT THEIR PROPER USE IS!
I'VE KNOWN MANY MEN LIKE YOU...
...I KNOW LESS OF THEM NOW.
WHO IS TO BE NEXT?

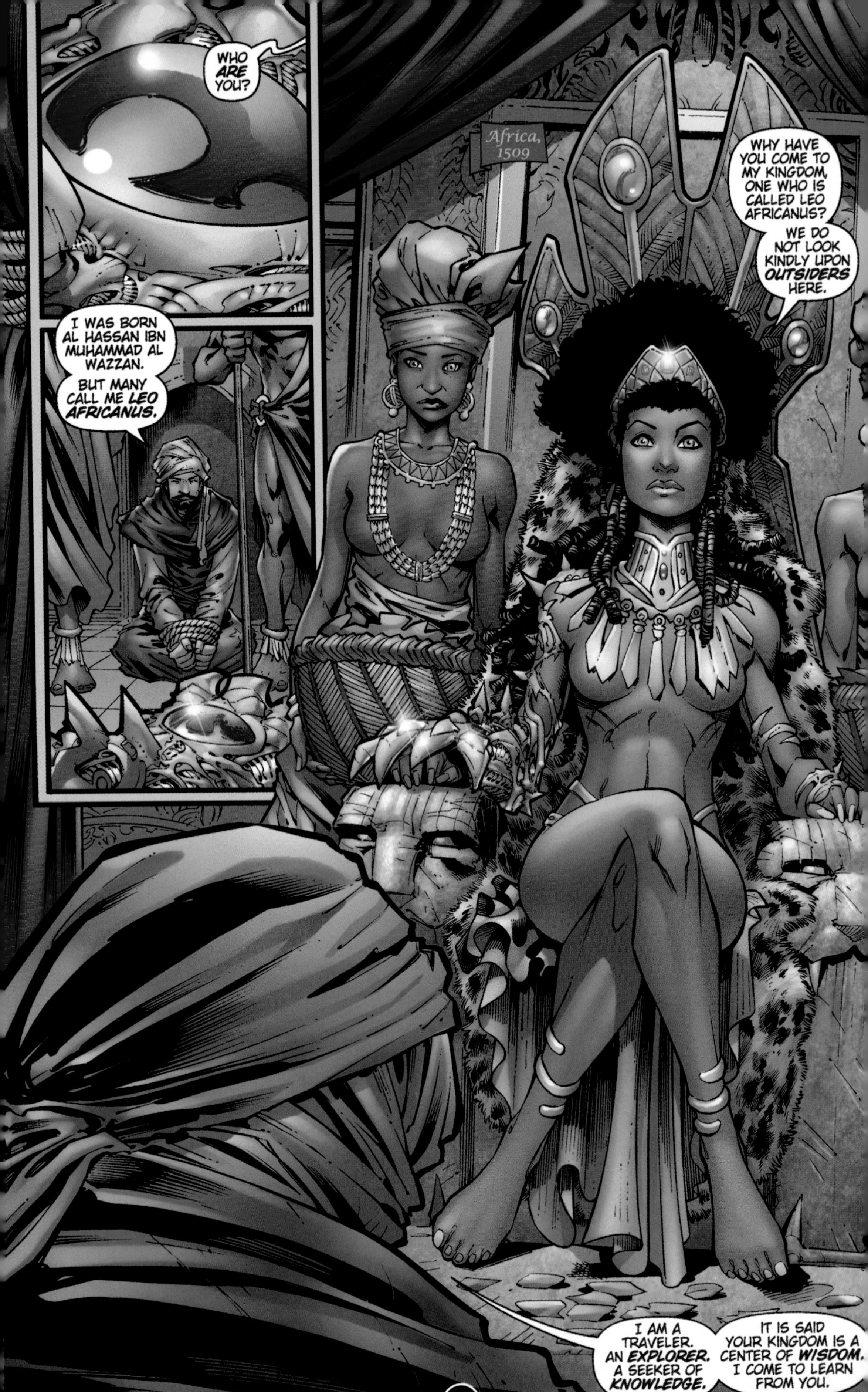

WHO ARE YOU?
Africa, 1509
WHY HAVE YOU COME TO MY KINGDOM, ONE WHO IS CALLED LEO AFRICANUS?
WE DO NOT LOOK KINDLY UPON OUTSIDERS HERE.
I WAS BORN AL HASSAN IBN MUHAMMAD AL WAZZAN.
BUT MANY CALL ME LEO AFRICANUS.
I AM A TRAVELER. AN EXPLORER. A SEEKER OF KNOWLEDGE.
IT IS SAID YOUR KINGDOM IS A CENTER OF WISDOM. I COME TO LEARN FROM YOU.

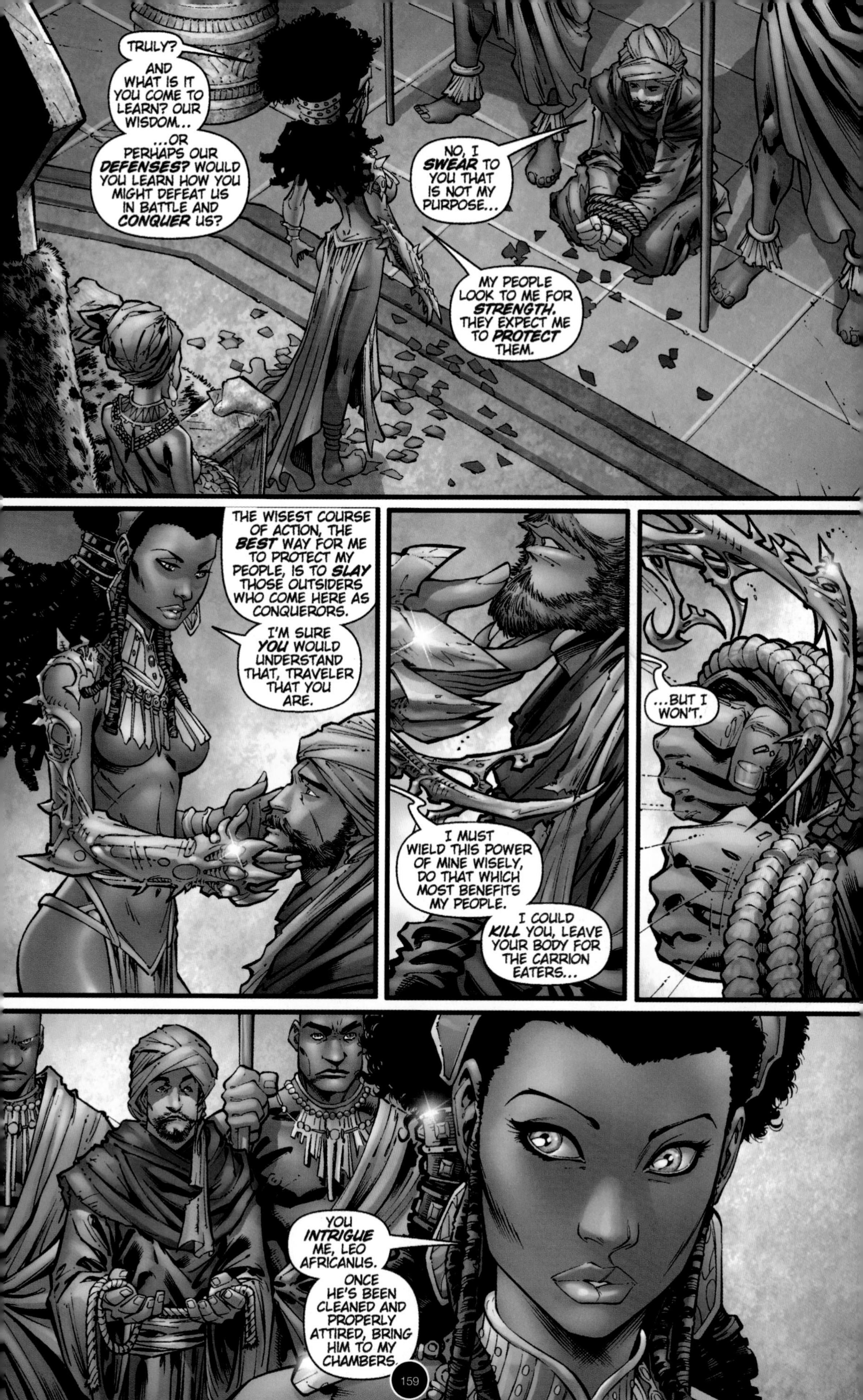
TRULY?
AND WHAT IS IT YOU COME TO LEARN? OUR WISDOM...
...OR PERHAPS OUR DEFENSES? WOULD YOU LEARN HOW YOU MIGHT DEFEAT US IN BATTLE AND CONQUER US?
NO, I SWEAR TO YOU THAT IS NOT MY PURPOSE...
MY PEOPLE LOOK TO ME FOR STRENGTH. THEY EXPECT ME TO PROTECT THEM.
THE WISEST COURSE OF ACTION, THE BEST WAY FOR ME TO PROTECT MY PEOPLE, IS TO SLAY THOSE OUTSIDERS WHO COME HERE AS CONQUERORS.
I'M SURE YOU WOULD UNDERSTAND THAT, TRAVELER THAT YOU ARE.
I MUST WIELD THIS POWER OF MINE WISELY, DO THAT WHICH MOST BENEFITS MY PEOPLE.
I COULD KILL YOU, LEAVE YOUR BODY FOR THE CARRION EATERS...
...BUT I WON'T.
YOU INTRIGUE ME, LEO AFRICANUS.
ONCE HE'S BEEN CLEANED AND PROPERLY ATTIRED, BRING HIM TO MY CHAMBERS.

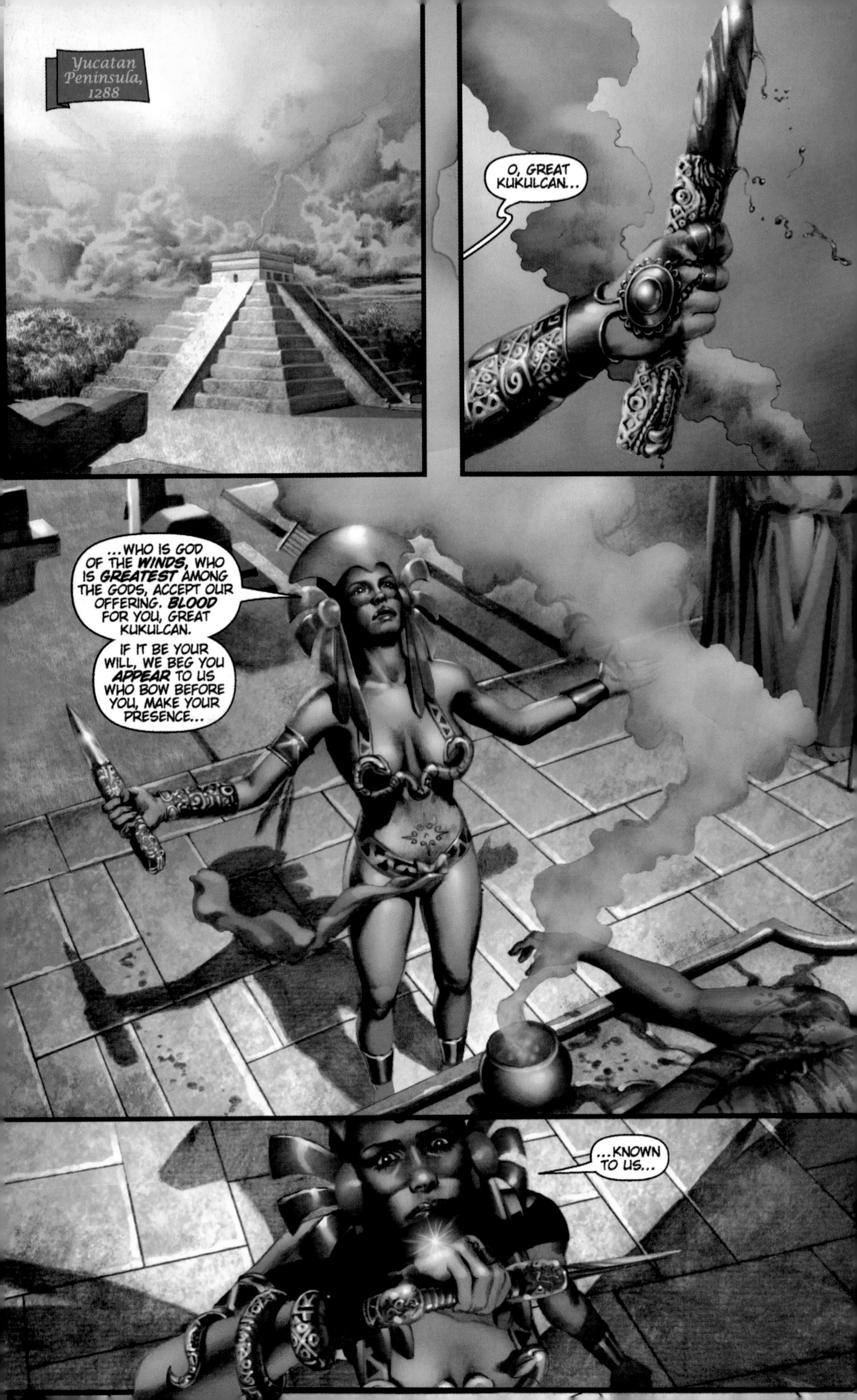
Yucatan Peninsula, 1288
O, GREAT KUKULCAN...
...WHO IS GOD OF THE WINDS, WHO IS GREATEST AMONG THE GODS, ACCEPT OUR OFFERING. BLOOD FOR YOU, GREAT KUKULCAN.
IF IT BE YOUR WILL, WE BEG YOU APPEAR TO US WHO BOW BEFORE YOU, MAKE YOUR PRESENCE...
...KNOWN TO US...

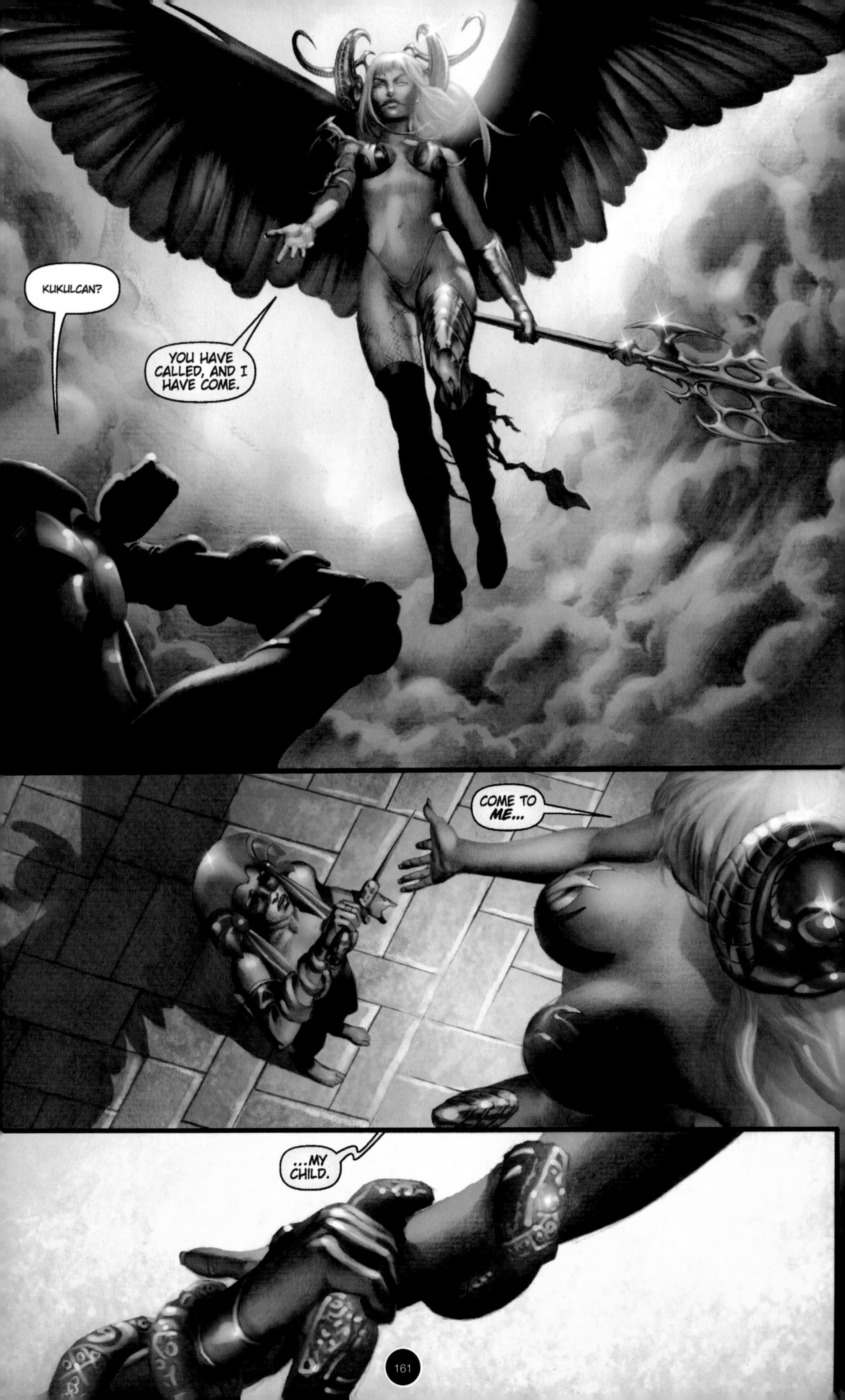
KUKULCAN?
YOU HAVE CALLED, AND I HAVE COME.
COME TO ME...
...MY CHILD.

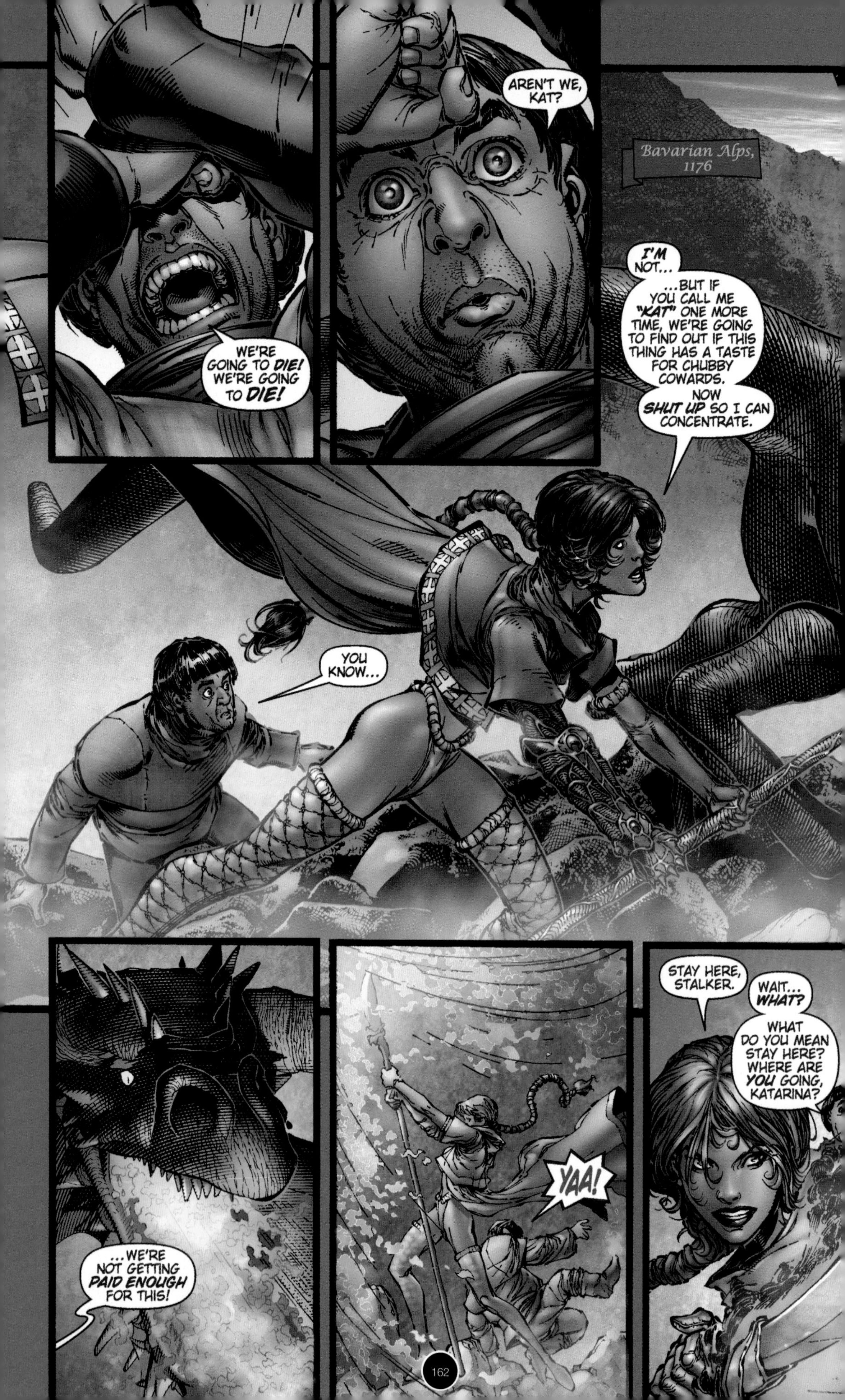
AREN'T WE, KAT?
Bavarian Alps, 1176
WE'RE GOING TO DIE! WE'RE GOING TO DIE!
I'M NOT...
...BUT IF YOU CALL ME "KAT" ONE MORE TIME, WE'RE GOING TO FIND OUT IF THIS THING HAS A TASTE FOR CHUBBY COWARDS.
NOW SHUT UP SO I CAN CONCENTRATE.
YOU KNOW...
...WE'RE NOT GETTING PAID ENOUGH FOR THIS!
YAA!
STAY HERE, STALKER.
WAIT... WHAT?
WHAT DO YOU MEAN STAY HERE? WHERE ARE YOU GOING, KATARINA?

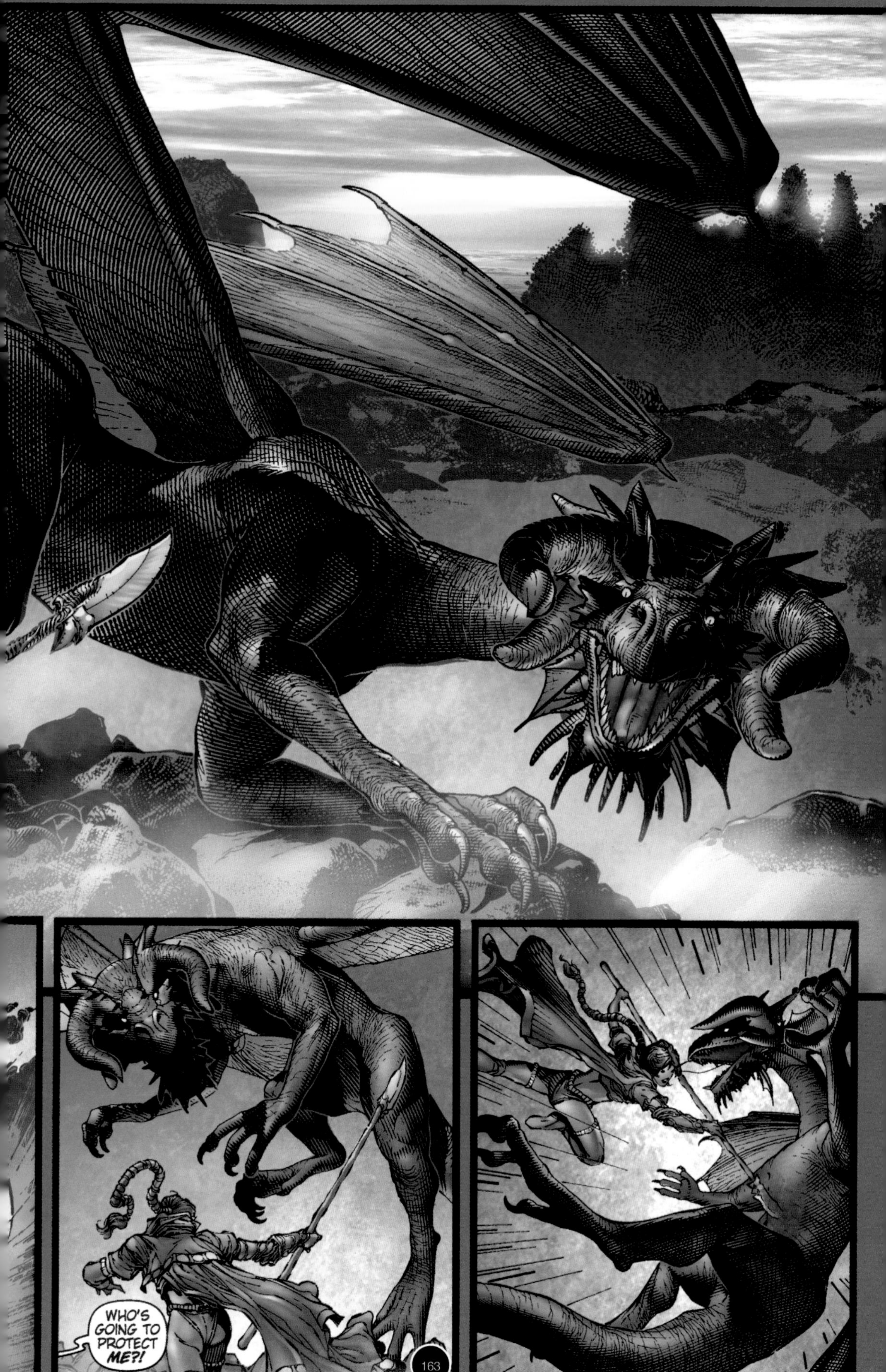
WHO'S GOING TO PROTECT ME?!

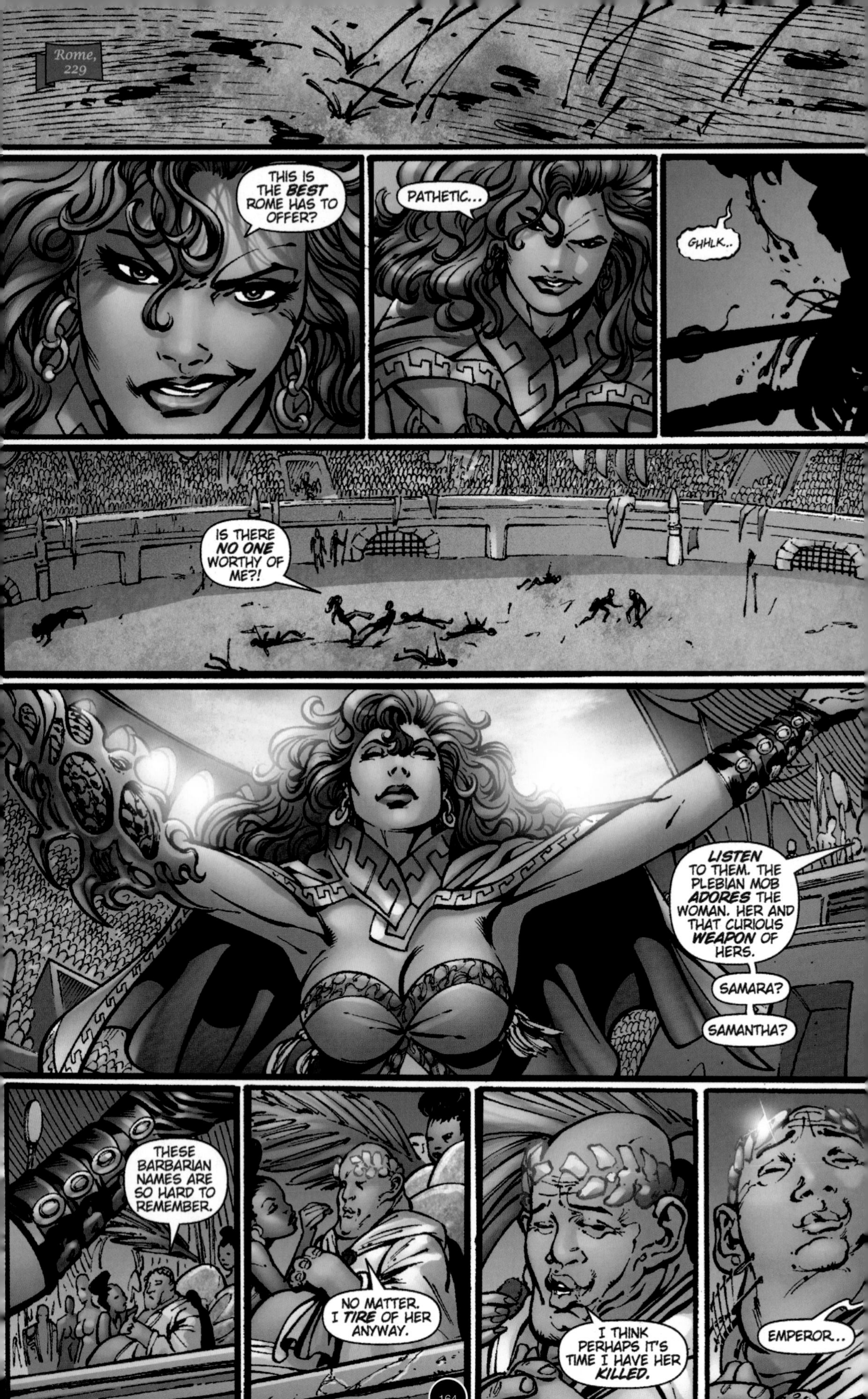
Rome, 229
THIS IS THE BEST ROME HAS TO OFFER?
PATHETIC...
GHHLK..
IS THERE NO ONE WORTHY OF ME?!
LISTEN TO THEM. THE PLEBIAN MOB ADORES THE WOMAN. HER AND THAT CURIOUS WEAPON OF HERS.
SAMARA?
SAMANTHA?
THESE BARBARIAN NAMES ARE SO HARD TO REMEMBER.
NO MATTER. I TIRE OF HER ANYWAY.
I THINK PERHAPS IT'S TIME I HAVE HER KILLED.
EMPEROR...

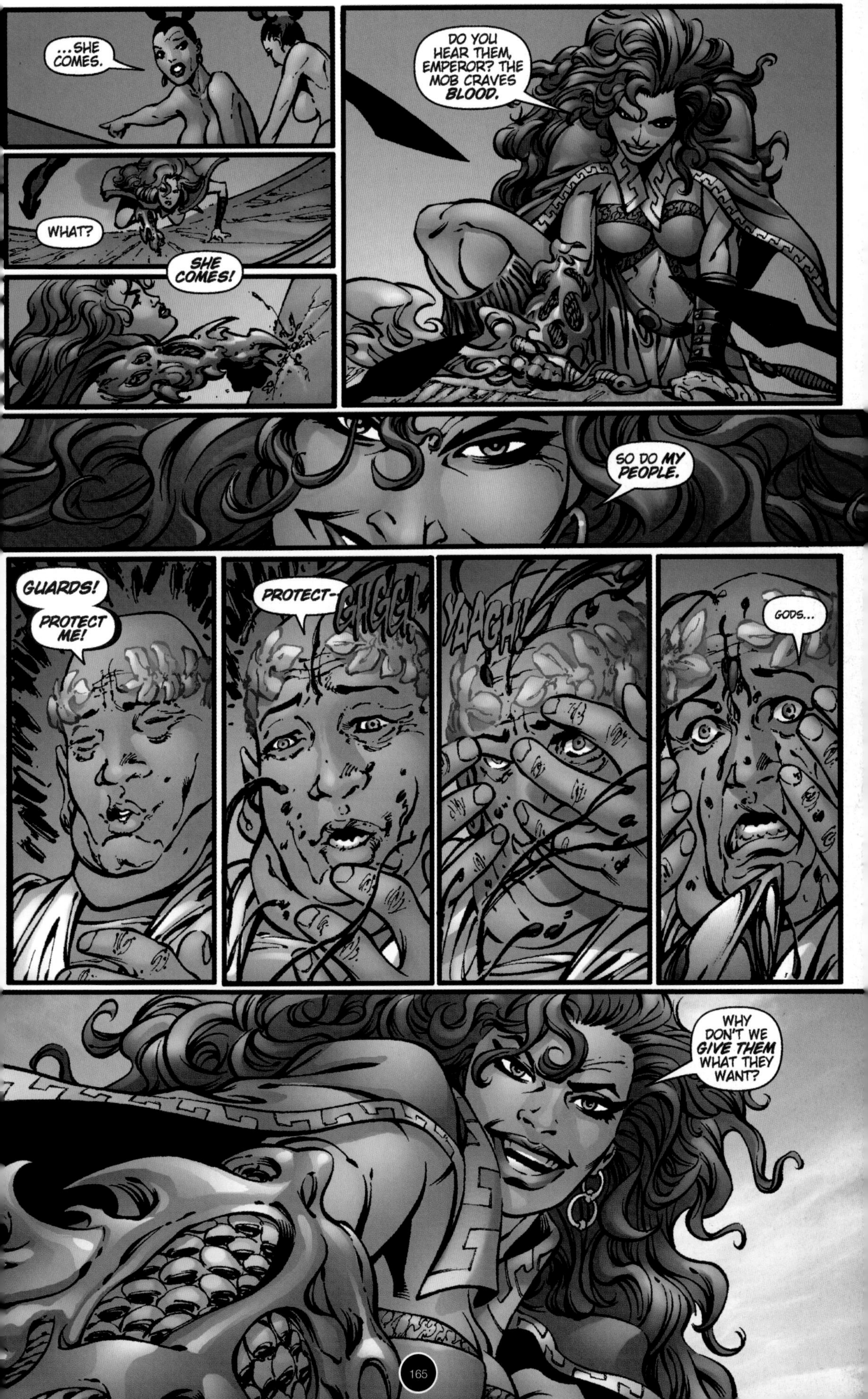
...SHE COMES.
DO YOU HEAR THEM, EMPEROR? THE MOB CRAVES BLOOD.
WHAT?
SHE COMES!
SO DO MY PEOPLE.
GUARDS!
PROTECT ME!
PROTECT--
GHGG!
YAACH!
GODS...
WHY DON'T WE GIVE THEM WHAT THEY WANT?

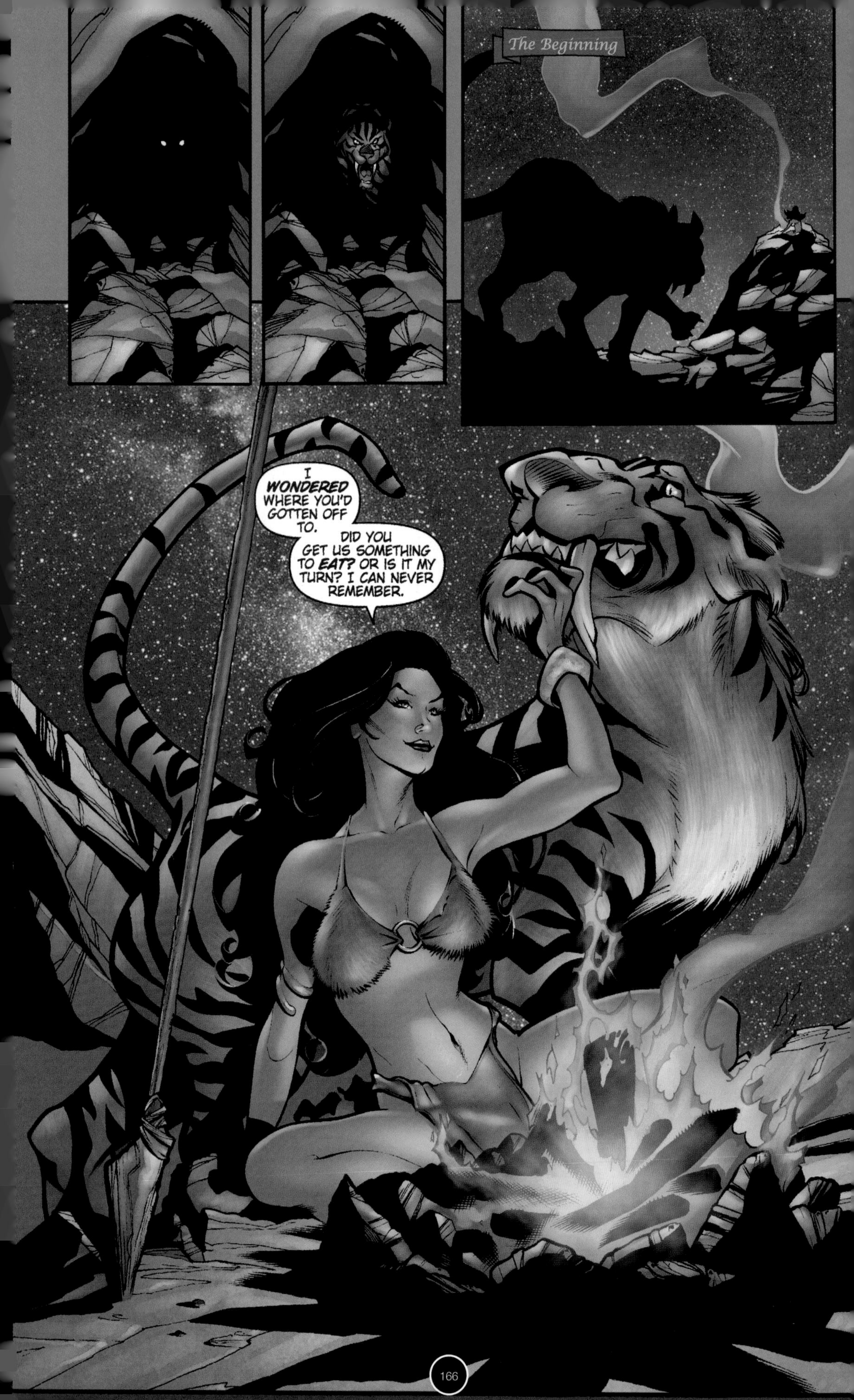
The Beginning
I WONDERED WHERE YOU'D GOTTEN OFF TO.
DID YOU GET US SOMETHING TO EAT? OR IS IT MY TURN? I CAN NEVER REMEMBER.

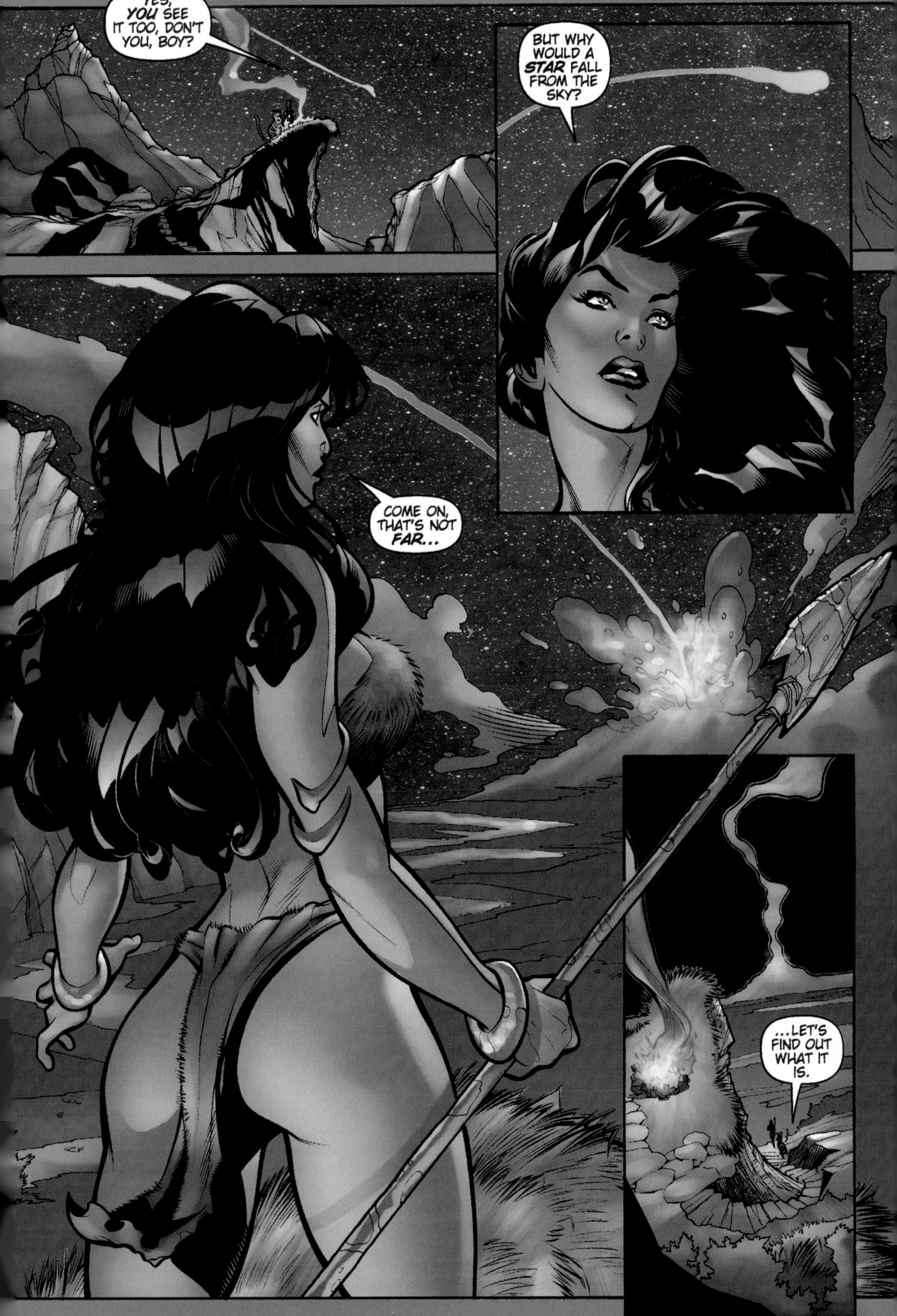
YES, YOU SEE IT TOO, DON'T YOU, BOY?
BUT WHY WOULD A STAR FALL FROM THE SKY?
COME ON, THAT'S NOT FAR...
...LET'S FIND OUT WHAT IT IS.

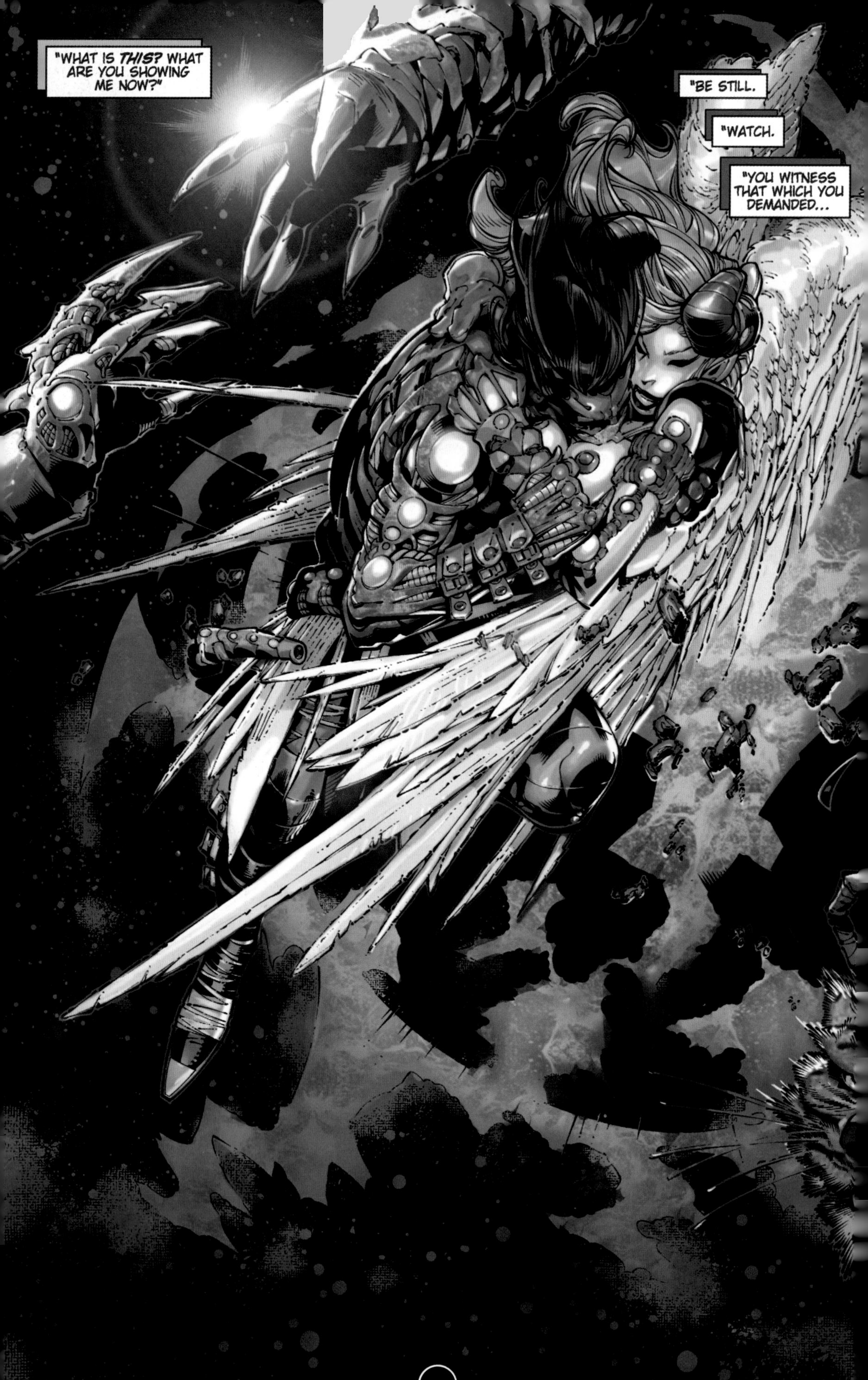
"WHAT IS THIS? WHAT ARE YOU SHOWING ME NOW?"
"BE STILL.
"WATCH.
"YOU WITNESS THAT WHICH YOU DEMANDED...

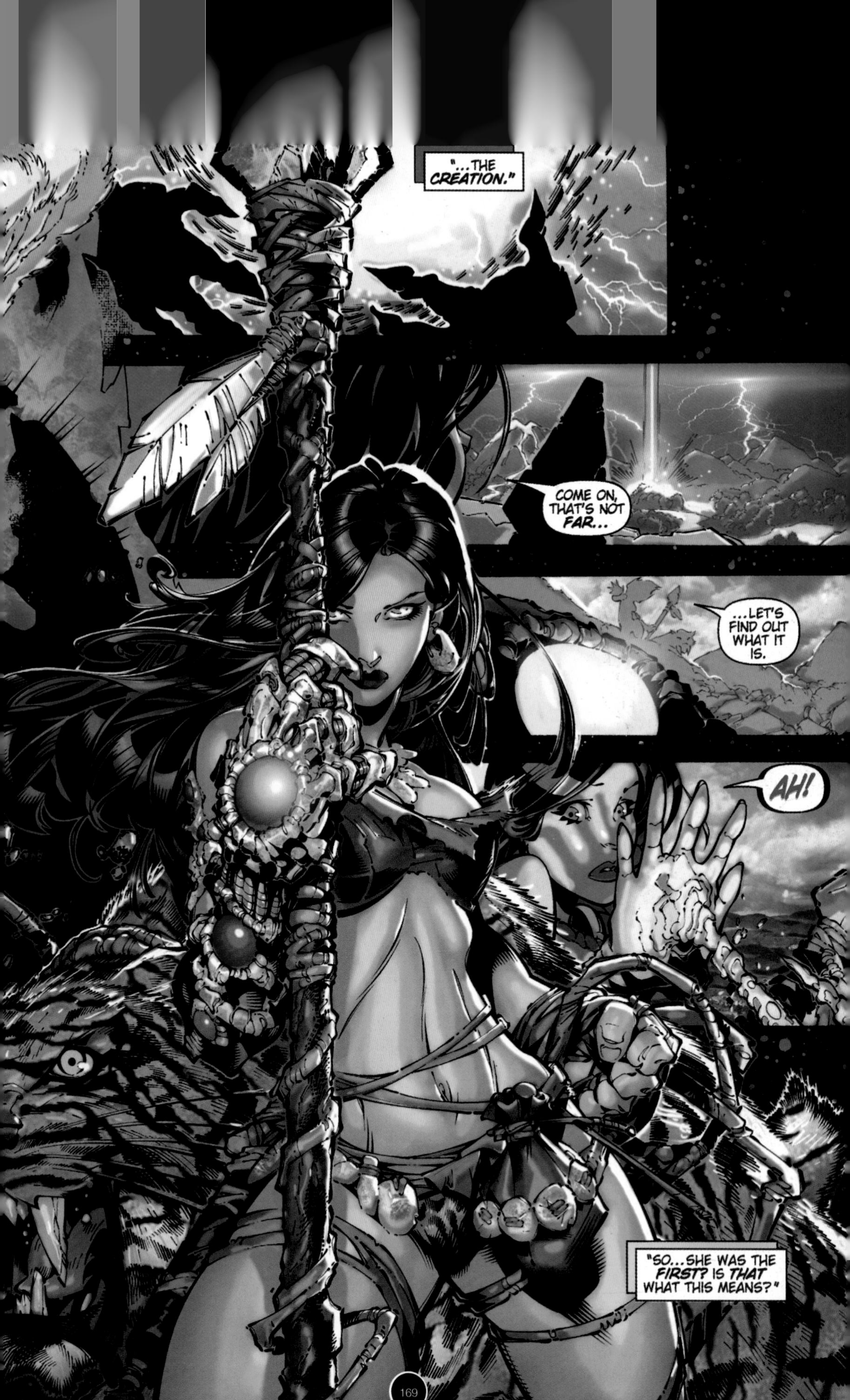
"...THE CREATION."
COME ON, THAT'S NOT FAR...
...LET'S FIND OUT WHAT IT IS.
AH!
"SO...SHE WAS THE FIRST? IS THAT WHAT THIS MEANS?"

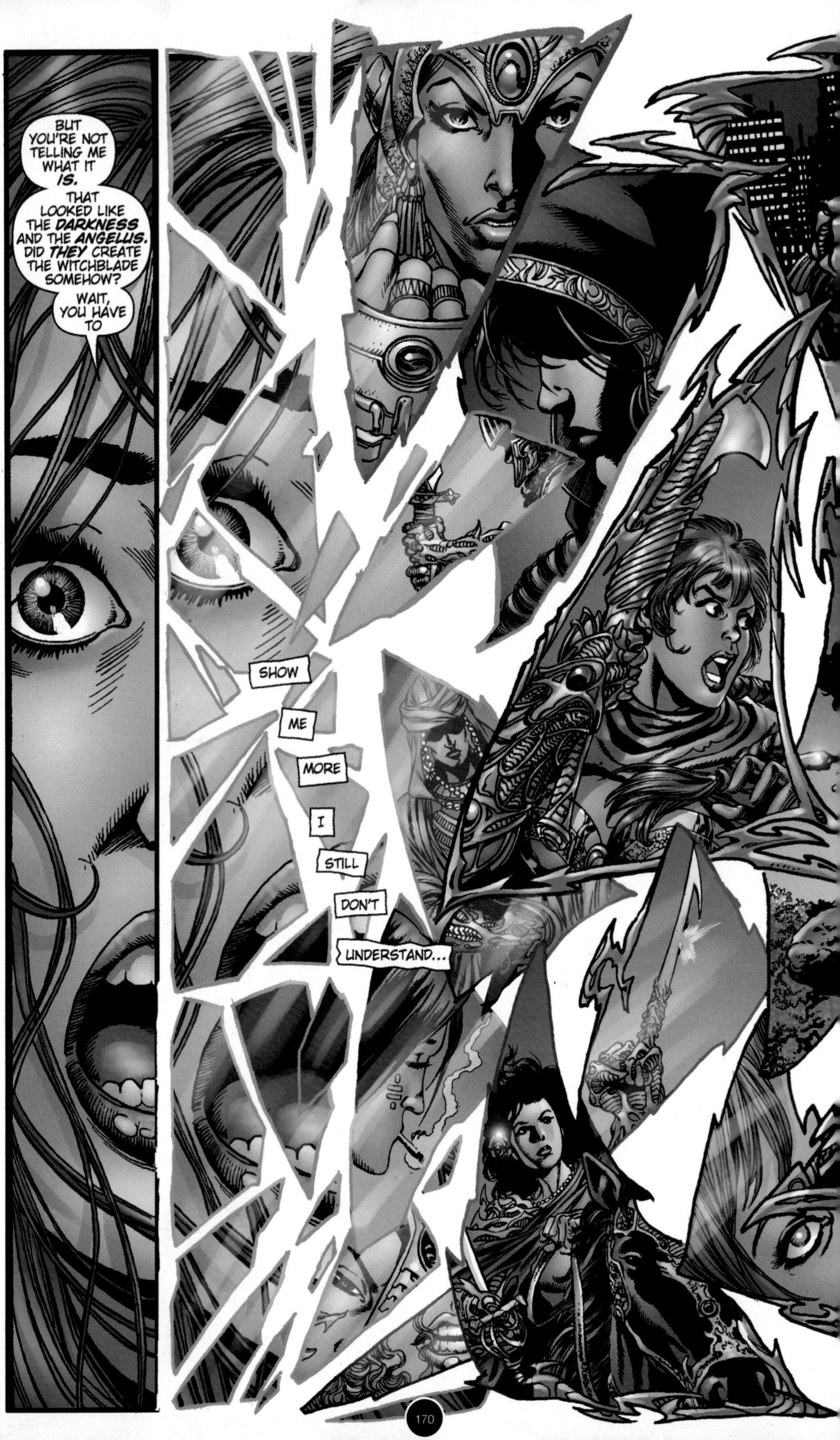
BUT YOU'RE NOT TELLING ME WHAT IT *IS.* THAT LOOKED LIKE THE **DARKNESS** AND THE **ANGELUS.** DID *THEY* CREATE THE WITCHBLADE SOMEHOW? WAIT, YOU HAVE TO
SHOW
ME
MORE
I
STILL
DON'T
UNDERSTAND...

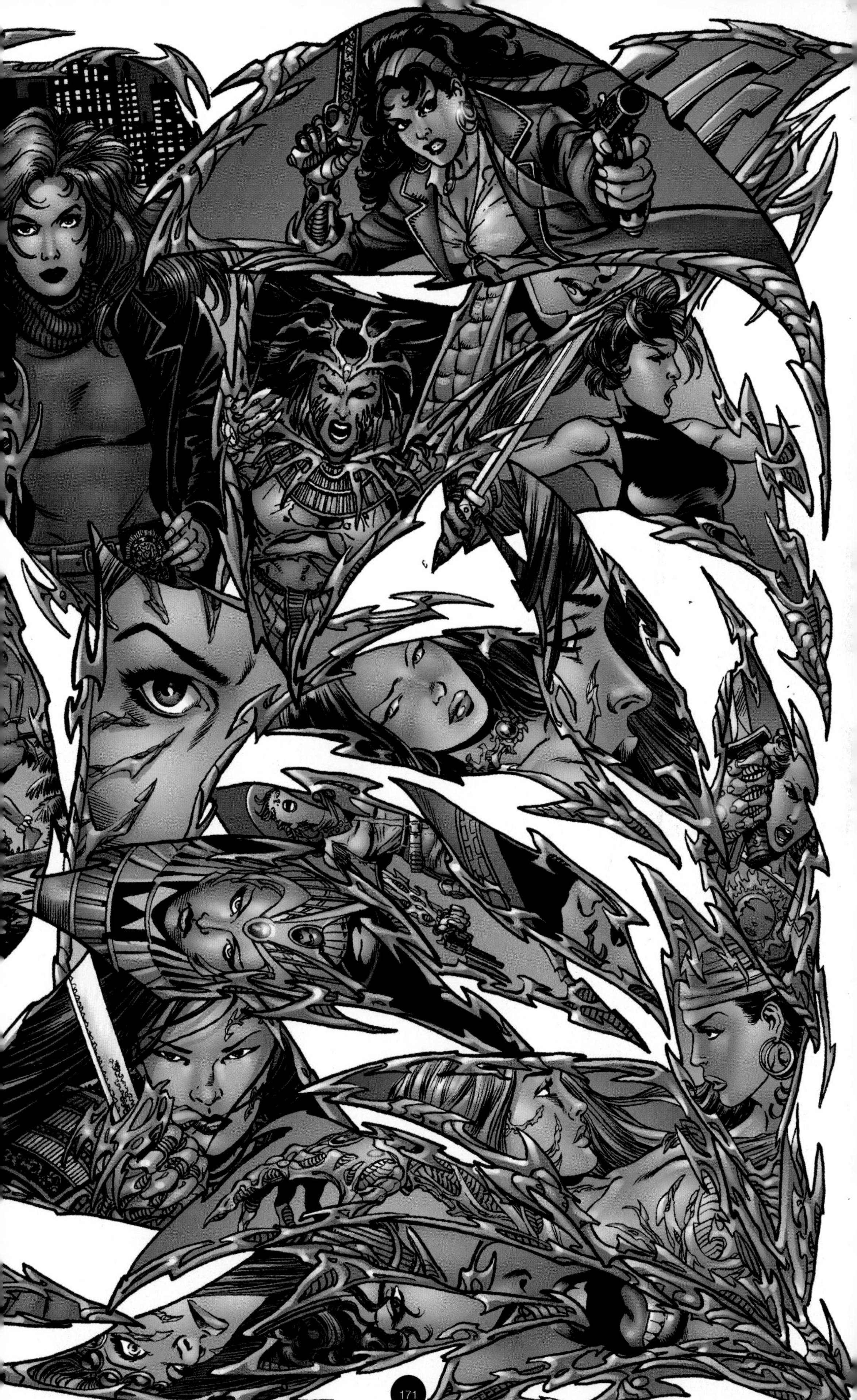

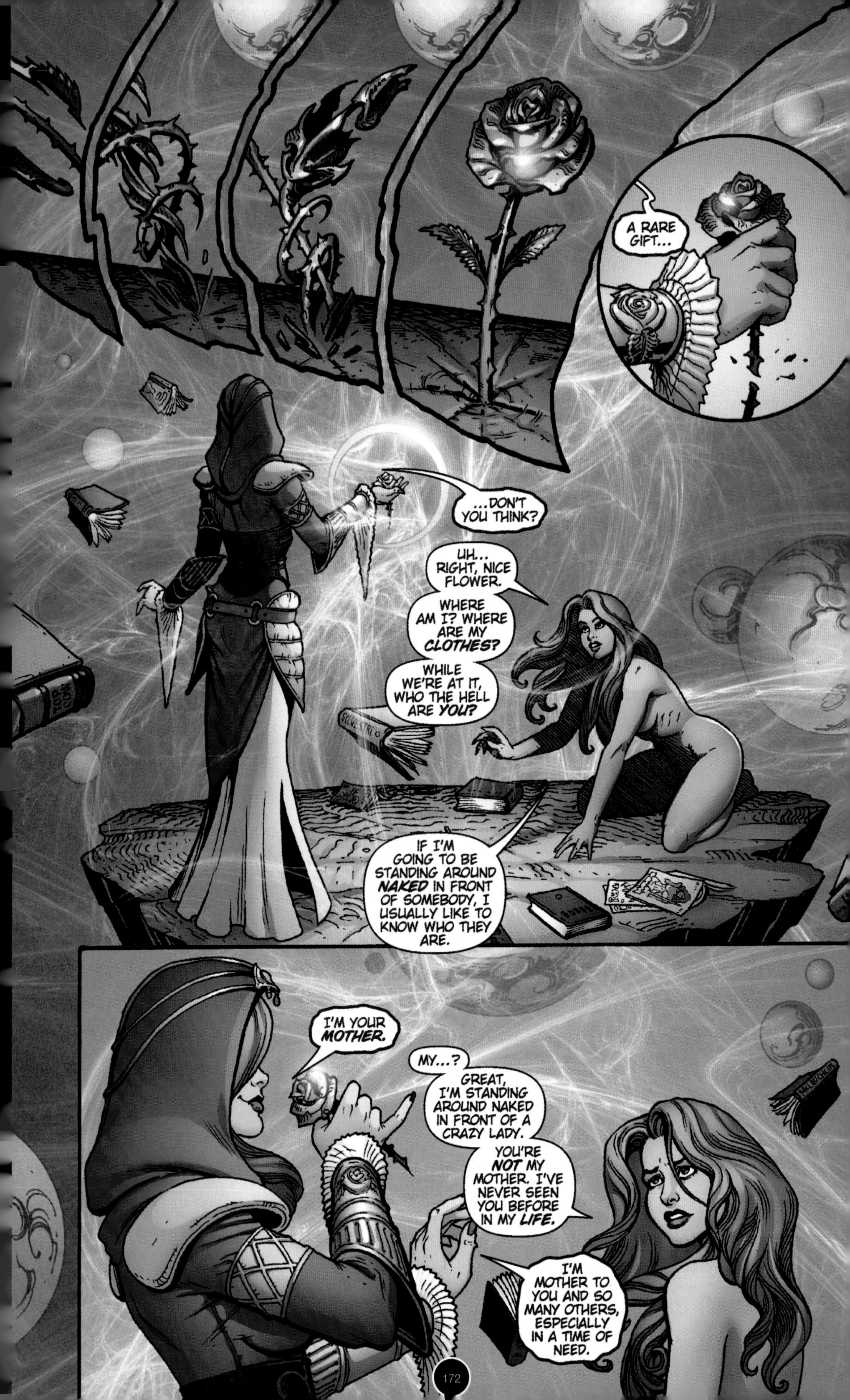
A RARE GIFT...
...DON'T YOU THINK?
UH... RIGHT, NICE FLOWER.
WHERE AM I? WHERE ARE MY CLOTHES?
WHILE WE'RE AT IT, WHO THE HELL ARE YOU?
IF I'M GOING TO BE STANDING AROUND NAKED IN FRONT OF SOMEBODY, I USUALLY LIKE TO KNOW WHO THEY ARE.
I'M YOUR MOTHER.
MY...?
GREAT, I'M STANDING AROUND NAKED IN FRONT OF A CRAZY LADY.
YOU'RE NOT MY MOTHER. I'VE NEVER SEEN YOU BEFORE IN MY LIFE.
I'M MOTHER TO YOU AND SO MANY OTHERS, ESPECIALLY IN A TIME OF NEED.

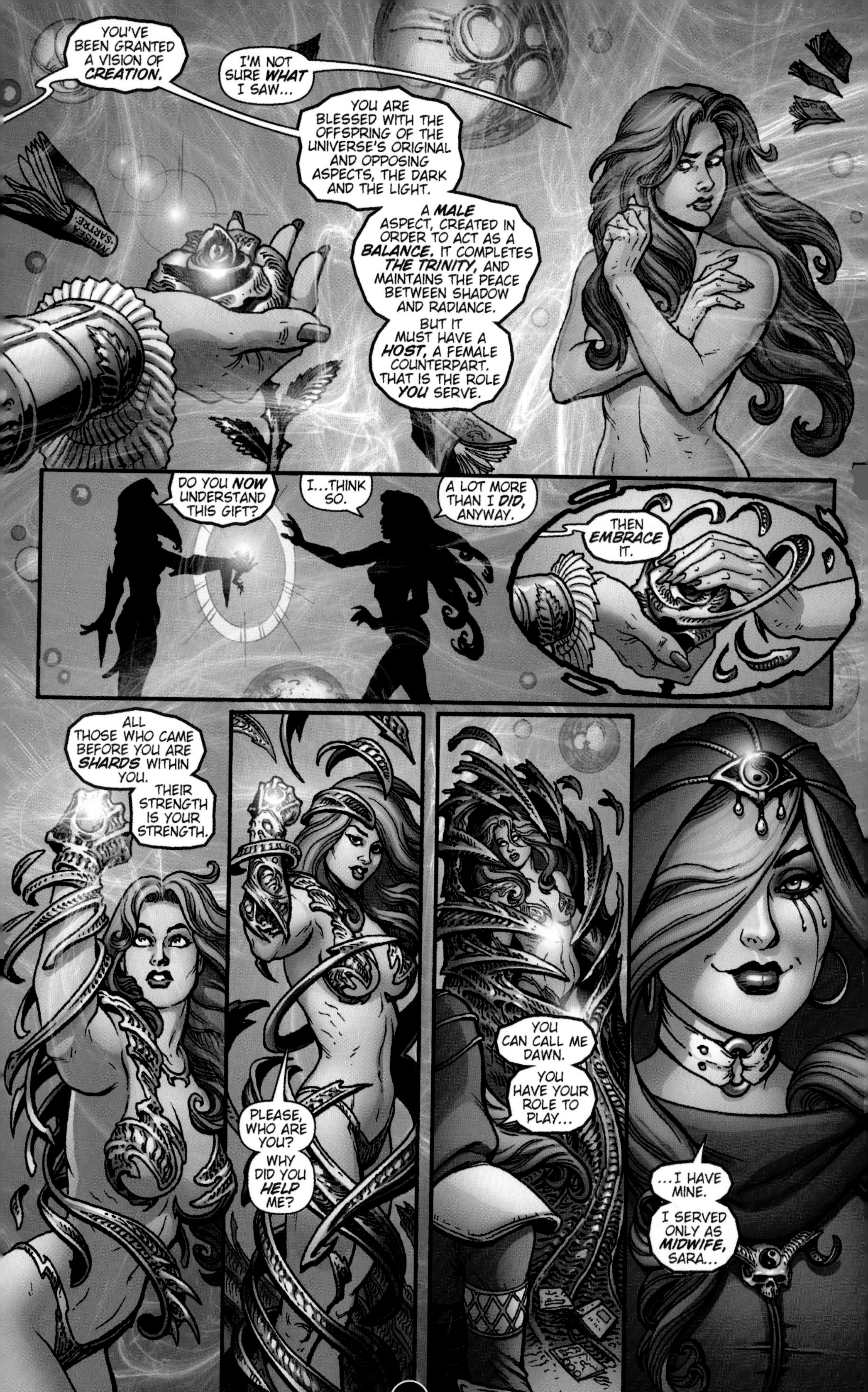
YOU'VE BEEN GRANTED A VISION OF CREATION.
I'M NOT SURE WHAT I SAW...
YOU ARE BLESSED WITH THE OFFSPRING OF THE UNIVERSE'S ORIGINAL AND OPPOSING ASPECTS, THE DARK AND THE LIGHT.
A MALE ASPECT, CREATED IN ORDER TO ACT AS A BALANCE. IT COMPLETES THE TRINITY, AND MAINTAINS THE PEACE BETWEEN SHADOW AND RADIANCE.
BUT IT MUST HAVE A HOST, A FEMALE COUNTERPART. THAT IS THE ROLE YOU SERVE.
DO YOU NOW UNDERSTAND THIS GIFT?
I...THINK SO.
A LOT MORE THAN I DID, ANYWAY.
THEN EMBRACE IT.
ALL THOSE WHO CAME BEFORE YOU ARE SHARDS WITHIN YOU.
THEIR STRENGTH IS YOUR STRENGTH.
PLEASE, WHO ARE YOU?
WHY DID YOU HELP ME?
YOU CAN CALL ME DAWN.
YOU HAVE YOUR ROLE TO PLAY...
...I HAVE MINE.
I SERVED ONLY AS MIDWIFE, SARA...

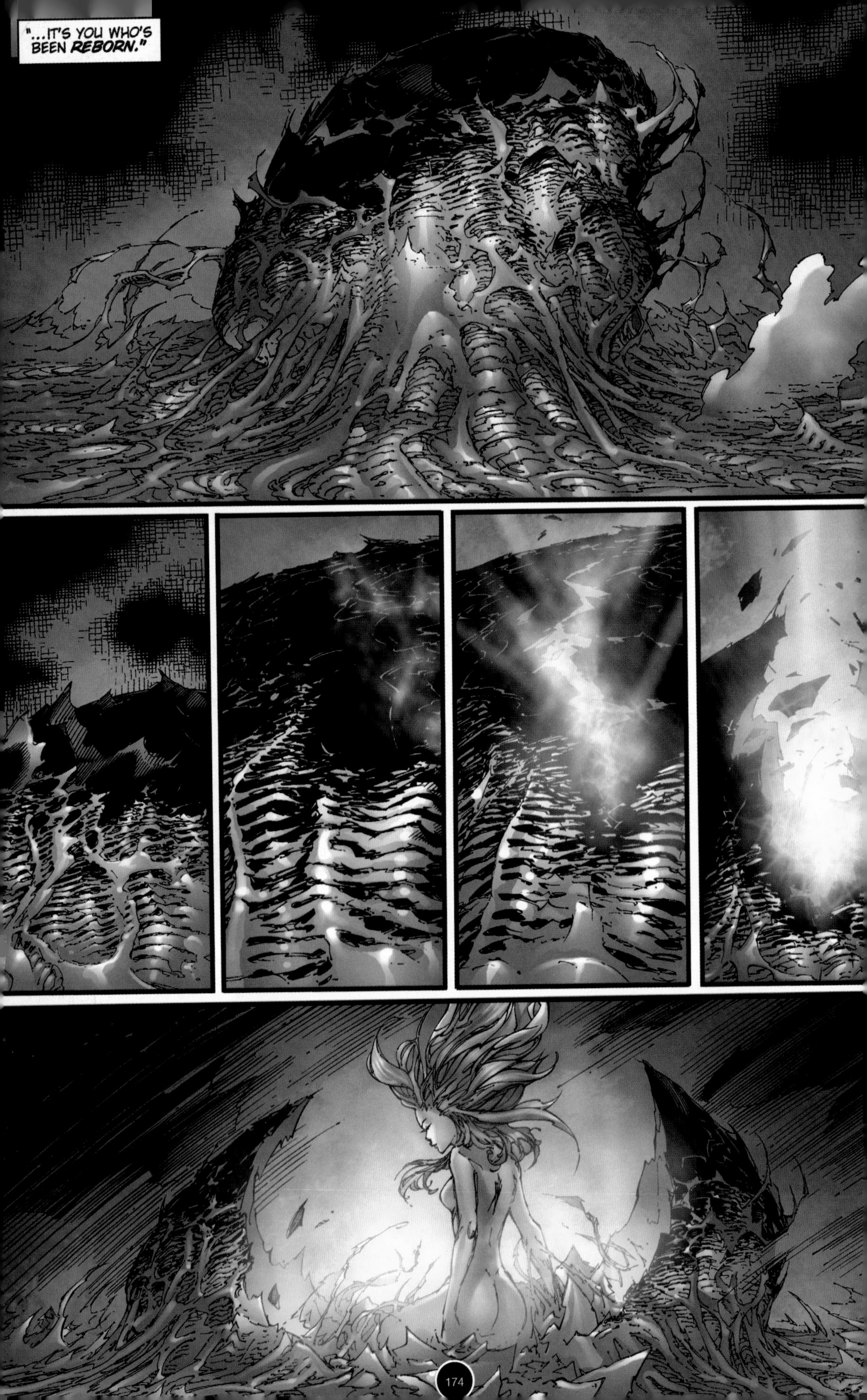
"...IT'S YOU WHO'S BEEN REBORN."

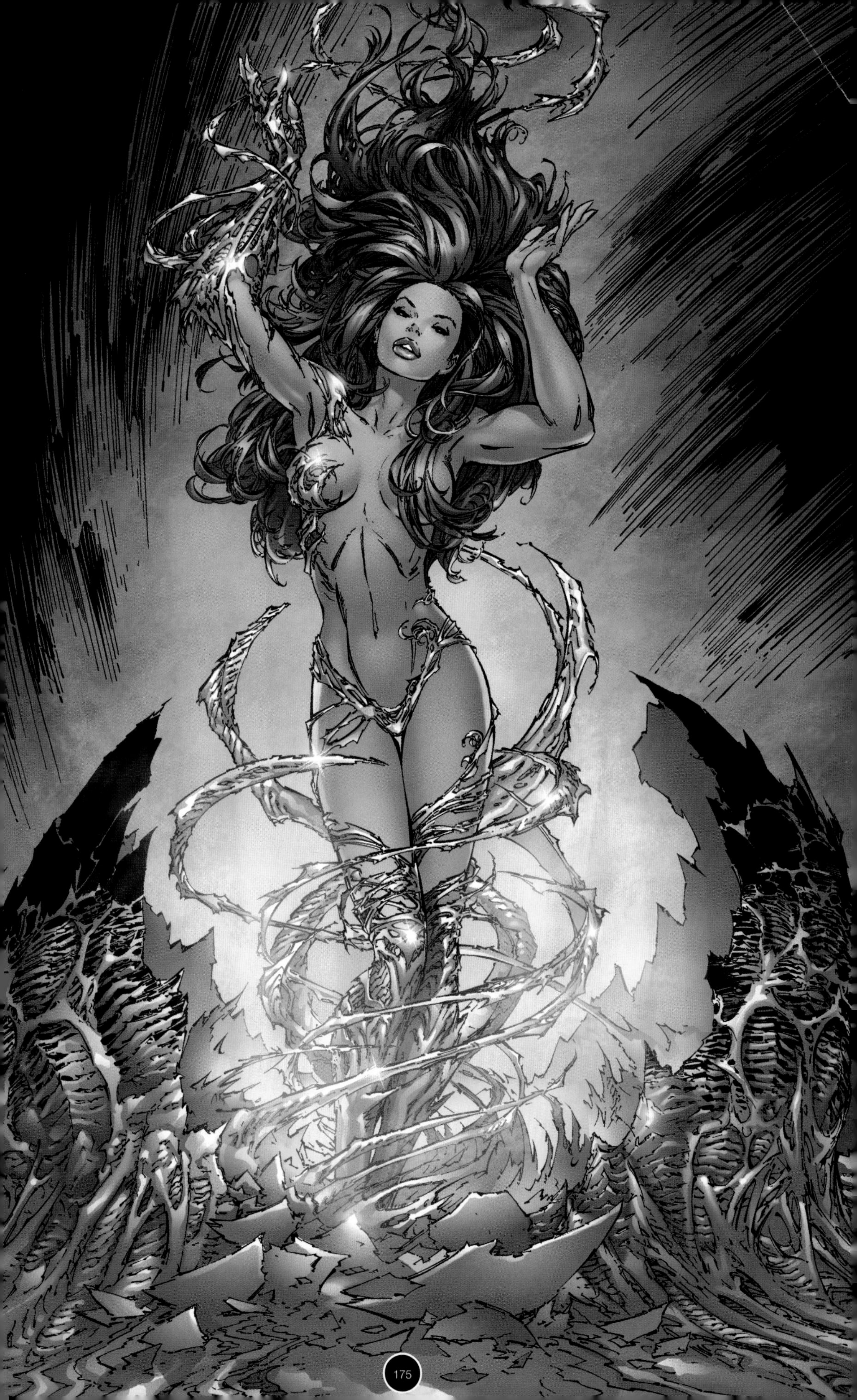

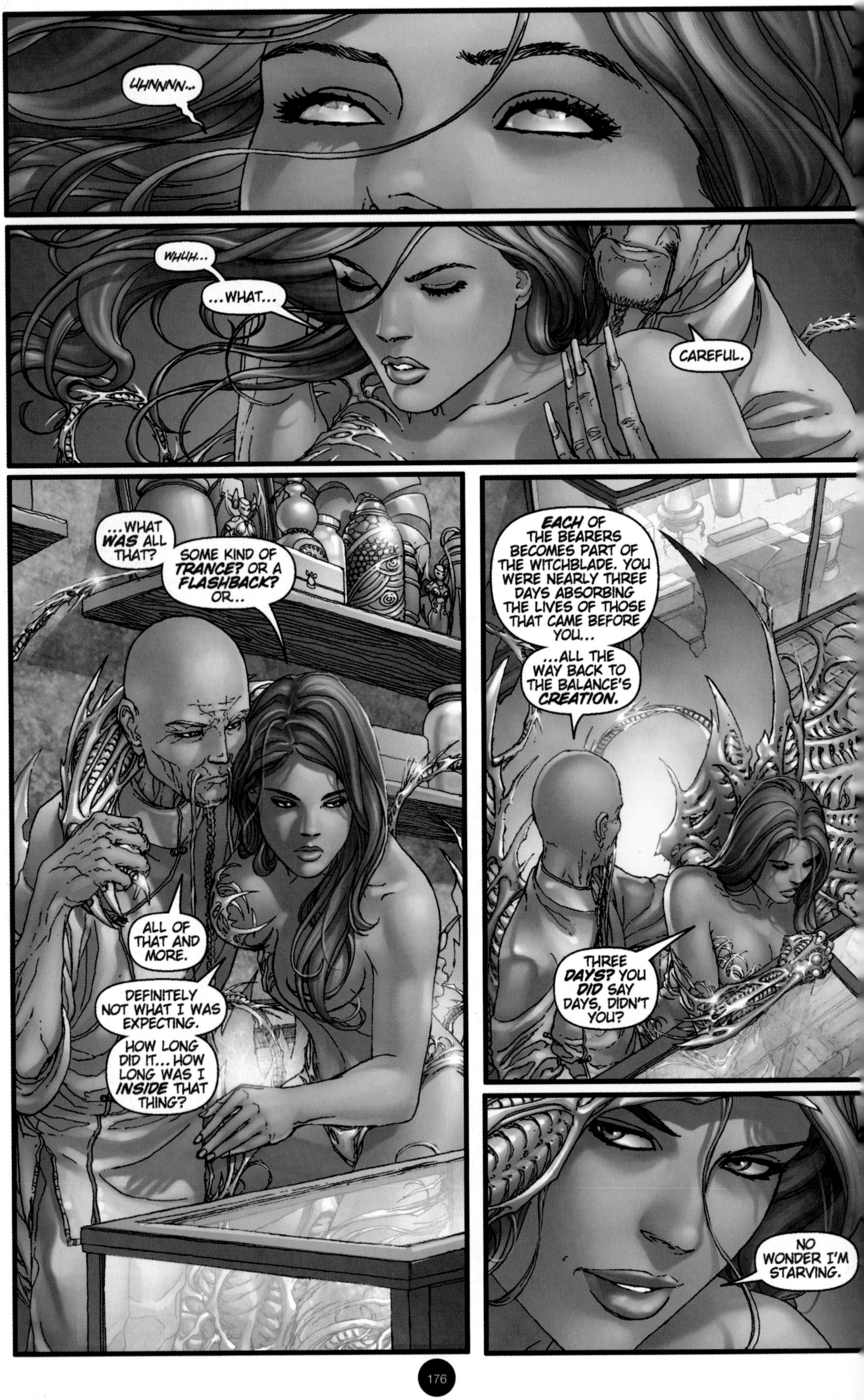
UHNNNN...
WHUH...
...WHAT...
CAREFUL.
...WHAT WAS ALL THAT?
SOME KIND OF TRANCE? OR A FLASHBACK? OR...
ALL OF THAT AND MORE.
DEFINITELY NOT WHAT I WAS EXPECTING.
HOW LONG DID IT... HOW LONG WAS I INSIDE THAT THING?
EACH OF THE BEARERS BECOMES PART OF THE WITCHBLADE. YOU WERE NEARLY THREE DAYS ABSORBING THE LIVES OF THOSE THAT CAME BEFORE YOU...
...ALL THE WAY BACK TO THE BALANCE'S CREATION.
THREE DAYS? YOU DID SAY DAYS, DIDN'T YOU?
NO WONDER I'M STARVING.

TAKE THIS.

THANKS. I WAS KIND OF HOPING MY DAYS OF SHOPPING FOR *NEW CLOTHES* EVERY WEEK WERE BEHIND ME.

YOU UNDERSTAND THE NATURE OF YOUR BURDEN NOW?

I DO.

YOU DO NOT HOLD THE WITCHBLADE IN COMPLETE CONTROL. YET NEITHER HAVE YOU ALLOWED *IT* TO CONTROL *YOU.*

MANY BEFORE YOU WERE NOT SO FORTUNATE.

SO THE WITCHBLADE IS BASICALLY *MALE,* HUH?

THAT EXPLAINS A LOT.

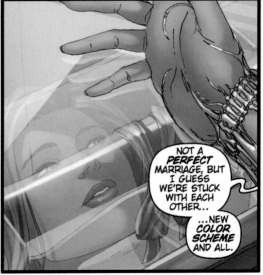

NOT A *PERFECT* MARRIAGE, BUT I GUESS WE'RE STUCK WITH EACH OTHER..

...NEW *COLOR SCHEME* AND ALL.

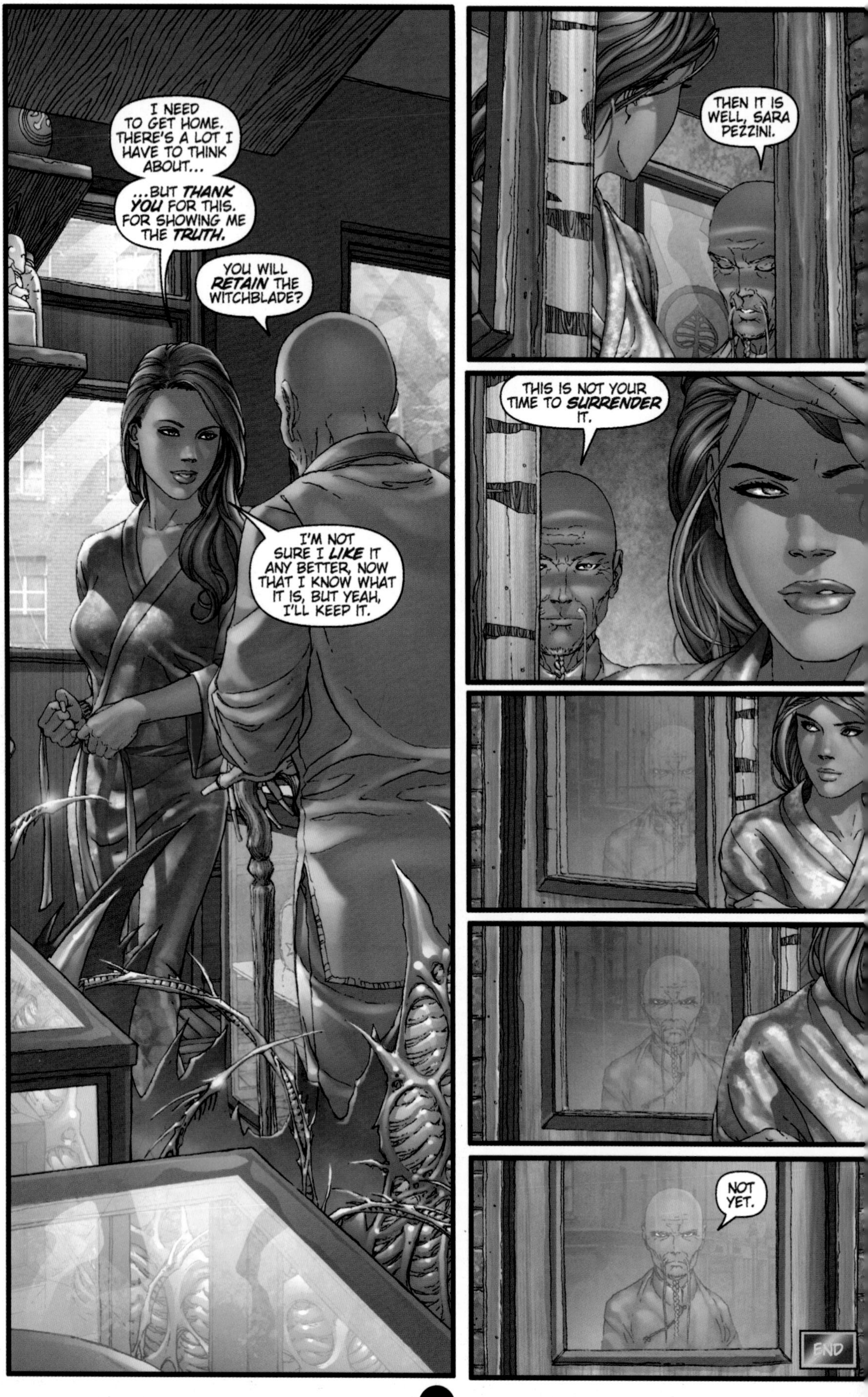
I NEED TO GET HOME. THERE'S A LOT I HAVE TO THINK ABOUT...
...BUT THANK YOU FOR THIS. FOR SHOWING ME THE TRUTH.
YOU WILL RETAIN THE WITCHBLADE?
I'M NOT SURE I LIKE IT ANY BETTER, NOW THAT I KNOW WHAT IT IS, BUT YEAH, I'LL KEEP IT.
THEN IT IS WELL, SARA PEZZINI.
THIS IS NOT YOUR TIME TO SURRENDER IT.
NOT YET.
END

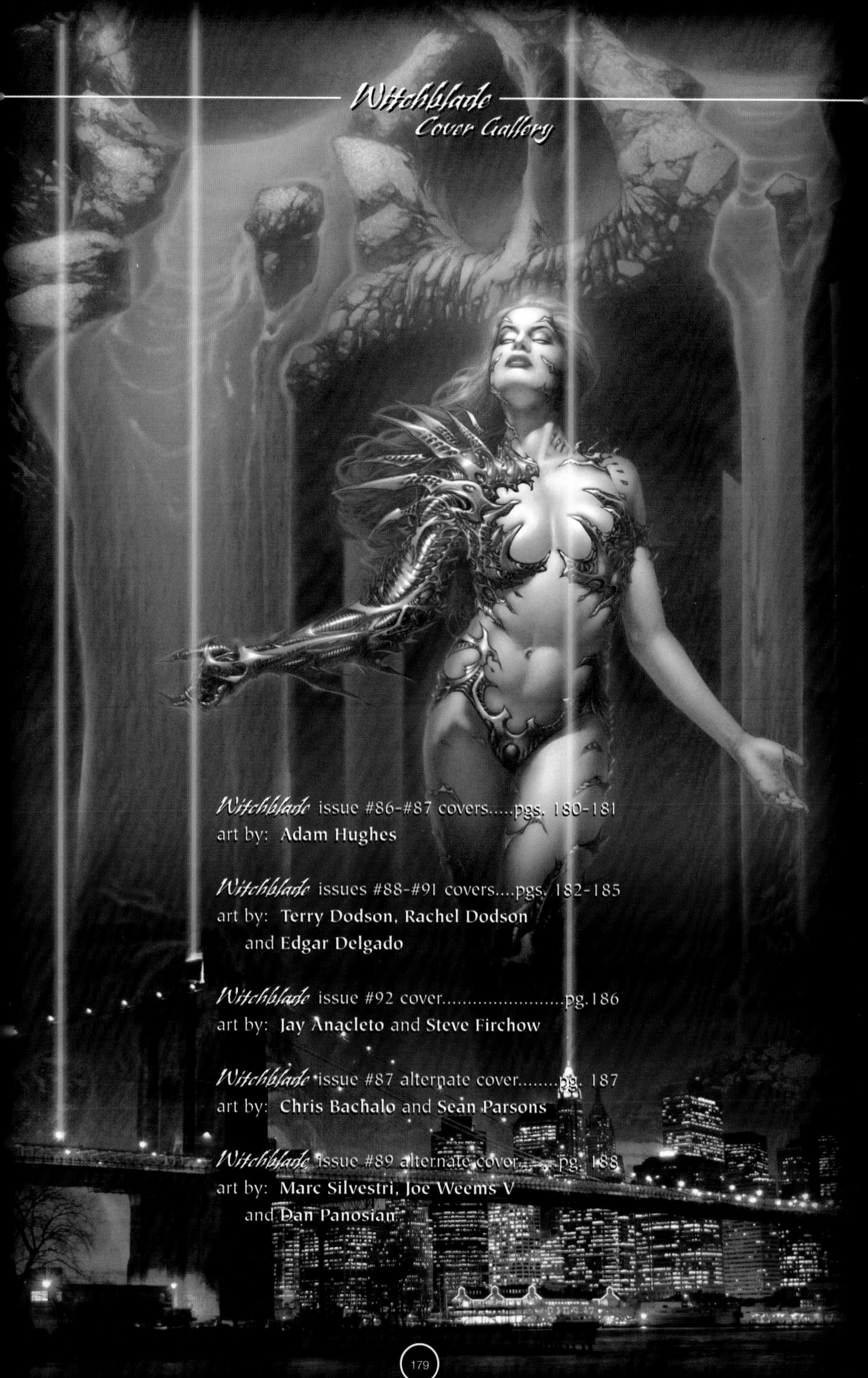

Witchblade Cover Gallery

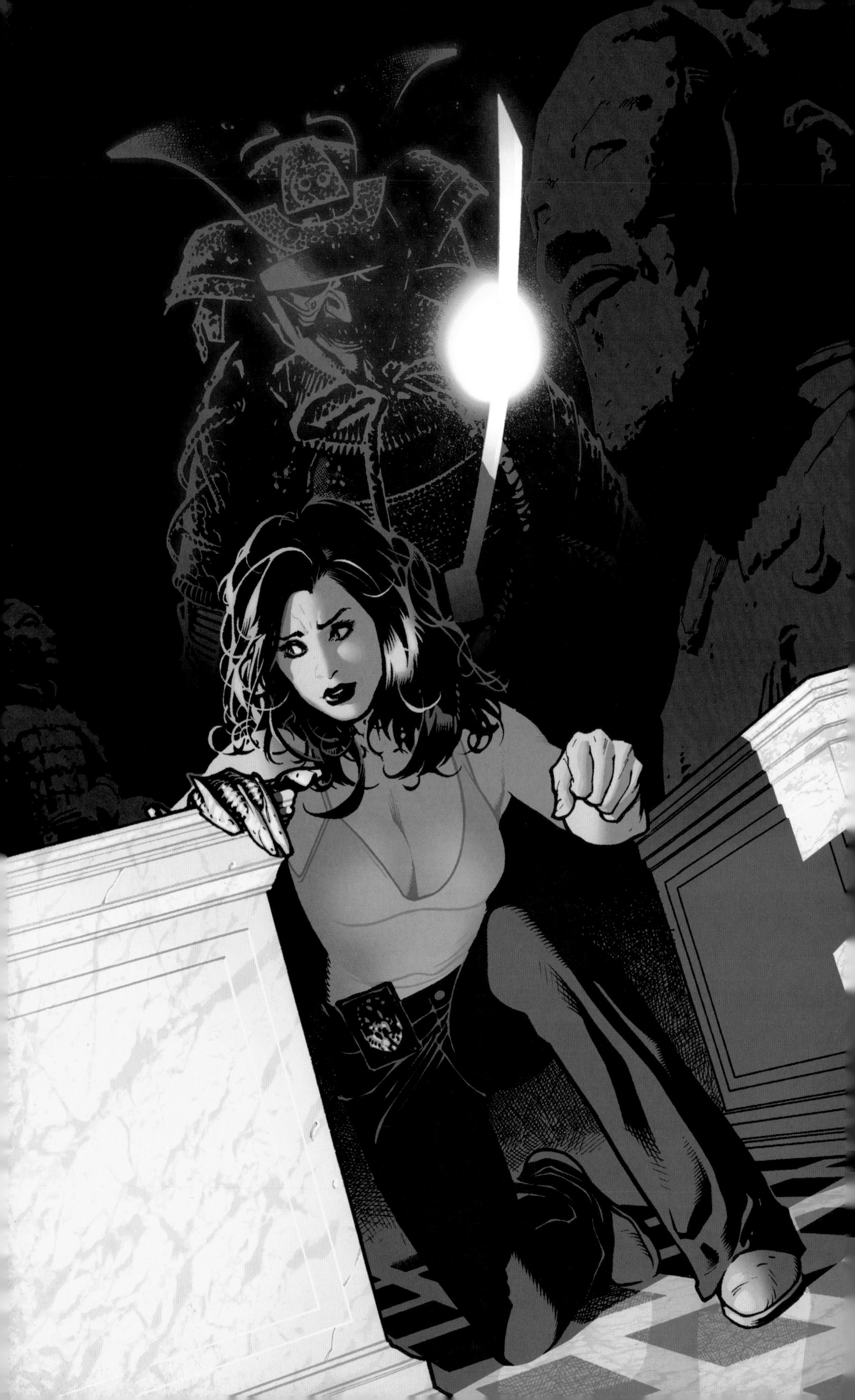

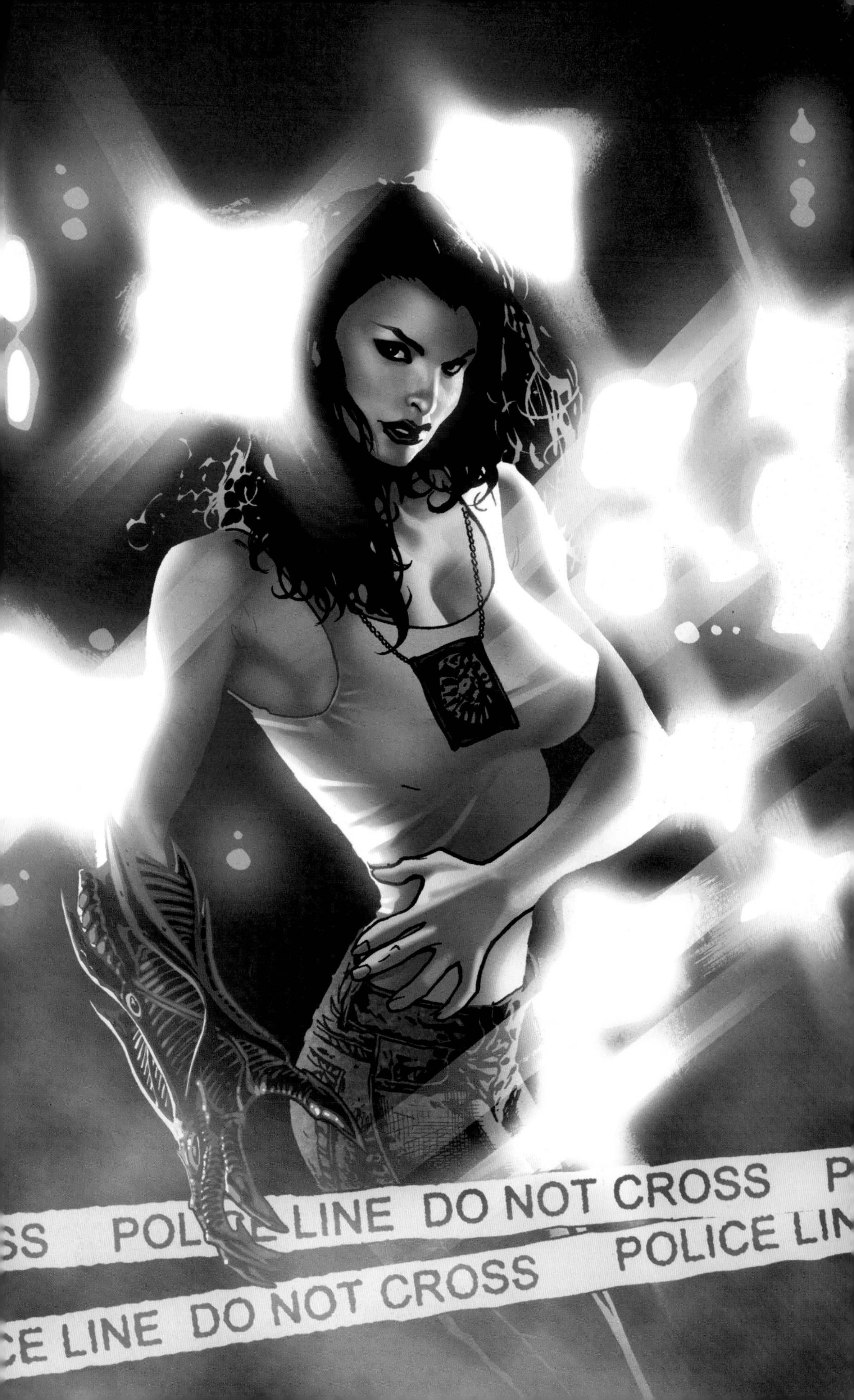

DO NOT CROSS
POLICE LINE DO NOT CROSS
POLICE LIN
CE LINE DO NOT CROSS

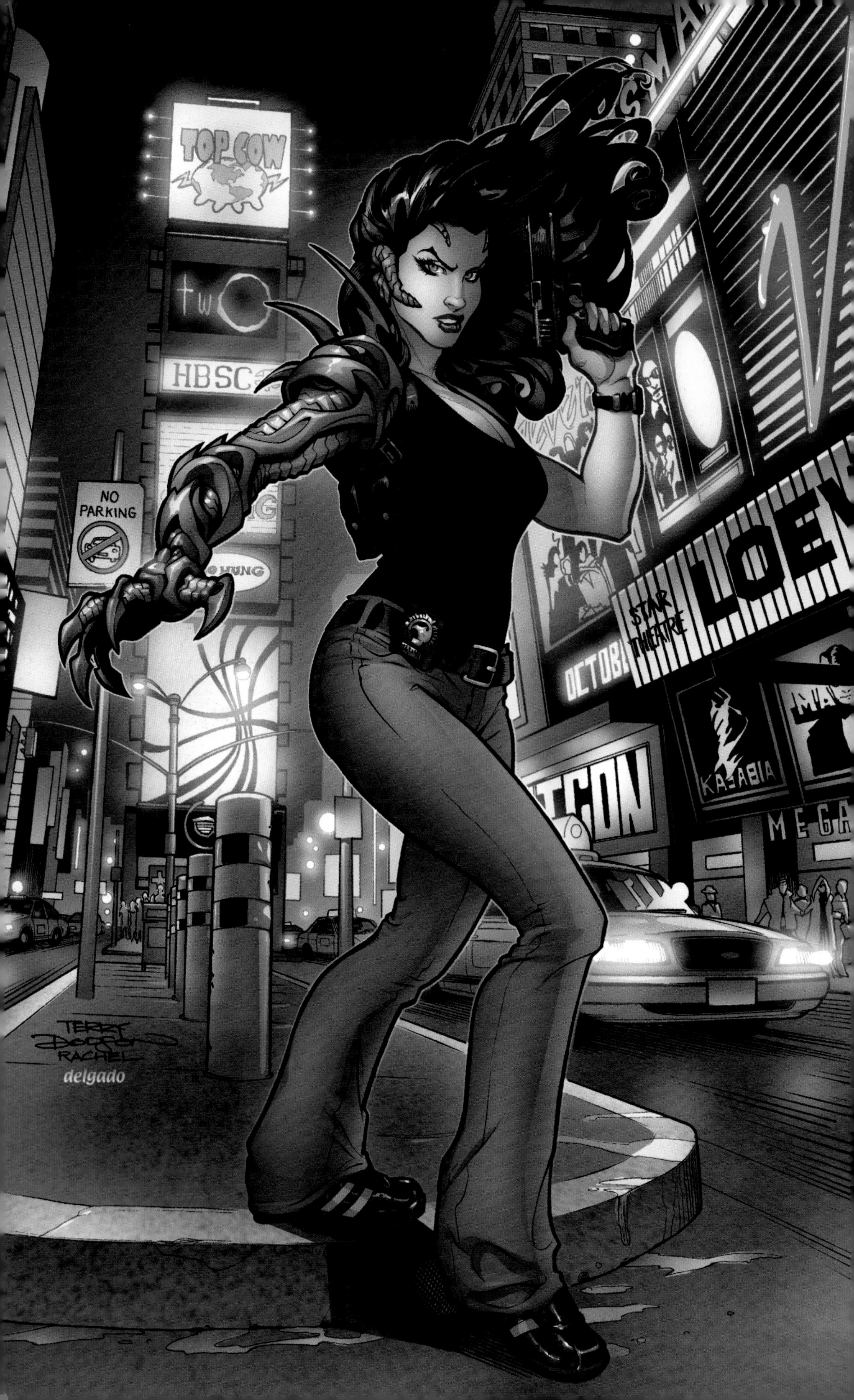
TOP COW
HBSC
NO PARKING
STAR THEATRE
KASABIA
TERRY DODSON
RACHEL
delgado

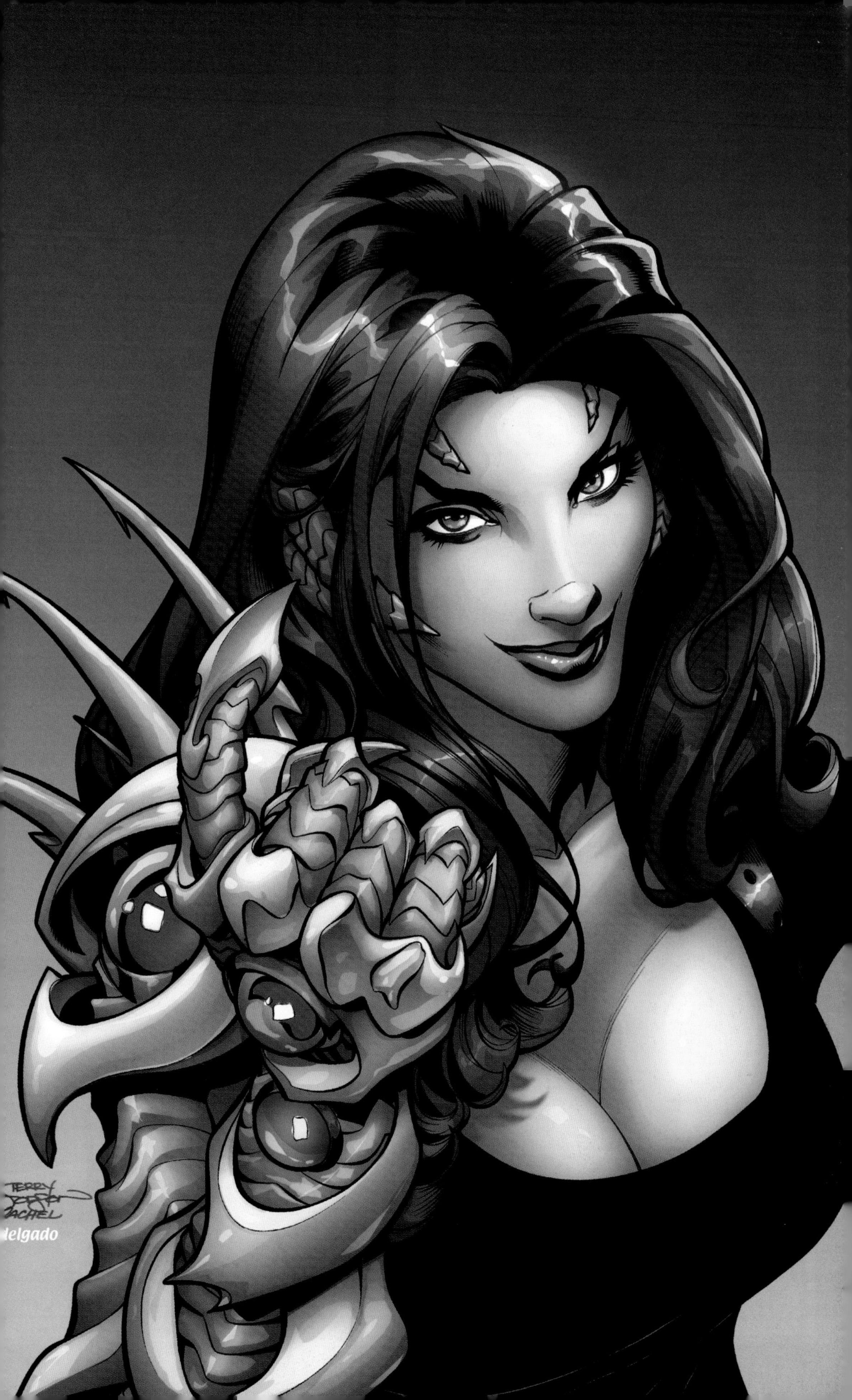
TERRY
RACHEL

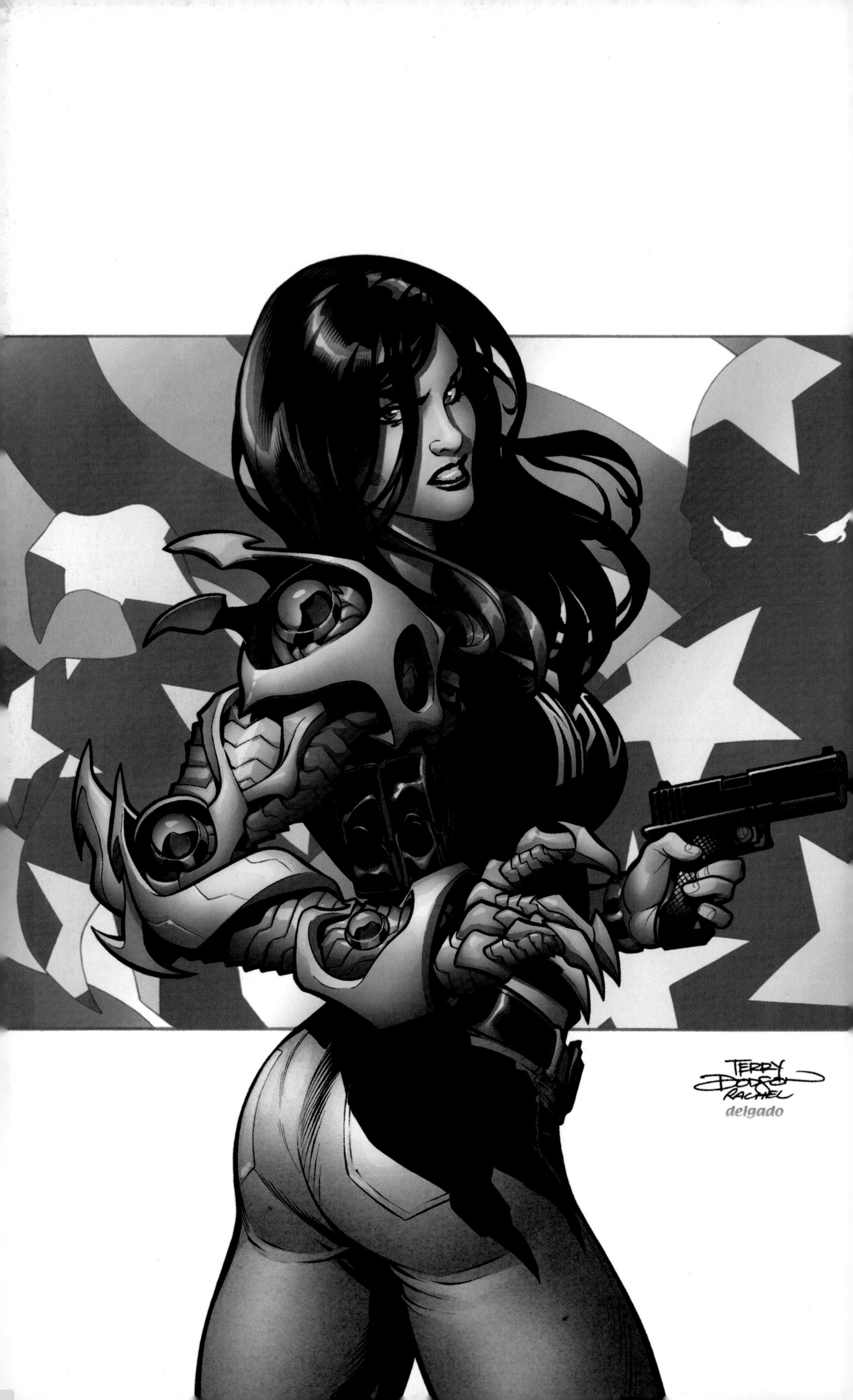
TERRY DODSON RACHEL
delgado

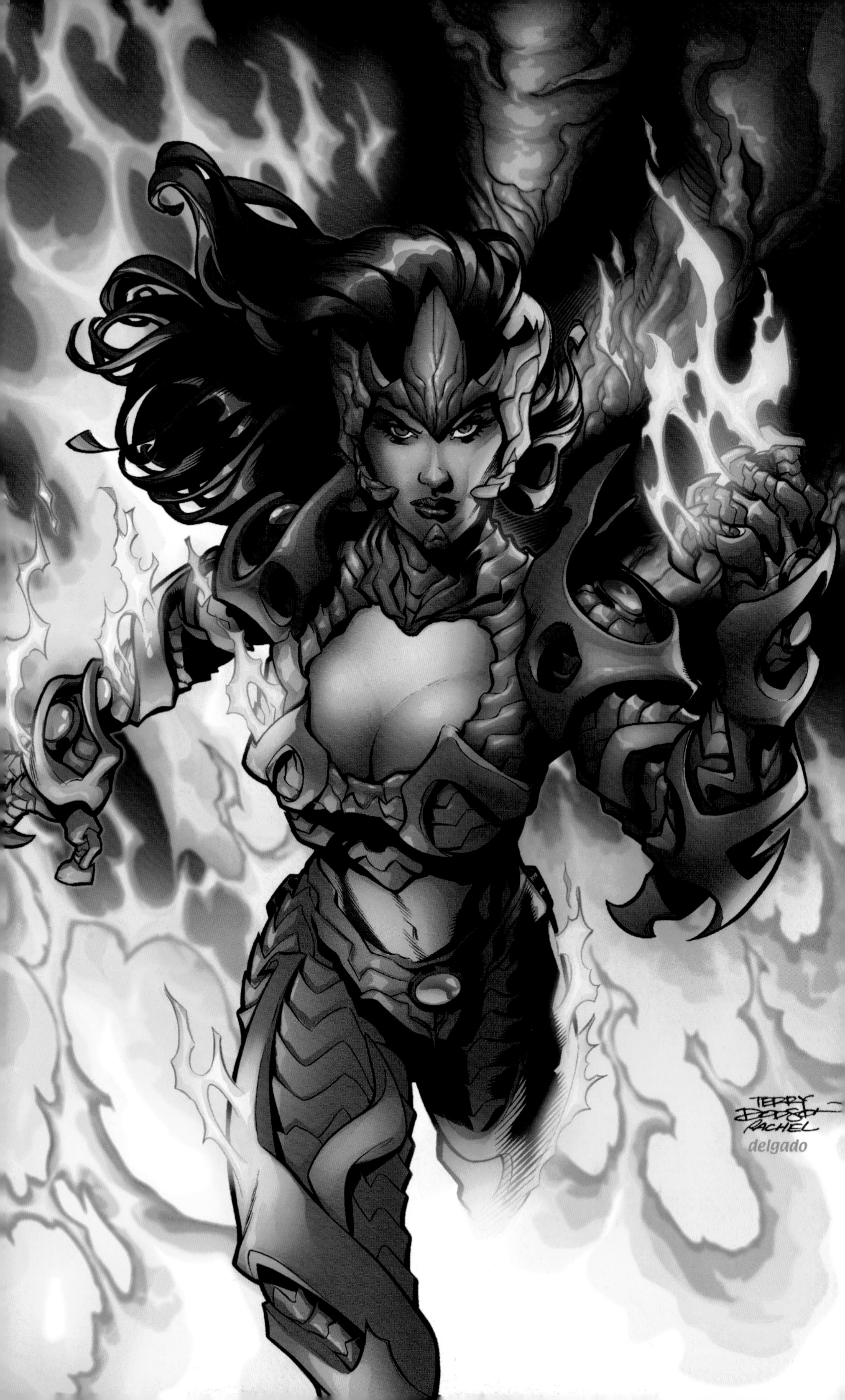
TERRY DODSON RACHEL
delgado

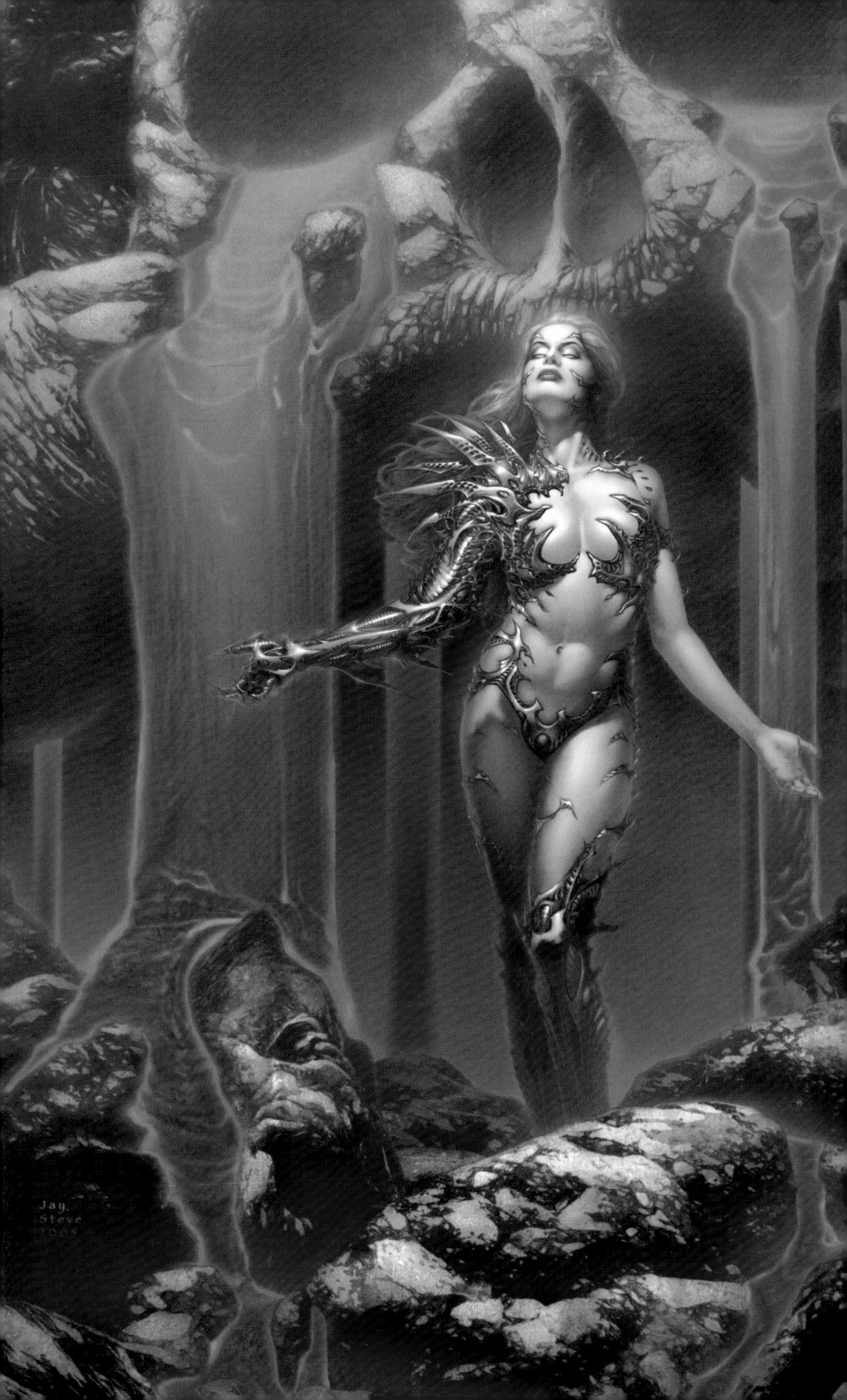
Jay,
Steve

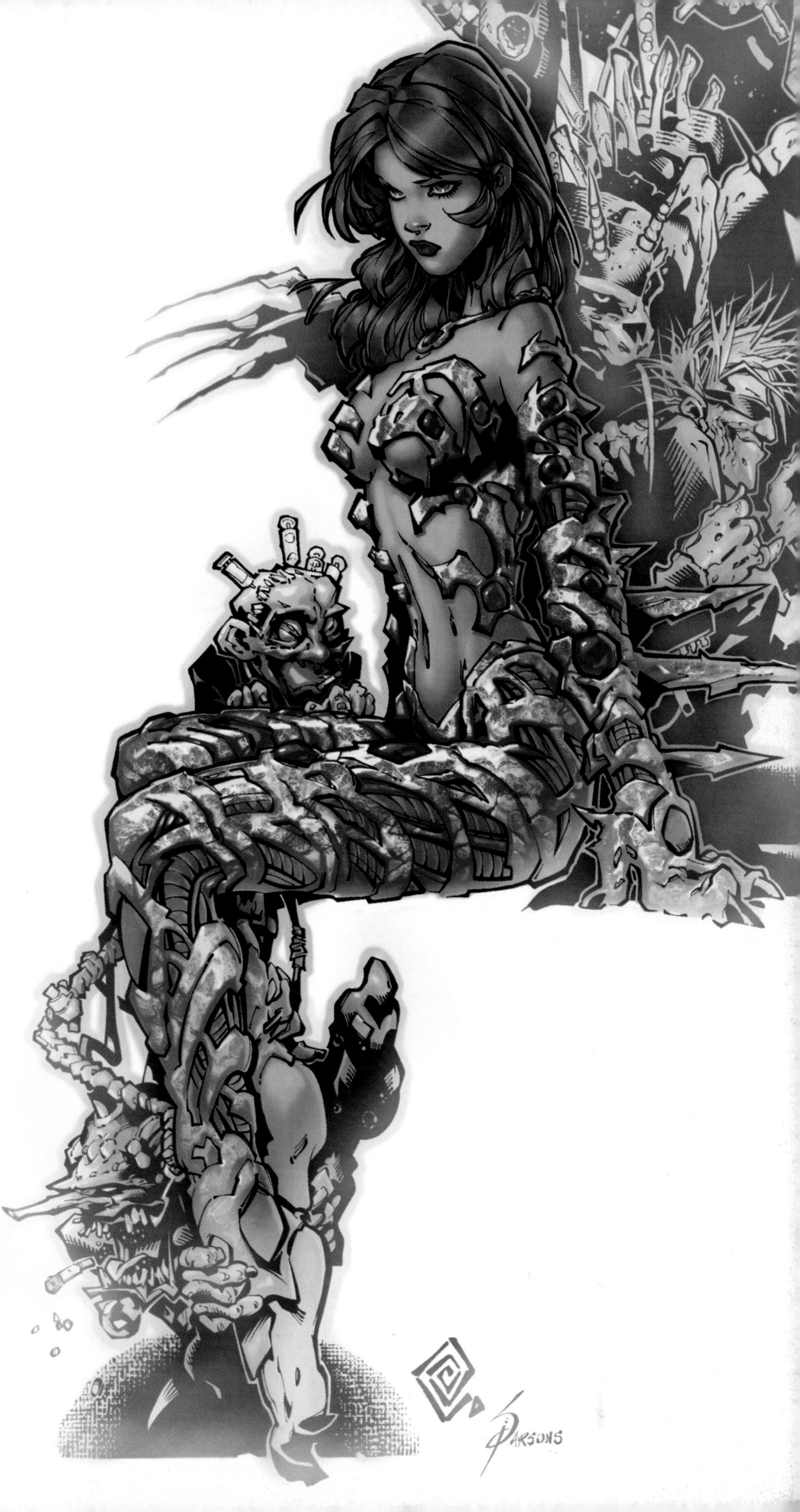
PARSONS

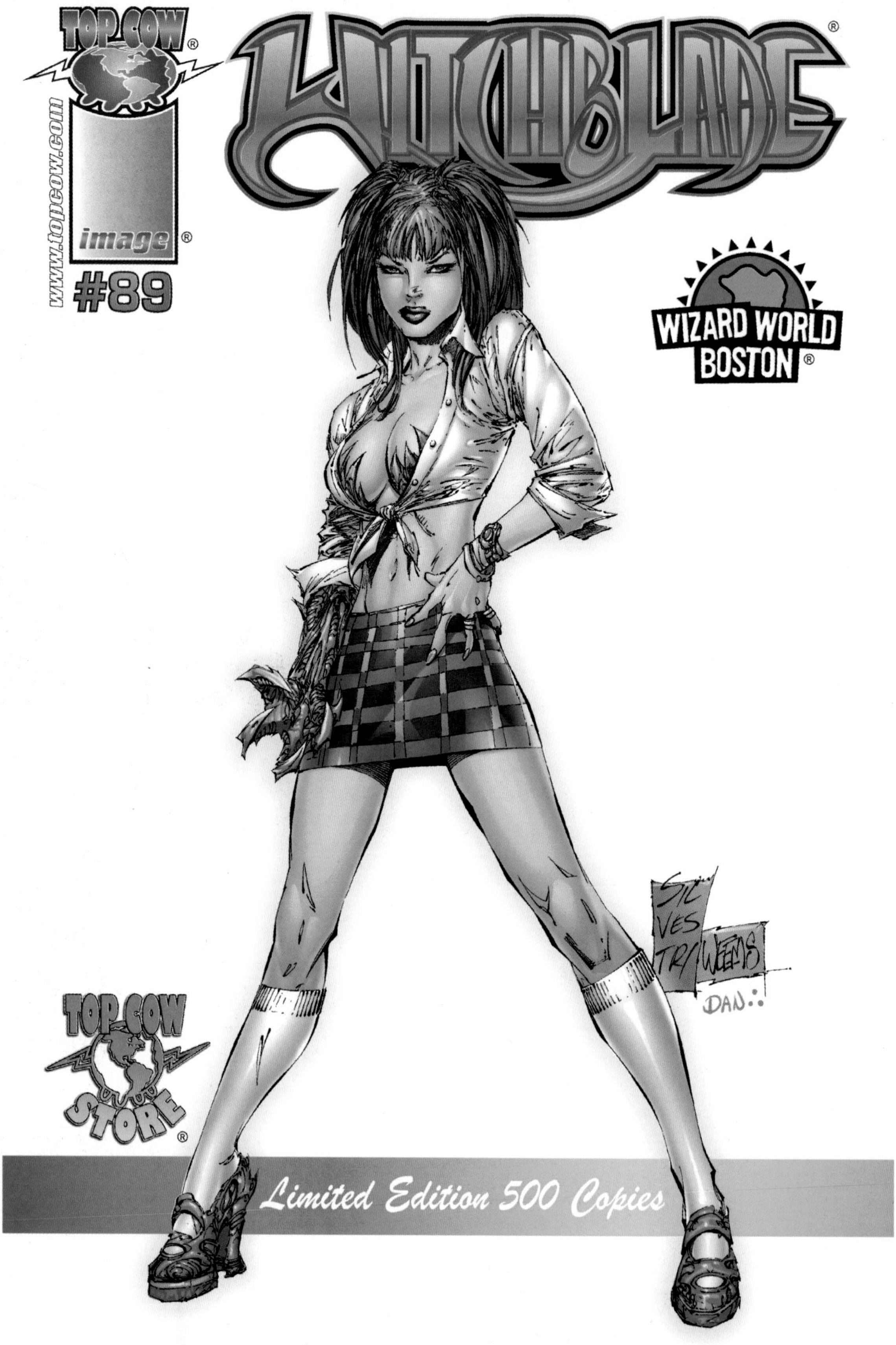
TOP COW
WITCHBLADE
image
www.topcow.com
#89
WIZARD WORLD BOSTON
SILVESTRI/WEEMS
DAN
TOP COW STORE
Limited Edition 500 Copies

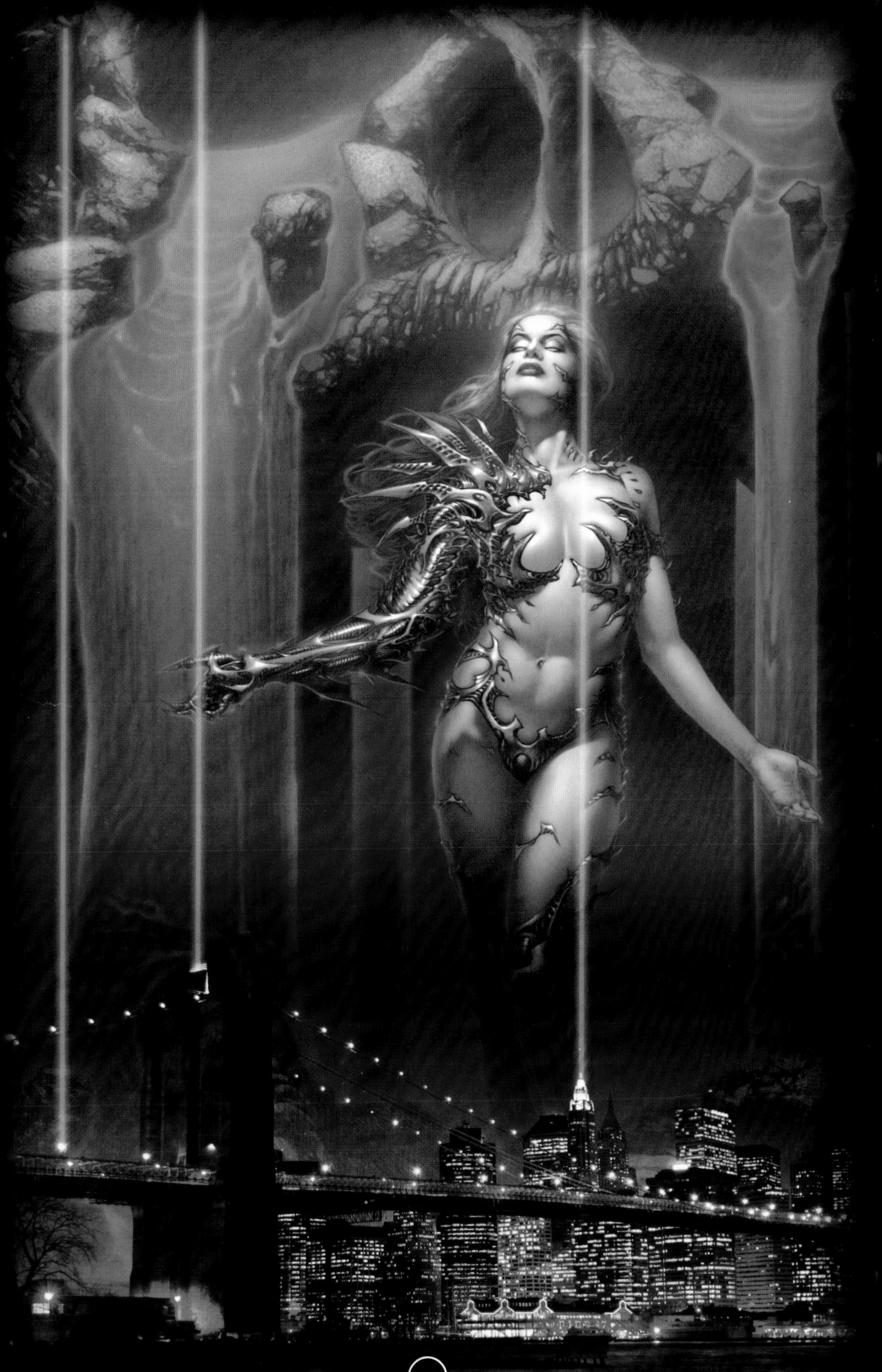

Check out these other trade paperbacks available now!

Freshmen!
collects *Freshmen* vol. 1 issues #1 - #6,
plus the *Freshmen Yearbook* and more!
co created by Seth Green and Hugh Sterbakov!
This edition features an all new bonus story by
writer Hugh Sterbakov!
(ISBN # 1-58240-593-X) US $16.99

"Super powered teens, angst, action and
comedy...I don't get it."
—Joss Whedon

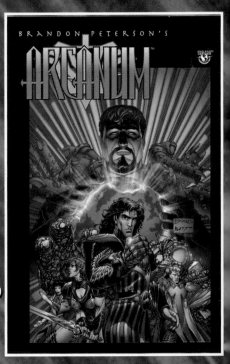

Arcanum: Millenium's End
collects *Arcanum* issues #1-8
plus issue #1/2!
Written and illustrated by industry
superstar artist Brandon Peterson
(*Ultimate Fantastic Four*)
(ISBN: 1-58240-538-7) US $16.99